WORDSWORTH'S POETIC COLLECTIONS, SUPPLEMENTARY WRITING AND PARODIC RECEPTION

The History of the Book

Series Editor: Ann R. Hawkins

Titles in this Series

1 Conservatism and the Quarterly Review: A Critical Analysis
Jonathan Cutmore (ed.)

2 Contributors to the Quarterly Review: A History, 1809–1825
Jonathan Cutmore

3 Wilkie Collins's American Tour, 1873–1874
Susan R. Hanes

4 William Blake and the Art of Engraving
Mei-Ying Sung

5 Charles Lamb, Elia and the London Magazine: Metropolitan Muse
Simon P. Hull

6 Reading in History: New Methodologies from the Anglo-American Tradition
Bonnie Gunzenhauser (ed.)

7 Middle-Class Writing in Late Medieval London
Malcolm Richardson

8 Readings on Audience and Textual Materiality
Graham Allen, Carrie Griffin and Mary O'Connell (eds)

9 Romantic Marginality: Nation and Empire on the Borders of the Page
Alex Watson

Forthcoming Titles

Socialism and Print Culture in America, 1897–1920
Jason D. Martinek

Elizabeth Inchbald's Reputation: A Publishing and Reception History
Ben P. Robertson

Art and Commerce in the British Short Story, 1880–1950
Dean Baldwin

WORDSWORTH'S POETIC COLLECTIONS, SUPPLEMENTARY WRITING AND PARODIC RECEPTION

BY

Brian R. Bates

Routledge
Taylor & Francis Group

LONDON AND NEW YORK

First published 2012 by Pickering & Chatto (Publishers) Limited

Published 2016 by Routledge
2 Park Square, Milton Park, Abingdon, Oxfordshire OX14 4RN
711 Third Avenue, New York, NY 10017, USA

First issued in paperback 2015

Routledge is an imprint of the Taylor & Francis Group, an informa business

BRITISH LIBRARY CATALOGUING IN PUBLICATION DATA

Bates, Brian R.
Wordsworth's poetic collections, supplementary writing and parodic reception.
– (The history of the book)
1. Wordsworth, William, 1770–1850 – Technique. 2. Wordsworth, William, 1770–1850 – Criticism and interpretation. 3. Wordsworth, William, 1770–1850 – Parodies, imitations, etc. 4. Wordsworth, William, 1770–1850 – Appreciation. 5. Authors and readers – England – History – 19th century.
I. Title II. Series
821.7-dc23

ISBN-13: 978-1-138-66163-9 (pbk)
ISBN-13: 978-1-8489-3196-1 (hbk)

Typeset by Pickering & Chatto (Publishers) Limited

CONTENTS

Acknowledgements   vii

Introduction   1
1 Reframing *Lyrical Ballads* (1800/1798)   21
2 Textual Travelling in the 1800 *Lyrical Ballads*   39
3 Short-Circuiting Wordsworth's 1807 *Poems*: Richard Mant's
    The Simpliciad   57
4 Wordsworth's 'Library of Babel': *The Excursion* and the 1815 *Poems*   77
5 Opening up Chapter 13 of Coleridge's *Biographia Literaria*   101
6 J. H. Reynolds's 'Peter Bell' and the Wordsworthian Reputation   121
7 *The River Duddon* Volume and Wordsworth's Canonical Ascent   141

Notes   161
Works Cited   217
Index   231

ACKNOWLEDGEMENTS

This book has benefited greatly from the continual support of Jessica Munns, who has lent a keen eye to several chapters and has provided helpful advice about my professional development. Initial thoughts on this project grew out of conversations with Jeffrey Robinson, Andrew Franta and Douglas Wilson. Jeff Cox has generously offered helpful suggestions about shaping this project into a book manuscript as well as providing insightful feedback on several chapters. During the book's preparation for press, I was fortunate to work with Stephina Clarke whose careful attention, patience and diligence have been remarkable. I am also grateful for the kind attention of Charles Rzepka, which came at a crucial moment in the development of the book, and for the warm encouragement of the series editor Ann Hawkins whose humour, critical insights and forthrightness I continue to appreciate. I would particularly like to thank Scott Howard who has been a wonderfully supportive colleague and friend, and a model of honesty, fairness and integrity. Finally, I offer my most heartfelt thanks and gratitude to Jennifer Kearny, my best reader in so many ways.

In Chapters 4, 5 and 6, I have adapted and expanded several previously published essays. Early versions of Chapter 4 were published as 'Wordsworth's Library of Babel: Bibliomania, the 1814 Excursion and the 1815 Poems', *Romantic Textualities: Literature and Print Culture, 1780–1840*, 14 (Summer 2005), at http://www.cf.ac.uk/encap/romtext/articles/cc14n01.pdf, and as 'Activating "Tintern Abbey" in 1815', in M. Lussier and B. Matsunaga (eds), *Engaged Romanticism: Romanticism as Praxis* (Newcastle upon Tyne: Cambridge Scholars Press, 2008), pp. 69–81. An early version of Chapter 5 was published in D. Lewes (ed.), *Double Vision: Literary Palimpsests of the Eighteenth and Nineteenth Centuries* (Lanham, MD: Lexington Books, 2008), pp. 83–102. The final section of Chapter 6 was published as 'Wordsworth, Milton, and Parodic Sonnets', *Appositions: Studies in Early Modern Literature & Culture*, 1 (Spring 2008), at http://appositions.blogspot.com/, and more completely as 'J. H. Reynolds Re-Echoes the Wordsworthian Reputation: "Peter Bell," Remaking the Work and Mocking the Man', *Studies in Romanticism*, 47:3 (Fall 2008), pp. 273–97.

INTRODUCTION

This study focuses on the poetry and prose relations, bibliographic forms, competitive poetry markets, readerly negotiations and parodic responses that informed the creation of Wordsworth's published collections of poetry from 1800 to 1820. Two intertwined stories govern the chapters that follow. The first describes how Wordsworth used supplementary writings to shape and engage readers in his poetic collections from *Lyrical Ballads, with Other Poems* (1800), to *Poems, in Two Volumes, by William Wordsworth* (1807), *The Excursion* (1814), *Poems by William Wordsworth* (1815) and *The River Duddon* volume (1820).[1] The second relates how Wordsworth's critics and parodists responded to and were connected with the designs of those collections.

Beginning with the publication of the 1800 *Lyrical Ballads*, Wordsworth employed a variety of supplementary writings to make a case for his poetry as a valuable addition to the 'Old Canon' of poets, an innovation on ballad collecting, and a means of lending authority to his singular poetic credentials.[2] Through prefaces, footnotes, endnotes, headnotes, half-title pages, epigraphs, advertisements and other paratexts,[3] Wordsworth not only presented himself as an important contemporary poet, but as an editor, anthologist, literary and cultural critic. The prose interlacing Wordsworth's collections from the 1800 *Lyrical Ballads* to his 1820 *The River Duddon* volume provided him with opportunities to guide readers through his poems and draw their attention to how his work as a collector and commentator added aesthetic, cultural and historic depth to his books of poetry.

As much as Wordsworth's supplementary writings chart how readers might engage with his poetry, they also play out his struggles in the first two decades of the nineteenth century to frame, reframe, combat and absorb the myriad responses of reviewing critics and parodists into his poetic collections. In those publications Wordsworth exercises two principal supplementary strategies – one that encourages connective sympathetic readings of his poetry and another that attempts to stave off reductive criticism. These vacillating interactions between poetry and prose, a poet and his readers, not only shaped Wordsworth's poetic collections; they led to his inclusion in what Jeffrey Cox has called Britain's 'living pantheon of poets in 1820'.[4]

Whether in *Lyrical Ballads, Poems in Two Volumes, The Excursion, Poems by William Wordsworth* or *The River Duddon* volume, Wordsworth's supplementary writings often comment on individual poems or highlight poetic pathways between poems within a collection.[5] His endnote to 'The Thorn' in volume 1 of the 1800 *Lyrical Ballads* exemplifies this type of supplement because it does both. The note reflects on how readers might interpret 'The Thorn', but it also asks them to consider the internal coherence of *Lyrical Ballads* and points out how the repetition of words – both within a poem and amongst poems – figures the aesthetic and cultural power of his collection. Prose notes such as the 'Note to *The Thorn*' feature Wordsworth as an interpretive guide who prompts readers to explore and weigh the cumulative, linguistic significance of a published collection through forward (visionary) and backward (revisionary) hermeneutic movements. Wordsworth's editorial presence appears even more frequently in his 1807 and 1815 collections in the form of footnotes, endnotes, headnotes and section headings. In these spaces he often reminds readers of how his particular brand of revision – poetic self-echoing and return – can animate words, as they redound upon poem to poem, and readers, as they journey through his volumes of poetry.[6]

Wordsworth also used supplementary writings to forge connections between his past, present and future publications. These paratexts usually take the form of prose essays or notes. However, they can be poems as well, such as his 'Prospectus' to *The Excursion* which maps out a variety of ways to link together his past, present and future poems. While the supplementary writing described in the previous paragraph deals with individual poems or the connective shape of a particular collection, this type of supplement often accounts for and juxtaposes the temporal and spatial confines of the real world with the physical and figurative layout of Wordsworth's books of poetry. Such writing operates, as Paul Magnuson maintains generally about paratexts, as thresholds that relate Wordsworth's poetry to particular public discourses.[7]

Wordsworth's projection in the 'Preface to *The Excursion*' of his amalgamating works as an ever-expanding Gothic cathedral exemplifies this second type of supplementary writing. His Gothic figuration describes each of his works as synecdoche and metaphor for an overarching poetic system in which each part of the whole offers a passageway from which readers can move forward and a vital place to which they can return.[8] This type of paratextual cycling underscores Wordsworth's poetics and reveals the cultural importance that he attributes to the power of his collected works.[9] Such cycling – a tracing and retracing of the biographical and psychological history of the poet – also provides readers with opportunities to piece together the development of an emerging national poet. Correspondingly, in his publications after *The Excursion*, several of Wordsworth's supplementary writings – such as his *Topographical Description of the Country of the Lakes* (1820) – invite readers to participate in the process of collecting together the origins and ends of his poetry as a means of creating a fictive history of Great Britain.

Locating Wordsworth in Romantic Period Book History

At the beginning of the nineteenth century, prefatory, marginal and end materials were common features of verse and prose publications. The currency of these supplementary writings underpinned a revolutionary print age in the last third of the eighteenth century that saw an enormous increase in the types and numbers of books made available to readers, the importance of mediating bibliographic professionals and the fashioning of authors for public consumption.[10] Like much of the burgeoning reading public in the 1780s and 1790s, Wordsworth encountered new and reprinted poetry in newspapers, magazines, periodicals, chapbooks, miscellanies, anthologies and single-author publications.[11] Moreover, in the wake of the French Revolution, authors and a nascent class of professional critics heatedly vied with one another in these print forms to explain how and why to write, publish and read poetry.[12] When Wordsworth published his first slim volumes of poetry, *Descriptive Sketches* and *An Evening Walk*, in 1793 with Joseph Johnson, he took part in a dynamic poetry industry driven by the complementary and competing interests of authors, publishers and reviewers.[13] All of these groups, however, were concerned with how the bibliographic and linguistic forms of the printed book might predict, respond to and direct the tastes of a rapidly expanding and fragmenting reading public.[14]

In *The Reading Nation in the Romantic Period* (2004), William St Clair traces this movement towards a more bookish and book-minded culture back to one court case in 1774, *Donaldson v. Beckett*.[15] The ruling on this case, which effectively ended perpetual copyright and upheld Queen Anne's statute of 1710, had several lasting effects on publishers, booksellers, writers and readers in Great Britain.[16] The House of Lords' decision in favour of the Scottish publisher Donaldson curtailed the monopolistic dealings and perpetual copyright practices of a cartel of London publishers and booksellers throughout much of the eighteenth century. This tightly-controlled publishing industry limited the access readers had to books through the price, number of editions and types of works printed. Following the Donaldson ruling, a frenzied competition began in Great Britain among publishers and booksellers to secure older printed materials that were returning to the public domain.

One result of this competition was a sharp increase in affordable books for middle-class readers that included a tremendous amount of poetry previously unavailable to that potential reading public.[17] London and Edinburgh publishers issued new miscellanies and anthologies of English language poets from Geoffrey Chaucer to Edward Young that established what St Clair calls the 'Old Canon': 'the first formal canon of poetry in English to be made widely and cheaply available, the most stable, the most frequently reprinted, and the longest lived'. St Clair also maintains that these Old Canon poets were so 'entrenched in the educational system' that 'the reading nation was probably, to a large extent, commensurate with the reach and availability of these texts'.[18] Furthermore, because the Donaldson ruling upheld Queen Anne's statute law of 1710, new publications by contemporary authors after 1774 were only guaranteed copyright protection for fourteen years, until copyright was extended conditionally to twenty-eight years in 1808, and then to an unconditional twenty-eight years or the life of the author in 1814.

Although intellectual property was a pressing concern throughout Wordsworth's career (and in the 1830s and early 1840s he did agitate to extend copyright beyond the poet's lifetime), how to sell books was Wordsworth's more immediate interest in the first two decades of the nineteenth century.[19] For a poet such as Wordsworth, intent on establishing himself as an important voice for contemporary English poetry, creating a collection of poetry required paying careful attention to the physical layout of the book.[20] When Wordsworth and Coleridge refer to readers' 'pre-established codes of decision' in the 1798 'Advertisement' to *Lyrical Ballads*, and when Wordsworth further describes the 'public taste' and readers' 'known habits of association' with poetry in the 1800 'Preface' to *Lyrical Ballads*, they certainly have aesthetic issues in mind, but 'how far this taste is healthy or depraved' depended on the bibliographic and linguistic forms of the books readers had access to as well as their content.[21]

Wordsworth's poetic collections imitate many of the design characteristics of 'Old Canon' miscellanies and anthologies of poetry in the last third of the eighteenth century, which were mediated by the presence on the page of editors re-presenting English poetry. However, his designs were more strongly influenced by the simultaneous ballad revival that brought attention to book layouts in unprecedented ways through the anthologizing and antiquarian practices of editors such as Thomas Percy in his *Reliques of Ancient Poetry* (1765).[22] Alongside these collections of the past, Wordsworth learned from and began to contend with contemporary poets who routinely employed prefatory, marginal and end materials in their books to create a brand and establish a market for their poetry.

These intensive decades of literary collecting, authorial presentation, repackaging, authorization and publicity have their own diffuse antecedents in the early eighteenth century when changes to page layouts gradually transformed printed books into multiform objects that dramatized the page as a conversation (or debate) among authors, editors, publishers, critics and readers. The footnote particularly facilitated these changes by making room on the same page for an author and an editor.[23] While footnotes initially were used as an objective scholarly tool for evaluating the accuracy and validity of a text,[24] editors – most notably Richard Bentley – also deployed them to re-author entire literary works.[25] Alexander Pope's *The Dunciad, in Four Books* (1743) satirically encapsulates many of these Augustan age print developments.[26] Replete with mock-editorial Scriblerus persona, accumulated prefatory documents, end materials and footnotes, *The Dunciad* depicts an impending cultural dark age brought about by hack writing and power struggles between authors, editors, publishers, printers, booksellers and critics. Pope's overwrought footnotes, which spatially overwhelm the poem, embody his fears that marginal print figures had usurped the primary role of the author. Ironically, Pope capitalizes on those same notes to defend and solidify his authorial identity. His footnotes provided him with contextual and spatially contiguous opportunities to engage in self-promotion, literary criticism, gossip and cultural reflections. Regardless of how strongly *The Dunciad* denigrates Augustan print culture, Pope's footnotes demonstrate that eighteenth-century authorship was shaped through the margins of the page and depended on the seemingly secondary producers of literature who trafficked in those margins.

Although writers in the second half of the eighteenth century proposed new definitions of originality and creative genius that would seem to have separated primary authors from secondary print producers, distinguishing how literary works were created and by whom became increasingly complex.[27] The antiquarian and popular vogue that began in Great Britain in the 1760s for recovering, collecting, translating, re-presenting and authenticating oral ballads, songs, tales and epics altered how late eighteenth-century readers, writers and publishers conceived of poetic publications. James Macpherson's *Works of Ossian* (1760–5),[28] Thomas Percy's *Reliques of Ancient Poetry*, and Thomas Chatterton's posthumously published 'Rowley' *Poems* (1777) challenged literary theorists, critics, authors and readers to reimage and redefine the roles that writers and readers, poetry and prose, might play in books of poetry.[29] Whether regarded as authentic or counterfeit, Macpherson's 'Ossian' and Chatterton's 'Rowley' poems provoked inquiries into the validity, value and identity of their editorial and authorial personae.[30] If the announced authors of these poems were fictional – Macpherson's 'Ossian' poems were purportedly the translated works of a third-century Scottish/Gaelic bard and Chatterton's 'Rowley' poems were supposedly the discovered writings of a fifteenth-century monk – then the editorial persona organizing each of these collections might also be held suspect. If every part of these books could be a fabrication, including the editorial framework, then all parts would need to be read closely, comparatively and contextually.

These authorial and textual controversies engendered new questions about what constitutes and authorizes a literary work. Could a counterfeit contain truth, or was a work divested of its authority if it did not faithfully testify to or mimetically portray the author's real experiences? As Marjorie Levinson argues, 'hoax poems not only impressed upon their readers the knowledge that reading is more than and different from the verbalizing of an inscribed content or the discovery of an authorizing authorial interest, they highlighted the fact that literary meaning is profoundly determined by the contexts within which a reader situates a work'.[31] Historical contexts, editorial reconstructions and authorial intentions came under intense public scrutiny – all of which empowered and placed a burden on readers to investigate and authenticate.

Numerous Romantic writers lauded the lyrical and emotional qualities of these poems as authentic and regarded the 'truths' in these works to be contingent on how their structural organization (poetic arrangements and supplementary materials) elicited imaginative responses from readers.[32] Furthermore, as Margaret Russett recalls, Macpherson and Chatterton were generic innovators, who mixed together poetry and prose in order to forge an authorial persona: 'If Macpherson's innovation was to publish prose as "poetry," Chatterton's was to produce a poetic corpus in the service of articulating novelistic character'.[33] While these authorial creations manifested themselves through the prosing of poetry and the poeticizing of fictional characters, they also were a function of how the editorial prose and margins of the page informed Macpherson's and Chatterton's poetic narratives.

Percy's *Reliques* was an equally influential and – in contrast to Macpherson's and Chatterton's works – critically authorized collection of poetry, which in the last third of the eighteenth century influenced the poetic and editorial practices of many Romantic poets, as well as the expectations of poetry readers.[34] Published in three volumes, the *Reliques* went through four editions between 1765 and 1794, and, with each edition, their editor Thomas Percy increasingly made his presence known as the guiding force behind the construction, organization and presentation of a poetic history. In the 'Preface' to the first edition, Percy points out, 'Each VOLUME, or SERIES, is divided into three books, to afford so many pauses, or reflecting places to the reader and to assist him in distinguishing between the productions of the earlier, middle, and the latter times'.[35] Percy's collection presents British history as the progress of poetry from age to age. His introductory materials, headnotes, footnotes, endnotes and glossary call attention to that progression by setting up a system of cross-references that sends readers backwards and forwards through the volumes in search of historical, lexicographical and poetic connections between the periods and poems he demarcates.

Percy fashioned the *Reliques* as a collection that would appeal to multiple audiences by combining antiquarian pursuits with new tastes for rustic ballads and lyric poetry that captures simple, unadorned emotional outpourings. Reflecting back on his editorial methods in the 'Preface' to the fourth edition, Percy declares that '[h]is object was to please both the judicious Antiquary, and the Reader of Taste; and he hath endeavored to gratify both without offending either'.[36] In his preface to the 1800 *Lyrical Ballads*, Wordsworth is aware and wary of the reading public's abiding interest in Macpherson's, Chatterton's and Percy's mediating presences and constructions of the poet[37] – a concern that Wordsworth explicitly addresses in his 'Essay Supplementary to the Preface' (1815) when he denigrates Macpherson's work while celebrating Percy's. Wordsworth also built on many of Percy's editorial manoeuvrings in his supplementary writings which highlight local histories and encourage textual and historical travel through his volumes.[38] However, Wordsworth's methods of authorial presentation more closely imitated the self-fashioning techniques of Charlotte Smith and Robert Burns who – through their mixing of supplementary prose and poetry – convinced the public of their authenticity as natural, lyric poets whose works simply and faithfully testified to their personal histories, emotional states and cultural moment.

In response to readers' and reviewers' interest in her volume *Elegiac Sonnets, and Other Essays* (1784), Charlotte Smith quickly published a second edition in 1784 that reprinted her dedication to William Hayley and 'Preface' while featuring several new poems.[39] By 1800 Smith's slim 1784 publication had gone through nine editions – expanded into two volumes in the 1790s – that reprinted old and added new prefaces (six in total), sonnets intermingled with other poems, footnotes and endnotes. Through these paratextual manoeuvrings and poetic reorderings, Smith weaves together a biographical narrative (interspersed after 1789 with engravings) for readers to follow, highlights her growing cultural acuity, foregrounds her desire for sympathetic responses and invites readers to testify to the cumulative value of her poetry volumes and novels. Even more resoundingly than these compounding editions, her posthumously published *Beachy Head, Fables, and Other Poems* (1807) prompts readers to reflect on her literary and cultural significance through an editor's elegiac preface offset by Smith's endnotes, which occupy nearly half the book and relate botanical and anthropological details, literary and folk traditions, British and world histories.

Like Smith, Robert Burns quickly responded to public interest in his *Poems, Chiefly in the Scottish Dialect* (1786) by adding new poems to a series of rapidly published editions that modified and expanded a mediating textual apparatus. After the first edition, Burns's paratexts, which include a growing list of his subscribers, deal with several problems of poetic authenticity with which Smith – whose title page grounds her English heritage in Bignor Park Sussex – was not confronted. In her multiplying prefaces and notes, Smith is concerned with how to authorize herself as a genuine lyric poet and female sonneteer. By contrast, Burns and his Kilmarnock publisher used the 1786 'Preface' and subsequent 'Dedication to the Noblemen and Gentlemen of the Caledonian Hunt' to establish Burns as an independent but humble rustic heir of Scottish bardolatry, while the accompanying footnotes and concluding glossary translate the language of this new Scottish bard for contemporary Edinburgh and London readers. These footnotes give English language explanations for Scottish words, oral traditions, heroes and customs while also identifying several of Burns's literary references, particularly those to Macpherson and Shakespeare. Correspondingly, the glossary, which grew with each single- and then two-volume edition, provides an extensive list of Scottish to English terms.

In contrast to the editorial prose in Burns's collections, which authorizes him as a modern Scottish bard for English readers, Erasmus Darwin's two-volume second edition of *The Botanic Garden; A Poem in Two Parts. Part I. Containing The Economy of Vegetation. Part II. The Loves of The Plants. With Philosophical Notes* (1791) attempts to substantiate his poetic credentials through scientific-minded supplementary prose. Darwin's 'Advertisement', 'Apology', and 'Preface', followed by extensive footnotes and endnotes, explain botanical and geological findings, examine creation stories and conceptions of the cosmos, and detail Carl Linnaeus's classification system of the natural world. Along with Smith's botanically picturesque and Burns's border-crossing notation, Darwin's volumes extended the possibilities for how a poet such as Wordsworth might appeal to multiple audiences and establish credibility by intertwining geographic touring and poetic exploration with newer scientific discourses. Marilyn Butler also maintains that after Darwin's publication,

> many of the most successful and intellectually ambitious poems of the period had footnotes, along with other features of *The Botanic Graden*: such as a narrative poem with an archaic, perhaps mythological setting and style, and footnotes, of necessity fragmented and nonholistic, that limited themselves to positivistic contemporary fact.[40]

Few poets around the turn of the century were as attuned to these late eighteenth-century authorial manoeuvrings, paratextual deployments and bibliographic forms as S. T. Coleridge, Wordsworth's 1798 *Lyrical Ballads* collaborator. Coleridge's letter on 28 May 1798 to their friend and printer/would-be publisher Joseph Cottle demonstrates how invested Coleridge and Wordsworth were in designing the layout of their volume:

> Cottle, my dear Cottle, I meant to have written you an Essay on the Metaphysics of Typography; but I have not time. – Take a few hints without the abstruse reasons for them which I mean to favor you – 18 lines a page, the lines closely printed, certainly, *more closely* than those of the Joan – (Oh by all means closer! W. Wordsworth) *equal ink and wide margins*. That is *beauty* – it may even under your immediate care mingle the sublime?[41]

Coleridge overtly juxtaposes his specifications about line spacing, lines per page, marginal width and ink blackness with Cottle's recent edition of his friend

Robert Southey's *Joan of Arc* (1796), but his letter also features Wordsworth's typographical presence – Wordsworth wrote in the parenthetical aside, 'Oh by all means closer!'. This redoubled excitement, undergirded by Coleridge's playful threat of writing Cottle an essay on 'the Metaphysics of Typography', reveals Coleridge's and Wordsworth's conviction that their particular page layouts for *Lyrical Ballads* could produce beautiful and even sublime effects.[42]

In contrast to the wide margins and – excepting the initial two-page 'Advertisement' –paucity of supplementary prose in the 1798 *Lyrical Ballads*, a year earlier Coleridge's *Poems by S. T. Coleridge. Second Edition. To which are Now Added Poems by Charles Lamb, and Charles Lloyd* is filled with prose writings that call attention to how he reorganized and revised *Poems on Various Subjects, by S. T. Coleridge, Late of Jesus College Cambridge* (1796). Coleridge struck out twenty-three of the 1796 poems while adding thirteen new ones, and opened up the second half of the volume to his friends Charles Lloyd and Charles Lamb. Following the contents page in the second edition, Coleridge included a new dedicatory poem about his formative relationship with the Reverend George Coleridge, an amended 'Preface to the First Edition', and a 'Preface to the Second Edition'. Beyond this stacking of new and old introductory materials, he transformed the endnotes from the 1796 volume – nearly twenty pages – into footnotes and added several new headnotes and footnotes. Roughly a third of the way through the 1797 volume, he also inserted a three-and-a-half page prose 'Introduction' to a sonnet section prefixed with the half-title page 'Sonnets, Attempted in the Manner of the Rev. W. L. Bowles'.[43] Another new half-title page inscribed 'Supplement' appears three-fourths of the way through the volume, followed by a three-page prose 'Advertisement' that prepares readers for the concluding mixed-author section of the volume.

Several of Coleridge's prose writings in the 1797 volume foreground his interest in Macpherson, Chatterton and Friedrich Schiller, and align his poetry with the recent tradition of sonneteering, poetic touring and picturesque border crossings practised by Charlotte Smith and William Leslie Bowles. However, other prose inserts style him as the editorial head of and mouthpiece for an emerging group of poets printed and sold through their fellow poet Joseph Cottle, who operated out of Bristol and London.[44] Coleridge's internal 'Advertisement' to the final mixed-author section of the volume lays out his connective role in this network of poetic association and highlights the contemporary sociability of his 1796 and 1797 volumes. In that 'Advertisement', Coleridge thanks Cottle for publishing his volume while also puffing the second edition of Cottle's 'Poems' – publicity re-echoed in the ensuing poem 'To the Author of Poems Published Anonymously, at Bristol'. Then, Coleridge announces that he has excised a note from the 1796 edition, connected to 'An Effusion On An Autumnal Evening; Written in Early Youth'. In its place he offers a lengthy apology to Samuel

Rogers and his readers because, in that 1796 note, he 'asserted, that the tale of Florio in Mr. Rogers' "Pleasures of Memory," was to be found in the Lochleven of Bruce'.[45] Although Coleridge retracts these plagiarism charges and dubs his explanation 'an unsolicited and self-originating apology', he continues to point out Rogers's lack of originality – 'I do (and still do) perceive a certain likeness between these two stories' – in contrast to his own poetry, mixed together with Lloyd's and Lamb's.

The 1796 endnote that he half-apologies for reads more like Coleridge's attempt to acquit himself of informal charges – 'I have been told' – that he has plagiarized from Rogers, as well as a strategy for distinguishing his growing poetry circle from Rogers's popular, eight-edition, heavily endnoted, associative, loco-descriptive poem *The Pleasures of Memory, with Other Poems* (1792–6). The ensuing 1796 endnote to Coleridge's poem 'Epistle I' offsets his slippery denial and defensive charge of plagiarism by touting Coleridge's borrowed expression 'green radiance' from 'MR. WORDSWORTH, a Poet whose versification is occasionally harsh and whose diction too frequently obscure: but whom I deem unrivaled among the writers of the present day in manly sentiment, novel imagery, and vivid colouring'.[46] Although Coleridge offers two major criticisms of this little-known poet of *Descriptive Sketches* and *An Evening Walk*, he also ranks Wordsworth in the vanguard of contemporary poets, which, according to Coleridge's 1796 and 1797 volumes, includes Lloyd, Lamb, Cottle, Coleridge and Southey.[47]

Southey's and Coleridge's separate collections of poetry between 1796 and 1800 particularly publicize their collaborative work while also mimicking each other's rearrangements of old with new texts. Southey's 'Preface' to *Joan of Arc* notes that the '450 lines at the beginning of the second book, were written by S.T. Coleridge',[48] while the last sentence of Coleridge's 1796 'Preface' explains that 'the first half of Effusion XV. was written by the Author of "Joan of Arc," an Epic Poem',[49] and Southey's footnote to 'The Soldier's Wife' in his 1797 *Poems* points out that the third stanza 'was supplied by S. T. Coleridge'.[50] Furthermore, like Coleridge's 1796 *Poems*, which he excised, reorganized and supplemented in the 1797 volume, Southey's 1797 *Poems* – stocked with headnotes and footnotes – was reconfigured in a second edition that also functions as volume 1 of his two-volume *Poems by Robert Southey* (1799). Wordsworth (with Coleridge's aid) further inflected Southey's revisionary and additive designs by reordering, excising and expanding the 1798 *Lyrical Ballads* into volume 1 of the 1800 *Lyrical Ballads with Other Poems. In Two Volumes. by W. Wordsworth*.

On the heels of these three poets reciprocally accumulating collections of poetry, Walter Scott meticulously built up his poetic credentials in *Minstrelsy of the Scottish Border* (1802; four editions by 1810) and *The Lay of the Last Minstrel* (1805; eight editions by 1810). The voluminous 'Introduction', appendices, footnotes, headnotes and endnotes in Scott's two-volume 1802 publication style him as an expert Scottish border historian as well as a careful ballad collector, translator and imitator, while the brief introduction and extensive endnotes in his 1805 volume present Scott as a contemporary poet who has learned and moved on from the reinvigorated ballad vogue, catalysed by William Taylor's 1796 translations of Gottfried Burger's ballads. Peter Murphy succinctly describes these cumulative manoeuvrings. *The Minstrelsy* 'collects together the various modes of [Scott's] apprenticeship into a kind of anthology of self-presentation', and '*The Lay of the Last Minstrel* appears at the end of a progress from translator to editor to imitator to author'.[51]

Scott's popularity and dominant commercial success were only rivalled in the second decade of the nineteenth century by George Gordon, Lord Byron. Byron rose to public attention through *English Bards and Scotch Reviewers* (1809), which lambasts reviewing critics and contemporary poets (including Wordsworth) with acerbic couplets and footnotes, and then became infamous through *Childe Harold's Pilgrimage* (1812) and a series of Eastern verse tales, all outfitted with prefatory materials and contextual notes. In his *Edinburgh Review* essay about Coleridge's *Christabel, Kubla Khan, A Vision: The Pains of Sleep* volume (1816), the Irish poet Thomas Moore describes the power that Byron's supplementary writings held, not only over readers of Byron's poetry, but over readers of other poets. Moore begins his review by singling out an advertisement for Coleridge's volume that 'carried in its front a recommendation from Lord Byron, who, it seems, has somewhere praised 'Christabel', as a 'wild and singularly original and "beautiful" poem'.[52] Moore questions Byron's capacity to reauthorize Coleridge's poetic credentials and doubts Byron's motives because his publisher John Murray also published the *Christabel* volume. However, Moore has no doubt about the impact that Byron's excerpted prose, taken from an endnote to 'The Siege of Corinth' (1816), would have on public opinion and sales of Coleridge's volume.

In 1809 Moore already considered prose notes to be so exploited and ubiquitous in poetry publications that he could play on readers' and writers' expectations in his 'Preface' to the second edition of *Corruption and Intolerance: Two Poems with Notes. Addressed to an Englishman by an Irishman*:

> The practice, which has lately been introduced into literature, of writing very long notes upon very indifferent verses, appears to me rather a happy invention; for it supplies us with a mode of turning stupid poetry to account; and as horses too dull for the saddle may serve well enough to draw lumber, so Poems of this kind make excellent beasts of burden, and will bear notes, though they may not bear reading. Besides, the comments in such cases are so little under the necessity of paying any servile deference to the text, that they may even adopt that Socratic dogma, 'Quod supra nos nihil ad nos.'

Moore, whose footnotes dominate the volume, wryly claims that prose notes need not refer to the 'indifferent verses' above them. Instead, these notes can command a place within poetry publications that upstages and even supersedes the poetic 'text'. Poetry just might be the 'beast of burden' that draws along, from page to page, the more practical and constructive prose 'lumber'.

However, Moore's final quotation from Socrates suggests a potential irony behind these seemingly strident observations. The quotation can be translated as 'what is above us does not concern us', or as 'what is beyond our comprehension does not concern us'. While the first translation echoes Moore's statement that prose notes have no need to pay 'servile deference' to the poetry looking down on them, the second translation suggests that poetry operates in a realm beyond the ken of such prose. Even though the bulk of Moore's commentary highlights the grounding and worldly practicality that prose can provide – 'turning stupid poetry to account' – this second possible translation reverses his argument and stations poetry at a height that prose can neither understand nor reach. According to Moore's shifty distinctions and upending of the top and bottom of the page, prose notation can supplant, make use of, ignore and misconstrue poetry – a set of possibilities that complicates the reception of poetic works by asking readers to measure the value of poetry with and against seemingly more matter-of-fact types of knowledge. In the midst of such slippery prose-poetry, primary-secondary divisions, Wordsworth's poetic collections foreground a poet intent on developing the prefatory, concluding and marginal spaces in his books to foster paths of connective reading through his volumes, relate individual poems to the whole of his poetic project and life, publicize and defend his poetry and establish an enduring place in an emerging contemporary canon of British poets.

Critical Contexts

Moore's comments in 1809 suggest that by the turn of the century prose notes were an established subgenre in poetry publications, deployed and read nearly as often as prose prefaces.[53] Wordsworth's Romantic reviewers and parodists often commented on his prefaces and supplementary essays, and they took note of the shifting paratextual and bibliographic forms in his poetic collections. By contrast, twentieth-century scholars have tended to focus exclusively on the relationship between his prose essays and poetry. Consequently, a great deal of critical attention has been paid to Wordsworth's (and Coleridge's) 'Advertisement' (1798), 'Preface to *Lyrical Ballads*' (1800), revised 'Preface' and the 'Appendix on Poetic Diction' (1802), 'Preface' and 'Essay Supplementary to the Preface' in the 1815 *Poems*, and his 'Essays Upon Epitaphs' (1810/14).[54] A similar Romantic/contemporary differential exists over Wordsworth's parodic reception. While parodic responses to Wordsworth's publications significantly defined his public standing as a poet in the first two decades of the nineteenth century, Romantic period scholars have tended to overlook or dismiss the substantial insights in those literary parodies about how to read his poetry. These historically differing views about the significance of Wordsworth's paratexts and the power of parody also point to a divide between how Wordsworth's contemporaries and Romantic period scholars have evaluated his poetic reputation and – what Andrew Franta has recently dubbed – his 'audience problem'.[55]

Part of why Wordsworth's paratexts have been neglected stems from the long-standing view that, in the second decade of the nineteenth century, the quality of Wordsworth's poetry declined in direct relation to his increasing roles as his own best editor and critic.[56] This argument about Wordsworth's 'anti-climax' also dovetails with Matthew Arnold's contention that Wordsworth needed a good editor (like Arnold).[57] While scholars since M. H. Abram's *The Mirror and the Lamp* (1953) have routinely treated Wordsworth's prose essays as manifestos that theorize about how to read his poetry, many of these same critics underplay, fudge or lament how these essays do not consistently provide a practical guide for how to read individual poems.[58] Wordsworth's Romantic reviewers and parodists had similar complaints, but they also commented (both seriously and derisively) on how, in his published books of poetry, Wordsworth attempted to bridge the potential gap between prose theory and poetic practice by intertwining his poems with interpretive, contextual and connective prose notation.[59]

A second lingering assumption, which relates Wordsworth's value as a poet to his perceived habits of oral composition, has further contributed to Romantic period scholars overlooking Wordsworth's paratexts. As Andrew Bennett maintains in *Wordsworth Writing* (2007), a long tradition of twentieth-century scholarship – typified by James Chandler's contention in *Wordsworth's Second Nature* (1984) that Wordsworth prefers speech rather than writing – has portrayed Wordsworth as a poet who did not like writing and who only produced inspired and, therefore, authentic poetry while walking outdoors and composing aloud.[60] From this perspective, Wordsworth's editorial work, process of revision, organization of poetic volumes and paratexts are separate from and secondary to 'authentic' composition. Bennett carefully debunks this conception of Wordsworth as a poet who did not often write and offers an insightful analysis of how the physical process of writing informed Wordsworth's poetic identity, choice of subject matter and passion for poetry. Bennett's argument provides a method for rethinking the significance of Wordsworth's writings and rewritings and an impetus to re-examine why and how Wordsworth collected together and published his poetry.

Paul Magnuson's *Reading Public Romanticism* (1998) offers a broader cultural horizon for theorizing about the significance of supplementary writings by Romantic poets. His book examines the precise 'location' of several canonical,

Romantic texts by reading the 'frames' in which those texts were originally published.[61] Beyond isolating particular versions and publication histories of a text,
Magnuson pays close attention to how Romantic paratexts often act as entrance-
ways into and exits from a particular text towards a variety of public discourses
– whether aesthetic, political, nationalistic or sexual. Magnuson's arguments shift
the terms of how scholars might engage with long-established histories of published poems in the Romantic period. However, his efforts to situate a poem or a
collection of poetry are often limited to an analysis of one or two paratexts. This
study builds on Magnuson's contention that Romantic texts must be explored
carefully in relation to their very public paratextual frames, and further maintains
the necessity of examining the numerous supplementary writings that appear in
publications by poets such as Wordsworth. These writings need to be located
and analysed in relation to each other, as well as in relation to the texts that they
supplement, and in relation to the field of texts within which they are placed.[62]
From this methodological perspective, Wordsworth's supplementary writings not
only define his brand of poetry and situate that poetry within particular cultural
debates; they also create for readers specific kinds of textual and cultural travelling
through the past, present and future forms of his poetic collections.

The relative lack of sustained scholarly interest in Wordsworth's paratexts has been mirrored by the treatment of his parodic reception.[63] Although
Wordsworth was one of the most parodied poets in what has long been referred
to as the 'Golden Age of Parody', parody holds a marginal place in Wordsworth
studies.[64] In 'The "Vile Art" of Romantic Parody', Graeme Stones attributes this
disregard to the 'myth that Wordsworth and parody are two separate and hostile entities'.[65] Coupled with Wordsworth's twentieth-century position as the
touchstone for British Romanticism, this 'myth' – grounded on Wordsworth's
own disparaging prose remarks about parody – has drawn attention away from
how parody shaped early nineteenth-century debates about authorship, reading and reviewing.[66] Though a resurgent interest in Romantic period parody has
begun over the last two decades,[67] parody is either conspicuously absent or plays
only a minor role in recent books about the vexed relationship between writers
and readers during the Romantic period,[68] and with similar studies focused on
Wordsworth, this type of omission has been even more prevalent.[69]

In the first two decades of the nineteenth century, Wordsworth's reputation
and readership were largely a function of the parodic framings and reframings of
his multi-voiced poems, shifting registers and supplementary prose.[70] As Mark
Jones recalls, Wordsworth's intermingling voices have been treated uneasily by
critics since Francis Jeffrey in the *Edinburgh Review* (1802) and S. T. Coleridge
in the *Biographia Literaria* (1817) who saw Wordsworth's multi-vocality – both
within and between his poetry and prose – as latently parodic forms that invite
further parody. Jones's Bakhtinian engagement with parody pits later nine-

teenth- and twentieth-century parody anthologies, which relegate parody to a singular and contained form of criticism, against 'how irreducible the contradiction is between Wordsworth's parodic practice and his explicit critical antipathy to parody'.[71] Through multi-faceted parody, Wordsworth's early critics and imitators found a means of representing, reframing and replying to the many voices in his poetic collections. By contrast, subsequent criticism of Wordsworth's poetry that mimics his 'critical antipathy' to parody tends to classify parodies of Wordsworth as parasitic and inconsequential forms. While such a practice may defend Wordsworth against his detractors, it runs the risk of flattening Wordsworth's dynamic engagements with his contemporary readers and, as a consequence, of misreading his variegated poetry and prose voices as either a unified authoritative perspective or a solely defensive practice.[72]

Wordsworth's supplementary writings and parodic reception were enmeshed in a wide-spread struggle between early nineteenth-century authors, reviewers and publishers to negotiate and create the tastes of contemporary readers.[73] Contrary to the critical thought established by Abrams and strengthened by Jon Klancher that by 1815 Wordsworth was writing for the 'people philosophically characterized' and not for his contemporaries, Wordsworth's increasingly complex, paratextual network and position as a parodic favourite reveal how intertwined his writings were with reader responses in the first two decades of the nineteenth century. During this period, Wordsworth's publications met with numerous literary parodies that critiqued his subject matter, poetic diction, uses of genres, political inclinations and choice of poetic associates. Nicola Trott has ably demonstrated how many of Wordsworth's reviewers in the first two decades of the nineteenth century contributed to Wordsworth's parodic treatment by drawing attention to Wordsworth's hopes that readers would have a sincere emotional response to his poems while also sarcastically pointing out how many of his poems sabotage his supposed purpose and read instead like self-parody.[74] Wordsworth's supplementary writings were at the forefront of this critique, and many of Wordsworth's parodists attempted to overwrite his aesthetic and cultural claims of authority by reconfiguring the very supplementary writings that called for these sympathetic responses. A significant part of parodying Wordsworth meant reproducing his poetic system – verse and prose – in order to obfuscate the line between parodic ridicule and complementary pastiche. The 'best' kind of Wordsworth parody – meaning the most popular – left readers unable to determine whether it was written in earnest or in jest, or if it was written by Wordsworth or someone else.

Satirical parodies of Wordsworth also offer a means for examining how authors such as Wordsworth were written into or out of particular literary markets and ideological frameworks. In his edited collection, *The Satiric Eye: Forms of Satire in the Romantic Period* (2003), Steven Jones points out how satire from 1780 to

1832 challenged emerging forms of what Jerome McGann has called the 'Romantic Ideology'. Romantic period satire often undercut developing myths of natural creativity, emotional sincerity and aesthetic sublimity, and, as a few scholars have demonstrated, several forms of satire rose to public prominence in direct response to the growing popularity of this Romantic sensibility.[75] Around the turn of the century, satire might be attached to the Whiggish ideology represented by the *Edinburgh Review* (1802); to Tory reviewing engines such as the short-lived *Anti-Jacobin* (1797–8), *Quarterly Review* (1809), *Satirist* (1807–14) and *Blackwood's Edinburgh Magazine* (1817); or to more radical publications such as William Cobbett's *Political Register* (1802) and John and Leigh Hunt's *Examiner* (1808).[76] Regardless of political affiliation, during this age of periodical satire, parody was a pliable critical and literary form used to disarm 'unsavoury' publications by rewriting authorial tones, rearranging literary forms, burlesquing language and, consequently, divesting authors of public credibility and possibly of sales as well.

Trott demonstrates that the ascendance of Romantic parody corresponded with and often mimicked journalistic criticism, particularly in the *Edinburgh Review*.[77] She maintains that this process led to the creation of a 'new school of criticism' intent on defining itself against and controlling what they perceived to be the poetic programme of writers such as Wordsworth, Coleridge and Southey – 'the new school of poetry'. In the midst of this prose onslaught, Wordsworth's reviewing critics and parodists singled out his poetry and supplementary writings as a means of debating the value and place of new types of literature, as well as what and how readers should read. While Wordsworth endeavoured to shape the trajectory of his career through his supplementary prose, reviewers and parodists attempted to mould those writings towards other ends by reframing them with their own political and aesthetic conceptions of literature. In the midst of this struggle, Wordsworth, his reviewing critics and parodists alternately aligned and pitted against one another the seemingly transcendent power of poetry and the corrective necessity of prose.

As a poet dependent on and constantly frustrated by the sales of his collections in the first two decades of the nineteenth century, Wordsworth could not afford to ignore parodic responses because they both damaged and highlighted how readers might grasp the particular qualities of his poetic collections.[78] Outside the feedback from his coterie circle of family and friends centred in the Lake District, Wordsworth could only hypothesize about how the rapidly expanding and diverse reading public was receiving his poetry by assessing reviews, literary parodies and imitations that represented and interpreted his publications for readers who had read, had yet to read, or, more likely, would not read his collections. As Lucy Newlyn's work has made abundantly clear, many of Wordsworth's contemporaries shared this 'anxiety of reception'. However, most authors did not express these concerns as directly or as confrontationally as Wordsworth did.

Particularly in his 1815 'Preface' and 'Essay Supplementary', Wordsworth's irritation can be attributed, in part, to his antipathy to antagonistic reviews and parodies, but these recurring frustrations also represent his desire and inability to distil the responses of contemporary readers from those sources.[79]

From the 1800 'Preface' to the 'Preface' and 'Essay Supplementary' in his 1815 *Poems*, Wordsworth's prose essays and other supplementary writings increasingly call attention to the necessity and difficulties of cultivating active rather than passive responses to his poetry. This enduring concern probably stems as much from his paradoxical views on reading his poetry as it does from his attempts to guard his poetry against criticism. Although many of Wordsworth's supplementary writings prescribe how to read his poetry, in some of the very same writings, he encourages readers to develop and exercise their own active reading strategies.[80] Wordsworth was convinced that his readers should follow his editorial directions, but he was also well-aware that many of his readers would exercise their own reading habits on his poems. His statement in the 1800 'Preface' that 'in some instances feelings even of the ludicrous may be given to my Readers by expressions which appeared to me tender and pathetic', demonstrates his deep and abiding concern that his choice of poetic language and style would be mocked.[81] Those 'pre-established codes of decision', which Wordsworth and Coleridge single out in the 1798 'Advertisement' to *Lyrical Ballads*, were difficult to change, and Wordsworth did not simply expect readers to adopt his views passively without question. On the contrary, he created rhetorical and bibliographic spaces before, within, between and after his poems for readers to reflect on and respond to his poetry.[82] Many of Wordsworth's contemporary readers did respond to his efforts to elicit a 'corresponding power' that would intermingle with his poetic collections. However, they often responded unsympathetically – as Wordsworth suspected they might – with the satirical power of parody.[83]

Satirical parodies such as Richard Mant's *The Simpliciad* (1808) and J. H. Reynolds's 'Peter Bell' (1819) provide incisive criticism into how Wordsworth styled himself –through the bibliographical setup of his books of poetry – as a poet, critic, editor, anthologist and cultural icon. These parodists sought to retard and render ridiculous the relationship between Wordsworth's supplementary prose and poetry. This satirical attention brought Wordsworth's poetry to a broader audience, and, in the cases of Mant and Reynolds, subversively demonstrated the very kind of active, readerly work that Wordsworth calls for in his supplementary writings. Their attempts to derange how readers might interpret Wordsworth's poems and progress through his volumes ironically offer rich models for how to reread his poetic collections. These parodies also highlight the degree to which Wordsworth's unsettled prose-poetry articulations were implicated in early nineteenth-century debates about the cultural importance of poetry and the collective work that poetry demands from a growing nation of readers.

Overview

Chapter 1 sifts the paratextual exchanges, reviewing practices and parodic recon-figurations that influenced Wordsworth's transformation of the single-volume 1798 *Lyrical Ballads* into a two-volume second edition. T. J. Mathias's *The Pursuits of Literature* (1794–8) and the *Anti-Jacobin* (1797–8) inaugurated a reviewing method that marked Wordsworth's early entanglements with parody and supplementary prose while Robert Southey's negative review of *Lyrical Ballads* led Wordsworth to develop prose endnotes that both prefigure the 1800 'Preface' and anchor his other more local supplementary prose in the volumes.

Chapter 2 examines more broadly Wordsworth's use of supplementary prose to reconstitute the anonymous 1798 volume as a new two-volume work dis-tinctly written and organized by William Wordsworth. This edition responds to the reading public's tastes for ballad collections, poetry anthologies, picturesque poetry and prose tours through the English Lake District, and takes readers of the 1800 volumes on a literal, metaphorical and affective journey through this highly travelled area of northern England. While the notes he includes in the second edition comment on the geographical terrain, customs and people of the Lake District, they primarily serve as directions on how to travel through his collection of poetry. In attempting to market his own brand of pastoral poetry, Wordsworth acts as a textual and cultural guide, who styles the 1800 edition as a revisionary collection that intertwines the future growth and stature of his poetry with how readers progress through and reread his poetic language.

Chapter 3 situates the publication of Wordsworth's 1807 *Poems* within the mocking responses of parodists and reviewing critics. Richard Mant's parody of Wordsworth's 1807 *Poems* in *The Simpliciad* (1808) reveals the extent to which Wordsworth's new volumes threatened the review culture's ability to define the criteria for public conversation about the nature and value of poetry. Reflect-ing reviewers' general dismay over Wordsworth's new volumes, Mant's parody is bifurcated between satirical-didactic couplets – a patchwork of poetic lines made up largely of Wordsworth's 1807 *Poems* – and footnotes – a wide selection of poetic passages also taken primarily from Wordsworth's 1807 *Poems*. *The Simpli-ciad* draws attention to how various poems in the 1807 volumes are purportedly connected to one another, and it distorts how Wordsworth's network of prose endnotes and footnotes, poem titles and section headings attempt to facilitate connective paths of reading. Through its prose-poetry juxtapositions and defor-mations, *The Simpliciad* presents Wordsworth's poetic language as a parodic echo of itself, which short-circuits the sympathetic engagement and hermeneutic activ-ity that the supplementary writings in his 1807 volumes encourage.

Despite enduring numerous and severe critical whippings from the press over his 1807 *Poems*, in 1814 and 1815 Wordsworth reengaged with his critics and the reading public armed with paratexts that outline the purpose and design of his past, present and future poems. Seeking to re-enter a book-filled market, Wordsworth attempted to capitalize on and direct the bibliomania sweeping Britain by developing his own anecdotal method of bibliographic organization. His network of supplementary writings attempts to separate his volumes from a saturated poetry market by placing them within an imagined coherent whole – a mini-library that unites his poems, presents a unified story of his poetic development and reveals a connection between the past, present and future cultural life of the nation. Through supplementary writings, in prose and verse, Wordsworth presents himself as a disinterested man of letters and recasts the values behind this bibliomania by recreating for and including his readers in the process of producing and collecting his poetry. Chapter 4 also demonstrates how, in one of his 1815 categories 'Poems of the Imagination', Wordsworth's prose notes describe his works as a modern classic, fit to be collected together and then re-collected by the public. These notes suggest how readers can gain control over the sheer mass of printed materials that they encounter, and they also identify 'Lines Composed a Few Miles above Tintern Abbey', the final poem in this category, as a composite form that has arisen not only out of the poet's developmental tale of imaginative growth but also out of the growth of a nation.

Chapter 5 focuses on the satirical letter from a 'Friend' in chapter 13 of the *Biographia Literaria* and examines why Coleridge's 'Friend' appropriates Wordsworth's Gothic church metaphor from his 'Preface to *The Excursion*' – the supplementary figuration that Wordsworth used to assert the unity of all his literary productions. The letter reconfigures the purpose of Wordsworth's Gothic church in order to reveal, by contrast, several allusive pathways that encourage Coleridge's attentive readers to move freely between his discursive prose and poetic compositions. Unlike the seemingly autonomous Wordsworth, whose prose manifestos and notes to his poems often attempt to direct public opinion by orchestrating particular frameworks within which to read his poems, the 'Friend' demonstrates how Coleridge's readers have often appropriated – and will continue to appropriate – his poetry and created the frameworks in which those poems might be read. Coleridge shadows Wordsworth's Gothic church with his own newly published *Sibylline Leaves*, and the 'Friend' provides readers with a humorously parodic opportunity to recollect and re-authorize the nation's recent literary heritage.

Coleridge was not the only poet-critic who responded satirically to Wordsworth's system for organizing his life's work. Several of Wordsworth's Regency parodists attempted to exploit and poke fun at his continued efforts to define a poetic contract, founded on the seemingly inviolable labour of the Wordsworthian poet and sanctified by the corresponding labour of the willing and able reader. Chapter 6 examines how J. H. Reynolds's 'Peter Bell' (1819) satirizes the Wordsworthian poet, who sings the praises of his own imaginative labour in the 'Preface' and 'Essay Supplementary to the Preface', which book-end volume 1 of his 1815 *Poems*. Bracketing his 'Peter Bell', Reynolds's own mock-essays, which ridicule Wordsworth's 1815 manifestos, are underwritten by parodies of Wordsworth's prose notes to his 1807 and 1815 volumes of poetry. In these notes, Reynolds seizes on the editorial persona in Wordsworth's footnotes, who puffs Wordsworth's poetic reputation and compulsively points backwards to his other poems and prose notes as unchallengeable reference points that solidify his present statements. In Reynolds's 'Peter Bell', one Wordsworth poem satirically builds on another so that every word or image from a poem triggers a mock-Wordsworthian response, which obsessively refers to another of his poems where that word was previously used. Seemingly lost in an insular world of his own creation, Wordsworth, Reynolds suggests, simply cannot help but refer to his earlier selves and idiosyncratic canon of poetry.

The final chapter probes how Wordsworth's *River Duddon* volume (1820) counters and absorbs this well-worn, parodic narrative of Wordsworth as an idiosyncratic and simple poet of the Lake District. The *Duddon* volume appeared in the midst of *Blackwood's Edinburgh Magazine's* celebratory, nationalistic and newly parodic treatment of Wordsworth's character and poetry. Through the *Duddon* volume, Wordsworth engendered a narrative of his literary life and national value that offset these portrayals and which many reviewers in 1820 began to credit and echo. The miscellaneous arrangement of the volume brings together sonnets (a genre that he was rarely criticized for using), extensive prose notes to those sonnets, narrative and lyric poems, and a lengthy prose *Topographical Description of the Country of the Lakes* – all of which position Wordsworth's poetry and prose as a cultural supplement to be revered because of his uniquely situated place in the Lake District. The *River Duddon* volume asserts this region as the moral seat of Britain and identifies Wordsworth as a guiding national poet, whose combination of poetry and prose speaks for an ideal British character articulated through his vision of the river Duddon. Concluded by four pages of advertisements for scientific, philosophical and agricultural books, the volume inflects numerous contemporary discourses about Britain's natural treasures and points the London print market and its readers to the origins of Wordsworth's poetry and the foundation of the nation's present identity – the Lake District.

1 REFRAMING *LYRICAL BALLADS* (1800/1798)

In the late summer of 1800 Wordsworth had several reasons to hope for the success of a second edition of *Lyrical Ballads*. First, the 500-copy print run of the 1798 edition had sold fairly well, the volume had received more positive than negative reviews, and its publisher Joseph Cottle had given the copyright to *Lyrical Ballads* back to Wordsworth.[1] Seven poems from the 1798 *Lyrical Ballads* had been reprinted between 2 April and 19 September 1800 in Daniel Stuart's newspapers the *Morning Post* and the *Courier*, and Coleridge had convinced a successful London publishing firm, held principally by Thomas Norton Longman, to publish a two-volume edition of *Lyrical Ballads* that announced Wordsworth as the author. Longman agreed to pay Wordsworth 80 pounds for two printings[2] – substantially more than he was paid for the first edition – and also provided for a more sizeable print run of the 1800 edition: 750 copies of volume 1 and 1,000 copies of volume 2.[3]

In the summer and autumn of 1800, William, his sister Dorothy, and their friends S. T. Coleridge and Sarah Hutchinson worked intensely on a manuscript of the new edition from which they intended Longman's Bristol printers Biggs & Cottle to prepare the final copy. In mid-July, with the help of his friends Wordsworth sent off a series of letters to Biggs & Cottle detailing a variety of revisions and instructions to reorder several poems from the 1798 volume.[4] The printers closely followed these directions and began printing the first volume of the 1800 edition. In contrast to this level of precision, the process of printing the second volume in the autumn of 1800 was chaotic and marked by slow, fragmented, ignored, lost and belated communications between Wordsworth's circle and the printers. Although publication was expected in mid-autumn, in early December Wordsworth was still fiddling with the ordering of poems, finishing the volume's concluding poem 'Michael', and working on a potential 'Preface' for that volume.[5] Amidst this flurry of activity, Wordsworth did not see most of the final proof pages. Instead, Coleridge arranged for Sir Humphry Davy, a twenty-one-year-old chemist and aspiring poet staying in Bristol, to read the final proofs.[6] The result was a second volume that in Wordsworth's opinion was 'throughout miserably printed'.[7]

Wordsworth's intensive manuscript preparations and negative reaction to the printing of the second volume reveal his concerns about the ordering of poems, the titles of individual poems, the insertion of prose notes, the layout of half-title pages, punctuation, spelling, capitalization and line spacing. When the volumes were finally published on 25 January 1801, Wordsworth was most upset by the omission of fifteen lines from 'Michael', and this printer's error was only partially rectified through an 'Errata and Corrections' page inserted three months later in unsold copies and which also pointed out twenty-seven other substantive errors in the 1800 edition. However, the bulk of what Wordsworth considered printing errors concerned capitalization and punctuation in his poems.[8] Although many of these differences might subtly shift how readers interpret a particular poem, most of the second volume appeared according to his specifications.

Wordsworth's dismay about these printing errors was tied to his hopes and anxieties about how the reception of the 1800 edition would shape his viability as a professional poet. As Susan Eilenberg has shown, Wordsworth's appropriation of *Lyrical Ballads* vexed him as much as it energized his work on the 1800 edition.[9] Wordsworth had his name *W. Wordsworth* placed on the title page in each volume, thereby claiming authority over the new (volume 2) and previously anonymous (volume 1) *Lyrical Ballads*.[10] Wordsworth's typographical concerns about the title pages during the printing process further suggest how preoccupied he was with weighing the impending significance of his name against the pre-existing title. In one of his final letters to Biggs & Cottle on 18 December, Wordsworth declares, 'I do not exactly like the Title-page though I do not know how to alter it to have a better effect. I must, however, particularly request that my name be printed in smaller character.'[11] His interest in achieving 'a better effect' for the title page, partially by reducing the printed 'character' of his name, demonstrates how absorbed Wordsworth was in creating *Lyrical Ballads* as a literary brand that would make his reputation.[12] At Wordsworth's request the words 'Second Edition' were omitted from the title page of the second volume; instead the title page specified that it was a new volume, signalling how Wordsworth's revisionary labour over volume 1 fostered his authorship and poetic authority over volume two.[13] Revision as progress animates the relationship between these two volumes – a process that Wordsworth understood as essential for mediating the critical reception of the 1800 edition in a competitive poetry market.

Several of Wordsworth's other letters in the autumn and winter of 1800, which focus on how many copies of the 1798 *Lyrical Ballads* had been sold and reveal his speculations about how much money the 1800 *Lyrical Ballads* might make, demonstrate how fixated he was on establishing a brand-name for his poetry and controlling how his volumes would be associated with other collections of poetry. In the same 18 December letter in which he 'particularly request[s]' that Biggs & Cottle alter the size of his name, Wordsworth also stipulates: 'It is my *particular desire* that no advertisements of Books be printed at the end of the volume'.[14] Wordsworth's '*particular desire*' was to disassociate the 1800 *Lyrical Ballads* from the common practice of advertising other books from the same publisher at the end of a work. Through this scrupulous request, which was carried out, Wordsworth attempted to ensure that his collection would neither serve as publicity for nor be associatively grouped with the works of past or present authors published by Longman. In asking that no advertisements be attached to the 1800 *Lyrical Ballads*, Wordsworth probably had Mary Robinson's forthcoming *Lyrical Tales* (1800) chiefly in mind. As Dorothy Wordsworth points out in a letter to John Marshall on 12 September 1800, when William heard that Longman intended to publish Robinson's poems, he proposed that the title 'Lyrical Ballads' be changed to 'Poems by W. Wordsworth' – a title that Longman rejected and then would later adopt for Wordsworth's 1807 *Poems*. Dorothy's letter, however, reveals more than her brother's simple annoyance with the similarity of their titles:

> This is a great objection to the former title, particularly as they are both printed at the same press and Longman is the publisher of both the works. The first volume sold much better than we expected, and was liked by a much greater number of people, not that we had ever much doubt of its finally making its way, but we knew that poems so different from what have in general become popular immediately after their publication were not likely to be admired all at once.[15]

While the similar titles are a problem, Dorothy makes clear that Longman's intention to publish them both is the pressing issue, and her next statement sheds light on the problem of such connective marketing.[16] The first volume of *Lyrical Ballads* had sold well, according to Dorothy, and gained an unexpected, because immediate, audience for poems advertised as 'different from what have in general become popular immediately'.[17] *Lyrical Tales* does not stand in the way of the second *Lyrical Ballads* 'finally making its way', but it does stand in the way of *Lyrical Ballads's* immediate market success, which is contingent on the public's perception of its newness and originality – a branding issue as much as a content-related one. In asking that Longman not advertise other books at the end of the 1800 *Lyrical Ballads*, Wordsworth sought to isolate his edition from publications like Robinson's and from the radical circle of poets that Longman had inherited from Cottle,[18] which was monitored closely by a review culture that commonly denigrated, recontextualized, parodied and sought to reform publishing poets.

The Pursuits of Literature and the *Anti-Jacobin*

Wordsworth's reception anxiety about the 1800 edition was, arguably more pervasive, neurotic and conspicuous than other Romantic poets, but his concerns were neither idiosyncratic nor without cause. Every publishing poet at the turn of the century was potentially subject to a personally and textually invasive kind of satirical parody popularized by T. J. Mathias's *The Pursuits of Literature: A Satirical Poem in Four Dialogues, with Notes* (1794–8) and the *Anti-Jacobin, or Weekly Examiner* (1797–8).[19] As quasi-government watchdogs, surveyors of contemporary publications, arch parodists, and astute paratextual framers, both reviewing engines attempted to illustrate and condemn 'Jacobin' principles by closely monitoring what they described as a corrupt British print culture beset by radical misrepresentations that threatened the morality and safety of the public. Though not directly affiliated with each other, their shared goals were to defend Burkean principles of constitutionalism against the incursion of French revolutionary philosophy, to develop the populace's tastes while encouraging their sense of civic duty, and to rescue the nation's character and literary tradition from illicit, immoral and politically marginal authors who had situated themselves into mainstream public discourses. Each of these publications attempted to subvert the major principles in such authors' works by correcting and parodying their central and supplementary writings. Fixated on transgressions of political and aesthetic boundaries, *The Pursuits of Literature* and the *Anti-Jacobin* waged a linguistic and bibliographic culture war against a radical margin encroaching on the traditional values of a central British narrative. Both works attempt to occupy and control those encroaching margins as a means to direct public discourses about socio-political, moral and literary hierarchies.

The central narrative of *The Pursuits of Literature* is an extended verse couplet conversation between the 'Author' and his sounding board 'Octavius'. However, in contrast to his sprawling prose footnotes, which dominate nearly every page, Mathias's poetry seems prosaic. The real innovative energy in his satire resides in footnotes that, he contends, 'are of a nature between an essay and an explanatory comment'.[20] Even though he denies on several occasions in his accumulating prefatory materials that his footnotes are the chief feature of his work, Mathias's notes were the most recognized, imitated and despised part of *The Pursuits of Literature*. Furthermore, his declarations about the centrality of his verse and the subservience of his rampant prose reveal Mathias's neoclassical concerns about focusing too much attention on indecorous and marginal forms. For example, in his 'Introductory Letter to a Friend' (inserted in the fifth edition), Mathias describes his notes as secondary to the poem and maintains that 'if the poem is read once without reference to the notes, the plan, connection, and manner of it will be perceived', while the 'Letter' announces that his couplets were 'not written as a vehicle for the notes, but the notes were composed to accompany the text'.[21] In the midst of these seemingly clear primary and secondary divisions, however, Mathias also makes a case for the indispensable and fortifying power of his prose notes: 'I know not whether I am mistaken, but as it appears to me, the power of legitimate Satire, thus extended and strengthened with the rampart of prose, and fully understood, is the best, if not the only literary support left'. According to this figuration, prose comes before, surrounds and defends poetry.

In fact, Mathias's prose was less an outward bulwark than a central platform from which to launch incisive attacks. His footnotes assault the character of individual writers, assail their political philosophies and dismantle the formal characteristics of their works. After contending in his 'Introductory Letter to a Friend' that 'Government and Literature are now more than ever intimately connected', Matthias claims that 'a variation is now required in the mode of conducting satirical writing. I mean, by calling in the reciprocal assistance of poetry and prose in the same work, for the great end; if it is designed for general perusal and extended application'.[22] Mathias describes his poetry/prose construction as a double containment that reframes and reconfigures the writings of particular authors as a means to actively engage readers in reassessing those writings. Mathias is also keen to point out that his reconstructions are not meant as a hermetic seal: 'I never desired to exhaust any subject, but to leave matter for the readers own suggestion'.[23] Seemingly far from exhausting any subject, Mathias's eighth edition in 1798 foregrounds his constant 'improvements and additions to the poetry and notes' and encourages readers to consider how his continual labour reifies the proper boundaries between the top and bottom of society by besieging and ironically writing through the bottom margin of the page.

While Mathias attacks a wide range of late eighteenth-century publications written in prose and verse, he seems most incensed by authors who, in his estimation, violate the boundaries between private opinion and responsible public service. His larger point, articulated in a scathing prose note about the 'Jacobin' defence attorney Thomas Erskine, is that Britain suffers from an 'Epidemick' – the 'Leprosy of Eloquence'.[24] This leprosy manifests itself in the productions of authors, politicians and orators who have foisted their personal and marginal notions onto what Mathias understands to be the central, governing set of constitutional principles codified by the 1688 Bill of Rights. Mathias regards 'Jacobin' rhetorical 'elegance' as deceitful misrepresentations that seek to upend the social and moral structure of Britain. *The Pursuits of Literature* tasks itself with identifying these marginal characters and invalidating their place in public discourse.

Mathias's irritation with and close attention to this 'Leprosy of eloquence' often correlates with how, and how much, a writer deploys marginal prose. Drawing on the 'hereditary dignity of the Satiric muse' carried on by William Gifford's *The Baviad* (1791) and *The Maviad* (1794), Mathias attempts to upset the inside of radical works (their language and formal qualities) and the outside of those works (their reception and socio-political ramifications) – a dual strategy that turns on how he reframes those writers' supplementary prose.[25] For example, Mathias's footnotes flatten Joseph Warton's editorial notes in his edition of Pope's works and take issue with numerous editorial comments in late eighteenth-century editions of Shakespeare's works. Preceding these attacks, his footnotes ridicule William Hayley's prose notes as 'prolix' and Erasmus Darwin's *The Botanick Garden and the Loves of the Plants* for 'the harlotry of [its] ornaments' contained in 'modish song or fashionable prose'.[26] Although Mathias acknowledges that Hayley's scholarly notes 'are very amusing, and not unfrequently afford much instruction', he sneers that Hayley's prose will ironically relegate his poetry to a marginal literary status: 'Had he but learned the art of blotting, he might possibly have attained considerable eminence, and preserved it'. Mathias's advice to avoid Darwin's illicit sensuality and corrupting social views centres on how Darwin's reciprocally-infected prose notes and poetry might influence 'all naturalists, whether poets or writers in prose'. In ironic contrast to his disdain for Hayley's and Darwin's prose, Mathias's parodic reframings of marginal discourses and supplementary prose established the authority and lasting notoriety of *The Pursuits of Literature* – a duelling practice the *Anti-Jacobin* celebrates as Mathias's 'mix'd mass', a 'stream of verse and many-languaged prose' from which 'Truth and Learning shine' (ll. 50, 51, 46).[27]

In its first issue (20 November 1797), the *Anti-Jacobin* describes its own mixed form as an innovation on satire that combines essayistic prose, personal attacks, parodic renderings and poetry.[28] Like Mathias, the authors of this periodical publication developed a capacious satiric form that would enable them to collect together, correct and root out Jacobinism from British print culture. In their 'Prospectus' to the first issue, the authors explain that every issue will single out 'Lies of the Week', 'Misrepresentations' and 'Mistakes' in the press while also identifying the publications spreading these falsehoods: 'To each of these several articles We shall carefully affix the name and date of the Publication from which We may take the liberty of borrowing it'.[29] Their rationale for citing specific works builds on Mathias's contention that contemporary satire cannot be effective 'without a personal application' to 'public men, and public books'.[30] From Mathias's point of view, satire should function as a court of public opinion that openly accuses and tries individuals in order to 'maintain and enforce publick order, morality, religion, literature, and good manners'.[31] The *Anti-Jacobin* carries out this methodology in each of its essay sections by recontextualizing and rewriting 'jacobinical' claims in newspapers, journals and single-author publications, and it conducts these reconfigurations most artfully in its treatments of 'Jacobin' poetry.

In their inaugural 'Introduction to the Poetry of the *Anti-Jacobin*', the authors lament that they have been unable to 'find one good and true Poet of sound principles and sober practice' to represent their public ideals and emerge as the voice of the British nation. However, instead of dispensing with poetry – 'a shabby expedient' – these authors proclaim their intention to reform the nation's poetry and shape public taste. By their estimation, they must rely on 'Jacobin' poetry –

Southey's and Coleridge's among others – because it can be found in 'the only market where [poetry] is to be had good and ready made'. Though they acknowledge the potential merits of 'Jacobin' poetry, these authors make clear that such poetry is perverted and a threat to 'the safety of our Readers principles and to the improvement of our own Poetry'. In order to safeguard readers and future poets against such 'an expedient full of danger, and not to be used but with the utmost caution and delicacy', the *Anti-Jacobin* announces that it will develop a triple 'frame' to help readers negotiate these dangers:

> we shall select ... such pieces as may serve to illustrate some one of the principles on which the poetical as well as the political doctrine of the NEW SCHOOL is established – prefacing each of them, for our Reader's sake, with a short disquisition on the particular tenet intended to be enforced or insinuated in the production before them – and accompanying it with a humble effort of our own, in Imitation of the Poem itself, and in farther illustration of its principle.[32]

First, the *Anti-Jacobin* will isolate specimens of 'Jacobin' poetry in order to shine a light on the singular purposes lurking therein. Then, they will recontextualize those specimens with new supplementary prose, and finally that prose will help guide readers through their parodic imitations of 'Jacobin' poetry.[33]

If nothing less, the *Anti-Jacobin* authors conjecture that their efforts to collect, contain and rewrite these poems discloses 'a *Jacobin Art* of Poetry' that will, ironically, shape the reading practices of the public and catalyse would-be writers to turn the *Anti-Jacobin*'s preliminary work 'to advantage'. These weekly gatherings of excerpted poetry, guiding prose and parodic imitations act as a roving literary miscellany that chiefly focuses readers on the *Anti-Jacobin*'s parodic renditions: 'By these means, though We cannot hope to catch *"the wood notes wild"* of the Bards of Freedom, We may yet acquire, by dint of repeating them, a more complete knowledge of the secret in which their greatness lies, than We could by mere prosaic admiration'.[34] The *Anti-Jacobin* maintains that parodic echoes provide a sharper method than critical prose for uncovering the illicit 'secret' veiled in Jacobin poetry. Their differential poetic echo purportedly redounds upon and homes in on the true 'principles' of Jacobin poetry, and the *Anti-Jacobin*'s supplementary 'prosaic admirations' help readers take note of those revealing parodic echoes.

The *Anti-Jacobin*'s farewell issue of 9 July 1798 forecasts its enduring influence on literary culture in 'The New Morality', a poem that calls for idling poets and reviewing critics to pick up its mantle and further exercise its 'keen shafts of satire and song' to 'animate the weak, unite the wise' and lead the country towards a cultural regeneration based on 'patriot pride'.[35] 'The New Morality' reflects back on many of the periodical's guiding prose principles and proclaims its central role in waging a successful print war against Jacobins and Whig opposition leaders. The poem also aligns the *Anti-Jacobin*'s power and success with

'Pope's satiric rage', carried on by Gifford in 'The Baviad' and Mathias, 'the name-less Bard-whose honest zeal / For Law, for Morals, for the Public Weal, / Pours down impetuous on thy Country's Foes' (ll. 43–5). In the midst of celebrating the *Anti-Jacobin's* heritage and influence, however, 'The New Morality' calls for more work to be done to ensure cultural victory. Reflecting back on its seven-month tenure, the prose and poetry in the final issue make the case that now, more than ever, poets need to guide an unsettled nation of readers. However, the poem also maintains that critical prose and parody should shape and monitor the terms of such a hypothetical poet/reader contract.

Through their politically charged reviewing practices, the *Anti-Jacobin* and *The Pursuits of Literature* style their prose and parody as indispensable guides for framing, monitoring and reforming the literary tastes of the nation. However, what seems unclear in 'The New Morality's' clarion call and in Mathias's own antagonistic relationship with other poets' marginal prose is what mediating roles (if any) poets' supplementary prose might play in such a system of poetry production and consumption legislated and judged by critical prose and parody.

From the 1798 'Advertisement' to the 1800 'Preface'

The two-page 'Advertisement' prefixed to the 1798 *Lyrical Ballads* remonstrates against such review culture governance by alternately refuting and adapting their multi-layered framework for judging poetry and legislating public taste. After initially celebrating the unlimited bounds of poetry – 'its materials are to be found in every subject which can interest the human mind' – the advertise-ment locates its 'evidence' for this proclamation in the writings of 'Poets' and not 'Critics'. As much as the advertisement asks readers to 'consent to be pleased' with the ensuing poems, it also maintains that the only valid prose frames from which to judge a poetic collection are the ones bound to it. This aggressive and possessive tone infuses the next three paragraphs, which challenge reviewing critics and general poetry readers to put aside their 'pre-established codes of decision' about poetry, work through their inevitable 'feelings of strangeness and awkwardness' and immerse themselves in a collection of 'experiments' made up of 'the language of conversation in the middle and lower classes of society'.[36] These reflections on poetry definitions, the cultivation of taste and judgement, and the differential process of 'perusing' *Lyrical Ballads* pointedly conclude with a paragraph about how to read five poems in the volume: 'Goody Blake and Harry Gill', 'The Thorn', 'The Rime of the Ancyent Marinere', 'Expostulation and Reply', and 'The Tables Turned'. Reviewers of the volume resoundingly heeded the advertisement. Whether positive (the majority) or negative, every 1798 and 1799 review quotes, paraphrases, mentions or echoes it.

From Coleridge's and Wordsworth's perspective, Southey's unsigned *Critical Review* essay in October 1798 was the most damaging to the integrity and market value of their volume, not only because Southey was one of its first reviewers and a definite part of their poetic circle, but also because Southey attacks several of their poems by taking issue with prose remarks about them in the 'Advertisement'.[37] Southey's largely negative review came as an unwelcome surprise to Coleridge and Wordsworth – who were in Germany – particularly since over the previous three years Coleridge and Southey had been close poetic collaborators and they were also brothers-in-law. Southey and Wordsworth also had become tentative admirers and imitators of each other's poetry. On a personal level, part of Southey's animus in the review may have come from his disappointment in Coleridge for giving up on their Pantisocracy scheme in America. However, Southey's specific criticisms and close attention to the linguistic and paratextual workings of the volume point towards another motive. The 1798 *Lyrical Ballads* was in direct competition with Southey's 1797 *Poems*, also published by Cottle, as well as Southey's plan for his two-volume 1799 *Poems*, made up of the revised 1797 volume and a new 1799 second volume to be published by Longman. Although Southey did not unmask Coleridge and Wordsworth as the authors of *Lyrical Ballads*,[38] his criticism reads like the work of an insider who has exposed the volume's 'Advertisement' as an artificial trapping that the author needlessly deploys to exercise his readers' 'ingenuity in attempting to unriddle what follows'.[39]

Southey declares the 'experiment' of *Lyrical Ballads* to be a failure and severs any governing plan to the volume by separating the bad poems – defined by worthless or absurd designs and subjects – from the volume's few 'serious pieces' and admirable poems.[40] 'The Idiot Boy' receives the most extensive ridicule as a 'Flemish picture in the worthlessness of its design', but Southey focuses much of the review on three poems singled out in the 'Advertisement' to *Lyrical Ballads*: 'The Thorn', 'Goody Blake and Harry Gill', and 'The Rime of the Ancyent Mariner'. Southey expressly disagrees with the interpretive contexts that the 'Advertisement' sets up for 'Goody Blake' and 'The Rime', and his criticism of 'The Thorn' seizes on the emphasis the 'Advertisement' places on the character of the poem's narrator, a Sea Captain. In response to the statement that 'Goody Blake and Harry Gill is founded on a well-authenticated fact that happened outside of Warwickshire', Southey asks, 'is the author certain that it is *"well authenticated?"* and does not such an assertion promote the popular superstition of witchcraft?'. Likewise, after rehearsing the claim that the 'Rime of the Ancyent Marinere was professedly written in imitation of the *style*, as well as the spirit of the elder poets', Southey chides, '[w]e are tolerably conversant with the early English poets; and can discover no resemblance whatever, except in antiquated spelling and a few obsolete words'.[41] Southey caustically charges that the prose of the advertisement has interfered with his reading experience and laid the groundwork for negative assessments.

Southey leads up to these two prose/poetry denigrations by turning one of the sentences of the advertisement about 'The Thorn' against the poem: 'The advertisement says, ['The Thorn'] is not told in the person of the author, but in that of some loquacious narrator. The author should have recollected that he who personates tiresome loquacity, becomes tiresome himself'.[42] Southey's rendition of that prose provides him with a rhetorical way to address the author, and his ensuing admonition implies that the author's prose sets up a parodic reading expectation. From Southey's perspective, the advertisement redoubles attention to what is 'tiresome' and mockable about the poem, the narrator's repetitious loquacity. Far from authorizing 'The Thorn', 'Goody Blake', and 'The Rime', the advertisement prompts readers to inquire into the limitations of these poems, and thus, seemingly opens them up to ridicule.

In volume 1 of the 1800 *Lyrical Ballads*, Wordsworth attempted to counter Southey's criticisms with more supplementary prose that would provide a connective framework for his poetic collection, separate his edition from similar publications (like Southey's), and alert readers to the particular reading experience that Wordsworth had created through revision and careful arrangement of his poems. While the 'Preface to *Lyrical Ballads*' is the most apparent prose supplement in this edition, Wordsworth also outfitted the reordered first volume with new endnotes to 'The Thorn', 'The Ancient Mariner', and 'Tintern Abbey', which ask readers to re-evaluate how they can 're-peruse' the poems in the first volume as well as the reprinted prose notation from the 1798 edition.

Wordsworth's 'Note to The Thorn' exemplifies his early experiments with how prose endnotes could mitigate mocking responses and foster a sympathetic reading. The note expands on the relationship set up in the 1798 *Lyrical Ballads* between the poem and the 'Advertisement' and reframes Southey's negative review of those prose/poetry interactions. Furthermore, the endnote stands in for an absent introductory poem which it mentions twice, extends Wordsworth's statements in the 1800 'Preface' about the limits of individual poems and projects the connective linguistic power of the entire two-volume collection.

Wordsworth's note provides a character analysis of the poem's narrator that no ballad could so succinctly detail. However, Wordsworth begins and ends this psycho-biography by asking readers to excuse his prose:

> This Poem ought to have been preceded by an introductory Poem, which I have been prevented from writing by never having felt myself in a mood when it was probable that I should write it well ... The Reader will have the kindness to excuse this note as I am sensible that an introductory Poem is necessary to give this Poem its full effect.[43]

According to this repeated apology, the endnote has been included only because an introductory poem, which would have given 'The Thorn' its 'full effect', has yet to be written. Though a compensatory supplement, the endnote does not complete 'The Thorn'. Moreover, the last half of the note suggests that the 'full effect' of the 'The Thorn' can only be experienced in conjunction with 'many other Poems in these volumes' – a projective and revisionary process guided by the 'few words' articulated in the remainder of the endnote. As Chapter 2 will explain more completely, this latter part of the note recontextualizes the repetitive language in 'The Thorn' as a projection of the connective poetic language throughout his volumes.

'The Note to The Thorn' acts as a defensive and corrective supplement for the poem itself, but it also mirrors the preface, which encourages readers to push beyond the limits and potential 'defects' of individual poems to create meaning through other poems and contextual prose.[44] In the preface Wordsworth tends to those limitations and defects by including several pages that stipulate the purpose and context through which to read over a dozen poems, including a direct response to Southey's attack on 'Goody Blake' as a dubious fact and promotion of superstition:

> 'I wished to draw attention to the truth that the power of the human imagination is sufficient to produce such changes even in our physical nature as might almost appear miraculous. The truth is an important one; the fact (for it is a *fact*) is a valuable illustration of it.[45]

Beyond these prose remarks about individual poems, Wordsworth offers readers oblique advice about how to 'perus[e]' and 're-perus[e]' all of the poems in the volumes:[46]

> If an Author by any single composition has impressed us with respect for his talents, it is useful to consider this as affording a presumption, that, on other occasions, where we have been displeased, he nevertheless may not have written ill or absurdly; and, further, to give him so much credit for this one composition as may induce us to review what has displeased us with more care than we should otherwise have bestowed upon it.[47]

This passage builds on several places in the preface where Wordsworth is at pains to express how his poems require rereading, not just individually but in relation to one another, and several other parts of the preface articulate how prose can facilitate and ameliorate this rereading process. Particularly in the middle portion of the preface, Wordsworth attempts to explain how prose informs his poetry by rehearsing the arguments of late eighteenth-century writers who challenged formal distinctions between poetry and prose, pointed out their commonalities and mixed them together, novelized poetry or poeticized the novel, and mediated the vogue for collecting oral ballads of the past in commercialized books with the modern language of prose.[48] The middle section of the 'Preface' works through several of these prose/poetry conflations in order to explain the particular value and purpose of Wordsworth's 'class of poetry', which borders on, runs into, and even depends on prose.[49]

From beginning to end, the 'Preface' posits a dynamic but unsettled relationship between Wordsworth's prose and poetry. In the first few paragraphs, Wordsworth privileges his poetry by contrasting the accessibility of his poetic language – 'a selection of the real language of men' – with the artificial, 'systematic' and potentially alienating '*reasoning*' of a preface.[50] However, throughout the preface Wordsworth also paradoxically relies on the explanatory power and limitations of his prose to encourage readers to engage with his poetry. By the end of the essay, Wordsworth remains fixated on how readers will move beyond both his prose exposition and the supposed defects in poems, which

> may frequently have suffered from those arbitrary connections of feelings and ideas with particular words, from which no man can protect himself. Hence I have no doubt that in some instances feelings even of the ludicrous may be given to my Readers by expressions which appeared to me tender and pathetic.[51]

Out of this unresolved but seemingly inextricable tension between the overlapping powers and limits of his prose and poetry, Wordsworth sets up a compensatory and additive reading experience in his volumes that interweaves its variegated poems and prose in a manner akin to what Neil Fraistat has called 'contexture'.[52]

Rereading Volume 1

Working both with and against the organizing principles of many collections of poetry and anthologies in the late eighteenth century, Wordsworth sought to alter the types of reading habits – such as skipping from poem to poem and perusing lyrical excerpts – that such collections encouraged as pleasurable for a growing middle-class readership. In his 'Preface' Wordsworth contends that readers can experience a more fulfilling kind of 'pleasure' when reading his collection of poems.[53] He aligns that pleasure, in part, with his editorial manoeuvrings – many of which follow Percy's editorial practices in *Reliques of Ancient Poetry* and counter the more common collecting techniques used at the end of the eighteenth century in anthologies such as Vicisimus Knox's *Elegant Extracts of Poetry: or Useful and Entertaining Pieces of Poetry, Selected for the Improvement of Youth* (1784).[54] Both Percy's *Reliques* and Knox's *Elegant Extracts*, in verse and prose, were popular during the last few decades of the eighteenth century. However, the different audiences, tastes and reading practices that these anthologies appealed to and cultivated led Wordsworth to side with Percy's guiding editorial presence.[55]

In 1794, Percy published a three-volume fourth edition of the *Reliques* which Wordsworth owned.[56] Percy prefixed an 'Advertisement' to that edition, which announced that nearly twenty years had elapsed since the *Reliques*'s last publication. Between its first publication in 1765 and its third ten years later, his volumes were attacked by antiquarians such as Joseph Ritson because Percy often altered, updated, abridged and corrected the language of many of the old heroic ballads and songs that he had collected for the public.[57] Conversely, these very same efforts were applauded by many poets, literary critics and editors, including Samuel Johnson, Joseph Warton, Southey, Coleridge, Scott and Wordsworth. While Percy's anthology met with a degree of public scorn, it also inspired a vogue for ballads and short, lyric poems. In his 'Advertisement to the Fourth Edition' Percy attributes a significant part of this popularity to his past and present efforts to correct printing errors, recur to original manuscripts, emend individual poems and situate connective prose notes, which introduce, interpret and occasionally defend the choice of ballads and lyric pieces that he has brought together. Given this editorial labour, Percy asks the public to 'judge how much they are indebted to the composer of this collection'.[58]

In contrast to Percy's pervasive editorial presence in his collection, Knox's *Elegant Extracts* was adopted widely as a text for school children because it was an anthology that seemingly required little mediation.[59] Knox advertised it as a collection that captured already existing public tastes for poetry and in the 'Preface' to the 1787 edition he assumes little credit for his role as an editor. Instead, Knox describes himself as an 'artisan', hoping to fall 'back into the shade of obscurity', and maintains that anyone could put together a collection in which the guiding principle focuses on picking that which is most popular. Knox demurs that in an anthology the 'best pieces are usually the most popular'.[60] When describing the organization of this anthology, he also calls his work an 'artificial disposition', a 'garland or nosegay ... carelessly mingled with all the ease and wildness of natural variety'. What he brings to this mixture of flowers is nothing of his own, except, in Montaigne's words, which he quotes, 'the thread that ties them'.[61] Knox intends his anthology to function as a means for school children to memorize, transcribe, recite and imitate, and he divides his volumes accordingly into four distinct sections. However, the anthology in no way encourages connective reading. The pleasure that Knox associates with reading his *Elegant Extracts* comes from his assertion that within the anthology 'such a number and variety [exist] as might furnish something satisfactory to every taste'.[62]

In chapter 7 of her *Strictures on the Modern System of Female Education* (1799), Hanna More offers an implicit critique of Knox's anthology making. More condemns the fashion of educating girls through 'the hot-bed of a circulating library' and through the widespread use of abridgements and anthologies, 'which form too considerable a part of a young lady's library'.[63] Although More understands the benefits of these excerpting devices and their purpose to control the overwhelming amount of information flooding the print market, she singles them out as mechanisms that produce a 'superficial mind'.[64] More maintains that in these collections:

A few fine passages from the poets (passages perhaps which derived their chief beauty from their position and connection) are huddled together by some extract-maker, whose brief and disconnected patches of broken and discordant materials, while they inflame young readers with a vanity of reciting, neither fill the mind nor form the taste: and it is not difficult to trace back to their shallow sources the hackney'd quotations of certain accomplished young ladies, who will be frequently found not to have come legitimately by any thing they know: I mean, not to have drawn it from its true spring, the original works of the author from which some beauty-monger has severed it.[65]

More's commentary relates directly to her ideas about how to reconfigure the education of women. However, her aesthetic criteria for published collections of poetry serve as a general criticism of poetry anthologies at the turn of the century. These collections erase the original 'position and connection' of a poem in its published context, which, in turn, destroys both the individual beauty of a poem and the organic unity of its place within a larger network of poetry. This process of dislocating individual poems and then reassembling them as an unrelated mass 'huddle[ed] together' also affects the minds of those who read them. While individual poems may 'inflame' readers' minds, inevitably, this passion is short-lived, 'neither fill[ing] the mind nor form[ing] the taste' in the long term. In sum, 'hackneyed quotations' will lead to a hackneyed mind – for More, a typically feminine, fragmented and incomplete one. To cure such a mind, More recommends entire books because they 'exercise the reasoning faculties, teach the mind to get acquainted with its own nature, and ... stir up its own powers'.[66] She specifically describes books that feature coherent and connective designs that encourage hard work, sacrifice and self-reflection on the part of readers.

While Wordsworth seems to have enjoyed Knox's *Elegant Extracts* and acknowledged the widespread currency of its poetic contents, his two-volume *Lyrical Ballads* features a guiding, editorial persona more like Percy's, and the 1800 'Preface' recalls More's aesthetic and educational criteria for collections of poetry. In that preface Wordsworth aligns his collection with the pleasure readers can experience when they closely attend to the special, connective qualities of his language. The 'Preface' develops what the 1798 'Advertisement' only vaguely touches on when it differentiates the language of the 1798 poems from the 'gaudy and inane phraseology of many modern writers'. The 1798 'Advertisement' reads as though it were publicizing a self-help manual, which requires readers to be vigilant and on their guard to inquire into, monitor, and alter their 'pre-established codes of decision'.[67] By contrast, the 'Preface' articulates a theory of poetic language that seeks to overthrow the seeming emptiness of eighteenth-century poetic phraseologies and reform reading habits.[68]

The 'Preface' describes a poetic language of elastic words that has the capacity to expand, in relation to the emotional ordeals of Wordsworth's characters, and be filled with the sympathetic responses of readers who encounter those characters. It also extends the self-monitoring declaration of the 'Advertisement'.[69] In the first paragraph of the 'Preface', Wordsworth briefly recounts the reception history of the 1798 edition by noting, '[t]he First Volume of these Poems has already been submitted to general perusal'. Wordsworth's use of the word 'perusal' in relation to the 1798 *Lyrical Ballads* perhaps recalls a Knox-like anthology-skimming; however, the revisionary context in which Wordsworth employs 'perusal' in the 'Preface' suggests that readers will need to engage in an intensive and sustained exploration of his expanded and reconfigured edition.[70]

Whether the 1798 poems elicited 'more than common pleasure' or 'more than common dislike', Wordsworth asserts that the collective value of his new volumes can be found in their capacity to elevate readers above the 'common' emotional responses conjured up by other contemporary poetry publications. The 'principal object' of the poems in these volumes is 'to make the incidents of common life interesting by tracing in them, truly though not ostentatiously, the primary laws of our nature: chiefly as far as regards the manner in which we associate ideas in a state of excitement'. Wordsworth also directly associates poetic pleasure with the poet's and his readers' capacities to trace 'the fluxes and refluxes of the mind when agitated by the great and simple affections of our nature' through the perception of 'similitude in dissimilitude, and dissimilitude in similitude'. Wordsworth predicates the pleasure and cultural importance of his poetic language on its ability to activate and energize the connective powers of his readers' minds.[71]

In a few of the prose notes that Wordsworth added to the 1800 edition, he extends this concept of how readers can fire their minds – through comparisons of words and dramatic situations – by asking readers to compare present poems to poems that are not included in either volume. These notes advertise the future development of Wordsworth's poetry and ask readers to imagine how a potential poem or poems might alter their current engagement with a particular poem or group of poems. For instance, Wordsworth's first footnote to 'The Brothers' in volume 2 begins: 'This Poem was intended to be the concluding poem of a series of pastorals, the scene of which was laid among the mountains of Cumberland and Westmoreland. I mention this to apologize for the abruptness with which the poem begins.'[72] This footnote serves as an apology to readers, perhaps excusing the overly familiar beginning of the poem – 'These Tourists, Heaven preserve us!' – and it reveals that 'The Brothers' was supposed to be part of a series of pastoral poems that Wordsworth either has yet to finish or has decided not to publish in the 1800 edition.[73]

Through these apologetic, self-advertising techniques, Wordsworth suggests to readers that his collection operates through a pattern of growth, which not only connects together present and future poems, but also – as his note to

'The Thorn' explains – relates the emotional contexts behind the composition of past poems to the writing of new ones. Wordsworth's significant reordering of the 1798 edition in the first volume of the 1800 collection plays out this pattern of continual growth by underscoring for readers the importance of how he places and replaces his poems. As many critics have pointed out, one the most notable changes to the 1798 *Lyrical Ballads* was that Wordsworth moved the opening poem to the second to last poem in volume 1 of the 1800 edition. He also convinced Coleridge to change the name of that poem from 'The Rime of the Ancyent Marinere' to 'The Ancient Mariner: A Poet's Reverie'.[74] In its place, Wordsworth moved 'Expostulation and Reply' and 'The Tables Turned' from their positions as the eighteenth and nineteenth poems in the 1798 edition.[75]

Even more explicitly than this shuffling of poems, in the second to last endnote in the first volume, Wordsworth uses the 'The Ancient Mariner' as an example to demonstrate the importance of reordering and revising for the overall development of his *Lyrical Ballads*. Sounding a bit like Southey in his review of the 1798 *Lyrical Ballads*, Wordsworth denigrates the Mariner's and the poet's (Coleridge's) character before defending the poem's republished value according to his own guiding principles, which purportedly connect together all the poems in the 1800 volumes:

> I cannot refuse myself the gratification of informing such Readers as may have been pleased with the Poem, or with any part of it, that they owe their pleasure in some sort to me; as the Author was himself very desirous that it should be suppressed. The wish had arisen from a consciousness of the defects in the Poem, and from a knowledge that many persons had been much displeased with it.[76]

Wordsworth addresses 'such Readers as may have been pleased with the Poem', suggesting those readers who have only read the 1800 version of the poem, as well as those readers who took pleasure in the poem in 1798 and have now reread the revised and resituated poem in 1800. In both cases, from Wordsworth's perspective, readers 'owe their pleasure in some sort to me'. The note openly incorporates the pleasure of readers – past and present – into the wider pleasure associated with Wordsworth's connective purpose, outlined in the 'Preface'.

Wordsworth, however, does not end the note by simply taking credit for that pleasure. By informing readers of past (and now) acknowledged defects in the poem, he seeks to make his readers aware of the emotional criterion from which to judge Coleridge's poem, and he also implicitly recalls the poems – 'Expostulation and Reply' and 'The Tables Turned' – that have displaced 'The Ancient Mariner'. Wordsworth offers three particular criticisms of Coleridge's poem: the mariner has no distinct character; he 'does not act, but is continually acted upon'; and the plot of the poem consists of unconnected events. These criticisms call to mind the contrast between the Mariner's lack of character and the distinctness of William's own character in 'Expostulation and Reply', long under the influence, but not the control, of natural impressions taken in from nature. Unlike the Mariner who is continually acted upon, 'William' remarks in 'Expostulation and Reply' that 'we can feed this mind of ours, / In a wise passiveness' and adds in 'The Tables Turned' that he (and readers) need to bring 'a heart / That [reciprocally] watches and receives'. Finally, in his third criticism, Wordsworth argues 'that the events [in Coleridge's poem] having no necessary connection do not produce each other'.

All three of these criticisms reveal Wordsworth's concerns about the Mariner's disembodied character, disconnected actions and displaced wandering. To explain the poem's new place and value in the 1800 volume, Wordsworth shifts attention away from the supernatural events and, at times, archaic language in the poem and instead connects the Mariner's passion with the type of passion exhibited in other poems throughout his volumes. While Wordsworth understands the plot of 'The Ancient Mariner' to be 'disjointed', he does find 'many delicate touches of passion, and indeed the passion is every where true to nature ... [giving] the Poem a value which is not often possessed by better Poems'.[77] The endnote classifies the mariner's passion as 'true to nature' and incorporates 'The Ancient Mariner' under the system outlined in his 'Preface', which 'distinguishes these Poems from the popular Poetry of the day' and asserts 'that the feeling therein developed [in a poem] gives importance to the action and situation and not the action and situation to the feeling'.[78] With a new title, a new prose 'Argument' and an endnote that resituates and reframes the poem, Wordsworth revises – and even reverses – the textual details and critical reception surrounding the poem's 1798 publication to make it conform to the principles of growth organizing his poetic collection. As an editor, Wordsworth takes credit for affording readers the opportunity to re-experience Coleridge's poem under his own watchful and reshaping eye. Moreover, his criticisms, recontextualization and reabsorption of Coleridge's poem model how readers can re-evaluate the poems in volume 1 and proceed through the pastoral ballads in volume 2.

2 TEXTUAL TRAVELLING IN THE 1800 *LYRICAL BALLADS*

Wordsworth's preface and endnotes in the first volume defend against criticisms levelled at the 1798 *Lyrical Ballads*, and they also link its lyrical ballads genre, ethos and tone to the new pastoral poems and emotional place-keeping maintained by the second volume. In contrast to the first volume's sparse (reprinted) footnotes, headnotes and subtitles, the second volume includes several poems with prose supplements that engage with the vogue for touring the English Lake District and exploring its local histories.[1] As a tour guide and editor Wordsworth takes readers of the first volume on a geographical, metaphorical and affective journey into the second volume,[2] which involves prose that juxtaposes the pleasures of reading his poems with picturesque touring in northern England. Many of Wordsworth's prose notes comment on the landscape, customs and people in the Lake District, but primarily they serve as directions for how readers can travel meaningfully through his poetic collection. While these scattered notes do not detail a systematic way of reading the poems in the 1800 volumes, they do ask readers to reflect on, adjust and amend their interpretations of individual and multiple poems.

As Stephen Parrish and David Duff have demonstrated, Wordsworth's experiments with the pastoral genre heavily mark the poetry and prose in the 1800 *Lyrical Ballads*.[3] Building on Parrish's incisive work about Wordsworth's 'pastoral ballad', Duff argues that Wordsworth's paratextual and bibliographic changes to 'The Brothers' – alterations were made to its half-title page, subtitle, or accompanying footnote nearly every time the poem was published – reveal how completely the 1800 volumes were bound up with Wordsworth's efforts to class his poems as a reinvigorated brand of pastoral poetry.[4] While Parrish and Duff describe Wordsworth's efforts to reinvent the often denigrated pastoral genre of the eighteenth century, Steven Jones argues further that Wordsworth challenged and attempted to reform typical eighteenth-century satirical responses to pastoral poetry and rustic characters.[5] This 'countersatiric' mode turns on Wordsworth's particular choice of pastoral language, supplementary prose and London publisher – all of which, Michael Baron maintains, separated his poetry in the commercial market from other Cumbrian poets, such as Robert Anderson, who wrote much of their ballad poetry in provincial dialect.[6] By contrast, Wordsworth aligns the significance of his new *Lyrical Ballads* with the nature poetry, rural settings and standard English language of widely read and often reprinted 'Old Canon' poets such as the lowland Scottish poet and celebrator of British liberty James Thompson.[7]

Through a variety of prose supplements and pastoral poems, Wordsworth makes a case for how his seemingly marginal collection offers an essential and abiding, communal space reified by the emotional and intellectual work of readers who modulate their responses as they travel through his multi-layered volumes.[8] Particularly in his 'Note to The Thorn' at the end of the first volume and internal 'Advertisement' to a group of five poems called 'Poems on the Naming of Places' towards the end of the second volume, Wordsworth describes how readers can trace and extend the recursive poetics played out in the 1800 edition. These prose notes suggest how the repetition of specific words from poem to poem engenders emotional touchstones to which readers can return and build on. Certain words, like 'stone', act as symbolic markers that situate how readers engage with individual poems, and which enable readers to record and connect together their emotional responses to multiple poems as they journey towards the unfinished, stone sheepfold in 'Michael, A Pastoral Poem'.[9]

Collecting Places and Advertising Emotion

Beyond advertising the revisionary qualities and connective patterns of growth in the 1800 edition, Wordsworth's prose in the second volume prompts readers to focus on contemporary customs, places and oral histories of the English Lake District.[10] These prose descriptions intertwine the poetic words and passions of his characters with specific locations, objects and inhabitants of the Lake District. In contrast to his prefatory denigration of London culture and city life – a place where 'a multitude of causes unknown to former times are now acting with a combined force to blunt the discriminating powers of the mind, and unfitting it for all voluntary exertion to reduce it to a state of savage torpor'[11] – these prose notes inscribe how his poems represent a healthier life, associated particularly with Cumberland and Westmoreland in the Lake District. As an editorial guide, Wordsworth informs readers about the textual condition and placement of his poems, but his prose notes also relate the pleasures of reading individual poems to the imaginative access he offers readers to the geographical places and histories behind those poems. Several of these notes highlight the picturesque landscape of the Lake District. For example, in 'Rural Architecture', Wordsworth adds a footnote that describes Great How Mountain: 'Great How is a single and conspicuous hill, which rises towards the foot of Thirl-mere, on the western side of the beautiful dale of Legberthwaite, along the high road between Keswick and Ambleside'.[12] Notes such as this one suggest that Wordsworth partially conceived of the 1800 *Lyrical Ballads* – published like the 1798 volume in foolscap octavo, pocket edition – as volumes that picturesque travellers could carry with them around the Lake District or Somersetshire.[13]

Particularly in the second volume, several notes, like the one above to 'Rural Architecture', portray Wordsworth as a tour guide, capable of directing readers to actual places. Accordingly, the first endnote to 'Michael' locates 'Ings Chapel' on 'the right hand side of the road leading from Kendal to Ambleside'.[14] Another internal note to a poem about Joanna's rock in 'Poems on the Naming of Places' carves out the geographical details of the area in which this poetic tale supposedly happened:

> The Rotha, mentioned in this poem, is the River which flowing through the Lakes of Grasmere and Rydale falls into Wyndermere. On Helm-Crag, that impressive single Mountain at the head of the Vale of Grasmere, is a Rock which from most points of view bears a striking resemblance to an Old Woman cowering. Close by this rock is one of those Fissures or Caverns, which in the language of the Country are called Dungeons. The other Mountains either immediately surround the Vale of Grasmere, or belong to the same Cluster.[15]

Wordsworth's attention to particular and expansive geographic detail is unmistakable, and several of Wordsworth's reviewers noted this particular emphasis on place.[16] In an unsigned review of *Lyrical Ballads* from the *British Critic* of February 1801, the reviewer – probably Wordsworth's friend John Stoddard – praises Wordsworth in a footnote to the review because Wordsworth has chosen rustic situations that portray the elemental passions of the heart in relation to the permanent forms of nature:

> Mr. Wordsworth seems to be peculiarly well situated for the subjects of such a study. The vicinity of the Lakes in Cumberland and Westmoreland (the scene of most of his Poems) is chiefly inhabited by an order of men nearly extinct in other parts of England. These are small farmers, called in that part of the country 'Statesmen,' who, cultivating their own little property, are raised above the immediate pressure of want, with very few opportunities of acquiring wealth. They are mild, hospitable people, with some turn for reading; and their personal appearance is, for the most part, interesting.[17]

The only footnote in the review, this sympathetic annotation draws readers' eyes downwards just as Wordsworth's footnotes do, and it also reads like a generous summary of Wordsworth's own notes in the second volume. Stoddard describes Wordsworth's specific perspective as 'well situated' and points out the universal value of his observations about 'small farmers' in Cumberland and Westmoreland. For this reviewer, Wordsworth has inscribed his poetic authority in the volumes not only because of how well situated he is in relation to his subjects, but also because of how carefully the prose notes, linked to his poems, inform and situate readers in relation to those 'subjects'.

The first volume of the 1800 edition often reminds readers of how 'well situated' they are and how a prose vantage point or a poetic injunction can afford them a particular kind of pleasure when reading Wordsworth's poems; and the second volume extends these poetry and prose groundings. On a few occasions, such place holders take the form of Wordsworth halting his readers with the first line of a poem, as in the opening line of 'Lines Left upon a Seat in a Yew-Tree', 'Nay, Traveller! Rest' – a direct address that he recurs to in the second volume with the first line of 'Michael' – 'If from the public way you turn your steps'. Wordsworth also includes several lengthy prose headnotes that provide brief cultural and geographical histories to situate readers before 'The Complaint of the forsaken Indian Woman' in volume 1, and 'Hart-Leap Well', 'Written in Germany', and 'The Old Cumberland Beggar' in volume 2.

At several points Wordsworth stops readers in the midst of a poem – or, depending on how one reads, at the end of the page – with footnotes that point out specific features of the geographic area in which a poem is set or that describe customs of the people inhabiting that area. For example, in the middle of 'The Female Vagrant', he includes the first footnote in volume 1: 'Several of the Lakes in the north of England are let out to different Fishermen, in parcels marked out by imaginary lines drawn from rock to rock'.[18] This note comments on the female vagrant's emotional description of how her father's fishing rights – 'marked out by imaginary lines' – were usurped by a new encroaching economy. The seemingly natural boundary line of her father's fishing range, marked 'from rock to rock', is erased by a greedy and powerful interloper, and father and daughter's goods and home are invariably seized. The note invites readers to pause, imagine, reflect on and evaluate their emotional responses to her story by considering what the shared boundaries are – whether natural or imaginary – that bind real communities, like this one in the Lake District, together.

Other reprinted footnotes in the first volume, such as the first footnote to 'Tintern Abbey', alert readers to the particular geographic perspectives that define individual poems: 'The river is not affected by the tides a few miles above Tintern'.[19] Although seemingly superfluous because it largely repeats what the title announces, 'Lines Written a Few Miles above Tintern Abbey', this note informs readers how different the poet's perspective is in the first verse paragraph from common picturesque framings of the tourist destination Tintern Abbey. Wordsworth connects that note to the lines, 'again I hear / These waters, rolling from their mountain-springs / With a sweet inland murmur' (ll. 2–4). The note reminds readers that what they might see from such a prospect is less important, from the poet's perspective, than how the continuity of the river – from its imagined 'mountain springs' origin, heard as a 'sweet inland murmur' – figures his emotional return and reflections on the landscape. In asking readers to hear the mild progress of the river, Wordsworth seeks not only to shift their expectations of a prospect view but to change the perspective from which they view the progress of his blank verse paragraphs.[20] In the poem, Wordsworth describes his extensive view of the landscape as a real site that readers could encounter on a tour. However, the note, which highlights his aural perspective on the river, transforms that site by singling out from where his acute pleasure flows.

The footnote aligns the origins and progress of the river with the capacity the poet and his readers have to hear the poet's language and commitment to his vocation 'again'. This note underscores the poet's and readers' place in the poem, and calls attention to how particular poetic words – heard and uttered 'again' – can engender a well-situated perspective from which to connect what has passed with the imagined twists and turns of what will come. The endnote that Wordsworth added to the poem for the 1800 edition draws further attention to the sounding of emotions and shifts in the poem: 'I have not ventured to call this Poem an Ode; but it was written with a hope that in the transitions, and the impassioned music of the versification, would be found the principal requisites of that species of composition'.[21] Beyond aligning his blank verse poem with the musicality and strophe, antistrophe, epode movements of the ode, Wordsworth's heading above the endnote, 'NOTE to the Poem ON REVISITING THE WYE', singles out the act of revisiting the Wye River from the many words in its long title 'Lines Written a Few Miles above Tintern Abbey, ON REVISITING THE BANKS OF THE WYE DURING A TOUR, JULY 13, 1798'.

This dual movement between revisiting (and revising) the past and turning towards what will come defines Wordsworth's brand of poetic pleasure, which he closely aligns with the journey that the second volume offers readers through the Lake District. When Alan Boehm maintains that the 1798 edition was meant to reform picturesque travel, he underplays how central this simulation of travel is to the 1800 volumes. 'Lines written' embodies Wordsworth's revisionary concerns in the first volume with establishing a unique relationship between poetic language, location, perspective and the emotional process of turning and returning to poems and places. Furthermore, the poem points through the endnote to 'The Thorn', which follows 'Lines Written' and precedes the endnote to 'The Ancient Mariner', towards the major focus of the second volume – the creation of monumental touchstones that mark specific places and encourage readers to reflect upon, return to and build up the emotional contexts of the first volume.

Placed before Wordsworth's endnote to 'The Ancient Mariner', the endnote to 'The Thorn' offers readers a concerted opportunity to reflect on Wordsworth's guiding presence. Following his defence of the perspective from which the poem is told, Wordsworth lays out a theory of poetic language that binds together the 1800 volumes. The note reaffirms that carefully chosen words maintain and build intense feeling and that – when repeated in several poems – such words create layers of meaning that can bind his readers and poems together.

In the note Wordsworth turns the Sea Captain's gossipy character, super-stitious nature and infatuation with certain words into an ironic model that demonstrates how readers can internalize repeated language in his poems. The note draws attention to the Sea Captain's obsessive and repetitious fascination with Martha Ray's miserable complaint –'Oh misery! Oh misery! / Oh woe is me! oh misery!' – which, even though the Sea Captain is painfully unable to answer 'why / Does she repeat that doleful cry?' (vol. 1, ll. 87–8), nevertheless demonstrates how the repetition of words creates and transfers the emotional power behind his story. These words, which are also the last two lines of the poem – 'Oh misery! Oh misery! / Oh woe is me! oh misery!' – entirely pos-sess the Sea Captain's mind, rendering him unable to think of the place without strong feelings and, as Wordsworth's note suggests, perversely inhabiting the built up and emotional force of those words.[22] Martha Ray's unending woe leads to the Sea Captain's repetitious, linguistic obsession with a place. These haunt-ing repetitions provide Wordsworth with an opportunity to suggest that readers consider how to distance their interpretation from the Sea Captain's sensational linguistic obsessions.

In this note the Sea Captain appears as a satirical caricature in need of cor-rection, which the second half of the note undertakes by guiding readers towards emotionally healthy linguistic associations: 'Upon this occasion I will request permission to add a few words closely connected with "The Thorn" and many other Poems in these volumes'. Wordsworth offers a set of instructions on how to read the repetition of words in individual and multiple poems and defends the propriety of repeating the same words, provided that they take on differ-ent meanings, against the ineffective practice of using different words that all have the same meaning. He further maintains that '[w]ords, a Poet's words more particularly, ought to be weighed in the balance of feeling, and not measured by the space which they occupy upon paper'.[23] Poetic words should be judged by the emotional contexts created through the repetition of a given word and not measured mechanically by how many times a word, or cluster of words, is repeated on a page.

To support his claims about word repetition, Wordsworth reminds readers of how poetry has the capacity to connect words to feelings: 'Poetry is passion: it is the history or science of feelings'. Poetry is not mere word play; it is a discipline like history or science that has as its object of study human 'feelings'. Wordsworth also suggests that an overabundance of language can even stand in the way of poetry's object: 'now every man must know that an attempt is rarely made to communicate impassioned feelings without something of an accompanying consciousness of the inadequateness of our own powers or the deficiencies of language'. Owing to these deficiencies in language, the human mind, he argues, when 'unsatisfied ... will cling to the same words, or words of the same character'. Wordsworth then offers three reasons to support his contention that repetition and apparent tautology often produce 'beauties of the highest' kind:

> Among the chief of these reasons is the interest which the mind attaches to words, not only as symbols of the passion, but as things, active and efficient, which are of themselves part of the passion. And further from a spirit of fondness, exultation, and gratitude, the mind luxuriates in the repetition of words which appear successfully to communicate the feelings.[24]

Such words can be symbolic of passion, and they can even become '*things*' that are intricately linked to that passion. Repeated words can gratify the mind as it exults in how those words have communicated and continue to communicate powerful feelings.

At the beginning of the second volume, the headnote to 'Hart-Leap Well' builds on this series of ideas by announcing how repetition and return to the same words and places can create monuments that connect together 'things' and 'passions':

> Hart-Leap Well is a small spring of water, about five miles from Richmond in York-shire, and near the side of the road which leads from Richmond to Askrigg. Its name is derived from a remarkable chace, the memory of which is preserved by the monuments spoken of in the second Part of the following Poem, which monuments do now exist as I have there described them.[25]

This headnote forecasts how, in the second part of the poem, the poet revisits the words in the first part of the story and reframes the meaning and place of three stone pillars.[26] The significance of the story told in that first section about these stone pillars only becomes apparent through the revisionary commentary about stones in the second section. The headnote also suggests how this process of reading backwards and forwards across Wordsworth's pastoral landscapes can transform words into monuments and intricately involves readers in the making of his poetic collection.

In volume 2 of the 1800 *Lyrical Ballads* such monumentalizing activities, which involve moving backwards and forwards not only between prose notes and poetry but also between poems, occur most prominently in Wordsworth's endnotes to 'The Brothers' and in his note to the second poem in the section 'Poems on the Naming of Places'. In these notes, Wordsworth recounts the oral histories behind the places identified in these poems, and he relates this information to the perceived habits of wandering tourists. In 'The Brothers' the Priest of Ennerdale begins the poem, 'These Tourists, Heaven preserve us! needs must live / A profitable life'. For the first ten lines, the Priest denigrates tourists as wayward butterflies or scribbling sketch artists wasting the day. Readers have no immediate basis for grasping to whom – could it be readers? – the Priest directs his discourse and are left to situate themselves in the poem in relation to these chastising comments.

The Priest only clearly addresses an individual milling around his churchyard in line 12. He describes this man as:

> one of those who needs must leave the path
> Of the world's business, to go wild alone:
> …
> The happy man will creep about the fields
> Following his fancies by the hour, to bring
> Tears down his cheek, or solitary smiles' (vol. 2, ll. 103–8).

He sees the man (Leonard) as a tourist bent on consuming the natural world to manufacture strong but artificial sensations. Consequently, when Leonard later asks the Priest about what has changed in the landscape over the last twenty years, the Priest responds with 'a feast / For folks that wander up and down like you' (ll. 149–50). He tells a story of destruction that involves two springs, one of which was destroyed by the effects of a blast of lightning that struck a nearby crag (l. 143). Wordsworth's endnote recontextualizes the Priest's tale, however, and explains the origin of these companion springs, which later in the poem come to symbolize Leonard and his deceased brother:

> The impressive circumstance here described, actually took place some years ago in this country, upon an eminence called Kidstow Pike, one of the highest of the mountains that surround Hawes-water. The summit of the pike was stricken by lightning; and every trace of one of the fountains disappeared, while the other continued to flow as before.[27]

Wordsworth's note relates this uncanny event in the poem to local lore that grounds the place of the Priest's story and Wordsworth's placement of the poem in the second volume.[28] As the third poem in volume 2, 'The Brothers' introduces readers to an oral history that prompts them to think through the written materials making up its emotional composition. The note encourages readers to consider what makes a poem such as 'The Brothers' valuable and emotionally transformative.

Wordsworth's next endnote to 'The Brothers' suggests how readers can engage in this process of making and remaking the value of his poems. Referring to the lack of gravestones in the churchyard, Leonard asks how the members of this community are able to distinguish 'the dead man's home' from 'that pasture field' (ll. 174, 175). The Priest's response links the dead and the living through shared oral discourses, 'plain tale[s]' that provide a 'second life' for the deceased and the community in which they are told. The endnote further explains,

> There is not any thing more worthy of remark in the manners of the inhabitants of these mountains, than the tranquility, I might say indifference, with which they think and talk upon the subject of death. Some of the country church-yards, as here described, do not contain a single tombstone, and most of them have a very small number.[29]

As in the previous endnote, Wordsworth frames his description of place according to how these mountain inhabitants measure their sense of community through shared tales and not through picturesque markings and solitary tombstones. This note suggests that meaningful tales are made and sustained – like the monuments recalled in the headnote to 'Hart-Leap Well' – by the communities that tell and retell them. Through the Priest's story, Leonard and Wordsworth's readers are initiated into and then dislocated from a pastoral community of monumental storytelling.

While Leonard is so haunted by 'such a weight' that he gives up his intentions to return home and instead goes to sea (l. 438), Wordsworth's readers are left to evaluate both that emotional 'weight' and the cumulative weight of storytelling as they turn towards other poems in the volume.

Even more explicitly than these endnotes to 'The Brothers', Wordsworth's note following the second poem in 'Poems on the Naming of Places' foregrounds how his poetry is made, can be shared and retold: 'In Cumberland and Westmoreland are several Inscriptions upon the native rock which from the wasting of Time and the rudeness of the Workmanship had been mistaken for Runic. They are without doubt Roman.'[30] This part of the note alludes to lines 29–32 in the poem when a vicar from a nearby house asks the poet why he has been carving into the nearby rocks. The vicar likens the poet's activities to

> a Runic Priest, [who] in characters
> Of formidable size, had chisel'd out
> Some uncouth name upon the native rock,
> Above the Rotha, by the forest side.

The poet corrects the vicar's explanation of this inscription by relating the story of how he and Joanna shared an experience that led the poet to carve her name 'upon the living stone'. Occurring years earlier, Joanna's derisive laughter – directed at the poet's delight in the expansive view in front of them – was echoed back all around them, and this 'work accomplish'd by the brotherhood / Of ancient mountains' (ll. 69–70) frightened Joanna and drew her closer to the poet. While the poem relates how Wordsworth alters the assumptions of an inhabitant of the area, the note corrects what appears to be a common anthropological and antiquarian misconception about the origin of such an inscription. The note demystifies the history of a commonly-visited place in the Lake District, but it also redoubles attention to how even common words or names, such as 'Joanna', can tell a story, foster a community and monumentalize emotional connections when they are revisited, re-echoed and reinscribed.

To explain the emotional significance of inscribing words like 'To Joanna', Wordsworth inserted an 'Advertisement' a few pages before this poem that introduces it and four other poems as 'Poems on the Naming of Places'. The 'Advertisement' calls attention to how 'well situated' the poet is, records the value of specific words and intimately connects particular places, through those words, with poetic pleasure. Appearing three-quarters of the way through the second volume and garnering its own half-title page, this advertisement temporarily arrests the progress of Wordsworth's readers, asks them to recollect how they have journeyed through his collection and shifts their attention towards the poems that they will encounter in the remainder of the volume. With the heading 'Advertisement', Wordsworth also implicitly reminds readers that the 'fluxes and refluxes of the mind', which he describes in his 'Preface', should not be governed by external forces, like advertisements for other works.[31]

Instead, Wordsworth includes an internal advertisement directed at readers already immersed in his volumes. Similar to the advertisement that introduces the 1798 *Lyrical Ballads*, this advertisement attempts to reconfigure the expectations of readers in order to turn their minds, once again, towards the collective significance of the volumes. It also instructs readers on how to proceed through the next five poems towards the concluding poem 'Michael':

> By Persons resident in the country and attached to rural objects, many places will be found unnamed or of unknown names, where little Incidents will have occurred, or feelings been experienced, which will have given to such places a private and peculiar interest. From a wish to give some sort of record to such Incidents or renew the gratification of such Feelings, Names have been given to Places by the Author and some of his Friends, and the following Poems written in consequence.[32]

Wordsworth deploys this advertisement to redouble his readers' attention to the places named in the ensuing poems. The capitalization of specific words – 'Persons', 'Incidents', 'Feelings', 'Names', 'Places', 'Author', 'Friends' and 'Poems' – outlines the scope and emotional significance of the places in the next five poems.[33] These capitalized words carry readers from persons to intimate friends by way of incidents that evoke feelings, which lead to affectionate naming by the poet and intimate connections with places that are recorded and shared through his poems.[34] Wordsworth's 'Advertisement' is a 'record' that relates oral telling to poetic writing and that describes the possibilities for community through written poetry. This record calls readers to witness emotions, concretized as if they were facts or things, and it even suggests that such records should be repeated, reread, or said over as a lesson. Situated as an internal reminder, place-keeper and monumental record, the 'Advertisement' acts as an invitation for readers to participate in and help 'renew' the 'gratification of such feelings' both in the ensuing poems and in poems that they have already encountered.

The advertisement may seem directed towards a coterie group of individuals – perhaps even as small as the select friends after whom the places in these poems have been named. However, at this point in the volumes, attentive readers would be conversant enough with the types of feelings developed in earlier poems to testify to, or at least to recognize, the value of such an advertisement, which shows Wordsworth as a collector, who gathers together emotions and words intimately connected with the places described in his poems. In the 'Advertisement', Wordsworth shows readers how emotions can be connected through words to places, and he reminds them of how particular words have aided them in journeying meaningfully through the 1800 volumes. Such words have become emotional touchstones, enabling readers to traverse and return to particular poems. And, many of those emotions have been inscribed through the word 'stone'.

The Weight of Stones

Because Wordsworth scatters supplementary prose throughout the volumes and attaches them to specific poems, their effect on readers is cumulatively uncertain. Instead of delineating exactly how readers should experience his poems, these notes suggest ways that readers can experience a distinct type of pleasure if they consider how specific words and contexts situate their emotional and interpretive participation in Wordsworth's collection. Furthermore, notes like 'The Note to the Thorn' and the 'Advertisement' discussed in the previous section maintain that Wordsworth's poems all linguistically supplement one another. For example, the first two poems in the 1800 *Lyrical Ballads* –'Expostulation and Reply' and 'The Tables Turned' – set forth the word 'stone' as a place-marker that grounds Wordsworth's poetic creed and suggests how readers can collectively experience the poems in these volumes.[35] Reciprocally, the last endnote in volume 2 reflects back on the value of stones in the final poem 'Michael', and this retrograde movement draws attention to the cumulative significance and emotional power of stones in *Lyrical Ballads*:

> It may be proper to inform some readers, that a sheep-fold in these mountains is an unroofed building of stone walls, with different division. It is generally placed by the side of a brook, for the convenience of washing the sheep, but it is also useful as a shelter for them, and as a place to drive them into, to enable the shepherds conveniently to single out one or more for any purpose.[36]

While this endnote describes the general structure and purpose of sheepfolds in the Lake District, it also refers to the unfinished, stone sheepfold in the poem 'Michael'. The 'old grey stone', which 'William' sits on in 'Expostulation and Reply', situates the first stone in Wordsworth's collection, points towards the final stone sheepfold, and grounds how stones serve in these volumes as weighty, though transferable, markers for reflection that allow the poet, his characters and readers to consider how feelings can be built up through the repetition of the same word. From 'Expostulation and Reply', 'Lines left upon a Seat in a Yew-tree', 'The Thorn' and 'The Ancient Mariner', in the first volume, to 'Hart-Leap Well', 'The Brothers', 'She Dwelt among th' Untrodden Ways', 'A Slumber did my Spirit Seal', 'Lines Written with a Slate Pencil upon a Stone', and 'Rural Architecture', in the second volume, stones serve as symbolic place-markers that challenge and expand the capacity readers have to record, recollect and consider how their emotional responses have shifted during their journey towards the unfinished sheepfold in 'Michael'.

After leading readers away from the 'old grey stone' in the opening poems, Wordsworth directs his readers, four poems later, to reflect on a seat under a yew tree, marked by a pile of stones in 'Lines left upon a Seat in a Yew-tree which stands near the Lake of Esthwaite, on a desolate part of the shore, yet commanding a beautiful prospect'. This poem asks readers to aid the poet in remaking the place-keeping power of an abandoned seat and pile of stones. The first line arrests the progress of readers with a dash ' – Nay, Traveller! Rest'. Rather than describing a quaint, picturesque prospect, which the title suggests, these cenotaphic words,[37] purportedly left on the seat, tell a story of 'one who own'd / No common soul' (ll. 11–12) and who 'pure in his heart' (l. 15) ended up turning away from the world. This man 'with the food of pride sustained his soul / In solitude' (ll. 19–20) by relishing the 'more distant scene' (l. 31) visible from this spot. The poet recounts the story of a disillusioned and solitary man who 'piled these stones' underneath a yew tree. Then, the poet admonishes readers to cultivate a new perspective on such artificial prospect views. Wisdom does not come from melancholy self-love and solitary views, but instead from he, '[w]ho, in the silent hour of inward thought / Can still suspect, and still revere himself, / In lowliness of heart' (ll. 58–60). The poem suggests that this man piled these stones and created this retreat for the wrong aesthetic and emotional reasons. Intent on building a spot that would isolate his thoughts from the rest of the world, the man missed the opportunity to turn this place, through his reflections, into a means for self-improvement that 'leads to love' of man (l. 56). The poet asks readers to reconsider this man's misanthropic bent – in a 'silent hour of inward thought' – and reflect upon their own motives and inclinations when imagining 'these barren rocks' and empty seat (l. 25). The significance of this abandoned place, the poet suggests, comes from what readers will make of it and of themselves in relation to it.

While Wordsworth asks readers to reflect upon an empty seat in 'Lines left', three poems later in 'The Thorn', Wordsworth's Sea Captain struggles to fill the gaps in his understanding by comparing an uncertain and shadowy thorn to a stone. The Sea Captain attempts to invest both the word and object 'stone' with a symbolic power that will explain Martha Ray's motives and actions – did she kill her baby or not? – and clarify the significance of the place where she allegedly buried her child. In the first stanza of the poem, the Sea Captain remarks that this thorn is 'so old and grey' (l. 4) that it resembles a stone overgrown by 'lichens' (l. 11), and in the next stanza he repeats this odd comparison: 'Like rock or stone, it is o'ergrown / With lichens to the very top' (ll. 12–13). Taken by itself, this repetition might seem needless. However, as Wordsworth's endnote reveals, the Sea Captain's search for answers will never conclude with definitive proof. To provide a solid basis for his interpretation of Martha's story, the Sea Captain transforms the uncanny qualities of the thorn into an old, grey, fixed stone, which also darkly recalls the stone in 'Expostulation and Reply'. However, the Sea Captain's interpretation and claims about Martha prove untenable because of his morbid fascination with every detail of her story and his inability to empathize with the emotional complexity of her situation. Unlike readers who have such a capacity, both in the poem and in Wordsworth's endnote, to probe and distance themselves from the Sea Captain's peculiar use of words and empathetic failings, the Sea Captain cannot open up and revolve his mind past his desire to transform the thorny details of her story into the certainty of 'stone'.

In 'The Ancient Mariner', the second to last poem in volume 1, Wordsworth exacerbates this difficulty of interpreting the value of stones by enjoining readers to sit on a stone that further taxes their emotional stability. 'The Ancient Mariner' rhetorically places readers in the same position as a wedding guest, who the Ancient Mariner stops with his 'glittering eye' and forces to sit 'on a stone, / [so that] He cannot choose but hear' (ll. 4, 13, 21–2). In contrast to Wordsworth's 'wise passiveness' on the 'old grey stone' and active imaginative powers in 'Expostulation and Reply', the wedding guest becomes enthralled and seemingly consumed by the Mariner's tale. By the end of the story, the Mariner renders the wedding guest unfit to join the communal celebration that he was supposed to attend. Mariner, wedding guest and readers all conclude the tale with words that seemingly alienate them from mankind and themselves: 'like one that hath been stunn'd / And is of sense forlorn' (ll. 656–7). Getting up from the stone (and turning the page) at the end of the tale, readers too are 'stunn'd', disoriented, and left without a definite sense of community to balance their emotional responses and guide their progress through the remainder of the volume. As in 'Lines left' and 'The Thorn' readers are left to measure and reconsider the emotional value of the barren places (and stones) where they have been detained.

While 'Tintern Abbey', the following and concluding poem in the first volume, supplies an immediate emotional and psychological counter to this stupor, the opening poem in the second volume, 'Hart-Leap Well', provides a revisionary context for stones that opens the word up to readers as a monument that can rejuvenate previous, and engender new, emotional contexts.[38] 'Tintern Abbey' may point the way towards an active, affective engagement with places and objects, but 'Hart-Leap Well' sets the tone for how readers can travel through Wordsworth's language in the second volume. In this second volume, stones serve as monumental place-keepers that mark the sympathetic capacity readers have to gather together and reconfigure the variety of emotional contexts in the 1800 *Lyrical Ballads*.

Written in two sections, 'Hart-Leap Well' first depicts Sir Walter's chase, which exploits his land and tenants all for the pursuit of a hart. The second section, a dialogue between the poet and a shepherd, then critiques Sir Walter's actions and reveals that, in the first section, the poet has rehearsed a shepherd's tale. In this first section Sir Walter, the knight who tracks the progress and fall of a hart to a place that gains its value from the hart's death-leap, exclaims: 'I'll build a Pleasure-house upon this spot'. Sir Walter also vows to make '[the hart's] praises known' by building 'Another monument ... / Three several pillars, each a rough hewn stone, / And planted where thy hoofs the turf have graz'd' (ll. 57, 65–8). Sir Walter leaves the hart 'stone-dead', and in its stead 'A cup of stone receiv'd the living well; / Three pillars of rude stone Sir Walter rear'd, / And built a house of pleasure in the dell' (ll. 82–4).

In the second section, the poet juxtaposes Sir Walter's motives for building this 'house of pleasure' and erecting three stone pillars with the poetic pleasure with which the poet hopes to provide readers through his revisionary commentary (l. 95). Through this retelling, the poet divides a lesson with a shepherd that he met after the poet paused in his journey homewards one day to gaze upon the sight of three aspins and 'three pillars standing in a line' (l. 107). Sir Walter's pleasure house has been reduced to 'dust' in this now cursed spot, but the poet points out that the three stone pillars, which mark the final steps of the hart, still stand. However, neither place marker seems an appropriate monument for the poet who grounds 'this second rhyme' on the 'small difference [that] lies between [a shepherd's creed] and mine' (ll. 95, 162). The poet asserts,

[t]he moving accident is not my trade
To freeze the blood I have no ready arts;
'Tis my delight, alone in summer shade,
To pipe a simple song to thinking hearts. (ll. 97–100)

The real monument to this place, the retold story of the hart, arises in the second part of the poem and challenges readers to reciprocate in the dialogue between poet and shepherd about the significance of the place marked by these stones. Through this second section, Wordsworth defines his brand of pastoral poetry as a kind of parodic retelling, which records the give and take between 'thinking hearts' and engenders transferable moments of sympathy and empathy.

Two poems later in 'The Brothers', Wordsworth asks readers to do without stone monuments – whether 'head [nor] foot stone' – and to divide another lesson with the characters in his poem (l. 171). Like the traveller Leonard in the poem, readers must negotiate a country churchyard without the aid of gravestones to mark the emotional context of their engagement. In fact, the only stone singled out in the area is 'the long stone-seat beneath the eaves / Of [the priest's] old cottage' from which the priest rises to address Leonard (ll. 18–19). Like the shepherd from 'Hart-Leap Well', the priest offers an oral link (albeit a fading one) between the past and present that chronicles a changed but still functioning rural economy. What the poem offers as recompense for a lack of gravestones is a sense of connection between the living and the dead, based on a communally held record from which Leonard guiltily turns away. Leonard chooses not to reveal his identity to the Priest 'from the weakness of his heart' and from his feelings of responsibility for his brother, who died in Leonard's absence after sleep-walking off of a summit (l. 446). At the close of the poem, readers are left somewhere between the communal perspective of the priest, marked by the foundation of the familial stone seat to which he returns, and the bewildered and alienated Leonard, bereft of community and unable to situate himself in his homeland without gravestones. Leonard follows in the footsteps of the ancient mariner in the first volume, 'he went on shipboard, and is now / A Seaman, a grey headed Mariner' (ll. 448–9), while Wordsworth's readers are further entrenched in his pastoral landscapes by a story told in the place of a stone marker.

In the next poem 'Ellen Irwin', Wordsworth fills the absence of guiding stone markers in 'The Brothers' with the gravestone of Adam Bruce, which represents the anguished love of a Scottish man for a woman who is killed by Bruce's rival, Gordon. This poem about forcibly separated lovers pushes readers towards a series of poems that meditate further on pastoral death. Two poems later in 'Song', followed by 'A Slumber did my Spirit Seal', readers learn from the poet's reaction to the loss of a loved one that stones only elusively connect together the living and the dead. While in the first poem, Lucy is a 'Violet by a mossy stone / Half-hidden from the Eye' (ll. 5–6), in the second poem she is 'Roll'd round in earth's diurnal course / With rocks and stones and trees!' (ll. 7–8). These last lines develop the poet's understanding of the continual motions of the physical world as he attempts to come to terms with the significance of her death and his life. In 'A Slumber' Lucy becomes a part of the natural world, a part of something larger, which her death has forced the poet to reconsider. These haunting poems open up a poetic space that Wordsworth neither ties directly to a specific landscape nor limits to his psychic valuations of Lucy's importance. Lucy occupies a space somewhere between the poet's sympathetic responses and where she lies 'Roll'd round in earth's diurnal course / With rock and stones and trees!' (ll. 7–8). She only exists through the tales that the poet continues to tell about her and through the stones in those tales that haunt his imagination and remain in her place.

While these 'Lucy' poems ask readers to commune with the living and the dead by imagining the significance and abiding place of this shadowy woman, several other poems in the second volume feature disembodied inscriptions – such as the poem 'Inscription for the Spot where the Hermitage stood' and the 'homely pile' in 'Inscription for the House (an Outhouse) on the Island at Grasmere' – or substantial stone buildings that encourage readers to reimagine and retrieve the emotional significance of their ruins.[39] Another poem, 'Lines Written with a Slate-Pencil upon a Stone, the Largest of a Heap Lying near a Deserted Quarry, upon one of the Islands at Rydale' warns:

> Stranger! This hillock of misshapen stones
> Is not a ruin of the ancient time,
> Nor perchance thou rashly deem'st, the Cairn
> Of some old British Chief (ll. 1–4).

Arrested again in their progress through these volumes, readers are asked to shift their perceptions of 'misshapen stones'. Unlike Sir Walter's pleasure house that turns to dust in 'Hart-Leap Well', in this poem Sir William's 'little dome/ Or pleasure house' has been left for a different purpose. While Sir Walter's pleasure house marks his conquest of land and animal, Sir William's unfinished house, 'the quarry and the mound / Are monuments of his unfinish'd task' (ll. 12–13). The poet admonishes would-be builders, to follow Sir William's example and realize that these stones are not meant to build a 'mansion destin'd soon to blaze / In snow-white splendour' (ll. 30–1). Instead, the poem, purportedly written on 'the corner-stone / Of the intended pile' (ll. 15–16), gives this advice:

> leave
> Thy fragments to the bramble and the rose,
> There let the vernal slow-worm sun himself,
> And let the red-breast hop from stone to stone (ll. 32–5).

A few poems later, readers encounter a Cumberland Beggar, who at the beginning of the poem sits on a pile of stones, 'a low structure of rude masonry', and whose existence embodies the building creed of 'Lines written with a Slate-Pencil'. In 'The Old Cumberland Beggar', these stones center the old man's presence in this community, and that continual presence offers a 'record [of communal pleasure] which together binds / Past deeds and offices of charity / Else unremember'd' (ll. 81–3). He is an aging touchstone, who reminds the community through which he travels that 'we have all of us one human heart' (l. 146) and who inspires people to continual 'acts of love' (l. 92). In the next poem 'Rural Architecture', Wordsworth playfully reminds readers that this shared heart must be tended to – like the building stones in this poem – again and again. The poem relates how three schoolboys climbed Great How and built a man, Ralph Jones, out of stone, who in a little over a week is destroyed by the wind. The response of these boys, the poet merrily declares, was simply to climb back up the hill and build another man of stone. He contrasts the attitude of these boys to the 'blind boisterous works / In Paris and London, 'mong Christians and Turks, / Spirits busy to do and undo' (ll. 19–21). The remembrance of such Paris and London 'works' – whether political philosophy or actual architectural building – causes the poet's blood to 'flag', and he readily turns to the boys and this local scene, crying out: 'Then light-hearted Boys, to the top of the Crag! / And I'll build up a Giant with you' (ll. 23–4). Energized by their actions, the poet joins the boys in building a natural structure based on constant change, renewal and the present emotional vigour of its builders.[40]

If 'Hart Leap Well' sets the tone for the monumental value of stones throughout the second volume and 'Rural Architecture' puts readers in mind of continual building, the ensuing 'Advertisement' to 'Poems on the Naming of Places' encourages readers to pause and 'record' the words and emotional touchstones that they have collected throughout *Lyrical Ballads*. Following these 'Poems on the Naming of Places', the closing poem 'Michael' charges readers with the further task of reflecting on the worth of that record in the face of broken compact – an unfinished sheepfold, 'a straggling heap of unhewn stones' (l. 17). This sheepfold remains unfinished because of a broken covenant between the shepherd Michael and his son Luke – an agreement meant to solidify Michael and Luke's relationship during Luke's absence in the city, where he has gone to remake and, ironically, retie his family's fortune to the land. Unfortunately, by the close of the poem, this sheepfold is defined by Luke's absence and subsequent degradation in the city, as well as by Michael's flagging labour – 'many and many a day he thither went, / And never lifted up a single stone' (ll. 474–5).

In the midst of this tragic heap of stones, the poem offers readers the opportunity to reflect on the emotional weight of the stones that they have accumulated during their journey through *Lyrical Ballads*.[41] Given the poet's initial address to readers – 'If from the public way you turn your steps' – and his avowal that he tells this story for 'the delight of a few natural hearts', as well as for the 'sake of youthful poets, who ... / Will be my second self when I am gone' (ll. 36, 38–9), 'Michael' offers readers the possibility of forging a new covenant out of the ruins of Michael and Luke's broken one. This new compact implies how the poet and his readers can figuratively carry on the labour left unfinished by Michael and Luke. That compact involves reconstructive reading and the writing of future poems.[42]

Unlike Luke, whose promise is degraded by the city, Wordsworth's readers can reify the past, present and future value of the 'stone' sheepfold and of Wordsworth's poems through the connective power of the words and places in *Lyrical Ballads*. Furthermore, unlike Michael, the poet – in good faith – can continue to labour on his poems in order to build a foundation of 'stone' to which readers can return and take part in. Through this imagined contract, *Lyrical Ballads* becomes a poetic collection that refuses to abridge Wordsworth's poetry of human emotion because it connects together the place and placement of his poems with how readers build up their emotional responses to those poems. In this context, Wordsworth's 'Preface' introduces a living body of poetry that seeks to keep readers in the 'company of flesh and blood' by asking them to keep a 'record' of the 'fluxes and refluxes' of their minds as they travel through his volumes. The final endnote, which describes this 'heap of unhewn stones', marks the culmination of that journey through the 1800 edition and readers' initiation into Wordsworth's brand of poetic pleasure. Unlike typical readers of poetry collections and pastoral poems, these readers are capable of perceiving and creating sustained connections between Wordsworth's poems because they can recognize and, like the poet, recollect the place-value and emotional contexts of his words. Such readers can travel meaningfully through the 1800 *Lyrical Ballads*, and they are prepared to encounter future poems – namely the 1802 *Lyrical Ballads, with Pastoral and Other Poems*.

3 SHORT-CIRCUITING WORDSWORTH'S 1807 *POEMS*: RICHARD MANT'S *THE SIMPLICIAD*

As neither preface, address, or advertisement informs us why these poems are published, we are unable to inform our readers of the author's design in so doing.[1]

nor can any thing give us a more melancholy view of the debasing effects of this miserable theory, than that it has given ordinary men a right to wonder at the folly and presumption of a man gifted like Mr. Wordsworth, and made him appear, in his second avowed publication, like a bad imitator of the worst of his former productions.[2]

Turn to the 'Moods of my own Mind' [in the 1807 Poems]. There is scarcely a Poem here above thirty Lines, and very trifling these poems will appear to many; but, omitting to speak of them individually, do they not, taken collectively, fix the attention upon a subject eminently poetical ...?[3]

Neither Wordsworth nor his publisher Longman could have predicted the surge of negative publicity that erupted from the review culture, the reading public, contemporary authors and parodists over the publication of his 1807 *Poems, in Two Volumes*. Before the 1807 volumes, Wordsworth's four editions of *Lyrical Ballads* had received more positive than negative reviews,[4] his poetry was discussed frequently by reviewing critics and his brand of poetry was slowly becoming a recognizable literary commodity.[5] To Wordsworth and his publisher, the reading public seemed primed for a new and original edition of his poems.[6] The 1807 volumes, however, neither achieved the market share, nor received the kind of sympathetic readings that Wordsworth expected. As sales languished, reviewers criticized his new poems for four related reasons.

First, many reviewers wondered why Wordsworth had not introduced the 1807 *Poems* with a preface that explained the poetic principles and purpose governing his poems.[7] Their confusion and frustration over this lack of a preface reveals the hold that Wordsworth's 'Preface to *Lyrical Ballads*' still had in 1807.[8] Second, several reviewers claimed that Wordsworth's new volumes should be considered as an extension of the poetic system outlined in that 'Preface'.[9] Third, because most of these critics were hesitant to read the 1807 *Poems* on their own terms, they often jokingly and seriously described Wordsworth's new poems as parodies of the poems in *Lyrical Ballads*. Finally, to explain how parody had made its way into Wordsworth's poetry, a few critics even jeered at the 1807 *Poems* as childish nursery rhymes that were the work of Wordsworth's inner child – father to the man who wrote *Lyrical Ballads*.[10] The consensus was that, wittingly or not, Wordsworth was 'making murderous attacks upon his own literary reputation'.[11]

This concentrated denigration of Wordsworth's 1807 *Poems* solidified an antagonistic, but symbiotic, relationship between what Nicola Trott in 'Wordsworth and the Parodic School of Criticism' has called a 'new school of poetry' (nominally headed by Wordsworth) and a 'new school of criticism' (headed by Francis Jeffrey and the *Edinburgh Review*). To make matters worse for Wordsworth, parodists such as Richard Mant exacerbated this negative press. In *The Simpliciad* (1808), Mant meticulously groups together the members of this 'new school of poetry' and then highlights the failings of their poetic theories by exercising the controlling powers of the 'new school of criticism'.[12] *The Simpliciad* reflects and extends the review culture's infatuation with Wordsworth's (purportedly failed) system of poetry. As Trott and Paul Magnuson have demonstrated, parody in the first two decades of the nineteenth century was often a direct outgrowth of the ideologies and language voiced by this 'new school of criticism'.[13] *The Simpliciad* exemplifies how early nineteenth-century parodies revivified reviews of Wordsworth's poetry by mocking his propensity to repeat simple words and ideas.

While a few early Wordsworth parodies like 'Barham Downs; or Goody Grizzle and her Ass' (1801) simply lambast his poetry as asinine or childish, several parodies in England and America offer incisive criticisms of Wordsworth's poetry.[14] These satiric poems suggest that *Lyrical Ballads* is marred by Wordsworth's obsession with babyish words, simplistic concepts and idiotic people. The most resounding of these works – from Wordsworth's, Southey's and Coleridge's perspective – was Peter Bayley's volume of *Poems*, printed first in London in 1803 and then in Philadelphia the following year. Part original poems, part imitative pastiche and parody of Wordsworth's poems, Bayley's *Poems* were greeted with reviews that alternately praised him as a poet with promise and labelled him a plagiarist. A few of these reviewers also blurred the line between original Wordsworth poems, imitative pastiche and mocking parody, when they playfully suggested that Bayley might be a *nom de plume* for Wordsworth.

Fueled by seething letters from Wordsworth and Coleridge,[15] Robert Southey responded to Bailey's poems with a scathing essay in the *Annual Review* (1804), meant to discredit Bailey's collection and literary reputation. The tone of Southey's first sentence betrays the extent to which Bayley's *Poems* threatened Wordsworth's reputation more than any negative prose review: 'STOP thief! Mr. Peter Bayley, jun. is a literary sharper, who has obtained credit upon false pretences, and made his way into good company by wearing stolen clothes'.[16] Southey attacks Bailey as a thief and a social climber, who has exploited

Wordsworth's reputation and capitalized on the cultural status and potential market created by *Lyrical Ballads*. Southey also contends that because many of Bailey's poems were 'made up from the Lyrical Ballads of Mr. Wordsworth', Bailey's poems are nothing more than a collection of Wordsworth imitations, 'one mass of patchwork' plagiarism.[17] However, Southey's attack on Bailey's 'patchwork' also inadvertently suggests that Wordsworth's poetry is particularly vulnerable to this kind of theft because any close imitation of Wordsworth's style might result in fragmented parodies.

To Richard Mant the poetic styles, shifting tones, loose organization and supplementary writings in Wordsworth's 1807 *Poems* were not only vulnerable to parody; they invited it.[18] Written as a satirical 'Art of Poetry' for the 'New School', Mant's *The Simpliciad* hijacks and attempts to implode Wordsworth's 1807 volumes by ridiculing the devolution of Wordsworth's poetry and poetic system. Mant bifurcates his parody into satirical-didactic couplets – a patchwork of poetic lines made up largely of Wordsworth's 1807 *Poems* – and footnotes – a wide selection of poetic passages also drawn together primarily from Wordsworth's new volumes.[19] Mant's couplets, which feature a dialogue between P – a Socratic/Horatian figure – and F – a student figure – link together Wordsworth's, Coleridge's and Southey's poems in a paratactic melee of seemingly unrelated titles and utterly simplistic lines that vacillate between gleeful parody, imitative pastiche and direct quotation. At the bottom of each page, Mant's footnotes isolate one stanza or several stanzas from a poem, or a series of poems, that seemingly prove the childish emotions and poor word choices marring these poets' works. Whenever Mant constructs a couplet that pieces together particular words from their poems, he also includes a footnote that identifies his sources, quotes the stanzas and italicizes the words he has reconfigured in the couplets above.

While *The Simpliciad* mocks the collective subject matter and poetic style of these poets, its footnotes and couplets distort, excise and overwrite how Wordsworth's endnotes, footnotes, headnotes, poem titles and section headings attempt to connect together individual poems in the 1807 volumes.[20] Through its prose/poetry juxtapositions and deformations, *The Simpliciad* presents Wordsworth's poetic language as a parodic echo of itself, which appears to short-circuit any sympathetic engagement and interpretive activity that the supplementary writings in the 1807 volumes might encourage. However, Mant's attempts to reduce Wordsworth's language to an utterly disjointed, perverse and repetitive simplicity ironically reveal how Wordsworth's poetic groupings – such as his three poems 'To the Daisy' – and individual poems – such as 'Resolution and Independence' – encourage readers to develop their own connective and sympathetic powers of reading by differentiating between a variety of redounding verbal echoes about individual liberty, shared duty and collective independence.[21]

Authority, Simplicity and Mant's Satirical Echo

Although Wordsworth did not publish a preface to introduce the purpose of and relationship between the poems in his 1807 collection, he did include a variety of section headings within the volumes that classify, divide up and loosely organize these poems.[22] Wordsworth arranged the 1807 volumes so that readers would encounter incisive correspondences and contrasts within and between these section headings that would encourage them to explore how ideas can be built up within a poem and between a series of poems.[23] This unmethodical method immerses readers in an uneven, but continual process of returning to ideas, objects and emotional states. And, much to the dismay of many critics, the vacillating, back-and-forth movements set up in these volumes involve subjects that border on the mundane, the cliché and the ridiculous. For example, Wordsworth included three poems 'To the Daisy' that stretch from the first section of the first volume to the final section of the second volume. Wordsworth underscores the connection between these poems with a footnote in the second volume that reminds readers to reconsider the first daisy poem in relation to the following two. Besides these three poems, consecutive poems 'To the Small Celandine' and 'To the same Flower' in the first volume are offset by 'The Small Celandine' in the second volume, which also includes a footnote that points backwards to the first 'Celandine' poem in the first volume. Prose footnotes such as this one, which identifies the page number of that first 'Celandine' poem, explicitly ask readers to return to the beginning of a poetic series and suggest that the first poem should be reread in relation to the last poem.

Wordsworth constructs many opportunities in his 1807 volumes for readers to reconsider the relationship between individual poems grouped under the same and different section headings. Perhaps most striking, he implies a connection between the last two lines of his final 'Ode' – 'To me the meanest flower that blows can give / Thoughts that lie too deep for tears' – and the first poem in volume 1, 'To the Daisy'. In his section of twenty numbered 'Miscellaneous Sonnets', Wordsworth links sonnets three and four together through an epigraph in sonnet four that renders part of the last two lines of sonnet three. He also constructs three consecutive sonnets 'To Sleep' and places three translated sonnets from Michael Angelo back to back. In his section of twenty-six 'Sonnets Dedicated to Liberty' (also numbered) his titles either link poems together through place (written in Calais) or through the year in which a poem was written (1802 or 1803). In the section headed 'The Blind Highland Boy and Other Poems' from the second volume, Wordsworth implies a titular correspondence between two consecutive poems, 'Incident, Characteristic of a Favourite Dog, which Belonged to a Friend of the Author' and 'Tribute to the Memory of the same Dog', that recalls the third poem in the first volume, 'Fidelity', which pays homage to the heroic virtue of a dog to its master.[24] Conceptions and reconceptions of liberty, fortitude, heroism and duty – both private and public – recur throughout these volumes, as well as 'metaphors of journey and home, past and present, freedom and confinement, gain and loss'.[25]

Beyond these thematic and titular groupings, Wordsworth inscribes his guiding presence in the volumes through a variety of footnotes, endnotes, and head notes that link together many of his poems about duty and heroism while also connecting together poems that provoke in the reader 'a continual readjustment of perspective between the simple and the complex, the quotidian and the cosmic'.[26] However, for parodists such as Richard Mant, these connections in the 1807 *Poems* only point to Wordsworth's ridiculous and unremitting simplicity. Accordingly, *The Simpliciad* mocks Wordsworth not only because he has a poem 'The Redbreast and the Butterfly' in the first section of volume 1, but also because he begins the section headed 'Moods of my own Mind' in volume 2 with a poem 'To a Butterfly', and then includes another poem 'To a Butterfly' as the penultimate poem in that section.[27] Likewise, Wordsworth's attempts to establish a connection between two poems about the cuckoo and echoes in volume 2 – one in the section headed 'Moods of my own mind' and the other in 'The Blind Highland Boy' – meet with derision in *The Simpliciad*.[28]

Mant's mockery of Wordsworthian repetition recalls several reviews of Wordsworth's 1807 *Poems* that single out childish nursery rhymes and dismiss him as the leader of a babyish and wrong-headed 'new school of poetry'. Mant had both personal and public reasons to echo these condemnations of Wordsworth and the 'Lake poets' and to parody their poetry. First, Mant was an Anglican clergyman who 'objected to the Laker's open-air nature-worship and déclassé innovations'.[29] Second, Mant's own *Poems* (1806) were subjected to uneven treatment in the same October 1807 issue of the *Edinburgh Review* in which Francis Jeffrey excoriated Wordsworth's 1807 *Poems*. Although separated by over forty pages from the review of Wordsworth's *Poems*, this review of Mant's *Poems* relates his poetry to Wordsworth's through their shared subject matter – nature – and secluded position of retirement in the country.

This anonymous reviewer closely links Mant and Wordsworth together when he describes a contemporary vogue for nature poetry in which 'village curates ... gather dandelions; and philosophers ... mourn and moralyze, and murmur over ponds "three feet long, and two feet wide"'.[30] The quoted line is from Wordsworth's 'The Thorn' in *Lyrical Ballads*, and the prosaic nature of that line illustrates this reviewer's assessment of how Mant's poetry suffers from stylistic failings similar to Wordsworth's poetry: 'Mr. Mant's principal fault is an extraordinary occasional feebleness, which sometimes entirely spoils the effect of what would else be pleasing description'.[31] Mant's poetry is riddled with faults similar to what Francis Jeffrey identifies as Wordsworth's bathos – a sudden sink-ing in style that, Jeffrey maintains, recurs throughout his poetry. The reviewer also criticizes him for including too many private addresses to friends and family, which might elicit 'the ridicule of the world, to whom their persons are uninteresting, and their characters are probably unknown'.[32] Although praised for a 'strong and manly train of virtuous sentiment', Mant is counselled to read his poetry privately to a coterie circle and not to 'push them out into the wide world' in the way of 'more unmerciful critics'.[33]

Instead of responding directly to this review, Mant grouped together Wordsworth, Coleridge and Southey in *The Simpliciad* as aesthetic and cultural whipping boys that would enable Mant to reassert his place as a writer in line with the principles of the 'new school of criticism'. He turns Wordsworth's, Coleridge's and Southey's own poetry against its authors, attempts to prove the 'new school of criticism's' political and aesthetic diagnoses of Wordsworth's 'Lake School' and elides Wordsworth's poems from *Lyrical Ballads* with his new, seemingly more puling 1807 *Poems*. As a means to carry out this critique, Mant fragments and simplifies Wordsworth's guiding voice – in his footnotes, endnotes and headnotes – and attempts to overwrite the emotional strength and connective meanings of Wordsworth's poems.

Somewhat surprisingly, Mant does not illuminate the review culture's charges against Wordsworth's poetry by focusing on his 'Preface to *Lyrical Ballads*'. Instead, he exaggerates Wordsworth's theory of poetic language from his endnote to 'The Thorn' – the very poem through which the *Edinburgh Review* had connected Mant with Wordsworth. If the 1800 preface provided critics with an uneven and potentially misleading rationale for the subject matter and style of the 1807 *Poems*, Wordsworth's note to 'The Thorn' gave Mant the satirical fodder to explode Wordsworth's paratextual statements about poetic diction and word repetitions in his new and old poems. In that endnote from volume 1 of the 1800 *Lyrical Ballads*, Wordsworth focuses on 'the interest which the mind attaches to words, not only as symbols of [a] passion, but as *things*, active and efficient, which are of themselves part of [a] passion'.[34] Mant reconfigures Wordsworth's supplementary prose to erase the literal and symbolic power of Wordsworth's poetic words, both in individual and multiple poems. *The Simpliciad* attempts to disable Wordsworth's poetic collection by usurping the very place of mediation – the emotional power behind his words – that Wordsworth hoped would draw readers into his poetic collections.

By foregrounding Wordsworth's repetitious word choices in *The Simpliciad*, Mant also exploits Wordsworth's acute anxiety in his note to 'The Thorn' about how readers will engage with his words:

> There is a numerous class of readers who imagine that the same words cannot be repeated without tautology: this is a great error: virtual tautology is much oftener produced by using different words when the meaning is exactly the same. Words, a

Poet's words more particularly, ought to be weighed in the balance of feeling and not measured by the space which they occupy on paper.[35]

In *The Simpliciad* Mant creates two separate verses that respond to 'The Thorn', both of which are footnoted with quotations from Wordsworth's poetry. Immediately preceding his first couplet about 'The Thorn', Mant gleefully offers up one poetic line from the 1807 volumes as an exemplary case of Wordsworthian repetition: 'And dance with dancing laughing daffodils' (l. 99). Mant forges this line out of the passages he provides in the footnote – the entire first stanza of 'I Wandered Lonely as a Cloud' and four more lines from the poem, which highlight in italics the pertinent words he reworks into the first line of his couplet.[36] Choosing not to quote the rest of the lines in the poem, Mant sarcastically remarks in the footnote, 'The whole poem, consisting of eighteen lines, is exquisite'[37] His own patchwork couplet places the repeated words next to each other and closes down what Wordsworth, in the note to 'The Thorn', calls 'the space which [words] occupy on paper'.

Throughout *The Simpliciad*, Mant attempts to dismantle the connective power of Wordsworth's theory of repetition by first rewriting Wordsworth's poetic lines and then in his footnotes implicitly asking if Wordsworth's words match the intensity of his feelings. As one of Mant's notes suggests, he intends readers to 'Judge of [Wordsworth's] emotions' by considering minutely the space that separates the repetition of the same words in a given stanza or on a given page.[38] The above passage, taken from 'I Wandered Lonely as a Cloud', highlights the central emotional difficulties that Wordsworth hoped to circumvent through careful word repetition and that Mant attempted to exploit satirically.[39] Mant's synthetic repetition of Wordsworth's words implies that Wordsworth's repetitions utterly fail to convey serious and lasting passions and, consequently, render readers unable to sympathize with the situations and objects described in his poetry. More than a simple critique of poetic diction, Mant's italicized words and couplet reconfigurations contend that Wordsworth's poetic system is nothing but a tautology.

Ironically, Mant's italicized words also suggest that Wordsworth's system works because his repetitions do prompt readers to connect together his poems. Mant's parody demonstrates how certain of Wordsworth's words become charged and cleave to one another, even through their potentially bizarre simplicity and emotional circularity. Mant seems all too aware of Wordsworth's cautioning tone in his note to 'The Thorn':

For the Reader cannot be too often reminded that Poetry is passion: it is the history or science of feelings; now every man must know that an attempt is rarely made to communicate impassioned feelings without something of an accompanying consciousness of the inadequateness of our own powers, or the deficiencies in language. During such efforts there will be a craving in the mind, and as long as it is unsatisfied the Speaker will cling to the same words, or words of the same character.[40]

For Mant, Wordsworth is unnaturally overcome by just such 'a craving in the mind' and has become infatuated with attaching the same simplistic words to the same objects.[41] His couplets seek to demonstrate 'the inadequateness of [Wordsworth's] powers' by offsetting the particular 'deficiencies in [his] language', which Mant catalogues in his footnotes.

Throughout *The Simpliciad*, Mant elides poem with poem and word with word, suggesting that any poem by Wordsworth and his 'Lake School' can be connected with any other because of their repetitive simplicity: 'A simple tale these artless bards rehearse; / The ditty simple, simple is the verse;' (ll. 124–5). Through his triple repetition and chiasmic mirroring of 'simple', Mant not only asserts that the subject matter and style of the 'Lake' poets are simple but also that all of their lines rehearse the same type of childish tale in quest of 'the nursery prize' (l. 127). Consequently, Mant writes of

> [p]oets, who fix their visionary sight
> On sparrow's eggs in prospect of delight,
> With fervent welcome greet the glow-worm's flame,
> Put it to bed and bless it by its name (ll. 94–7).

While two of Mant's footnotes quote the passages, pages and volume numbers underpinning the above lines, his couplets splice 'The Sparrow's Nest' from the section 'Moods of my own Mind' in volume 2 of Wordsworth's 1807 *Poems* with 'Among All Things my Love had Been' from the opening section of volume 1, which Wordsworth intended to advertise as 'Orchard Pathways'. Mant's footnoted patchwork suggests that there is no difference between these two Wordsworth poems. Furthermore, his couplets erase Wordsworth's placement of these poems, remove the contexts suggested through Wordsworth's section headings, and imply that these poems might as well follow one another chronologically in Wordsworth's *Poems*. Mant does acknowledge two of the section headings when he remarks in another footnote that '"Musings", and "Moods of my own mind" are the titles prefixed by our poets to some of these effusions'.[42] However, his comments label these categories as random effusions and idiosyncratic pleasures and, consequently, level the significance of the eight sections in the 1807 *Poems*.

The spatial competition between Mant's couplets at the top of the page and the excerpts from the 'Lake' poets' poems at the bottom of page would seem to give Mant control over Wordsworth and 'the new school of poetry'.[43] However, read separately from the couplets above, Mant's supporting quotations from these 'Authorities' do not always maintain the satirical tone that he seeks to establish in his couplets. As Priscilla Gilman asserts in 'To Kill and Bury the Poor Thorn Forever', *The Simpliciad* attempts to narrow and shut off multivalent interpretations of Wordsworth's poetry. However, Mant's attempts to control how readers interpret Wordsworth's words, individual poems and series of poems are occasionally undone by the very evidence that he provides in his footnotes. In his 'Dedication' to *The Simpliciad*, Mant claims that Southey's, Coleridge's and Wordsworth's poems are already parodies of themselves without their authors' awareness,[44] but such an assertion belies Mant's ability to fully render and control the purportedly self-parodic aspects of their poetry. Without poetic passages at the bottom of the page, which succinctly prove Wordsworth and the 'Lake School's' utterly ridiculous simplicity, Mant's couplets become overwhelmed by the accumulated power of their poetic language. Consequently, *The Simpliciad* enacts an uneven dialogue between poetry and prose notes that calls into question the authority of Mant's parody as well as the poetry of the 'Lake poets'.[45]

Mant's Satirical Echo and Wordsworth's Poems 'To the Daisy'

Mant's first footnote in *The Simpliciad* singles Wordsworth out as the head of the 'Lake School' and announces that Mant will assemble, abridge, and respond to their poetry by placing it in dialogue with itself. Above this footnote, Mant's couplets first praise the 'Classical Muse of Simplicity' for inspiring scenes that imitate heroic and virtuous emotions before then denigrating the effects of contemporary 'Simplicity', which leads to a 'perverted taste' attended by 'Enthusiast Folly' and a 'vapid chorus [that] louder swells' with noise (ll. 74, 73, respectively).[46] Mant first suggests that this enthusiastic, but flat, chorus grows louder because it is obsessed with itself and then asserts that the 'Lake School' muse of 'Simplicity' is a perverted echo of the 'Classical Muse of Simplicity':

> thine is the song that wakes
> Echo, who sleeps by Albion's northern lakes,
> Echo, whose birth the cuckoo cannot tell,
> Though that 'tis sound the bird must know full well; (ll. 86–9)

With this first overt reference to a Wordsworth poem, Mant frames his ensuing critique of the Lake School within a satirical tradition that can be traced back to Ovid's myth of Echo in the *Metamorphosis*.

In *The Figure of Echo* (1981), John Hollander identifies two major classical traditions associated with the personified figure of Echo – one from Longinus and one from Ovid. While Longinus's myth of Pan and Echo becomes associated with the lyric as an authentic echo of nature, Ovid's tale of Echo and Narcissus becomes associated with satire. Hollander points out that satirical and 'negative readings of Echo come from associations of fragmentation of the anterior voice, the hollowness of her concavities of origin transferred to the figurative hollowness of her words, and the progressive diminution of successive reverberations'.[47] By asserting that the 'Classical Muse of Simplicity' has a new and perverted echo, an '*Echo, who sleeps by Albion's northern lakes*', Mant links the Lake poet's geographic location, surrounded by mountains (and some caves), with the final resting place of the scorned Echo in Ovid's myth. *The Simpliciad* carries out the satiric tradition of Echo to correct the Lake School's misplaced assumption that its lyrical echoes are natural and authentic. Mant's footnote to these lines, which quotes the first two stanzas of Wordsworth's 'Yes! full surely 'twas the Echo', proclaims that Wordsworth's song, inspired by the contemporary muse of 'Simplicity' and voiced through the cuckoo, is a degenerative echo that has, in turn, awoken Mant's own satirical echo. This footnote encourages readers to see the sources of Mant's echoes as deranged, and it singles Wordsworth's poetry out as the pinnacle of the Lake School's ridiculous simplicity.

Mant's footnote quotes particular passages from Wordsworth's poem about echoes, ridicules Wordsworth's poetry as idle and meaningless chatter, describes Wordsworth as a poet who combines the qualities of Narcissus and the cuckoo, and reduces the effects of Wordsworth's poetic language to a misplaced self-referential void. In that note, Mant provides the following passage:

> Yes, full surely 'twas the Echo,
> Solitary, clear, profound,
> Answering to Thee, shouting Cuckoo
> Giving to thee Sound for Sound.
> Whence the Voice? From air or earth?
> *This the Cuckoo cannot tell;*
> But a startling sound had birth,
> *As the bird must know full well.* (original emphasis)

Mant's corresponding couplet only partially echoes these footnoted stanzas: 'Echo, whose birth the cuckoo cannot tell, / Tho' that 'tis sound the bird must know full well'. The two lines repeat most of the italicized lines in his footnote, including the two end rhymes, but Mant eliminates the first word of each italicized line – the indefinite pronoun and deictic 'This' and the adverb 'As'. The couplet also replaces 'This' with the word 'Echo', which repeats the last word of the first line in the footnote, and includes the word 'birth', which echoes the last word of the seventh line in the footnote. In the second line of his couplet, Mant poaches the word 'sound' from the seventh line in the footnote, disrupts Wordsworth's enjambment of line seven into line eight, and, consequently, breaks the link between what the cuckoo cannot tell and its sudden recognition, which accompanies the birth of a startling sound. Mant's elided couplet highlights the disjunction between source and echo in the poem and also equates Wordsworth's Lake School with cuckoos.

Cuckoos, incidentally, often do not recognize their progeny because they lay their eggs in other birds' nests, and Mant's reading of Wordsworth's cuckoo suggests that Wordsworth might not recognize his own words echoed back to him – either because that echo would be satirical or because Wordsworth is a cuckold to his own debauched poetry. Mant's mockery of Wordsworth also plays upon the male cuckoo's voice, which can be heard incessantly – especially during mating season – projecting its uniform and unvaried call, 'cou-cou'. The cuckoo calls its own name, and the cuckoo's name is an echo. Furthermore, this satiric association with the cuckoo's echo points back to Narcissus, who is drawn to the response of what he perceives – the call back of his own voice – only to be disappointed that this voice is the disembodied echo of his own.

Mant's couplet reconfiguration of Wordsworth's lines also implies that readers are privy to a dramatic irony of which the poet is unaware. Unlike Wordsworth, readers, like Mant, can see from whence Wordsworth's echo originates and where it will go. Mant maintains that any echo originating from a Wordsworthian source will rebound on itself, satirically disembodied. Through this couplet, Mant attempts to disable the power of Wordsworth's poetic language to resonate beyond its own singular utterance and to reduce Wordsworth's words to monotonous, satirical and self-referential echoes – without origin or end – that undercut any meaningful application for Wordsworth's readers. This first footnoted reference to Wordsworthian repetition characterizes Wordsworth as foolish and also ridicules the public value of his poetry.[48] From Mant's perspective, Wordsworth's poetry epitomizes the Lake School's self-referential trifles.

Mant's footnotes to his couplets about Wordsworth's series of poems 'To the Daisy' and his poem 'Resolution and Independence' demonstrate most acutely his attempts to satirically echo the essential simplicity of Wordsworth's language. For Mant, these poems exemplify Wordsworth's repetitions of lowly subject matter and bizarre emotional responses to those subjects. When describing the insular, cult-like behaviour of these 'Lake' poets, Mant exclaims, 'Of apostolic daisies learn to think, / Draughts from their urns of true devotion drink' (ll. 108–9). His couplet refers to Wordsworth's first and third daisy poems in the 1807 *Poems* and points back from the last stanza in that third daisy poem in volume 2 to the seventh and eighth stanzas of the first poem in volume 1. At the bottom of the page, Mant devotes nearly two pages of footnotes to his couplet and remarks that the 'daisy is a favourite with one of our poets; and with reason: for it is fitting that the flower which is "Nature's favourite", also should be "the Poet's darling"'. While Mant seems disturbed by the poet's seemingly bizarre praise and – in Mant's estimation – perverse worship of this flower, his footnotes reveal that he is also bothered by the number of times that Wordsworth addresses the flower in the volumes.

In his 1807 *Poems*, Wordsworth not only draws attention to these three poems by including a footnote in the second volume; at the end of the first volume, he supplies readers with an endnote that explains:

> This Poem, and two others to the same Flower, which the Reader will find in the second Volume, were written in the year 1802; which is mentioned, because in some of the ideas, though not in the manner in which they are connected, and likewise even in some of the expressions, they bear a striking resemblance to a Poem (lately published) of Mr. Montgomery, entitled a Field Flower.[49]

Wordsworth admits that some of the ideas and even the expressions in his poems 'bear a striking resemblance' to Montgomery's 'Field Flower', but he points out that the ideas, which connect together these poems, are substantially different. The next part of the note explains that Wordsworth need not apologize to Montgomery for any form of plagiarism, although he does include a comic five-line apology taken from a poem by Chaucer. Beyond acquitting himself of plagiarism, Wordsworth seems concerned with establishing two degrees of authority for his poetry. First, he points out that these three poems are not the same as Montgomery's poem and, consequently, should not be read in the same vein. Second, he establishes a connection between his poems based on language that extends beyond the ideas expressed in each poem singly.

The choice of words was undoubtedly an important element for these three poems. In a letter to Sir George Beaumont, 20 February 1808, Wordsworth bristles at the criticism he had received about one of these daisy poems from a friend of Lady Beaumont's. Responding to her remarks about his poem, which she calls 'on a daisy', Wordsworth retorts, 'by the bye, it is on *the Daisy*, a mighty difference', and then asserts, 'My language is precise, and therefore, it would be false modesty to charge myself with blame'.[50] For Wordsworth, the fault lies with Lady Beaumont's friend, and his peevish remark implies that inattention to his words divests readers of the authority to criticize his poetry. His letter challenges readers to attend to his particular uses of language within individual poems, and asks them to engage with the precision of that language, before grappling with the mental contexts that connect such 'overflowings of the mind'.

Mant's criticisms of Wordsworth's poems to the daisy satirically exploit Wordsworth's directions in the 1807 volumes about how readers should connect together words, ideas, and poems. Mant's footnote, which quotes four stanzas from three separate Wordsworth poems – the first poem begins volume 1 and the other two appear next to each other in the last section of volume 2, 'The Blind Highland Boy' – alludes to Wordsworth's own footnote 'To The Daisy' in volume 2: 'The two following Poems were overflowings of the mind in composing the one which stands first in the Volume'.[51] Mant sneers at Wordsworth's footnote – 'I select one or two passages from "the overflowings of his mind", in praise of that "sweet silent creature"' – which maintains that the two daisy poems in the second volume are connected to the initial poem in the first volume because they extend the emotional context of that first poem. Furthermore, Mant places these poems under the same categorical designation, 'the overflowings of his mind' because, to him, they represent the same bizarre, retarded simplicity. Ironically, his attempts to level these three poems into one both follow and creatively extend Wordsworth's suggestions in the 1807 volumes for how to read this group of poems.

Mant does not present his footnoted excerpts from Wordsworth's daisy poems as they appear chronologically in Wordsworth's two volumes. Instead, he traces the backward and forward looking directions in Wordsworth's footnote to the second daisy poem. Mant first quotes from the second poem and fixates on the second half of its last stanza. Then, as if heeding Wordsworth's connective footnote, Mant returns to the first poem and quotes the first half of stanza six and the second half of stanza seven. Finally, he turns to the third poem and quotes the last stanza. Although Mant seemingly undercuts the fact that the last two poems come from a different section heading than the first one, he also replicates the kind of emotional and recuperative attention to the daisy that Wordsworth asks readers to attend to from the first poem to the third poem. Furthermore, Mant's return to the opening poem in the first volume retraces the path that attentive readers might have taken through the 1807 *Poems* up to the second daisy poem. Such readers have travelled from the first daisy poem through the rest of the first section, which ends with the 'Ode to Duty', through the section 'Poems Composed during a Tour, Chiefly on Foot', which ends with another type of tribute to duty in 'Resolution and Independence', through 'Miscellaneous Sonnets' and 'Sonnets Dedicated to Liberty', and past the endnotes to volume 1 – one of which asks readers to attend to the daisy sequence. The second volume begins with another tour, which mirrors the one in section I with 'Poems Written during a Tour of Scotland', and then moves readers through the section 'Moods of my own Mind' toward the two other daisy poems, which appear in the section 'The Blind Highland Boy'. Finally, the second volume ends with an 'Ode' that concludes by pointing back to the first daisy poem in volume 1.

Although Mant seeks to erase the accumulated weight of this textual travelling through his parodic reconstructions, he engages in the kind of attentive reading of repetition for which Wordsworth calls. Mant constructs a synthetic poem out of these three daisy poems that, far from showing all of Wordsworth's stanzas to be the same, ironically highlights the differences and intricate relationship between them:

> Thou breath'st with me in sun and air,
> Do thou, as thou art want, repair
> My heart with gladness, and a share
> Of thy meek nature!
> Again:
> If stately passions in me burn,
> And one chance look to thee should turn,

> I *drink* out of an humbler *urn*
>   A lovelier pleasure.
> Again:
> At dusk I've seldom mark'd thee press
> The ground, as if in thankfulness,
> Without some feeling more or less,
>   *Of true devotion.*

But I know not whether a more perfect instance of silliness is to be detected in the whole farrago of the school than the following stanza; mark ye! addressed as well to the foregoing daisy:

> Thou wander'st the wide world about,
> Uncheck'd by pride or scrupulous doubt,
> With friends to greet thee, or without,
> Yet pleased and willing;
> Meek, yielding to occasion's call,
> And all things suffering from all,
> *THY FUNCTION APOSTOLICAL*
> *IN PEACE FULFILLING.*[52]

While in many places in *The Simpliciad*, Mant allows a quotation to speak for itself, in this extended footnote, he is unable to resist supplying a connective tissue through his own annotations to Wordsworth's three poems. These annotations link the first three stanzas together with the word 'again' and suggest that each stanza is merely a repetition of the same. Furthermore, his final prose statement before the last stanza attempts to highlight the repetitive 'silliness' of these continued addresses to the daisy.

In poaching from Wordsworth's three poems, Mant selects passages in which Wordsworth's speaker hovers at the emotional height of his epideictic praise for the daisy. Through these selected quotations, Mant attempts to overwrite the manner in which Wordsworth's speaker modifies his praise of the daisy over the course of these poems. The reparative passage from the second daisy poem that Mant initially quotes represents a point of transition for the poet, who hovers between his past delights with the daisy in the first poem and his newfound vision, only fully developed in the third poem. Mesmerized by the daisy in the second poem, Wordsworth's speaker plays a fanciful game of similes; he alternately compares the flower to a nun, a maiden of court, a queen, a starveling, a cyclops, a 'Faery bold' and a star. However, when all of these 'reveries' vanish, he maintains, 'I call thee, and to that cleave fast' (l. 43), and then reveals the daisy's newly perceived ability to 'repair / His heart' (ll. 46–7). The daisy cannot be described through fanciful comparisons; it is a flower that stands on its own and, therefore, demands a singular definition. In the second poem, the poet also discovers qualities about the daisy that signal an evaluative change in his own character. This internal development stands in marked contrast to the initial daisy poem in which the poet praises the daisy in conjunction with his new found ability to make his 'own delights' (l. 5) in nature as opposed to his past when,

> In youth from rock to rock [he] went
> From hill to hill, in discontent
> Of pleasure high and turbulent,
> Most pleas'd when most uneasy; (ll. 1–4)

This first poem highlights the poet's perception of

> [a]n instinct ... a blind sense;
> A happy, genial influence,
> Coming one knows not how nor whence,
> Nor where going (ll. 69–72)

The poem also indirectly praises the youthful poet who reads the variety of intrinsic qualities of the daisy that, occasionally, give him 'some chime of fancy wrong or right' and, at other times, 'a lowlier pleasure'.

Mant's next movement, from this first poem to the third poem, demonstrates the most profound shift in Wordsworth's conception of himself and his poetic duty to the world. In the third poem, the poet modifies his view of the daisy when he recognizes the flower as 'a Pilgrim bold in Nature's care' (l. 2) that possesses '[s]ome concord with humanity' (l. 7). He foregrounds the importance of the daisy as an instrument that not only brings him joy and helps him to repair his emotional state but also ministers to humanity. He relinquishes his personal and idiosyncratic associations with the daisy to his perception of the universal and exemplary qualities of the flower. The daisy becomes a ubiquitous reminder of what humanity should strive for. Its qualities of humility and a kind of 'negative capability' render it a fit emblem for the poet to reread and reflect on as he considers the relationship between his poetic development and his responsibility to mankind. In fact, unlike the other three stanzas that Mant quotes, in this final stanza, the daisy's qualities efface the poet's idiosyncratic fancies and very presence.

Mant's attempts to render Wordsworth's series of poems as idiotic 'overflowings of his mind', which only speak to Wordsworth, ironically highlight the power that these poems have to redouble attention to a simple object and to remind readers of their shared humanity. This redoubled attention also prompts a re-evaluation of the perceiving individual's place and purpose in the world. Such acts of attention do not simply occur by progressing from the first to the second to the third poems. Instead, they require readers to pause over the second poem, return to the first, and then trace the movement between the first and the third. The internal reflection, growth, and renewed sense of duty that these poems facilitate, both for the poet and his readers, occur through backward and forward readings of the daisy poems. Far from proving their torpid sameness, Mant's engagement with these three poems reveals that Wordsworthian repetition engenders difference, independent thoughts and energetic renewal.

Repeating 'Resolution and Independence'

If Mant unwittingly emphasizes these nuanced connections between Wordsworth's three poems to the daisy, in his footnoted commentary on 'Resolution and Independence' he foregrounds the very transformative power of Wordsworthian repetition that *The Simpliciad* attempts to render flatly ridiculous. Mant's couplets and footnoted quotations single out moments in the poem when the poet and the leech gatherer repeat the same dialogue. In 'Resolution and Independence' this encounter between the poet and leech gatherer, and their subsequent conversation, are marked by variations of seemingly the same question, which the poet asks at two different points in the poem – 'What kind of work is that which you pursue?' (l. 95) and 'How is it that you live, and what is it that you do?' (l. 126).

Wordsworth's leech gatherer provides Mant with the opportunity to liken Wordsworth's poetic failings to the leech gathering activities of an old man:

> See! Motionless he stands, and like a cloud,
> That heareth not the winds which call so loud,
> And now upon the water he doth look;
> And readeth there as if he read his book;
> And stirreth now the pond about his feet,
> And tho' with not a leech he there can meet,
> He smiles so sweetly on his state forlorn,
> That gazing bards may laugh themselves to scorn. (ll. 323–32)

Mant's couplets reduce the stages of the poet's personal journey in 'Resolution and Independence' to a distended gaze that mocks the poet's subject matter and the poet for choosing such a subject. What Mant leaves out is the significance of this encounter. Following each of his questions to the leech gatherer, Wordsworth's poet both listens and allows his mind to wander so that, invariably, he does not fully comprehend the leech gatherer's speech. By the end of the poem, the poet has engaged in three different readings of the leech gatherer's significance marked by the repetition of the old man's speech. The poet's continual return to sameness – the leech gatherer's speech – engenders differential acts of reading that transform the poet's view of the leech gatherer from an impressive object into a touchstone for continued sympathy, personal evaluation, perseverance and independence. Mant overwrites the importance of this repetitive conversation and instead depicts the leech gatherer as a dotard, who cannot hear 'the winds' and is unable to perform his simple labors. In Mant's parody the leech gatherer remains inert and stares fixedly at the water as if passively reading a book while smiling at his own ineptness.[53]

For Mant the leech gatherer stands as a figure for Wordsworth, both as a poet and as a reader of his own poetry. Accordingly, Mant's couplet renders Wordsworth's lines, which are quoted in Mant's footnote – '*Upon the muddy water, which he conn'd / As if he had been reading in a book*' – as, 'And now upon the water he doth look; / And readeth there as if he read his book'. Self-contained, unmoving, and pleased with what he sees – his own reflection in the water according to Mant's reconstruction – Wordsworth spends his time reading and rereading the same figure of himself in 'his book'. As a word- (leech-) gathering poet,[54] Wordsworth repetitively pores over and 'cons' his own pages, unsuccessfully looking for new words just as the leech gatherer repeatedly scans the barren pond for leeches. Through Mant's depiction, Wordsworth's word search stagnates just as the old leech gatherer seemingly fails in his vocation.

Mant carefully selected his footnoted excerpts from 'Resolution and Independence' to support his charges against Wordsworth's empty, meaningless repetitions. However, instead of flattening the poem, these passages foreground the complexity of repetition in 'Resolution and Independence' and reveal that the poem is about how to read Wordsworth's brand of poetry. Consequently, when Mant aligns the poet with the leech gatherer in his couplets, he is half right. 'Resolution and Independence' sets up a continuum not only between leech gatherer and poet but also between the poet and his readers. If the activities of the leech gatherer conjure up the vocation of the poet, then the poet's responses to the old man suggest the challenges that Wordsworth's poem offers readers. The repetitious conversation that the poet tends to and the revolutions of his mind, which figuratively respond to that conversation, describe the possibilities that Wordsworth's language opens up for readers to engage closely with and wander imaginatively through not only this poem, but his entire poetic collection.

At the beginning of 'Resolution and Independence', the poet mimics the hermeneutic activities of many readers of poetry.[55] Similar to how readers might approach a poem through their own personal thoughts and associations, the poet is preoccupied with his own 'fears and fancies' when he first encounters the leech gatherer (ll. 25–7). After noticing the leech gatherer, he immediately imagines the import of the man's presence in the landscape (text) spread out before him. This initial transformation of the leech gatherer turns on the poet's recent sense of despair and pressing need to ground his emotions by reading the man's external strength and fortitude as sublime and awesome. He imagines the leech gatherer as a physically impressive 'huge stone' on 'the bald top of an eminence' and then transforms this figuration into 'a sea-beast' sunning itself on a shelf. From these massive prehistoric images, the poet examines more closely the man's physicality, though he still understands him as subhuman, 'not all alive nor dead' with his body 'bent double', plagued by a 'more than human weight'. Finally, in reaction to the old man's stillness, the poet illustrates him as standing 'Motionless as a cloud'. These initial readings of the leech gatherer, however, give way to a series of corrective acts of attention that reconceptualize the old man's significance.

After asking the leech gatherer a question – 'What kind of work is that which you pursue?' – the poet's grandiose imaginings of the leech gatherer's outward form shift towards a literal engagement with the old man's words. The poet does not completely grasp the import of the leech gatherer's speech the first time that the old man tells his tale, but those words have a decided impact on the direction of the poet's already vexed thoughts:

> each [word] in solemn order follow'd each,
> With something of a lofty utterance drest;
> Choice word, and measured phrase; above the reach
> Of ordinary men; a stately speech! (ll. 100–3)

The leech gatherer's particular word choices, ordering, style and measured pace arrest the poet's mental activity and prompt him to engage closely with the old man's answer. Like a well-crafted poem, the form of his speech enmeshes the poet in the content of his story. However, as the leech gatherer continues his discourse, the poet's attention to that form flags so that 'his voice ... was like a stream / Scarce heard; nor word from word could I divide' (ll. 107–8). This trailing off and slackening of attention is less a function of the poet's inability to concentrate on the old man's words than a matter of what those words prompt him to imagine.[56] Wading through the leech gatherer's speech, the poet's mind revolves outward into a reverie in which 'the whole body of the Man' appeared as if sent in a dream 'To give [the poet] human strength, by apt admonishment' (l. 112). Far from the impressive physical being into which the poet initially transforms the leech gatherer, the poet now rereads him as an agent who can speak to the poet correctively and fortify him internally.

This second reinvigorated, imaginative act results from the poet's ability to feel for the leech gatherer as he relates the old man's speech and circumstances to his own life. Once this sympathetic connection is achieved, the poet attends more closely to the leech gatherer's actual discourse. Then, the poet 'eagerly' asks his question again: 'How is it that you live, and what is it you do?' In response to the poet's question, the leech gatherer smiles and then repeats his words (l. 120). In his footnote, Mant seizes on this moment of double repetition as proof of Wordsworth's repetitive simplicity. However, while Mant's couplet claims 'he smiles so sweetly on his state forlorn', his footnote quoting Wordsworth's line – 'He with a *smile* did then his words repeat' – demonstrates that Wordsworth's leech gatherer actually smiles at the poet because the poet has not yet understood the complete import of the old man's words. Wordsworth's poet has been an attentive and an inattentive listener, but, as a reader, he has travelled a great interpretive distance. To extend this logic, if the poet can imaginatively assume the role of the leech gatherer, and if readers can take on the searching inward and outward, mental activity of the poet as reader, then the leech gatherer's smile is also directed at readers. Pointedly, after this smile, the leech gatherer speaks for the first time in the poem.[57]

In his footnote, Mant quotes the entire stanza with the leech gatherer's speech as a 'fair specimen of the solemn buffoonery' of the poem. What he excises, however, is how the leech gatherer's words immediately affect the poet. Troubled by both 'the old Man's shape, and speech' (1. 128),[58] the poet's mind sets the leech gatherer's words in motion, unfixing the old man from his rooted spot so that 'in [his] mind's eye [he] seemed to ... pace / About the weary moors continually, / Wandering about alone and silently' (ll. 136–8). Correspondingly, the leech gatherer halts his repeated discourse in a purposeful manner that enables the poet to pursue his thoughts. This lull facilitates the poet's final transformative reading of the leech gatherer, who 'having made a pause, the same discourse renewed' for the third time in the poem (1. 140). However, any final self-corrective reading of the leech gatherer's significance remains unstated. The last stanza of the poem only suggests that the previous reading of the leech gatherer as a perpetual vagrant or figure of the Wandering Jew is not a conclusive one.

This unstated recognition occurs as the poet attaches his thoughts to the leech gatherer's final, '[c]hearfully uttered', and 'stately' words (ll. 142, 143). What the poet achieves is a resolution based on his reflections about how he has read and reread the leech gatherer's significance. The poet has recovered his sense of independence through revisionary reading – a vacillating process of mediating his own thoughts and imaginatively transforming the leech gatherer through varying degrees of attention to the old man's repeated words. Strength of mind comes in the form of the poet's continual attention to the leech gatherer's speech, as well as through the repeated imaginative forays that the poet has undertaken when not closely listening to his words. This dual realization prompts the poet to remark, 'I could have laugh'd myself to scorn, to find/ In that decrepit man so firm a mind' (ll. 144–5). Deriding his earlier fears of mental stagnation and madness (ll. 43–9), the poet also chides himself for his misapprehensions earlier in the poem about the leech gatherer as a bastion of outward strength.

This final stanza in 'Resolution and Independence', which Mant's couplets ridicule, acknowledges that the poet has only begun to grasp the real strength that lies in the leech gatherer's continual acts of mental engagement with a potentially stagnant, circular and unyielding vocation. The old man's strength comes from his cheerful willingness to keep searching, rereading and retelling his life and profession anew. '[T]hink[ing] of the Leech-gatherer' provides the poet with 'help' and a 'stay secure' by recalling a process of attending both to his own mind and to the object in front of him. To avoid stagnation, the poet must return to the same objects and words and continually adjust his former thoughts in relation to his new perceptions. 'Resolution and Independence' shows how vacillating degrees of attention to repetition – even deformations like Mant's – can lead to self-discovery, sympathy, strength and independent reading. A significant part of the poet's resolution is to read words, things and people anew. 'Resolution and Independence' extends this pledge to readers and challenges them not only to consider how they might actively engage with this poem and with Wordsworth's poetic collection, but also to reflect on their duty to themselves and to one another. With that shared responsibility, Wordsworth turns his readers towards the final two sections of volume 1 – 'Miscellaneous Sonnets' and 'Sonnets Dedicated to Liberty' – which pit ideals of British liberty, free-thinking, heroism, independence, tradition and national unity against selfishness, venality and the threatening presence of Napoleon Buonaparte's imperial France.

Mant overlooks and overwrites Wordsworth's concerns in his 1807 *Poems* with public duty, independent thinking, British nationalism and pressing political and martial action.[59] Moreover, in attempting to short-circuit the connective power of Wordsworth's volumes, *The Simpliciad* loses control, at times, over Wordsworth's poetic language. Consequently, his parodic reconfigurations of Wordsworth's poems to the daisy and 'Resolution and Independence', which aim to demonstrate the simplistic, fragmented, and disjointed nature of Wordsworth's poetry, ironically replicate the kinds of hermeneutic mobility and revisionary reading that Wordsworth's paratexts and poems attempt to encourage in readers. Far from definitively asserting 'the new school of criticism's' control over the 'new school of poetry', Mant reveals that poetry and parody, verse and prose, writers and reviewers, redefine one another through continual acts of transformative reading. Mant's redounding echoes of the 'Lake poets' and their reviewers create a complex satire that ridicules the 'Lake School' and inadvertently points out how many reviewers had missed the mark in their evaluation of Wordsworth's poetic system and 1807 volumes. Through his revisionary reading of Wordsworth's poetry, Mant's parody reveals how Wordsworth's repetitious language and linked poems open up spaces throughout his 1807 volumes for readers to exercise and evaluate their roles as active and creative agents, who – by engaging with his poetic collection – are also asserting their capacity to uphold Wordsworth's ideals of British liberty.

4 WORDSWORTH'S 'LIBRARY OF BABEL': *THE EXCURSION* AND THE 1815 *POEMS*[1]

Wordsworth's poetic reputation was severely damaged by the mocking criticisms levelled at his 1807 *Poems*, and sales of these volumes languished over the next few years.[2] Wordsworth did not publish another collection of poems until 1815.[3] And, before hazarding the publication of such a collection, he carefully advertised its lasting cultural significance and massive size in a 'Preface' and 'Prospectus' to his epic, philosophical poem *The Excursion* (1814). Through his 1814 and 1815 publications, Wordsworth sought to prove his critics wrong, demonstrate the high sincerity of his poetic project, establish a market share for his poetry and direct the bibliomania affecting the reading public in Great Britain.

Philip Connell argues that the 1810s saw the rise of diverse strains of bibliomania involving the aristocratic gentleman, the burgeoning reading public and the man of letters. Citing the famous sale of the great library of the fifth duke of Roxburghe, James Innes-Ker, Connell relates the aristocratic vogue for purchasing and collecting expensive literary treasures to a larger public interest in assembling the nation's literary heritage. In the early nineteenth century, an aristocratic bibliomaniac might be understood publicly either as a self-absorbed collector, gratifying an insatiable desire for collecting rare and valuable books, or as a benefactor to society, accumulating a library of books that would add to the cultural capital of the nation. Connell suggests that this latter view developed largely in the late eighteenth century in conjunction with the reading public's broadening interest in collecting the literary past – a pursuit made economically possible with the end of perpetual copyright in 1774. Such widespread interest led to cheap and expensive editions of literary classics and to a concern with establishing and collecting together the literary heritage of Great Britain. With this vogue for book collecting, Connell maintains that even an aristocrat's private library could be understood, 'symbolically at least, as a national resource'.[4]

Such antiquarian cravings for books, in both the upper and middling classes, was offset in the 1810s by what many critics – most prominent in the *Edinburgh Review* and the *Quarterly Review* – described as a deluge of modern books. These critics maintained that what was needed to contain this onslaught of books was a standard for measuring the national value of literary productions – a yard stick for deciding what should be read and why. And, with a public intent on collecting literary treasures, questions about what should be collected, how collections should be made and how such collections might be read were common.[5] The emerging nineteenth-century literary class of the man of letters[6] responded to this call for bibliographic and hermeneutic order, in part, by fashioning themselves as disinterested readers and writers gathering together the cultural life of the nation.[7] Connell singles out Isaac D'Israeli as such a leading man of letters who developed an anecdotal method of writing, meant to bridge the gap between the learned and unlearned, by constructing a personal history that also pointed to a shared national history. Such a method featured 'a collection of discrete particulars whose diligent accumulation and tasteful arrangement gestures toward a cohesive, organic conception of collective national culture'.[8]

Connell's article offers a means for understanding the cultural dialogue about books in the second decade of the nineteenth century, to which Wordsworth responds through the network of supplementary writing attached to *The Excursion* (1814) and his collected *Poems* (1815). Seeking to re-enter a book-filled market, Wordsworth sought to capitalize on and redirect the bibliomania sweeping Great Britain. He developed his own anecdotal method, which sets his works apart by placing them within an imagined coherent whole – a mini-library that unites his poems, presents a unified story of his poetic development and reveals a connection between the past, present and future cultural life of the nation. This chapter investigates several of the hypertextual principles that organize Wordsworth's 1815 categories, which function as both a portion and a reflection of his collecting and organizing tendencies for his larger hypothetical *oeuvre*, outlined in his 'Preface to *The Excursion*' of 1814.[9] Wordsworth presents himself in his supplementary writings as a disinterested man of letters, and he recasts the cultural significance of this bibliophilia craze by including his readers in the process of collecting together and producing his volumes of poetry. Furthermore, in one of his 1815 categories, 'Poems of the Imagination', his prose notes describe his poetic volumes as a modern classic, fit to be collected together and then re-collected by the public. These notes suggest how readers can gain control over the sheer mass of printed materials that they encounter, and they also identify 'Tintern Abbey', the finishing poem in this category, as a composite form, constructed not only out of the poet's developmental tale of imaginative growth but also out of the growth of a nation.

The 'Prospectus' and 'Preface to *The Excursion*' (1814)

The publication of *The Excursion being a Portion of The Recluse* (1814) marked Wordsworth's re-entrance into the poetry market.[10] His dedicatory sonnet 'To the Right Honourable William, Earl of Lonsdale, K.G.', 'Preface to the Edition of 1814' and the ensuing poetic 'Prospectus' leave no doubt that Wordsworth was marketing his works and himself as a valuable, cultural monument, which his dedicatory sonnet relates directly to the reception of *The Excursion* – 'may it prove a monument!'. Responding to critics who derided his 1807 *Poems* as ephemeral and childish, Wordsworth surrounded, guarded and attempted to monumentalize his fragmentary epic, *The Recluse*, with paratexts, both seen and unseen.

As Stephen Gill points out, *The Excursion* was beautifully printed in a large quarto of 447 pages, including a dedicatory sonnet 'To the Right Honourable William, Earl of Lonsdale, K.G. &c. &c.' and a six-page summary of the contents in each of the poem's nine books. Six pages of notes and a sixteen-page *Essay upon Epitaphs* accompanied by notes also follow these nine books.[11] While *The Excursion* was kept from the majority of the reading public by its high price, its book size also announced the poem as an enduring monument. Not since his 1793 publication 'An Evening Walk' had Wordsworth chosen, or been given, the opportunity to publish in quarto. Wordsworth re-entered the poetry market by announcing his enduring presence in a book size that was typically placed in a library and not toted around, like his pocket-size octavo editions of *Lyrical Ballads* might be. *The Excursion* was designed as a portion of a literary treasure, which appealed directly to Wordsworth's aristocratic patron William, Earl of Lonsdale. However, its supplementary writings also describe the collective, but as yet unactualized, potential of his works for a wider audience. These paratexts announce the monumental value of his epic in terms of its capacity to activate the collecting and collective powers of its readers.

Wordsworth's dedicatory sonnet,[12] prose 'Preface' and poetic 'Prospectus' set up the centrality of *The Excursion* for the, as yet fragmentary, *Recluse* and for all of his poetic productions, in the past and future. These supplementary writings function as introductions to *The Excursion*, and they operate as advertisements that both remind readers of what Wordsworth has already accomplished and announce what he will accomplish. In several places, Wordsworth's preface highlights the 'laborious Work' that he has undertaken to write the enormous *The Recluse*.[13] In this preface Wordsworth strives to connect together the fragments of all he has written and all that he will write, and he foregrounds the importance of collecting the life of the poetic mind and the life of his poetic works. Wordsworth explicitly points out that his purpose in retiring 'to his native mountains [was founded on] the hope of being enabled to construct a literary Work that might live'.[14] In order to construct a living work, such as *The Recluse*, he collected his thoughts by 'tak[ing] a review of his own mind', and this recollection has led to the construction of *The Prelude*, '[a]s subsidiary to this preparation'.[15]

Curiously, Wordsworth uses the word 'review' to describe the activity that led to his writing *The Prelude*. He styles himself as a poet-critic, engaged in a type of pre-reviewing activity – even before the act of writing – which leads to a preparatory poem that acts as a critique of his powers and as a guiding force that enables him to construct *The Excursion*.[16] Wordsworth announces that he has studied his subject before writing this poem, has considered the past in order to write the present, and has been his own best critic. He also foregrounds his decision to publish 'the second division of the Work' because it 'was designed to refer more to passing events, and to an existing state of things' than the other two, as yet unpublished, parts of *The Recluse*.[17] Wordsworth implies that his sense of public responsibility has influenced his decision to publish this middle part of the poem first.

By contrast, in his November 1814 review of *The Excursion*, Francis Jeffrey relates Wordsworth's publishing propensity to a distinct lack of public responsibility. Jeffrey diagnoses Wordsworth with a sickness – the type of bibliomania that was often associated with the idiosyncratic and self-serving collecting habits of aristocrats. The book size and material style of *The Excursion* might have prompted Jeffrey towards such an evaluation, but Jeffrey also provides a detailed rationale, confiding to his readers that 'had [Wordsworth] condescended to mingle a little more with the people that were to read and judge of [his poems], we cannot help thinking, that its texture would have been considerably improved'.[18] While throughout the review Jeffrey strongly denigrates Wordsworth's choice of rustic characters, bathetic fallings in language and passion for overwrought simplicity, Jeffrey's choice of the word 'texture', which suggests the structure given to an object by the size, shape and arrangement of its parts, also recalls his major criticism of Wordsworth's 'peculiar system'. For Jeffrey, Wordsworth's value to the public, or lack thereof, is to be found in this system: 'His former poems were intended to recommend that system, and to bespeak favour for it by their individual merit; – but this, we suspect, must be recommended by the system – and can only expect to succeed where it has been previously established'.[19] Jeffrey's commentary inverts the familiar part/whole Wordsworthian proposition to whole/part and evaluates *The Excursion* against the whole of Wordsworth's past publications. Because *The Excursion* is a part of that past system, Jeffrey argues that it will fail to win over readers just as Wordsworth's 1807 *Poems* had.

Jeffrey saves some of his most caustic and exasperated remarks for Wordsworth's preface to *The Excursion*:

> it is stated in the title – with something of an impudent candour – to be but 'a portion' of a larger work; and in the preface, where an attempt is rather unsuccessfully made to explain the whole design, it is still more rashly disclosed, that it is but 'a part of the second part of a *long* and laborious work' – which is to consist of three parts.[20]

After lamenting 'Mr. Wordsworth's ideas of length', Jeffrey asserts that this

> small specimen ... and the statements with which it is prefaced, have been sufficient to set our minds at rest in one particular. The case of Mr. Wordsworth, we perceive, is now manifestly hopeless; and we give him up as altogether incurable, and beyond the power of criticism.[21]

Jeffrey publicly deserts his patient Wordsworth and acknowledges the Lake poet's case as hopeless because he has so continually 'been for twenty years at work on such matter as is now before us', and 'is at this moment working up for publication upon the old pattern ... it [is] almost hopeless to look for any change'.[22]

Although Jeffrey contends that Wordsworth is beyond critical and clinical help, he does maintain, '[w]e cannot altogether omit taking precautions now and then against the spreading of the malady'.[23] Jeffrey associates this malady with the longstanding perversion of taste that has marred Wordsworth's genius, but he seems most upset with Wordsworth's plans to continue writing and collecting together his works under the same system. He recognizes 'The Preface to *The Excursion*' as Wordsworth's announcement of an idiosyncratic system that enables the poet to collate and organize his poems into a seemingly unending series of tomes. Jeffrey regards Wordsworth's poems as too self-involved, too attached to his '[l]ong habits of seclusion, and an excessive ambition of originality',[24] and Wordsworth as bent on collecting his poems so that he can obsessively look at them all together. For Jeffrey, the health of the reading public can only be debilitated by the spread of Wordsworth's collecting malady, and 'This will never do'.[25]

Like Jeffrey, ironically, Wordsworth also was intent on delimiting the public's cravings for unhealthy stimulation fed by the deluge of printed works in the 1810s. However, while Jeffrey describes Wordsworth's sickness as if it were an idiosyncratic taste for publishing and hoarding together his own books in a private library, Wordsworth describes his collecting tendencies as a system for evaluating and combating the overwhelming production and circulation of books. Wordsworth's supplementary writings in *The Excursion* encourage his readers to transform themselves from passive buyers who are inundated by books into active agents, empowered by their capacity to recognize and take part in creating the organizing principles behind the collections that they purchase.

In his poetic 'Prospectus' to *The Excursion*, Wordsworth demonstrates how readers' cravings for ephemeral productions might be reshaped into a lasting appreciation for and desire to collect past and contemporary literary classics.[26] Through his prospectus Wordsworth attempts to include readers in the process of producing and collecting together his poetry. While this prefatory, epic proemium links together the poet, the powers of his mind, his task and his subject matter with his readers, it also foregrounds the poet grappling with the difficulties of an extended moment of pre-writing, pre-reading and pre-editing.

The prospectus functions as a poetic index and overview of what is, what was and what will come – all of which hinge on how it prompts and intermingles the creative powers of the poet with his readers.

The prospectus encourages readers to follow what Coleridge would describe as the 'revelations of [the poet's] own mind, producing itself and evolving its own greatness'.[27] Its subject matter and form invite readers to evaluate Wordsworth's poetic labour and to regard him as a poet that follows Milton's narrator, who traces Satan's descent and ascent through hell, chaos and heaven. However, Wordsworth also describes the space that he explores as more awful and more fertile than the path of Milton's narrator because Wordsworth 'must tread on shadowy ground, must sink / Deep – and, aloft ascending, breathe in worlds / To which the heaven of heavens is but a veil' (ll. 28–30). After passing through that veil, he reveals that the 'haunt, and the main region of [his] song' is 'look[ing] / Into our Minds, into the Mind of Man' (ll. 41, 40).

Such a journey into the mind of man necessitates a more detailed poetic inquiry and heightened psychological journey than the exposition in *Paradise Lost*, which, like *The Recluse*, begins in the middle and works forwards and backwards as the narrative progresses. However, Wordsworth also proclaims the necessity of invoking a muse, like the muse in *Paradise Lost*, to aid him in his journey: 'Urania, I shall need / Thy guidance, or a greater Muse' (ll. 25–6). Like the narrator of *Paradise Lost* who, on several occasions, calls for Urania's guidance so that he will not lose the theme of his epic and become lost in the midst of the design that he constructs, Wordsworth too foregrounds his need to find an organizing framework for his epic that will speak of more than *Paradise Lost* could ever encompass – even with Milton's temporal design, which reaches backwards to creation and forwards to revelation. Wordsworth's prospectus further privileges his organizing framework over Milton's because Wordsworth attempts to bridge the psychological gap between the poet and his readers.

His burden as a poet, the prospectus makes clear, is to chart the evolving and revolving relationship between the developing mind of an individual life (Wordsworth's) and 'Man', 'Nature', and 'Human Life' (l. 1). The prospectus connects together all of these focal points – to 'chant ... the spousal verse / Of this great consummation' (ll. 56–7) between the 'Mind of Man' (l. 40) and 'Beauty – a living Presence of the earth' (l. 43), between high subjects and low, between himself and mankind, and sets up the possibility for such a consummation through its engaging form. Wordsworth interrupts his blank verse on a number of occasions with dashes that divide and align his thoughts as they twist and turn between his narrative argument and apostrophic invocations. In fact, nearly all of the revolutions of the poet's mind are divided by dashes, which parse his proemium into six sections that draw the reader on toward his '[t]heme this but little heard of among men' (l. 68). While in the first third of the prospectus

Wordsworth identifies 'the main region of *my* Song' (l. 41), by the end of line 71 he asserts, 'this is *our* high argument' (emphasis added). Lines 70–1 signal the climax of this shift from the poet's song to a song shared by the poet and his readers: 'And the creation (by no lower name / Can it be called) which they with blended might / Accomplish – this is our high argument' (ll. 69–71).

The rhetorical construction of these lines suggests why such mutual 'creation' is contingent. Although Wordsworth implies that the 'blended might' of mind and world can produce a type of creation that is almost divine, the construction of 'blended might / Accomplish' followed by '*our* high argument' (my emphasis) implies the necessity of 'fit' readers contributing to Wordsworth's poetic project. His use of 'might', which directly precedes 'Accomplish', leaves readers to actualize the poet's claim that 'this is our high argument'. These words suggest to readers – who have been informed, a few lines earlier, that Wordsworth would 'arouse the sensual from their sleep / Of Death, and win the vacant and vain / To noble raptures' (ll. 60–2) – a possible consummation with the poet through the word 'our'. This 'blended might' suggests how readers are connected to the poem – as an extension of the poet – and, reciprocally, how the poet is connected to the poem – as an extension of readers.

Directly preceding 'Accomplish', 'might' implies both the poet's advice and request that readers enact the latent strength inherent in a union between the text, the poet, and readers, which could produce 'creation (by no lower name / Can it be called' (ll. 69–70). If readers respond to the poet's call for 'blended might', then those inspired readers can move through this 'Prospectus' – a multivalent, paratextual threshold, which opens up access to all of Wordsworth's works. Because the entire 107 lines of the prospectus are set off in quotations and identified as the end of *Home at Grasmere*, they not only point backwards to the end of the absent *Home at Grasmere*, but also forward to *The Excursion* and the design of the future *Recluse* that follows the prospectus. Furthermore, the prospectus points backwards through the 'Preface to *The Excursion*' to *The Prelude*, which enabled Wordsworth to take a review of his mind and design his entire poetic project; and, the prospectus also provisionally points outward to all of the other 'minor Pieces' that Wordsworth would collect together in 1815.[28] From this multivalent perspective, the 'Prospectus' bridges all of Wordsworth's works. It is proleptic because it continues forward *The Prelude*; it is analeptic because it recounts events that led up to *The Excursion*; it is elleptic because it links together *Home at Grasmere* and *The Excursion*; and it projects a contiguous, paralleptic movement between all of Wordsworth's 1815 poems that prepares readers for how to read Wordsworth's collected 1815 *Poems*.

If readers faithfully and sympathetically cross the threshold of the 'Prospectus' into the poetic world of '*our* high argument', then instead of remaining 'a doorway to incompleteness, fragmentation and ruin',[29] it offers a doorway into a process of continual growth, where readers can take part in the 'creation' of what is no longer just the shadowy Gothic church that Wordsworth describes in the preface, but the construction of '*our* high argument'. Through the prospectus Wordsworth prompts readers not only to begin 'extracting the system for [themselves]', as he asserts in that preface, but to take part in the creation of his system.

The prospectus recalls and illustrates the temporal and spatial dimensions of his collected works, which Wordsworth describes through his Gothic church figuration in the preceding preface to *The Excursion*. In this preface Wordsworth compares the relationship between *The Prelude* and *The Recluse* to the construction of 'the Anti-Chapel … to the body of a gothic Church'.[30] The word 'Anti-Chapel' suggests not only an entranceway into another part of a church, but the intimacy of a private, preparatory space. Wordsworth implies that readers should enter the main body of his works only after crossing through the recess of a subordinate, private, and, as yet, publicly absent place of worship – the threshold of *The Prelude*. Like the poet, Wordsworth suggests, readers must pass imaginatively through a personal and meditative chamber in order to properly enter his Gothic structure. Then, Wordsworth contends, readers can begin to imagine the shape of his poetic oeuvre:

> His minor Pieces, which have been long before the Public, when they shall be properly arranged, will be found by the attentive Reader to have such connection with the main Work as may give them claim to be likened to the little Cells, Oratories, and sepulchral Recesses, ordinarily included in those Edifices.[31]

Here, Wordsworth intertwines presence with absence, past with future, and parts with overarching design. He asks readers to construct the presence of the unfinished *Recluse* by passing through an absent *Prelude*, to project his past works into a coherent future 'main Work', and to imagine the reordering of the smallest, seemingly disparate 'Cells' as intricately necessary for the larger design. Since the 'Public' has long been exposed to his 'minor Pieces', Wordsworth hopes that 'attentive Reader[s]' will be able to construct the absent parts of this Gothic church and imaginatively inhabit the fragmented structure that he asks readers to complete. Faced with an incomplete, Gothic church missing its central piece, as well as many of its subsidiary parts, and filled with areas of light offset by uncertain 'Oratories, and sepulchral Recesses' clouded by darkness, readers are asked to work through their dismay and attune themselves to the grandeur of a structure in the process of being constructed. As Mark Schoenfield suggests, Wordsworth is not only building a figurative Gothic church, which he hopes readers will help him to complete; he is building an entire poetic community of readers based on how this structure is built over time.[32] Readers, however, would need to decide whether and how they want to participate in the fictive construction of this poetic oeuvre.

Recollecting Literary History in the 'Essay Supplementary to the Preface' (1815)

Wordsworth published two essays that explain how readers might participate in his life's work, and, fittingly, this 'Preface' and 'Essay Supplementary to the Preface' function as book-ends to the first volume of his *Poems by William Wordsworth*.[33] Before this preface Wordsworth included a table of contents, which elucidates his cataloguing and collating system for his poems while also asserting the overarching purpose and collective design behind his life's work.[34] Beyond relating when Wordsworth first composed and published various poems, this table of contents suggests how the 1815 volumes outline the growth of Wordsworth's mind, divides his life's work into different categories and foregrounds Wordsworth's efforts to order his life, his work and his readers. Drawing on these outlined narratives, Wordsworth's two volumes present him as a professional poet intent on grappling with a hostile print market and review culture, but they also identify him as a man of letters, attempting to add on to the store of human knowledge through the design of his collection. If in the 'Preface to *The Excursion*', Wordsworth depicts his collected works as a Gothic church – a figuration that perhaps reflects a growing public interest in gothic churches as national treasures – in the 'Essay Supplementary to the Preface', he places himself and his works squarely within a library of his own creation.

A few reviewers of the 1815 *Poems* identified Wordsworth's collecting propensity as an example of the frenetic bibliomania besetting the public in the face of a flooded book market. In the *Theatrical Inquisitor* of June 1815, one anonymous reviewer summarizes this exasperation with the number of books overwhelming the public:

> If the present race of authors was to be judged of from the quantity, and not the quality of their productions, the voice of censure would be wholly silenced; quarto succeeds to quarto, and poem to poem, in such rapid succession, that the public has no time to pause or doubt.[35]

This reviewer laments how general readers and reviewers are so overwhelmed by books that they neither have the capacity to stop and reflect on these productions, nor the ability to question the wisdom behind publishing any of them. Arguing that at 'the very instant [readers] are adjusting their critical scales to weigh the merit of one production, their attention is called off to the perusal of another', the reviewer laments, '[t]here is, indeed, scarcely one of our modern poets, who could not, out of his own works, furnish a very decent library, although it may not be so extensive as the Bodleian'.[36]

Though perhaps unintentionally, this reviewer captures the tone and subject matter of Wordsworth's 'Essay Supplementary to the Preface'. The overwhelming deluge of books, the need to properly judge those books and concerns with how and what to collect together are all central to Wordsworth's supplementary essay. This essay criticizes ignorant critics, diverse segments of the reading public, unrelenting market forces, and greedy booksellers, while also providing a brief and skewed history of the circulation and popularity in England of writers since Shakespeare.[37] Throughout this critique of the print market, which paves the way towards Wordsworth's assertion that the poet must 'create the taste by which he is to be enjoyed',[38] Wordsworth turns on the offensive and moulds literary history, his contemporary reception and his own conception of his works to fit into a library that he imagines as a future treasure for the 'People, philosophically characterized'.[39]

Tellingly, the only moment in the 'Essay Supplementary' when Wordsworth reveals himself as writing from a specific place occurs in the midst of his attack on how reviewing critics have tampered with the reception of poetic works. Wordsworth defends his position by turning to his own private library[40] and criticizes Dr Johnson for what he sees as Johnson's flawed assessments of the reception and success of *Paradise Lost*: 'Dr. Johnson has fallen into a gross mistake when he attempts to prove, by the sale of the work, that Milton's Countrymen were "*just* to it" upon its first appearance'.[41] He disagrees with Johnson's explanation that the demand for *Paradise Lost* after its first publication was low because of a lack of poetry readers. Wordsworth's response is both measured and biting: 'How careless must a writer be who can make this assertion in the face of so many existing title pages to belie it! Turning to my own shelves, I find the folio of Cowley, 7th Edition, 1681. A book near it is Flatman's Poems, 4th Edition, 1686; Waller, 5th Edition, same date'.[42] Wordsworth insists that the market for *Paradise Lost* was full of readers buying other editions of poetry; if Milton's epic did not sell better, Wordsworth contends, it was because readers were directed towards other poetic purchases.

Furthermore, the manner in which Wordsworth locates and identifies these volumes in his bookshelves suggests how inconsequential and randomly organized such popular groupings of books can be. From the folio of Cowley, his eye trails off to 'a book near' Cowley's, Flatman's and then he happens upon Waller's book. Beyond the general period when these writers published, these books appear grouped together on Wordsworth's shelves only because they went through enough editions to render them popular. After condemning Johnson's argument with this evidence from his private library, Wordsworth then implicitly dismisses the very collection of books that has proved his point. Such groupings of writers do not, he suggests, represent the values of a shared national culture, validated over time. These books only represent the popular taste of the late seventeenth century, and Wordsworth pushes them aside as a way to clear space for a new, imagined library of his own making – a library that he hopes will be built up, passed down and sustained from one generation to the next.

A few pages later, Wordsworth further bolsters his literary history over Johnson's by drawing attention to Johnson's *Lives of the Poets*. After denigrating the false language, descriptions and feelings in Macpherson's *Ossian*, Wordsworth turns to Johnson, who:

> was solicited not long after to furnish Prefaces biographical and critical for some of the most eminent English Poets. The Booksellers took upon themselves to make the collection; they referred probably to the most popular miscellanies, and, unquestionably, to their Books of accounts; and decided upon the claim of Authors to be admitted into a body of the most Eminent, from the familiarity of their names with the readers of the day, and by the profits, which, from the sale of his works, each had brought and was bringing to the Trade.[43]

Controlled by booksellers, who 'allowed [him] a limited exercise of discretion' to choose writers for *Lives of the Poets*, Johnson, Wordsworth maintains, has produced a collection that is 'scarcely to be mentioned without a smile' because it begins with Cowley and does not include Chaucer, Spenser, Sydney or Shakespeare.[44] From Wordsworth's perspective, Johnson's collection lacks integrity and, consequently, the ability to embody any sense of Britain's literary heritage because it was constructed under the direction of fashionable taste and a fickle market, where 'the Booksellers stalls in London swarmed with the folios of Cowley'.[45] By contrast, Wordsworth implies that his own 1815 collection possesses integrity because his disinterested judgement has governed its making and not money-grubbing booksellers and publishers.

Wordsworth then shifts his analysis of the print market to align his collection with Shakespeare's constructive genius and lasting cultural importance. Praising Shakespeare as more than a 'wild irregular genius', Wordsworth maintains 'that the judgment of Shakespeare in the selection of his material, and in the manner in which he has made them, heterogeneous as they often are, constitute a unity of their own, and contribute all to one great end [and] is no less admirable than his imagination, his invention, and his intuitive knowledge of human Nature!'.[46] Instead of referring directly to Shakespeare's dramatic works, which Shakespeare did not collect together, Wordsworth praises Shakespeare's sonnets because Shakespeare grouped them together, they were ignored or denigrated by critics in the seventeenth and eighteenth centuries, and recently their value had been widely acknowledged. However, Wordsworth's turn to Shakespeare also has a material as well as literary purpose. Throughout the eighteenth century, the market for publishing Shakespeare's collected works soared. Wordsworth's mention of Pope's Shakespeare edition before this passage offers just one example of how many poets and critics produced edited collections of his plays. By the end of the eighteenth century, Shakespeare's works had become an institution, a national heritage to be passed down from generation to generation – a self-contained library of beauties that inhabited the bookshelves of every man of taste and to which Wordsworth sought to add his own poetic collection.

Following this analysis of Shakespeare's cultural significance, Wordsworth singles out Percy's *Reliques* for particular praise as an anthology that links together the nation's past, present and future literary history through its form. Wordsworth describes the *Reliques* as 'collected, new-modelled, and in many instances (if such a contradiction in terms may be used) composed, by the editor Dr. Percy'.[47] As a seemingly overlooked and often slighted '[c]ompilation [that] was however ill-suited to the then existing taste of City society', the *Reliques* draw Wordsworth's praise because Percy has done more than simply collect and edit them. Although Wordsworth criticizes Percy for the unfortunate occasions in which he appears 'in his own person and character as a poetical writer' and replicates the characteristics of the 'unfeeling language of the day',[48] he warmly praises Percy's editorial endeavours for providing a standard or example ('new-modelled'), placing and forming these poems in the proper order ('composed') and drawing together materials from different sources ('Compilation').

From Wordsworth's point of view, Percy is also a poet-creator and not just an editor because the first publication of his collection drew so many imitators. Percy's composition of his *Reliques* drew together new and old materials that united Britain's past and present literary culture. Unlike Macpherson's *Ossian*, which showed an 'incapability to amalgamate with the literature of the Island', Wordsworth readily asserts, 'with a public avowal of [his] own', that Percy's *Reliques* has strongly influenced German literature 'and for our own Country, its Poetry has been absolutely redeemed by it. I do not think that there is an able Writer in verse of the present day who would not be proud to acknowledge his obligations to the Reliques.'[49] According to Wordsworth, Percy's collection has succeeded because it brings together diverse forms from the past that spur on present writers into the future.[50]

The *Reliques* provide a continuum and continuity for British literature – the same status that Wordsworth accords to *Lyrical Ballads* when he points out 'to what degree the Poetry of this Island has since that period been coloured by them'.[51] Wordsworth argues that literature, which is valuable, durable, worthy of being collected and kept 'is at once a history of the remote past and a prophetic annunciation of the remotest future'.[52] However, he also suggests that such works seemingly must wait to receive the recognition that they deserve, and he consoles himself by asserting that with literature such as his own, 'the *individual*, as well as the species, survives from age to age' while 'of the depraved, though the species be immortal the individual quickly *perishes*'.[53] Wordsworth's quasi-evolutionary stance of strong literature (and poets) seems to beg the question of how such literature survives. How can the 'individual' survive, and how can poets, such as Wordsworth, ignore the reading public, when that public provides the only sure means by which a poet's work can survive? Wordsworth obliquely answers these questions with his avowed devotion to 'the People, philosophically characterized, and to the embodied spirit of their knowledge, so far as it exists and moves, at the present, faithfully supported by its two wings, the past and the future'.[54]

Who such philosophic 'People' are (or will be) remains unclear,[55] but regardless of who they might be, Wordsworth's ability to appeal to these people was still contingent on contemporary publishers, reviewers and readers, who were willing to keep his works alive in the present so that they could be read in the future. The answer to these reception problems would seem to depend on the shifting and uncertain forces that governed the print market. Furthermore, Wordsworth needed a literal place[56] where his works could be collected and kept – bookshelves in libraries that would place him at the end of the great line of works that he catalogues before his own. Such cataloguing spaces, whether in bookshops or circulating libraries, would (by necessity) have some connection with the literary market, which was overrun by new publications, governed by the opinions of the review culture and inflected by the ephemeral tastes of the public. Wordsworth openly acknowledges that his poems cannot succeed against the popular and ephemeral tastes of the day, so he counters that the public's taste for poetry must change.

In the 'Essay Supplementary', Wordsworth distances his 1815 collection from the current literary market and maintains that his poetry, beginning with *Lyrical Ballads*, has carried on and helped to develop Britain's literary heritage, which he traces back through Percy to Shakespeare. Wordsworth differentiates his poetry, and the market for his works, from other contemporary publications by asserting their antiquarian, prophetic and lasting monumental value for Great Britain. *Lyrical Ballads* has captured the spirit of the past, through its descent from Percy's *Reliques*, and has proved the future worth of his poems through the number of writers who have imitated *Lyrical Ballads*. Wordsworth also suggests that readers should consider his newer works, which had failed thus far as popular, marketable poetry, according to his history in the 'Essay Supplementary' of treasured classics – Shakespeare, Milton, Percy – which initially were unpopular and seemingly unmarketable.

Classification and Anecdotal History in the 1815 'Preface'

Wordsworth's 'Essay Supplementary' engages closely with the immediate reception of his collected works. Rounding out the first volume of his 1815 *Poems*, the 'Essay Supplementary' describes why Wordsworth's contemporary readers should consider his works as a modern classic, and the 1815 preface catalogues how readers can experience, through his volumes, Britain's past and future literary heritage. In that preface, he introduces the 1815 poems as a mass of hybrid genres that can be divided, but not separated, from the schema that he develops for his entire poetic *oeuvre*. Wordsworth asserts the value of these 1815 poems by describing the number of ways that they can be connected with one another. The 'Preface' offers an anecdotal history of the poet's mind and of recent literary and cultural history by relating the collected pieces of his literary life to fragments of early nineteenth-century culture.[57] Through this preface his volumes appear as a miscellany of English life, accessible to readers who wish to reconstruct it by tracing the footsteps of the poet re-collecting in tranquillity.

Wordsworth begins the 1815 preface with a discussion of how he creates poetry, and he specifically outlines what he perceives to be the six elements necessary for the 'production of poetry'.[58] These six categories are related chronologically in two ways. Each of these categories describes a progressive step in the process of poetic composition, and, collectively, they also suggest that the process of composing strengthens over the course of the poet's development. Wordsworth maintains that the poet's powers of observation and description come first, but he renders these powers subservient to an exquisite sensibility, which incites the poet 'to observe objects, both as they exist in themselves and as re-acted upon by his own mind'.[59] He then details a third power, reflection, which mediates between and weighs the value of the two former poetic powers. Fourth, Wordsworth adds, 'Imagination and Fancy, – to modify, to create, and to associate'. Fifth, he articulates the importance of invention, which operates as a power that uses the first four categories to create characters in relation to incidents worked upon by the imagination and 'most fitted to do justice to the characters, sentiments, and passions, which the Poet undertakes to illustrate'. Last, he calls attention to the need for judgement, 'to decide how and where, and in what degree, each of these faculties ought to be exerted'.[60]

Wordsworth then describes this hierarchy of poetic faculties as 'cast, by means of various moulds, into divers [*sic*] forms', which include narrative, dramatic, lyrical, idyllium, didactic and philosophical satire. Although Wordsworth distributes these six poetic faculties amongst the forms in which poetry can be written, he neither stipulates which forms have which faculties nor points out how those faculties might be employed, given the type of mode in which they are employed. Even more confusing, Wordsworth contends that '[i]t is deducible from the above, that poems, apparently miscellaneous, may with propriety be arranged either with reference to the powers of mind *predominant* in the production of them; or to the mould in which they are cast; or lastly to the subjects to which they relate'.[61] Following these three seemingly separate categories for organizing his poems – powers of the mind, mould and subjects – Wordsworth further subdivides his poems into:

classes; which, that the work may more obviously correspond with the course of human life, for the sake of exhibiting in it the three requisites of a legitimate whole, the beginning, a middle, and an end, have been also arranged, as far as it was possible, according to an order of time, commencing with Childhood, and terminating with Old Age, Death, and Immortality.[62]

Beyond the three classes he describes, Wordsworth declares that he has organized his poems according to a time scheme, which points from childhood to death and immortality.

Wordsworth also declares that his system of classification affects the relationship between groups of poems in the 1815 volumes and even involves poems that do not appear in the 1815 volumes: 'My guiding wish was, that the small pieces of which these volumes consist, thus discriminated, might be regarded under a two-fold view; as composing an entire work within themselves, and as adjuncts to the philosophical Poem, "The Recluse".[63] Although Wordsworth hopes that 'individually' the 1815 poems will have a 'natural effect' on readers, his preface also details possible ways to read his poems connectively. Readers can consider the mental faculty behind the creation of a given poem and group of poems, the poetic form in which a poem and group of poems are written, the subject matter of a poem or group of poems and the interlocking time schemes that connect his poems together. Furthermore, Wordsworth asks readers to ponder the effects of individual poems in relation to the collective effect of his two volumes, as well as the relationship between all of the 1815 poems and the hypothetical whole of *The Recluse*. Wordsworth's descriptions of how readers can connect individual poems to a larger whole suggest that nearly any poem in his collection offers a psychological, formal, temporal or spatial window that links together aspects of Wordsworth's poetic life with the overarching development of that life.

While Wordsworth constructs a complex, organizing apparatus for these poems and alerts readers to the necessity of paying heed to this apparatus, he also leaves readers at liberty to discover the relationships between the poems that he has classified. What seems most important to Wordsworth in this preface is that readers recognize that they can approach his classification schema from various interlocking perspectives. Accordingly, he points out that his works are readily available to readers with different levels of hermeneutic competence. Such a belief leads him to declare, 'I should have preferred to scatter the contents of these volumes at random, if I had been persuaded that, by the plan adopted, anything material would have been taken from the natural effect of the pieces individually, on the mind of the unreflecting reader' and, alternately, to assert that 'for him who reads with reflection, the arrangement will serve as a commentary unostentatiously directing his attention to my purposes, both particular and general.[64] While Wordsworth asks that all of his readers actively engage with his poems because, '[p]oems, however humble in their kind, if they be good in that kind, cannot read themselves', he also maintains that readers' minds must be 'left at liberty' after first being 'summoned, to act upon [their] thoughts and images'.[65]

Through this dizzying classification system, Wordsworth sets up interlocking categories that encourage readers to wander connectively through the imaginary library of his works. In fact, Wordsworth bases the coherence and value of this library on the activating powers of his readers and suggests that readers who carve out imaginative pathways through his collection are taking part in ordering Britain's cultural future. Wordsworth's 'Preface' and 'Essay Supplementary to the Preface' announce the 1815 volumes as a living collection that can be activated only through his readers' participation in his textual design and anecdotal history of British culture. Similar to Connell's description of D'Israeli's anecdotal method, which attempts to construct Britain's national character, Wordsworth's method 'imparts "a certain activity to the mind" ...function[ing] as a kind of Arnoldian touchstone, restoring ties of 'remote or latent connexion' within the canons of literary history and thus imposing a fluid yet coherent and adaptive structure upon the ever-increasing multiplicity of books'.[66] Wordsworth's 1815 volumes project a collection of books not just to admire on a shelf, but a library to enter into imaginatively, where the activity of reading is tantamount to collecting together, organizing and becoming a part of a living culture. Furthermore, Wordsworth's footnotes to the 1815 volumes underscore how books can become a part of readers and how readers can become a part of books.

Poems of the Imagination, 'Tintern Abbey' and National Identity

Many critics of the 1815 volumes denigrated Wordsworth's 'Preface' and 'Essay Supplementary to the Preface'. However, in the *Monthly Review*, one particular reviewer (probably Francis Hodgson) also draws attention to several of Wordsworth's poems in the section 'Poems of the Imagination' because of the network of footnotes that Wordsworth attached to them. After quoting a portion of Wordsworth's 'Essay Supplementary', which anticipates Wordsworth's fame in posterity, the reviewer sarcastically 'beg[s] permission to subjoin to this extraordinary passage, as we cannot help considering it, the following still more extraordinary quotation and note'.[67] This exasperated reviewer feels the need to beg permission of his readers to relate these passages because he fears that this kind of attention might be seen as a digression. In fact, the reviewer's attention to Wordsworth's footnotes cleverly parodies the purpose of Wordsworth's anecdotal movements within his 1815 volumes. He pauses over Wordsworth's connections between his poetry and supplementary prose to prove his evaluation of Wordsworth's overarching classification system, 'that we do not remember to have ever met with so "Much Ado about Nothing" in any author'.[68]

The reviewer quotes two stanzas from 'I Wandered Lonely as a Cloud' (untitled in the 1815 *Poems*), and he attaches Wordsworth's footnote at the bottom of the page:

> The subject of these stanzas is rather an elementary feeling and simple impression (approaching to the nature of an ocular spectrum) upon the imaginative faculty, than an *exertion* of it. The one which follows is strictly a Reverie; and neither that, nor the next after it in succession, 'The Power of Music', would have been placed here except for the reason given in the foregoing note.

As the reviewer points out, this other 'foregoing' note refers to 'The Horn of Egremont Castle' and to the following ballad 'Goody Blake and Harry Gill': 'This POEM, and the ballad which follows it, as they rather *refer to the imagination than are produced by it*, would not have been placed here, but to avoid a needless multiplication of the *classes*'.[69] Wordsworth's footnotes focus on the rationale behind the placement of poems, and each note supports the other in declaring Wordsworth's need to expand the category 'Poems of the Imagination' to include poems that refer to the imagination as well as to those that are produced by it.

These two notes defend Wordsworth's poetic groupings as a method for him to gain control over his massive poetic collection, but this reviewer can only regard them satirically as representative examples of the compendious apparatus that readers must confront in Wordsworth's collection. Such notes appear ridiculous to this reviewer because they treat Wordsworth's collection as if it were a modern classic that would merit extensive notes about the subject matter or history behind why one poem was grouped with another. The reviewer's exasperation implies that no reader would be interested in the minute details that connect together Wordsworth's poems. Through his attempts to dismiss these notes as hapless and laborious parts of Wordsworth's system, however, this reviewer redoubles attention to how those notes monumentalize Wordsworth's poems and attempt to guide his readers. Wordsworth's notes provide contexts from which to consider a given poem, set up continuities between poems within the two volumes and establish connections between the 1815 poems, *The Prelude* and *The Recluse*.

One of these prose notes in 'Poems of the Imagination' encourages readers to consider 'Lines Composed a Few Miles above Tintern Abbey' as a poem that exemplifies the connective, amalgamating power of single poems within his collected works. Placed two poems before 'Tintern Abbey', this footnote to the poem 'French Revolution, as It Appeared to Enthusiasts at its Commencement' reads: 'This, and the Extract, vol. I. page 44, and the first Piece of this Class are from the unpublished Poem of which some account is given in the Preface to *The Excursion*'. The note links together 'French Revolution' with two poems in the first volume – 'Influence of Natural Objects', from the section 'Poems Referring to Childhood', and 'There was a Boy', the initial poem of 'Poems of the Imagination'. While this note identifies and draws together three poems excerpted from Wordsworth's unpublished *Prelude*, it also points from 'French Revolution' through the next poem, 'It is No Spirit', to 'Tintern Abbey', the final poem of 'Poems of the Imagination', and encourages readers to reassess how seemingly unrelated poems can be recomposed together.[70] The note provides a context for considering the relationship between individual poems within the 1815 volumes, but it also suggests connections between single poems within those volumes and *The Prelude*, which in the preface to *The Excursion* (1814), he announces as subsidiary, but necessary to his larger project, *The Recluse*.[71]

The fragments from *The Prelude*, which this note connects, set up a particular vantage point from which to read 'Tintern Abbey', and this poetic alignment compounds the meanings of Wordsworth's title change from 'Lines Written' (1798–1805 *Lyrical Ballads*) to 'Lines Composed' (1815 *Poems*). Through its new title and connections with other poems in the volumes, 'Tintern Abbey' appears as a 'composite species'[72] – a poetic form that Wordsworth briefly describes in his 1815 'Preface' as a mixture of at least three classes of poetry and that he classes with Edward Young's 'Night Thoughts' and William Cowper's 'The Task'.[73] Another note in the 1815 collection also suggests why 'Tintern Abbey' might be considered a composite species. Wordsworth reprinted a footnote to the lines 'half create / and what perceive' from 'Tintern Abbey' in *Lyrical Ballads*. The footnote reads: 'This line has a close resemblance to an admirable line of Young, the exact expression of which I cannot recollect.'[74] While in *Lyrical Ballads*, this note might allude to a tradition of spontaneous writing often attributed to 'Night Thoughts', read in the context of Wordsworth's 1815 preface, this footnote draws attention to another aspect of 'Night Thoughts' – its blank verse description and meditation, which mixed together various modes of writing through a process of serial expansion and revision over several years.

In prompting readers to recognize how three fragments from *The Prelude* create a mixed context in which to read the newly titled 'Tintern Abbey', Wordsworth weaves together a historical basis and textual network from which to consider the value of the poem in relation to his collected works. This textual alignment draws together three seemingly unrelated moments of emotional enthrallment by juxtaposing youthful revolutionary fervour, elemental and formative childhood interactions with nature, and a boy's feverish, but deathly calming intercourse with the natural world. Mediated through a fourth transcendental poem that immediately precedes 'Tintern Abbey', 'It is No Spirit', these three poems set up a return to 'Tintern Abbey', not only as an amalgamation of the poet's insights in 1815 but also of his past mistakes.[75] 'Lines Composed' announces itself as an aggregating form that assimilates visionary and revisionary poetic pieces into an ever-changing poetic structure whose meaning depends upon its placement and the context that readers bring to bear on it. As a form that declares its internal makeup and meaning to be dependent upon the web of connections brought to bear on it, 'Lines Composed' offers a prospect overlooking all of Wordsworth's poetic works, past and future, and it models a process of continual return for readers to re-collect and compose a national psyche that had been fractured by over twenty years of war.[76]

Wordsworth's commentary in the 'Essay Supplementary' on how Percy composed his *Reliques* provides a distinct, textual perspective from which to approach the title change to 'Tintern Abbey'. Instead of highlighting the oral or musical nature underpinning the act of composing, the 'Essay Supplementary' draws attention to the poetic ordering and rhetorical organization of Percy's poetic compilation, which Wordsworth aligns with the methods underpinning his own 1815 collection. This section of the 'Essay Supplementary' also coalesces with Wordsworth's' major focus throughout the essay on active mental labour. Regardless of whether 'Lines Composed' is understood as a blank-verse meditative or loco-descriptive poem, a quasi-ode, an effusion, a conversation poem, an elegiac inscription or a ballad that has been lyricized – the position that 'Lines Composed' occupies in the 1815 category 'Poems of the Imagination' announces the poem as a locus for continual work.[77] 'Lines Composed' provides a connective, poetic space through which the poet and his readers can station themselves to consider how the various contexts surrounding the poem in the 1815 volumes can be brought to bear on that poem. In drawing attention to its own making, not just as a single poem in 1798, but as an amalgamation of all of Wordsworth's poetry in 1815, 'Lines Composed' asks readers to 'half create' the context of what they have perceived in the collection.

Instead of hiding, eliding or closing down history, biography, physical or cultural space, 'Lines Composed' opens these issues up for Wordsworth's contemporary readers and prompts them to reflect upon and recompose what Wordsworth perceived as the psychological discontinuities of a war-torn nation.[78] Although in his 'Fenwick Note' to 'Lines Composed',[79] Wordsworth is at pains to highlight the oral nature of the poem by tying it directly to his biography and seemingly spontaneous composition of the poem, the Wordsworth who worked so closely with the production of his 1815 *Poems* appears more concerned with establishing a two-volume edition that would, in no small way, resurrect the reading practices and health of Great Britain.[80]

Appearing two poems before 'Lines Composed', the poem 'French Revolution' – originally printed in the *Friend* and part of book 10 of *The Prelude*[81] – describes Wordsworth's renewed faith in the French Republic. Purportedly set in France in 1792, the poem precedes Wordsworth's first trip to the Wye Valley by one year, which 'Tintern Abbey' draws attention to through the specificity of its title and its first verse paragraph. 'French Revolution' illustrates a seemingly limitless prospect – both internal and external – for everyone caught up in the fervour of the revolution, to aid in creating, through the 'plastic' 'stuff at hand', the present social world and its institutions (l. 34). This forward-looking, idealistic prospect opens the world up to the shaping powers of the generations at hand. Rousing even the 'inert', the promise of renewal conjoins both the meek and the lofty in a 'pleasant exercise of hope and joy!' (l. 1). This unbounded, potential energy draws human beings together because it seemingly enables individuals to create and fulfill their own senses of selfhood – 'to their heart's desire' – amidst a collective rewriting of human law (l. 33). However, in the next linked poem 'Influence of Natural Objects', the grandeur of an English landscape, governed by natural laws beyond the construction of individual reason, reconfigures this time of communal enthrallment in France – 'When Reason seemed the most to assert her rights' (l. 9).

This movement backward to the first volume and 'Influence of Natural Objects' – a fragment from book 1 of *The Prelude* – re-engages readers with a childhood world of natural and direct, sensual experience – a world that appears foreign in contrast to the revolutionary fervour and prospective state depicted in 'French Revolution'. In 'Influence' the English landscape is imbued with a soul that gives 'everlasting motion' and continually enthrals by impressing the mind with acute pain, fear and pleasure (l. 4). Unlike the collective rapture engendered through the prospect of creating an ideal community in 'French Revolution', in this poem a child has a solitary intimation of his inclusion in the continual motions of the natural world. What the child recognizes intuitively, albeit unclearly, gives way to internal and external tranquillity as he simultaneously composes himself into nature. The poem pits the calming effects of this singularly organic, English epiphany against the seeming prospect of a fervour constituted through French reason.

Moving forward from this poem to 'There was a Boy' – a poem first published in the 1800 *Lyrical Ballads* and then incorporated into book 5 of *The Prelude*[82] – readers are prompted to reflect upon another act of attention to nature in a scene that features the poet, in the latter half of the poem, reflecting on the import of the seemingly failed, but fervent exchanges between a boy shouting into nature and the ensuing natural din responding to him. What has been impressed on the boy 'unawares' through this interaction provides a 'gentle shock' that echoes through the poet as he overlooks the boy's grave – a monument to the boy's all too sudden death and unfinished development (ll. 22, 19). Cut short in the midst of his interaction with nature, the boy has experienced a 'gentle shock' that transfers to the poet, whose subsequent activity of mind – both composing and composed by the tale on which he meditates – enacts the boy's potential, though unfulfilled, later state of mind.[83] Far from the mechanical, self-willed revolutions of mind described in 'French Revolution' and pushing further than the child's singular apprehension of connected grandeur in the previous poem, in 'There was a Boy' the poet's reflections hang suspended between silence and sound, listening and response, as he composes his mind through a landscape that enables him to look backward and echo forward through the amalgamating power of the boy's 'gentle shock'.

Leaping forward from this poem in the first volume to 'It is No Spirit', which, in the second volume follows 'French Revolution', readers encounter the poet as he is startled by the appearance of Hesperus into an intimation of his own immortality. This textual travelling moves the reader beyond the poet's epitaphic reflections on the death of a child, towards the poet imagining his own death and transcendence above a world of uncertainty, censure, and past mistakes. Disembodied at the end of the poem, the poet imagines that he too 'might one day trace / Some ground not mine' (ll. 14–15) in an ethereal sphere 'that no one shall reprove!' (l. 17). The poet's final projected apparition of his soul – 'tread[ing] there, with steps that no one shall reprove!' (l. 17) – seemingly places him at a complete remove from the criticisms and ridicule that had so often and, in 1814, so lately greeted his earthly steps as a poet.[84] In this ethereal sphere, his life's work seems as secure as his poetry's reception and enables him to 'trace / Some ground not mine'. However, just when Wordsworth seems to have left behind his contemporary audience and his guide and anchor, the English landscape, the next poem grounds readers in a particular time and place of self-reckoning and cultural revision.

Returning to 'Tintern Abbey' through these four poems, readers encounter a prospect view that aligns the past with the present, connects the landscape with the 'quiet of the sky' and places the poet with his readers, 'Here', in a specific location that appears the same, but whose meaning is 'once again' in the process of being created. Both concretely located and disconcertingly trans-located – hanging betwixt and between the certainty of the landscape and the uncertainty of the mind – the poet and his readers are left to reconfigure the discontinuity of the four states of mind that they have encountered in the four preceding linked poems. Each of these states can readily be found in 'Lines Composed', slipping and sliding into one another, as the poet vacillates backwards and forwards through remembered, projected and reflective states of physical sensation, despair, uncertainty, faith and hopeful transcendence.

No longer just a poem about a return to a physical place a few miles above Tintern Abbey, 'Lines Composed' reveals a poet returning with his readers to overlook the prospect of his poetic works – a return that Wordsworth hints at in his 1815 preface when he explains the fragments that he has chosen to place in the section 'Juvenile Pieces' with a quotation from 'Lines Composed'.[85] In describing this early poetic context through 'Lines Composed', Wordsworth opens the poem up as a 'mansion for all lovely forms' that offers an expansive window looking out onto all of his poetry. Providing both a backward and forward vantage point, the poem encourages such returns and positions itself as a vehicle for evaluating the context of the poet's life and the lives of Wordsworth's British readers. 'Lines Composed' testifies to how the poet has connected together the discontinuous pieces, changes, twists and turns that make up his 1815 collection, and the poem acts as a threshold, which offers readers contiguous access to the forms, states of mind and reflexive time schemas that the 1815 preface sets up.

Read from this perspective in 1815, the unseen Abbey, which Wordsworth only mentions in the title and no where else in the poem, materializes as Wordsworth's Gothic church structure – the metaphor for his poetic oeuvre, which he outlines in his 1814 'Preface to *The Excursion*'. As Anne Janowitz points out, the 'English landscape, studded with ruined abbeys and other half-enclosed gothic ruins, was an icon for the image of some structure that would be both rooted in the visible world, yet kin to an invisible whole'.[86] 'Lines Composed' suggests that the key to making the visible, fragmented structure of Wordsworth's poetic works into such an imagined, invisible whole lies in the work of his readers.[87] Similar to Wordsworth's return to the poem of 1798 in 1815, readers have the opportunity to station themselves through a process of continual return, based on a paralleptic movement both within and between the surrounding poems. That process of experiencing a return – 'Once again / Do I behold' – engages readers with a poetic structure based on change and shifting contexts, which can be revisited, reordered and recreated by the power of the mind that sets to work on it.

'Lines Composed' provides an experiential explanation of Wordsworth's poetic system, which enables readers to participate in constructing and exercising the poetic networks and historical contexts that compose his works. While taking part in this first-hand collecting experience may aid readers in negotiating Wordsworth's volumes, it also offers them an opportunity to trace the revolutions of their own minds as they engage with the poet's attempts to cope with discontinuity, missteps and misimaginings. Seen in this way, the prospect in 'Lines Composed a Few Miles above Tintern Abbey' materializes for readers as a stable but ever-changing communal point of return that offers pathways for recovering the psychological health of a nation not at war for the first time since the winter preceding Wordsworth's trip to the Wye Valley in 1793. Through 'Lines Composed', Wordsworth's Gothic church becomes a space for realizing mistakes, and it also asserts the power of the mind to put back together the pieces of a fractured psyche. Such a path of continual return provides readers with opportunities to find themselves together, again and anew – just as Wordsworth rediscovers, once again, the necessity of the poem, not only for Dorothy, but as a communal point of return that concludes and connects together his 'Poems of the Imagination'.

From this perspective, the poem still occupies its field in *Lyrical Ballads* (1798–1805), and it still looks back on the French Revolution from 1792 to 1793. However, it also allows for a wider view of where Wordsworth and the nation have gone and can go in 1815. 'Lines Composed' makes room for interlocking, and even conflicting, perspectives and historical contexts that encourage Wordsworth's readers to view themselves as a self-creating community with the potential to grow more interconnected as readers work to find a point of return that will provide fodder for future years. Far from a singular, solitary and spontaneous act of creation, the word 'composed' in Wordsworth's 1815 volumes signals the power of the mind to piece together fragments of the past, present and future – a practice that connects the value of poetic collections with the working health of a nation.

5 OPENING UP CHAPTER 13 OF COLERIDGE'S
BIOGRAPHIA LITERARIA

Dear C.

You ask my opinion concerning your Chapter on the Imagination, both as to the impressions it made on myself, and as to those which I think it will make on the PUBLIC, i.e. that part of the public, who from the title of the work and from its forming a sort of introduction to a volume of poems, are likely to constitute the great majority of your readers.

As to myself, and stating in the first place the effect on my understanding, your opinions and method of argument were not only so new to me, but so directly the reverse of all I had ever been accustomed to consider as truth, that even if I had comprehended the premises sufficiently to have admitted them, and had seen the necessity of your conclusions, I should still have been in that state of mind, which in your note, p. 72, 73, you have so ingeniously evolved, as the antithesis to that in which a man is, when he makes a bull. In your own words, I should have felt as if I had been standing on my head.

The effect on my feelings, on the other hand, I cannot better represent, than by supposing myself to have known only our light and airy modern chapels of ease, and then for the first time to have been placed, and left alone, in one of our largest Gothic cathedrals in a gusty moonlight night of autumn. 'Now in glimmer, and now in gloom;' often in palpable darkness not without a chilly sensation of terror; then suddenly emerging into broad yet visionary lights with coloured shadows, of fantastic shapes yet all decked with holy insignia and mystic symbols; and ever and anon coming out full upon pictures and stone-work images of great men, with whose names I was familiar, but which looked upon me with countenances and an expression, the most dissimilar to all I had been in the habit of connecting with those names. Those whom I had been taught to venerate as almost super-human in magnitude of intellect, I found perched in little fret-work niches, as grotesque dwarfs; while the grotesques, in my hitherto belief, stood guarding the high altar with all the characters of Apotheosis. In short, what I had supposed substances were thinned away into shadows, while every where shadows deepened into substances:

If substance may be call'd what shadow seem'd
For each seem'd either!
Milton.

Yet after all, I could not but repeat the lines which you had quoted from a MS. Poem of your own in the FRIEND, and applied to a work of Mr. Wordsworth's though with a few of the words altered:

> – An orphic tale indeed,
> A tale *obscure* of high and passionate thoughts
> To a *strange* music chaunted![1]

Many reviewing critics contested Wordsworth's supplementary efforts in *The Excursion* of 1814 and his 1815 *Poems* to shape the reading public's tastes, construct a literary miscellany of British life, and advertise his collected works as a monumental Gothic church and contemporary classic. However, no one challenged the poetic and paratextual grounds on which Wordsworth based these assertions more acutely than his long-time friend and collaborator Coleridge in his two-volume *Biographia Literaria* (1817). Throughout the *Biographia* Coleridge measures his philosophical insights, his status as a literary and cultural critic and his poetry's continued popularity against the genius, faults and troubled reception of Wordsworth's poetry and supplementary prose. Particularly in chapter 13 of the *Biographia*, Coleridge parodies Wordsworth's Gothic church figuration, revisits the difficulties of negotiating public opinion and suggests how his life's work – and not Wordsworth's – can gather together, parody, re-present and actualize the nation's literary character.

Coleridge's above letter, written by a 'Friend', which interrupts his philosophical 'disquisition' on the imagination in chapter 13 of the *Biographia Literaria*, is a Gothic counterfeit.[2] The letter wryly challenges reviewing critics, parodists and the reading public to weigh the past and present literary value of Coleridge's works against Wordsworth's recent canonical claims. Coleridge's 'Friend' reconfigures Wordsworth's architectural metaphor in the 'Preface to *The Excursion*' of his collected works as an ever-expanding, Gothic church and revamps Wordsworth's definition of the imagination in his 1815 'Preface'. This fictitious 'Friend' further enables Coleridge to include, in the very middle of his two-volume work, a reader's testimony that voices the potential concerns of the reading public and reviewing critics while also manufacturing a mysterious, Gothic response to Coleridge's (absent) philosophical prose. That response parodically highlights the significance of the publication and reception histories following Coleridge's poetry.

The 'Friend's' turn to the Gothic recalls a host of aesthetic, cultural and genre-related issues that Michael Gamer traces back to late eighteenth- and early nineteenth-century debates – involving readers, authors and reviewers – which played out an emerging ideology of high romantic literary forms against the seemingly low literary forms of the Gothic.[3] In the midst of his efforts to articulate his transcendental views on the imagination, Coleridge inserts a letter that ties the continued success of his works to, potentially, the lowest common denominator – the popular tastes of the reading public and the literary marketplace. In that letter the 'Friend' responds to 'about one hundred pages', which he recommends Coleridge withdraw from chapter 13, with a Gothic anecdote that mixes together high and low literary aesthetics, and which Bradford Mudge claims, 'closely resembles the climax of *The Mysteries of Udolpho*, a scene that Coleridge had quoted at length in his 1794 review'.[4]

The 'Friend's' response overwrites Wordsworth's high aesthetic Gothic church figuration, which prescribes how fit readers might understand the construction of his collected works, with the generic conventions of Radcliffe's widely read and often imitated Gothic narratives. If Wordsworth's 1814 preface and prospectus offer Wordsworth's lofty testimony about the imaginative power that his literary works hold out to readers, Coleridge's 'Friend' provides a reader's first-hand response to the infectious feelings, suspenseful engagement and imaginative freedom that define the Gothic character of Coleridge's literary works and their popular, enduring appeal.[5] By contrast, Wordsworth's seemingly expansive, Gothic church appears more like the 'light airy modern chapels of ease' with which the 'Friend' is familiar – chapels that do not readily elevate the feelings, adequately encourage intellectual work or memorably foster a communal touchstone for its viewers.

A wry, tongue-in-cheek humour energizes the 'Friend's' letter, which alternately praises and denigrates Coleridge's literary character. In *Romanticism, Nationalism, and the Revolt Against Theory* (1993) David Simpson suggests the importance of such humour to Coleridge's understanding not only of his own character, but of England's literary character. Simpson contends that in the *Biographia* Coleridge 'attempts to establish the national literature as the most important cohering principle for both the individual psyche and the national culture as a whole'. To this end, Coleridge presents his own philosophical principles and evolving literary character as 'exemplary of a general potential in the national literature for the constitution of a national personality'.[6] Simpson traces this endeavour back to Coleridge's earlier periodical publication the *Friend* (1809–11), which lauds a triad of characteristics that Coleridge claims are distinct to the English character – 'genius, sense, and humor' – in contrast to the German character – 'typified by genius, talent, and fancy' – and the French character – defined 'by cleverness, talent, and wit'.[7] Coleridge's desire in the *Friend* to define the literary character of England as the basis for a national personality is central to the *Biographia*,[8] and nowhere is this desire foregrounded more provokingly than the letter in chapter 13, supposedly written by a 'Friend'.[9] Through this letter, Coleridge demonstrates the 'genius, sense, and humor' of the English mind in the act of interpreting and connecting together a dizzying hodgepodge of literary material. This 'Friend' adopts a commonsense approach to Coleridge's mystifying prose by recommending that Coleridge withdraw nearly one hundred pages from chapter 13, and he displays an amalgamating, Gothic 'genius' that attempts to explain Coleridge's prose through allusions to Coleridge's poetry. Finally, the 'Friend's' vacillation between sense and genius is actuated through a humorously parodic, Gothic anecdote that juxtaposes the 'Friend's' desires as a reader with Coleridge's lofty ascent towards his exposition of the imagination. This humour, 'which gives the air of ease to genius, and of lightness to sense', ironically takes the air out of Coleridge's prose and refocuses attention on the lasting significance of his poetry.[10] Half-seriously and half-parodically, the 'Friend' weighs the possibility and impossibility of other readers engaging meaningfully with Coleridge's chapter by placing Coleridge's scattered life's work in allusive dialogue with Wordsworth's recently published supplementary writings.[11] Particularly through his gothic church appropriation, the 'Friend' reveals that, in contrast to Wordsworth, Coleridge encourages readers to question and test the relationship between his prose and poetry. The 'Friend' also suggests that Coleridge possesses two qualities that Wordsworth does not – openness to and a sense of humour about the mixed reception of his works. Finally, the 'Friend's' mixing of a popular Gothic form with high, philosophic principles demonstrates how Coleridge's collected works have shaped and embody the desires of the reading public not only because they allow readers to participate in the construction of Coleridge's works, but also because the aesthetic and cultural value of his works can be measured by the intensity and duration of his readers' participation.[12]

The letter disrupts Coleridge's philosophical prose about the imagination in volume 1 and sets up his literary criticism of Wordsworth's poetry in volume 2. However, it also creates a space that invites readers to join this counterfeit 'Friend' in constructing what is distinct about English literature and the Gothic character of the nation.[13] Offering up his own literary character for public inspection and commentary in the letter, Coleridge creates a palimpsestic[14] end to volume 1 of the *Biographia* that encourages readers to reconfigure the relationship between Coleridge's past poetry, gossip about his life in the review culture, and his recent political and philosophical prose.[15] The 'Friend' describes a Gothic labyrinth of connective possibilities, and, somewhat laughingly, he asserts the rights that Coleridge's readers have to make their own cultural and textual forays into his works. The letter, however, does not simply license promiscuous readings and rewritings of the meanings and value of Coleridge's works. Occupying a central position in the *Biographia*,[16] the Gothic trappings in the letter provide readers with a distinct opportunity to recall the nation's recent literary heritage.[17] Book-ended by Coleridge's reference to 'The Rime of the Ancient Mariner' at the close of chapter 13, which follows the 'Friend's' allusions to 'Christabel' and 'To William Wordsworth', the 'Friend's' letter reminds readers of how Coleridge's unmethodical, literary character has opened up numerous possibilities for them to actively read and write themselves into a literary collection that embodies the present character of the nation.

Openness and Reception

Following this interrupting letter, Coleridge reasserts his voice over a chapter that he nearly relinquished at the 'Friend's' suggestion. When Coleridge renews this discourse, it follows the 'Friend's' advice in the 'very judicious letter'.[18] After providing abbreviated definitions of the primary and secondary imagination and the fancy, Coleridge stops short of his goal – a complete exposition of the powers of the imagination – and offers instead an elliptic, concluding commentary:

> Whatever more than this, I shall think it fit to declare concerning the powers and privileges of the imagination in the present work, will be found in the critical essay on the uses of the Supernatural in poetry and the principles that regulate its introduction: which the reader will find prefixed to the poem of The Ancient Mariner.[19]

As if following his 'Friend's' commonsense directions, Coleridge opted not to publish a critical essay on the imagination as an introduction to 'The Ancient Mariner'.[20] Instead, he leaves readers at the end of volume 1 with a textual gap that, much like the 'Friend's' allusions in the letter, is obscurely filled by poetic allusion. Coleridge's reference to 'The Rime', which takes the place of any discursive explanation of the imagination, only seems to further obfuscate the announced design of chapter 13. Is Coleridge playing a trick or a textual joke on readers?[21] Perhaps, but the humour he employs here also helps to ease a double-bind: the impossibility either of renewed philosophical explanation – from the 'Friend's' point of view – or of further reductive definitions – from Coleridge's point of view. Furthermore, in 1817 the reading public was able to investigate Coleridge's poetic reference because he had revised 'The Rime of the Ancient Mariner' and placed it at the head of his poetic collection *Sibylline Leaves*,[22] which he published in the same month as the *Biographia*.[23]

Appearing for the first time in a collection with Coleridge's name on it, the restructured poem calls attention to its reception history through its restored and amended paratexts: the original 1798 title, 'The Rime of the Ancient Mariner In Seven Parts', new Latin epigram, fifty-seven marginal glosses and two footnotes. As the final reference point for the closing words of chapter 13, 'The Rime of the Ancient Mariner' sheds little direct light on Coleridge's definitions of the imagination. However, in its 1817 published form, 'The Rime' asserts itself as the ultimate example of an English, Gothic poem which had so continually vexed the reading public's imagination into activity through its chequered reception history, shifting textual forms, and troubling relationship to any prose theory about poetry.[24] Coleridge's republication of the poem also follows his own advice from one of his footnotes closing chapter 12 of the *Biographia*, written to young authors about the difficulties of publishing too early and too often: 'what medical physiologists affirm of certain secretions, applies equally to our thoughts; they too must be taken up again into circulation, and be again and again re-secreted in order to ensure a healthful vigor, both to the mind and to the intellectual offspring'.[25] Revision and recirculation, the footnote maintains, are the keys to successful authorship because they allow the author to re-present himself and his works to the public in so many variable forms.[26]

Coleridge's closing reference to 'The Rime' in chapter 13 also recycles the 'Friend's' conjecture from a few pages earlier about the effects of that chapter on 'the PUBLIC, i.e. that part of the public, who from the title of the work and from its forming a sort of introduction to a volume of poems, are likely to constitute the great majority of your readers'.[27] The 'Friend' estimates that Coleridge's readers will not only understand chapter 13 as a preface to *Sibylline Leaves* but will also expect a systematic relationship between such introductory prose and collected poetry.[28] However, when passing from chapter 13 to *Sibylline Leaves*, readers in 1817 would find that Coleridge's poetic collection contains its own introductory preface, which, instead of describing a clear organizing system for his poetry, offers a dizzying journey into a nearly system-less system that calls into question the very concept of a finished poetic collection.[29]

Written in Gothic script, much like the title 'The Rime of the Ancient Mariner', the title of Coleridge's volume of poems, *Sibylline Leaves*, points to the Gothic instability of his collection and highlights the unsteady relationship between its author, his poems and readers. Several critics who reviewed the *Biographia* and *Sibylline Leaves* together laboured over the meaning of Coleridge's poetic collection. For example, in the *Literary Gazette* of July 1817 one anonymous reviewer remarks:

> 'Sibylline', says our Dictionary, 'of or belonging to a Sibyl or Prophetess' ... But on refreshing our classic memory we grasp the essence and soul of this mysterious title. The Sibyl wrote her prophecies on leaves; so does Mr. Coleridge his verses – the prophecies of the Sibyl became incomprehensible, if not instantly gathered; so does the sense of Mr. Coleridge's poetry.[30]

This analysis of Coleridge's title quickly devolves into ridicule and scorn – 'we do not thank the author for allotting us time-pressed Critics the trouble of turning over Varro, Aelian, Diodorus, Pliny, Ovid, Sallust, Cicero, and even Pausanias and Plato, for the manifestation of his recondite enigmas'. This irritation with Coleridge's title, and satirical dismissal of the subsequent poems as recondite and publicly useless drivel, suggests a more general difficulty that reviewing critics had with figuring out how to grasp the form and purpose of Coleridge's poetic collection.[31]

As the title suggests, textual instability occurs whenever an author's works leave his personal control and are circulated in public. Although Coleridge has gathered together his poems for *Sibylline Leaves*, the preface points out how his poetry has long been scattered by winds throughout his earliest collaborative book, periodical and newspaper publications, and manuscript versions. And, like those people who were disappointed by the counsel offered through the disordered leaves of the Sibyl, Coleridge's readers run the risk of departing from his 'leaves' disgruntled with their author because he has provided neither sustained nor systematic counsel. Far from asserting his control over the volume, Coleridge's preface details the disconnected and fragmented nature of the poems' relations to one another – and to their author – from his earliest to his most recent productions:

> THE following collection has been entitled SIBYLLINE LEAVES, in allusion to the fragmentary and widely scattered state in which they have been long suffered to remain. It contains the whole of the author's poetical compositions, from 1793 to the present date, with the exception of a few works not yet finished, and those published in the first edition of his juvenile poems, over which he has no controul.[32]

Instead of including a table of contents, Coleridge uses the preface to divide his poems into three general categories,[33] prompting one *Literary Gazette* reviewer to sigh, 'but as no clue is furnished whereby we can unravel the complexity of the labyrinth, we are compelled to take the Poems, unclassed, in the way they are divided and subdivided on the Sibylline Leaves, price ten and sixpence'.[34] The preface announces Coleridge's first class/division as made up of a selection of poems taken out of the 1797 and 1803 editions of his poetry, 'together with those originally published in the LYRICAL BALLADS, which after having remained many years out of print, have been omitted by Mr. Wordsworth in the recent collection of all his minor poems, and of course revert to the author'.[35] This first class is made up of poems that have been mixed with other poets' works, namely with Charles Lamb's and Charles Lloyd's poetry in 1797. Furthermore, Coleridge only appears to claim ownership over his poems from *Lyrical Ballads* because Wordsworth has not chosen to republish them, so by default they revert back to their original author.

The second class consists of poems 'published at various periods, in various obscure or perishable journals, &c. some with, some without the writer's consent; many imperfect, all incorrect'.[36] This class calls attention to how Coleridge's poems have been so widely disseminated and read – with and without his knowledge – over the last twenty years in such a wide variety of places and forms that their complete recovery in an authoritative collection appears to be a textual and cultural impossibility. Finally, Coleridge describes a class 'formed of Poems which have hitherto remained in manuscript'. Given the manuscript history of 'Christabel' – related in the next section of this chapter – such a category in no way provides Coleridge with authorial control over this grouping of poems. Coleridge's last summarizing remark about these three classes draws particular attention to this problem: 'The whole is now presented to the reader collectively with considerable additions and alterations, and as perfect as the author's power and judgment could render them'.[37] Although collected together and authorized by Coleridge for publication, these poems are far from perfect, and the alterations and additions that Coleridge has made – even as late as the 'Errata' list prefixed to these poems – testify to their unstable, ever-changing and seemingly uncontrollable textual status. *Sibylline Leaves* announces itself as a work in progress. It appears as a collection defined by its incompleteness, textual mobility, changeableness and capacity to continually engage the reading public in its creation.[38]

In the letter in chapter 13, the 'Friend' recalls and demonstrates for readers the textual mobility and adaptability of Coleridge's poetry not only within *Sibylline Leaves* and in relation to the prose of the *Biographia*, but also within recent literary history. In the second sentence of the letter, the 'Friend' describes his personal attempt to understand Coleridge's bewildering pages about the imagination by recalling the journalistic debates throughout the first two decades of the nineteenth century about the relationship between supplementary prose and poetry – a controversy that the *Biographia* dates back to the publication of Wordsworth's 'Preface to *Lyrical Ballads*' (1800). Through his remarks, the 'Friend' creates a historical continuum that explains how the relationship between Coleridge's poetry and prose differs, not only from Wordsworth's supplementary poetry/prose system but from any of his contemporaries, because the relationship between Coleridge's supplementary prose and poetry recalls and facilitates the Gothic workings of a characteristic English mind. The 'Friend' remarks:

> As to myself, and stating in the first place the effect on my understanding, your opinions and method of argument were not only so new to me, but so directly the reverse of all I had ever been accustomed to consider as truth, that even if I had comprehended the premises sufficiently to have admitted them, and had seen the necessity of your conclusions, I should still have been in that state of mind, which in your note, p. 72, 73, you have so ingeniously evolved, as the antithesis to that in which a man is, when he makes a bull. In your own words, I should have felt as if I had been standing on my head.

Here, the 'Friend' relates the process of trying to understand Coleridge's prose to the disorienting experience of feeling 'as if [he] had been standing on [his] head'. However, the words are not directly his. The 'Friend' recirculates Coleridge's words from a footnote in chapter 4, titled 'The *Lyrical Ballads* with the Preface', and this ventriloquism draws readers into a spatial and a temporal journey.[39] It encourages them to remember – to move backwards to chapter 4 – and it transports them from a present tense commentary on Coleridge's chapter in 1817 back to Coleridge's description in chapter 4 of the review culture's difficulties with and distaste for Wordsworth's 1800 preface to *Lyrical Ballads*.[40] Through this reference to chapter 4, the 'Friend' traces the apparent failures of

Wordsworth's poetic system back to the irritation that Wordsworth's preface engendered in reviewing critics. The 'Friend' implicitly likens his estimation of how the *Biographia* will be received to the reception of *Lyrical Ballads*, and he compares his own difficulties with chapter 13 to the difficulties reviewing critics had with Wordsworth's preface. These comparative prose/poetry alignments also encourage Coleridge's readers to distinguish between Wordsworth's and Coleridge's reputations, literary currency and burgeoning, canonical place in the early nineteenth century.

In the section of chapter 4 amended by the footnote to which the 'Friend' refers, Coleridge explains the rationale behind the numerous heated responses to Wordsworth's *Lyrical Ballads*:

> Not able to deny that the author possessed both genius and a powerful Intellect, they felt very positive, but were not quite certain, that he might not be in the right, and they themselves in the wrong; an unquiet state of mind, which seeks alleviation by quarrelling with the occasion of it, and by wondering at the perverseness of the man, who had written a long and argumentative essay to persuade them, that
>
> Fair is foul, and foul is fair;
>
> in other words, that they had been all their lives admiring without judgment, and were now about to censure without reason.[41]

Coleridge maintains that when reading Wordsworth's poetry from *Lyrical Ballads*, critics felt that Wordsworth possessed 'genius and a powerful Intellect'. However, when they read his preface, which explains the theory on which his poems were based, they disagreed with that theory and, subsequently, disliked the poetry that they previously had thought ingenious. As the footnote in chapter 4 explains, these critics were experiencing the opposite psychological state of what Coleridge calls 'making a bull'. When making a bull, a person brings 'together two incompatible thoughts, with the sensation [feeling], but without the sense [understanding], of their connection', and exhibits 'such disproportionate vividness of two distinct thoughts, as distinguishes or obscures the consciousness of the intermediate images or conceptions, or wholly abstracts the attention from them'. Someone who makes a bull is completely absorbed in each concept singly and rendered unable to see the relationship between those two concepts.[42]

In Wordsworth's case, critics were in a state opposite to 'making a bull'. They felt that his poetry was 'in the right', but his prose convinced them that his poetry was wrong-headed. Coleridge further implies that this critical devaluation could have been avoided. Had *Lyrical Ballads* been 'perused without knowledge of, or reference to, the author's peculiar opinions [in the preface], and [if] ... the reader had not had his attention previously directed to those peculiarities', then 'the lines and passages which might have offended the general taste, would have been considered as mere inequalities, and attributed to inattention, not to perversity of judgment'.[43] For these critics, Wordsworth's supplementary prose destroyed any certainty of his poetic genius, leaving them irritated with only a vague 'sensation' of the power of that poetry in opposition to their certainty of the senselessness of his poetic theories.

In the chapter 13 letter, the 'Friend' exhibits a psychological state similar to Wordsworth's critics seventeen years earlier. Like those critics, whose minds were conflicted because of their impressions of Wordsworth's poetry and the troubling implications of applying his prose explanations to that poetry, the 'Friend' is caught between his sensation of the genius of Coleridge's prose and his sense that Coleridge's philosophy is the reverse of all that he has been taught and holds to be true. Grappling with his 'distinct sense of the connection between two conceptions, without that sensation of such connection which is supplied by habit',[44] the 'Friend' struggles as his mind wavers between ideas, working back and forth between their seemingly antithetical relationships. He attempts to break away from connecting ideas through habit and association, which makes the juxtaposition of new and old ideas seem irritating and incongruous. The 'Friend' does not remain in such an irritable state throughout the letter. Instead, in the next paragraph, he makes sense of the disorienting sensation (feeling) of reading Coleridge's prose through a Gothic anecdote filled with allusions to his poetry.

Turning to Coleridge's poetry as a figurative mediator between his dizzying prose and past theoretical preconceptions, the 'Friend' attempts to make intuitive, and not systematic sense (understanding) of, Coleridge's philosophy by relying on a popular, Gothic narrative. Michael Gamer's claims about how turn of the century Romantic authors employed the Gothic as a genre that appealed to a variety of readers and was shaped by that reception is particularly relevant here. Gamer maintains that such genre uses reveal a strategy 'not only of targeting a particular audience but also of potentially negotiating *between* audiences ... It becomes, in short, a way for authors to *market* texts to imagined audiences'.[45] In the letter Coleridge's 'Friend' represents a popular, Gothic affectation – representing the tastes of the reading public – and a more critical response to the Gothic – carried out largely by periodical, reviewing critics. The 'Friend' models how low and high aesthetics, general readers and critics, prose and poetry, all have a potential place in Coleridge's collected works. Furthermore, the 'Friend's' efforts to bridge these seeming dualities distinguish his reading experience and subsequent commentary from the negative reactions of many reviewing critics who responded to Wordsworth's preface to *Lyrical Ballads* and from Wordsworth's vitriolic reaction to his critics in the supplementary writings surrounding his 1814 and 1815 publications.

Remembering 'Christabel' and Reconstituting Coleridge's Gothic Church

As a collection within but also seemingly beyond its author's control, *Sibylline Leaves* announces itself as a group of poems that necessarily will be reshifted, disrupted and even rewritten by public intrusions, not unlike the interrupting letter that Coleridge inserted in chapter 13. Through his reference to the footnote in chapter 4, the 'Friend' also calls attention to the reception histories preceding Coleridge's poetic collection by juxtaposing his disorienting experience of reading Coleridge's prose with the critical turmoil surrounding the reception of Wordsworth's poetic system as described in his preface to *Lyrical Ballads*. To fill in the prose gaps during his present engagement with Coleridge's chapter, the 'Friend' draws on a collective, literary memory – one constructed by the critics who attacked Wordsworth – a series of attacks that also introduced his poetic brand and name to the wider reading public. After rekindling this memory, in the next paragraph the 'Friend' reveals that when reading the withdrawn pages from chapter 13, he feels left on his own to make sense of his reactions and interpretations. As the 'Friend' points out in the second half of the letter, Coleridge has 'been obliged to omit so many links' in the chain of his argument that his philosophical prose appears like 'the fragments of the winding steps of an old ruined tower'.[46] In order to bridge the philosophical holes that confront him as he ascends the winding steps of Coleridge's argument, the 'Friend' turns to Coleridge's 'Christabel' and 'To William Wordsworth'. After first alluding to 'Christabel' in order to describe his feelings of confusion and enthrallment, the 'Friend' relies on his sense of humour to reappropriate 'To William Wordsworth' and consequently ground his conclusions about Coleridge's prose argument.

The 'Friend's' first poetic allusion demonstrates how Coleridge's Gothic reputation had been continually built up, reworked and reconstructed through the public's seemingly unremitting attention to and appropriations of poems such as 'Christabel'.[47] As the letter unfolds, it functions like a reader's prospectus that forges textual pathways connecting together Coleridge's works. The letter also serves as a supplementary essay that reflects on the historical import and current value of those works. Less like the preface to *Lyrical Ballads* and more like Wordsworth's 1814 prospectus to *The Excursion*, which stands in the middle of and seemingly links together all of Wordsworth's works, the letter connects volume 1 of the *Biographia* to volume 2, projects forward Coleridge's great book on the constructive philocophy, and sets up correspondences between Coleridge's Christabel volume (1816) and *Sibylline Leaves* (1817). However, unlike Wordsworth's prospectus, this letter does not provide a central and unshakeable authorial perspective that firmly establishes the relationship between all of Coleridge's works. Instead, the letter represents an absent middle, and any definitive connections between Coleridge's works – either in reference to volume 1 and 2 of the *Biographia* or to any of his poems – are complicated by the 'Friend's' account of his difficulties when trying to make sense of the very pages about the imagination that Coleridge withdraws from public view. While Wordsworth's prospectus describes where its author will go and what he will prompt readers to do, the 'Friend's' Gothic prospectus, seemingly written by someone other than Coleridge and inserted as an epistolary stop-gap, relates the value of Coleridge's literary works to how his readers imaginatively supplement, connect together and recreate the relevance of those works. Consequently, instead of providing an account of the chief features of his forthcoming work, the letter plays out the responses that his works can elicit from his readers.

The 'Friend's' poetic allusions might seem like a personal, even idiosyncratic, reaction to reading Coleridge's prose. However, the propensity to conjure up Coleridge's older poetry when reacting to his newer prose was not idiosyncratic.[48] Throughout the 1810s, several reviewing critics questioned, or even dismissed, any connection between Coleridge's older poetry and his burgeoning role as aesthetic, cultural and political critic.[49] Much of the journalistic focus on Coleridge the prose essayist, both immediately pre- and proceeding the publication of the *Biographia*, demonstrates this compulsion to recall his earlier poetry while at the same time excoriating and disconnecting his newer prose and politics from that earlier poetry.

In describing his reaction to Coleridge's pages on the imagination, the 'Friend' turns this critical propensity on its head by connecting Coleridge's prose directly with his past poetry. He remarks,

> [t]he effect on my feelings, on the other hand, I cannot better represent, than by supposing myself to have known only our light airy modern chapels of ease, and then for the first time to have been placed, and left alone, in one of our largest Gothic cathedrals in a gusty moonlight night of autumn. 'Now in glimmer, and now in gloom.'[50]

Here, the 'Friend's' prose description gives way to a direct quotation from Coleridge's recently published 'Christabel' – a poem that the 'Friend' seizes on as a means to illustrate his dizzying entrance into such a shadowy and uncertain Gothic space.[51] From its composition in 1797/8, 'Christabel' proved itself to be a mysterious, mesmerizing, elusive and powerful poem. When Coleridge's 'Friend' makes this allusion to the poem in the autumn of 1815 – the period when this section of the *Biographia* was drafted – Coleridge was planning to publish 'Christabel' in order to capitalize on its uncommon, seventeen-year manuscript history. Even before its publication, 'Christabel' had gained a kind of cult status through Coleridge's private readings of the poem, subsequent public commentaries and several published works imitating its meter and alluding to particular parts of the poem.[52]

If the mysterious acclaim attributed to Coleridge's manuscript poem were not enough to create its notoriety, in the months preceding the poem's publication in 1816, Lord Byron whetted the reading public's and review culture's appetite with a footnote in 'The Siege of Corinth' advertising 'Christabel'.[53] In that supplementary notice – what one reviewer in the *Anti-Jacobin* describes as 'a new species of puff direct' – Byron acknowledges that he has been so spellbound by Coleridge's poem that he has done all but directly plagiarize from it. The reviewer relates all of the private details of Byron's introduction to Coleridge's poem: '[Byron], as the newspapers informed the public, had read them in manuscript, and, in a letter, to the author, had called "Christabel", it seems, "a singularly wild and beautiful Poem"'. After noting this occurrence, the reviewer points out that this private endorsement made public will translate into financial gain (for Coleridge and the publisher John Murray) and immediate, cultural currency among readers (for Coleridge and Byron).[54]

The 'Christabel' volume, though not critically well received, was a popular success and went through three editions in less than a year. In anticipation of the public's curiosity about 'Christabel', Coleridge included a preface that explains the long manuscript history of the poem and suggests how his literary works have gained their cultural staying power from the diverse readings and plagiarisms that a poem like 'Christabel' has attracted. In the preface Coleridge describes 'Christabel' as an incomplete but ever-expanding structure, and he explains that the first part of the poem was written in 1798 and the second part in 1800. He further maintains that 'I shall be able to embody in verse the three parts yet to come, in the course of the present year'.[55] Using the word 'embody' to describe his proposed composition of three unwritten parts to 'Christabel' superimposes an eerie context onto Coleridge's assertion that he will author the 'parts yet to come'. While the word 'embody' seems to invest Coleridge with an almost divine ability to incarnate thoughts into words, his use of it in the preface to arguably his most Gothic poem also suggests a ghostly presence lingering behind the poem's conception. Although Coleridge states that he soon will 'embody' forth these three parts, they are for the time being disembodied – left to float, hauntingly and somewhat laughingly, before the public's curiosity.

The remainder of the preface only further obfuscates Coleridge's credibility as the controlling author and proprietor of his 1816 poetic publication. Coleridge singles out his indolence as the chief reason for the tardy publication of 'Christabel', and he acknowledges that the poem would have appeared more original in 1800. He even remarks that the 'dates are mentioned for the exclusive purpose of precluding charges of plagiarism or servile imitation from myself'.[56] Ostensibly a defence against charges of plagiarism or self-imitation that could be levelled at him, Coleridge's claim also calls attention to the fact that over the previous seventeen years 'Christabel', though a manuscript work, had been embodied in diverse ways through the reimaginings of contemporary writers such as Scott, Byron and Wordsworth.[57] In defending the tardy appearance of 'Christabel', Coleridge points out,

> I am confident, however, that as far as the present poem is concerned, the celebrated poets whose writings might be suspected of having imitated, either in particular passages, or in the tone and the spirit of the whole, would be among the first to vindicate me from the charge.[58]

Here, Coleridge seems less interested in clearly demarcating his poem as an original production than in pointing out that it has been often imitated. Curiously, although Coleridge heads off any possible charges of self-plagiarism, he does not accuse those poets who might have stolen from him, and the fact that Coleridge leaves the 'celebrated poets' unnamed who have stolen from him only further underscores the poem's ubiquity, continuing currency and mysterious power. According to Coleridge's preface, authors, reviewers and general readers have brought this disembodied manuscript poem to life through their constant attention; and, after its appearance in 1816, the poem would haunt the review culture and the literary market continually, like a ghostly presence that can neither be concretely located nor adequately dismissed.[59]

In the letter in chapter 13, the 'Friend's' particular use of Coleridge's line from 'Christabel' – 'Now in glimmer, now in gloom' – demonstrates how the imagination of general readers and critics has been vexed into activity. Seemingly the only way that the 'Friend' can make sense of his prose-reading experience is to quote from an unfinished poem that still needs completion. The allusion refers to the moment in the poem just after Christabel has brought the beautiful, but shadowy and vampiric, Geraldine back from the woods into her father's castle. Christabel lifts the seemingly overcome Geraldine '[o]ver the threshold of the gate', and then the two sneak up to her bedroom (l. 131). They

> [s]teal their way from stair to stair,
> Now in glimmer and now in gloom,
> And now they pass the Baron's room
> As still as death, with stifled breath (ll. 168–71).

As the two climb the stairs to Christabel's bedroom, they – alternately – appear partially illuminated and partially shrouded in darkness. Their wavering, uncertain appearance on their climb towards Christabel's room, where she mysteriously falls from innocence after bedding with Geraldine, foreshadows how Christabel and Geraldine will change places the following morning when the fair Christabel is cast aside while the dark and deceptive Geraldine usurps her position as her father's favourite.

Like Christabel, who is at first spellbound by Geraldine, only realizing too late what she really is, Coleridge's 'Friend' appears spellbound by the pages that he has read. The 'Friend's' allusion to this portion of 'Christabel' suggests the mental dangers surrounding his decision to read Coleridge's prose (could readers lose their identity and mind to a similarly vampiric author?). After all, Christabel loses her identity to the vampiric Geraldine and becomes an unwitting part of the new narrative that Geraldine constructs for Sir Leoline's household. In contrast to Christabel, however, the 'Friend' attempts to imaginatively assess his transforming and nearly debilitating experience by appropriating lines from the poem. Instead of becoming completely overmastered by Coleridge's prose or poetry, he responds to Coleridge's prose with a line of poetry that illustrates and attempts to conceptualize his own painful transformation.[60]

Undergoing a conversion experience, which the 'Friend' compares to wandering through a Gothic church at night, the 'Friend' finds himself 'often in palpable darkness not without a chilly sensation of terror; then suddenly emerging into broad yet visionary lights with coloured shadows, of fantastic shapes yet all decked with holy insignia and mystic symbols'. He is surprised, overwhelmed, and awed on seeing 'great men, with whose names I was familiar, but which looked upon me with countenances and an expression, the most dissimilar to all I had been in the habit of connecting with those names'. What he has known and taken for truth is transformed into its opposite so that those people 'whom [he] had been taught to venerate as almost super-human in magnitude of intellect, [he] found perched in little fret-work niches, as grotesque dwarfs; while the grotesques, in [his] hitherto belief, stood guarding the high altar with all the characters of Apotheosis'. Wavering between past certainty and a peripatetic revelation, the 'Friend' reorients his mind so that he can weigh and make sense of these oppositions through his Gothic poetry/prose description.

Although the 'Friend' stretches his mind to appropriate and recontextualize Coleridge's poetry in order to make sense of Coleridge's prose, he also stipulates in the letter the limits of how far he will entertain Coleridge's philosophical explanations: 'I will not promise to descend into the dark cave of Trophonius with you, there to rub my own eyes, in order to make sparks and figured flashes, which I am required to see'.[61] The 'Friend' relies on humour to mediate between Coleridge's ingenious, and perhaps excessive, philosophical leaps and his own need to ground Coleridge's prose through good sense.[62] He illustrates this mark of a tempering, English mindset by reappropriating Coleridge's lines from his poem 'To William Wordsworth':

> Yet after all, I could not but repeat the lines which you had quoted from a MS. Poem of your own in the FRIEND, and applied to a work of Mr. Wordsworth's though with a few of the words altered:

>   – An orphic tale indeed,
> A tale obscure of high and passionate thoughts
> To a strange music chaunted![63]

Here, the 'Friend' changes several words and alters the referent of 'To William Wordsworth', which Coleridge had first printed in his failed periodical the *Friend* and then published in *Sibylline Leaves* under the title 'To a Gentleman. Composed on the Night after his Recitation of a Poem on the Growth of an Individual Mind'.[64] Instead of referring to *The Prelude*, the 'Friend' alters Coleridge's lines of praise for Wordsworth's epic, autobiographical poem into a commentary that evaluates the aesthetic and communal power of Coleridge's withdrawn pages on the imagination.[65] This reappropriation inflects Coleridge's poem in *Sibylline Leaves* and places Wordsworth's as yet unpublished *The Prelude* in relief against the suppressed pages of chapter 13. In 'To a Gentleman', Coleridge testifies to how Wordsworth's recitation of *The Prelude* moved him intellectually and emotionally because of Wordsworth's attention to his inner life, descriptions of influential external forces, and commitment to the 'Social Sense' / Distending wide' (ll. 28–9). Following this praise, he envisions Wordsworth 'in the choir / Of ever-enduring men', imagines 'triumphal wreaths / Strew'd before [Wordsworth's] advancing', and claims that Wordsworth will be placed 'with gradual fame / Among the Archives of Mankind' (ll. 51–2, 59). The 'Friend's' compulsion to draw on several lines from 'To a Gentleman' would seem to grant Coleridge a similar 'triumphal wreath', crowning him with an impending, canonical status because of the emotional and intellectual power the withdrawn pages have elicited from the 'Friend'.

    However, the 'Friend's' rewriting of the three quoted lines in his letter significantly changes the terms of this praise, as well as the literary forms and type of aesthetic being celebrated. First, this reappropriation draws attention to a poem that also features Coleridge lamenting his own literary failings – even imagining his own death with 'Flowers / Strew'd on my course' – in the midst of Wordsworth's sublime poetic powers and strong authorial presence (ll. 75–6). Second, the words that the 'Friend' substitutes for Coleridge's invert Coleridge's high aesthetic and philosophical praise for Wordsworth's epic poem into a low aesthetic set of terms that recall the Gothic. The 'Friend' changes Coleridge's assertion in the poem that *The Prelude* is 'An orphic *song* indeed, / A song *divine* of high and passionate thoughts / To *their own* Music chaunted' (emphasis added), by replacing 'song' with 'tale', 'divine' with 'obscure', and 'their own' with 'a strange'. In 'To a Gentleman' Coleridge announces the supreme excellence of Wordsworth's epic, its god-like truth ('divine'), and its revelatory, poetic music ('orphic song'), which grows organically ('their own') out of Wordsworth's genial powers. By contrast, the 'Friend' describes Coleridge's pages as a kind of fabulous but communally held story ('tale') that darkly conceals ('obscure') and reveals secreted knowledge that astonishes through its surprising newness ('strange').[66]

If the 'Friend's' words celebrate Coleridge's mystifying, philosophical genius, they also sensationalize the process of reading the 'tale' withdrawn from chapter 13 and tease Coleridge's readers with a narrative trick that plays on their curiosity about the promise of secret knowledge being revealed. Set up by the 'Friend's' appropriations and reconstructions of Coleridge's poetry, this trick invites readers to first indulge their curiosity by reading his literary works – a provocation, perhaps, to read volume 2 of the *Biographia* as well as *Sibylline Leaves* – and then reflect on how those works have affected them. This second act of reflection also turns on the 'Friend's' final description of his Gothic reading experience as 'hard thinking' and 'hard reading'.[67] Far from a dismissal of Gothic narrative, Coleridge's textual trick relies on suspense to first draw readers in and then encourage them to examine and exercise their own secondary powers of imagination. The 'Friend's' sensational description piques curiosity and then defers gratification by enjoining readers to discover the mixture of independent thinking, practicality, idealism and humour characteristic of Coleridge's literary works and, Coleridge suggests, of the English character.

To bring out these characteristics, Coleridge draws on Radcliffe's popular Gothic narrative and on the high literary aesthetics with which Wordsworth imbues his Gothic church figuration. Independently, neither of these aesthetics appears to adequately represent the appeal or power of Coleridge's literary works. However, in conjunction these aesthetics contribute significantly to how the 'Friend' evaluates his reading experience. The 'Friend's' anecdote mimics Radcliffe's common practice of interleaving poetry in her prose narratives – an additive that disrupts how readers progress through her plots and which opens up a host of poetic beauties that offset the seeming terrors and horrors unfolded in her novels. Several reviewing critics commented on these qualities of Radcliffe's embedded poetry, and Coleridge was one of them. He was particularly intrigued and troubled by how readers might understand the relationship between Radcliffe's prose narrative and interrupting poetry.[68] If Radcliffe's prose encouraged a kind of vulgar reading, her embedded poetry upset readers' desires for sensational intrigue. As Leah Price contends, Radcliffe's 'inscribed verse can be understood as a formal corollary to [her] rationale supernatural ... Both strategies substitute edification for the pleasure that readers were tricked into expecting...and replace immediate gratification by the discipline of delay'.[69] Radcliffe's prose/poetry model drew praise from reviewers who branded her Gothic novels as distinctly English because of her high moral purpose and attention to how readers perused her unfolding narratives.

Though Radcliffe's critical and popular successes in the 1790s established a high water mark for Gothic tales in Great Britain,[70] her much-imitated Gothic conventionality was often denigrated in the early nineteenth century by reviewers who considered such authors' works as ephemeral, repetitive, self-indulgent and feminine. On a seemingly higher aesthetic plain, Wordsworth's critics also had repeatedly deemed his poetic system to be out of touch and irrelevant, boring and too simplistic, or simply idiosyncratic. For Coleridge in 1817, what both of these low and high literary aesthetics seemed to lack was flexibility. By contrast, the 'Friend's' literal and metonymic rewriting of 'To a Gentleman' suggests the highly transformable and translatable nature of Coleridge's poetry. His words inflect Coleridge's experience of listening to *The Prelude* and shed light on the difference between Coleridge's experience and the 'Friend's', whose mind appears curiously invigorated and at liberty to play with the dizzying uncertainties of his reading experience. In 'To William Wordsworth', Coleridge has Wordsworth's strong sense of self to guide him, and Wordsworth's authorial presence nearly overwhelms him as a listener. Unlike Wordsworth's *The Prelude*, which identifies a specific role for Coleridge to serve as a model reader/listener, the *Biographia* and the poems that the 'Friend' makes use of celebrate Coleridge's Gothic creations of conflicting multiple perspectives, uncertain authorship, textual adaptability and readerly engagement.

As the 'Friend's' anecdote also subtly recalls, Wordsworth had long since turned away from the Gothic forms and subject matter that marked his collaborative work with Coleridge in the first and second editions of *Lyrical Ballads*. The allusions in chapter 13 to 'Christabel' and 'The Rime of the Ancient Mariner' recall and celebrate those earlier Gothic collaborations, and draw attention to Wordsworth's anxieties about and subsequent rejections of the mixed Gothic character of *Lyrical Ballads* (1800).[71] Set in relief against the 'Friend's' Gothic church experience, Wordsworth's figuration in 1814 appears illegitimate – a kind of sham Gothic that lacks the capacity to adequately engage readers in its design because it fails to make room for their tastes while also challenging them to engage in independent acts of emotional and intellectual self-discovery. Wordsworth may in fact be a better poet, as Coleridge readily admits throughout the *Biographia*. However, the 'Friend's' parodic rendering of Wordsworth's Gothic church metaphor reveals that, in contrast to Coleridge, Wordsworth has buried his Gothic past and attempted to replace it with his all too personal vision of the nation's pastoral character. As a parodic rendering of Wordsworth's second-self presented as Coleridge's own second-self, the 'Friend' suggests that Wordsworth has lost a significant part of his authorial appeal to the reading public, as well as his sense of humour about the mixed, critical reception of his literary works.

The 'Friend's' letter sets up Coleridge's collected literary works as an embodiment of England's high literary heritage and seemingly low Gothic character. The letter recalls how often reviewing critics, contemporary authors and readers have commented on, recirculated, reappropriated and re-envisioned the unmethodical character and troubling power of his literary works. In attempting to make sense of Coleridge's prose by conjuring up the textual histories, cultural importance and transformative nature of his poetry, the 'Friend' also checks Coleridge's progression towards fixed principles by asserting a distinctly English need for self-adjustment and practical, first-hand engagement. The 'Friend' maintains that he will only follow Coleridge so far in his philosophical prose before turning to find his own way through appropriations of Coleridge's poetry. At the mid-point of the *Biographia*, arguably the centrepiece of Coleridge's life's work – a work saturated by its relationship with Wordsworth's poetry and supplementary prose – Coleridge's 'Friend' invites the public to reaffirm England's literary character by continuing to read and write their tastes and personalities into Coleridge's collected works. What this humorous, Gothic counterfeit calls attention to is the possibility for an ever-changing literary miscellany – a touchstone that facilitates the continual growth of the nation's literary culture according to how readers engage with Coleridge's unmethodical life and literary works. The 'Friend' articulates this possibility by capitalizing on Radcliffe's popularized, Gothic conventions at the expense of Wordsworth's Gothic church metaphor. He suggests that, unlike Wordsworth, Coleridge knows when to have a sense of humour about the reception of his works, and how readers – and not authors – create and recreate the supplementary frameworks that establish the enduring value of a writer's literary collections.

6 J. H. REYNOLDS'S 'PETER BELL' AND THE WORDSWORTHIAN REPUTATION

In the short term Coleridge's mixed defence of Wordsworth's genius, criticisms of his poetic diction and subject matter and parodic treatment of his poetic system did little to dissuade – and may have fuelled – further attacks by reviewing critics and parodists who scoffed at Wordsworth's elaborate claims for how and why his poems were 'bound each to each'.[1] Along with J. H. Reynolds's 'Peter Bell, A Lyrical Ballad' (1819), a handful of other Regency parodies call attention to the laborious and repetitious construction of Wordsworth's poetic *oeuvre* by singling out a particular Wordsworth poem as a pathetic, simplistic and ridiculous microcosm of his entire poetic works.[2] Undoubtedly, they developed this satirical part/whole focus in response to Wordsworth's own prose remarks about how to read his poetry in his 'Preface to *The Excursion*' (1814) and in the supplementary prose surrounding his 1815 *Poems*. Most troubling for many of these critics were Wordsworth's claims in the preface that *The Excursion* acts as the completed centrepiece for his fragmentary, unpublished epic *The Recluse* and connects together all of his minor poetic pieces.[3] Responding to Wordsworth's amalgamating poetic system, these parodists sought to effect a wholesale revision of the relationship between the part (a particular poem) and the whole (the entire projected Wordsworthian oeuvre).[4]

While an earlier parody like *The Simpliciad* attempts to reduce the whole of Wordsworth's poetic *oeuvre* into inconsequential parts, Reynolds's 'Peter Bell' expands a part into an empty and displaced whole. Through their supplementary prose notation, both parodies attempt to divest Wordsworth's individual poems of their metaphoric unity and metonymic significance and to redirect the emotional, political and economic contexts surrounding his poems. In 'Peter Bell' Reynolds ridicules Wordsworth's poetic project and poetic persona by creating a mock-Wordsworth who calls attention to how his readers are mired in a surfeit of paratexts that ask them to understand and evaluate his continued labour and current poems against former and future poetic productions. Reynolds's parody jeers at Wordsworth's efforts to foster a sympathetic attentiveness from his readers through the notes in his books of poetry. In singling out Wordsworth's supplementary prose, Reynolds wryly turns against the Lake poet his system of classifying and connecting together his poems and his penchant for word repetition. Although Wordsworth articulates a basis for his use of repetition as early as his note to 'The Thorn' in the 1800 *Lyrical Ballads*, for parodists such as Reynolds, Wordsworth's repetitions only highlight a lack in his poetic system that draws needless attention to his poetic persona.

Reynolds's 'Peter Bell' pokes fun at Wordsworth's efforts – through the supplementary prose in his books of poetry – to create the taste by which he was to be judged. His parody represents a hyperbolic version of Wordsworth's own system, which – through poetic groupings, echoes and prose notes – attempts to bind together past and future poems and to maintain Wordsworth's claims of continued original labour. Reynolds's 'Peter Bell' mockingly replicates Wordsworth's supplemental prose and reduces the supposed continuity of his reader-involved project to an over-inflated, egotistical and repetitive opportunism for building his reputation. However, in his sonnet, 'On the Detraction which Followed the Publication of a Certain Poem' (1820), Wordsworth responds, showing that he too could re-echo the language and parodic labour of his detractors. This sonnet demonstrates Wordsworth's awareness that in order to engender a sustainable cultural place for his poetry he must relocate and reappropriate his own poetic discourse in relation to the very cultural forces that seek to dismantle the collective power of his works.

Reputing Wordsworth: 'Here lie the remains of W. W.'

Two weeks before Wordsworth published his 'Peter Bell', Reynolds published his parody to pre-empt and shape the public's response to yet another Wordsworth publication.[5] Reynolds's satirical attack mimics Wordsworth's paratextual practices and mocks the seeming continuity of his poetic career, which Wordsworth based heavily on the relationship between his past and future poetic productions – a method with which Coleridge, Wordsworth's former *Lyrical Ballads* collaborator, was well-acquainted.[6] In a letter to Reynolds's publishers Taylor and Hessey, which refers to the parodist's 'Peter Bell', Coleridge admits, 'I laughed heartily *at all the prose*, notes included'. Coleridge seems delighted by Reynolds's paratextual apparatus,[7] including his mock preface, supplementary essay and footnotes to the poem, which poke fun at Wordsworth's poetic system, egotism and seemingly extravagant valuation of his profession. Reynolds's supplementary writings, particularly his footnotes, ridicule Wordsworth's prose notes, which point out the significance of repeated words and continuities between his poems. Fittingly, Reynolds begins his concluding supplementary essay by burlesquing Wordsworth's prose:

> *I BEG* leave, once for all, to refer the Reader to my previous Poems, for illustrations of the names of the characters and the severe simplicity contained in this affecting Bal-

lad. I purpose, in the course of a few years, to write laborious lives of all the old people who enjoy sinecures in the text, or are pensioned off in the notes, of my Poetry.[8]

Through this satiric Wordsworthian pose, Reynolds highlights Wordsworth's inability to leave the characters in his poems and notes alone. Reynolds's mockery might have been directed at the 1819 advertisement for Wordsworth's forthcoming 'Peter Bell' – which followed rumours that Wordsworth finally would publish a poem that he had been working on for twenty years – or at Wordsworth's revised and reordered collected 1815 *Poems*, or at his announced intention to publish another collected edition of poems in 1820. Reynolds colours his supplementary critique of Wordsworth's continual poetic resurrections with the Anglican connotations of 'sinecure' and the economic stigma of 'pensioned off'. This depiction of the Lake poet's characters as 'enjoying sinecures' in his poems not only aligns Wordsworth with conservative principles; it implies that his characters occupy a position that involves little or no responsibility, labour or active service. Wordsworth and his characters seemingly have been bought off.

Reynolds maintains that Wordsworth's characters – reconceived under the aegis of political conservatism – have no active or useful poetic function because they are old and static. Reynolds also ridicules the supplementary prose surrounding these poems, in which Wordsworth has 'pensioned off' or given payment to various characters – some fictional and some real. Such a characterization suggests that Wordsworth seeks to curry favour with influential and wealthy living people, not unlike William Earl of Lonsdale and Sir George Beaumont, to whom Wordsworth inscribes a dedication as well as notes that accrue from his *Poems of William Wordsworth* (1807), to his 1814 preface to *The Excursion* and 1815 *Poems*. Reynolds implies that Wordsworth aligns himself with a history of landed and quasi-Tory principles – an accusation not unfounded, given Wordsworth's long description in a note to 'Song, at the Feast of Brougham Castle' from the 1807 *Poems*, which catalogues the family history and character of Sir Clifford and dwells on various castles from that family, now 'preserved from all depredations' by Wordsworth's contemporary the Earl of Thanet.[9]

Reynolds also accuses Wordsworth of trying to construct his own reputation through 'laborious' repetition, and his mock preface portrays Wordsworth as unable to resist making references to his own works:

I have persevered with a perseverance truly astonishing, in persons of not the most pursy purses; – but to a man of my inveterate morality and independent stamp, (of which Stamps I am proud to be a Distributor) the sneers and scoffings of impious Scotchmen, and the neglect of my poor uninspired countrymen, fall as the dew upon the thorn, (on which plant I have written an immortal stanza or two) and are as fleeting as the spray of the waterfall, (concerning which waterfall I have composed some great lines which the world will not let die.)[10]

After satirizing Wordsworth's purported indifference to public opinion, obsession with his own poems and claims for poetic independence by pointing out Wordsworth's own quasi-sinecure as a government stamp collector, Reynolds portrays Wordsworth not as a bard labouring to produce new and original poetry but as a gossipy professional poet. Reynolds's Wordsworth 'laboriously' rehearses and rehashes his past productions (even in the face of a hostile public) as a means to create his reputation and obtain a poetic 'sinecure' in the public eye. Until such a time comes, Reynolds suggests, Wordsworth remains pensioned off in a poetic world of his own 'old people'.

Coleridge's concept of reputation, outlined by Andrew Bennett in *Romantic Poets and the Culture of Posterity* (1999), sheds light on Reynolds's critique. In a letter to Lady Beaumont in January 1810, Coleridge writes a brief etymological account of the word reputation and maintains that reputation is nothing more than 'the opinions of those who *re-suppose* the *suppositions* of others'.[11] Coleridge then translates the Latin *reput* as 'echo' and asserts that reputation 're-echoes an echo'; it is an echo of an echo that is displaced and that has nothing to do, necessarily, with the original referent itself. The word 'reputation' re-supposes or (from the Latin *supponere*) puts one thing in the place of something else. Reynolds's parodic notes exemplify this type of displacement, which occurs when re-echoing an echo. His notes echo and underline the import of Wordsworth's words by pointing back through those words to an earlier poem with the same words. Reynolds does not dispute the fact that Wordsworth relates poem to poem through such echoes. Instead, Reynolds's notes suggest that Wordsworth's re-echoing only draws readers' attention away from his poetry and towards the poet himself. Reynolds's reconfigurations imply that Wordsworth's network of prose functions as public gossip that sensationalizes and rehashes the seeming importance of how poems relate to poems. From Reynolds's perspective, Wordsworth's repetitions only seek to aggrandize his reputation.

Reynolds's 'Peter Bell' concerns itself directly with Wordsworth's efforts to build his reputation through continual self-references that re-echo other echoes, which seem to refer back to a poem or a word but actually displace those echoes from his poetry to 're-suppose' the continuity of his professional identity. In a footnote that provides a self-supporting quotation from 'Simon Lee', Reynolds's mock-Wordsworth admits, 'I cannot resist quoting the following lines, to shew how I preserve my system from youth to old age. As Simon was, so he is. And one and twenty years have scarcely altered (except by death) that cheerful and cherry-cheeked Old Huntsman'.[12] Here, Reynolds suggests that Wordsworth's rigid continuities only lead to the suspended animation or even death of his poetry. By the close of the poem, Reynolds lays Wordsworth's reputation to rest in the graveyard where he already has interred many of the Lake poet's characters: 'The death they say was suicide; / ... "Here lieth W.W. / Who never more will trouble you, trouble you'" (stanza 43). In his essay 'J. H. Reynolds's "Peter Bell"', Gerald Pyle argues that Reynolds probably gleaned these lines from a letter in the *Literary Gazette* from 6 December 1817.[13] In this letter, a 'Sexton' complains about too much levity on tombstones, and he singles out the epitaph on the grave of one William Williams to prove his point: 'Here lie the remains of W.W. / Who never more will trouble you, trouble you'. Pyle remarks that the *Literary Gazette*'s review of Reynolds's parody refers to these lines as an old joke. Similar to Richard Mant's repetitions in *The Simpliciad* of the *Edinburgh*'s language, ideology and critical prose, Reynolds twists the currency of the review culture's language.

By the time Reynolds employed these words in his parody, they were recognizable to many periodical readers as a new turn on an old joke. Likewise, by the spring of 1819, publicly poking fun at Wordsworth was a return to an old joke. Through these lines Reynolds mocks Wordsworth's treatment of epitaphs in his 'Essay upon Epitaphs' – published both in Coleridge's the *Friend* and as an endnote to *The Excursion* – by assigning Wordsworth the kind of epitaph, which he purportedly disdained, that severs the connection between the community of the living and the dead, and by extension Wordsworth and his audience. Reynolds also ends his poem by having Wordsworth's character Peter Bell repeat, '"W. W. / Never more will trouble you, trouble you"'. He lays Wordsworth to rest with the repetition of a common joke – a tired phrase, which ends Wordsworth's continual laborious activities. This double repetition of a repetition – punctuated as much by the repeated namesake W. W. as by this final construction – points to Wordsworth's repeated 'laborious' efforts to impose himself and his poetic system on readers. These two lines place Wordsworth's career in the context of a repeated and hackneyed phrase, founded and built upon a repeated name that is not even Wordsworth's.

Reynolds's footnotes also mock how Wordsworth has undertaken this reputation building. They accuse Wordsworth of doing exactly what many reviewers do – gossip – and, in Wordsworth's case, build his reputation by recirculating and echoing his own poems. Throughout his notes, Reynolds constructs a satiric family lineage, which stretches from Wordsworth's forthcoming 'Peter Bell' to his earliest characters in *Lyrical Ballads*. When elaborating on this genealogy, which explains that Betty Foy is the aunt of Peter Bell, whose nephew is Simon Lee and niece is Alice Fell, Reynolds adds the following footnote: 'Mr. Sheridan, in his sweet poem of the Critic, supplies one of his heroes with as singularly clustering a relationship'.[14] The scene that Reynolds refers to occurs in Act III, Scene I of *The Critic* – a play about playwrights and critics in which Puff, a writer/director and a 'Professor of the Art of Puffing',[15] and his critic-friends Dangle and Sneer comment on the practice performance of Puff's tragedy *The Spanish Armada*. Reynolds's footnote draws attention to the 'underplot' of the play, which in *The Critic* has 'as little connection with your main plot as possible'.[16] In the 'underplot', an orphan is reunited unwittingly and quickly with his relatives in a brief court scene, and this farce ends with all of the characters fainting happily into each other's arms.

While Reynolds's allusion further renders Wordsworth's poetic characters farcical, it also places Wordsworth in the position of Puff, an avid self-promoter and manipulator of public opinion. Puff is an opportunist and a flatterer, skilled in appealing to and constructing the opinions of the public through the new information technologies of the newspaper. Puff abuses the power of advertisements and critical reviews to create public opinion and contends that 'the number of those who go through the fatigue of judging for themselves is very small indeed!'.[17] Reynolds's allusion portrays Wordsworth as a public manipulator who is intent on manufacturing the responses of his readers through a prose apparatus that guides readers' responses to his poetry. Wordsworth appears as an opportunist, engaging in relentless 'Puffery'. As Puff, Wordsworth is unconcerned with how different poems and plot lines in his master-work are linked to one another, so long as they are linked together and please the public. Reynolds's footnote characterizes Wordsworth's habitual references in his prose – about how his poems are bound together and how the repetition of words within and between poems builds emotional context – to the denouement of a play within a play, a farcical simulacrum that displaces the action and significance of that play.

Repeating Wordsworthian Labour

Reynolds's mock-Wordsworth further carves out this farcical genealogy by exaggerating in other footnotes the manner in which Wordsworth has constructed his cast of poetic characters. His mock-Wordsworth reveals that Susan Harvey is 'Dairy-maid to Mr. Gill'; that 'Harry Gill was the original proprietor of Barbara Lethwaite's pet-lamb; and that he bred Betty Foy's celebrated pony, got originally out of a Night-mare, by a descendent of the great Trojan horse'. Furthermore, when establishing a strict, genealogical relationship between characters is impossible, he remarks in a footnote, 'Peter Bell resembleth Harry Gill in this particular: "His teeth they chatter, chatter, chatter", I should have introduced this fact into the text, but that Harry Gill would not rhyme. I reserve this for my blank verse.'[18] Reynolds implies that such a resemblance between characters, brought together through the repetition of 'chatter', detracts from the emotional contexts that might be built up by such repetition. Instead, such a resemblance opportunistically advertises Wordsworth's other blank verse productions. In his preface Reynolds's mock-Wordsworth further announces, 'Copies of my previous works may be had in any numbers, by application at my publisher'.[19]

Beyond ridiculing Wordsworth's cast of poetic characters, Reynolds attacks Wordsworth's theories about poetic language and repetition. He constructs a footnote for the line 'Four brown bugs are feeding there' – a commentary on a stanza about Peter Bell's foster child beset with fleas – which explains, 'I have a similar idea in my Poem on finding a Bird's Nest: – "Look *five* blue eggs are gleaming there". But the numbers are different, so I trust that no one will differ with the numbers.' Reynolds jeers at the supposed similarity between 'four' and 'five' and 'feeding' and 'gleaming' – disparaging Wordsworth's idea of similitude in dissimilitude from his 1800 preface to *Lyrical Ballads*. He also has the mock-Wordsworth defend a line of poetry, 'Catch as many as you can', with the footnote, 'I have also given these lines before; but in thus printing them again, I neither tarnish their value, nor injure their novelty'.[20] Reynolds portrays Wordsworth asserting the 'value' of his repetitions not as self-plagiarism but as original labour, and his mock-Wordsworth maintains that the value of his lines only increases the more he repeats them.

In another footnote that parodies several of Wordsworth's notes 'To the Daisy' in his 1807 and 1815 *Poems*, Reynolds's mock-Wordsworth privileges his own poetic construction of the daisy over Chaucer's. Reynolds manipulates Wordsworth's 1807 endnote – in which Wordsworth acquits himself of plagiarism by distinguishing his poems to the daisy from a similar poem, 'Field Flower' by a Mr Montgomery – into an explicitly defensive claim by relating it to Wordsworth's footnote 'To the Daisy' in *Poems of the Fancy* (1815): 'See, in Chaucer and the Elder Poets, the honours formerly paid to this flower'.[21] Reynolds's footnote – 'It was a favourite with Chaucer, but he did not understand its moral mystery as I do'[22] – elides the two notes, which both appear in Wordsworth's 1815 edition, and transforms Wordsworth's concluding quotation from Chaucer's poem 'The Flour'. Reynolds's mock-Wordsworth uses this quotation, which comically defends plagiarism as a reflection of love and service to the daisy, to privilege his labour over Montgomery's and Chaucer's.

Throughout his parody, Reynolds answers other 'moral' mysteries with footnotes that mockingly refer to Wordsworth's earlier poems and echo specific words and characters. These footnotes call attention to how Wordsworth binds his concept of the poet's labour to the value of his poetic system. In the preface Reynolds's mock-Wordsworth asserts that 'Peter Bell' is 'written in that pure unlaboured style, which can only be met with among labourers'.[23] Reynolds highlights Wordsworth's propensity to foreground his poetic labour while also proclaiming that labour to be economically unquantifiable. He catches Wordsworth in the act of showing off the product of his labour while attempting to hide the process of that labour, and he implies that Wordsworth should have spent more time composing his poetry than striving to highlight the value and products of his imaginative labour. Far from a guarantee that acts as the basis for a contract between poet and readers, which Mark Schoenfield describes in *The Professional Wordsworth: Law, Labor, and the Poet's Contract* (1996),[24] Reynolds implies that Wordsworth's labour and laborious assertions guarantee little to nothing for readers.

His mock-Wordsworth adds to these declarations about the value of this unlaboured labour by proclaiming the sublimely bathetic difficulties and unaccountability of his poem: 'I can safely say, that while its imaginations spring beyond the reach of the imaginative, its occasional meaning occasionally falls far below the meanest capacity'.[25] Reynolds distorts Wordsworth's claims about the value of his imaginative labour through his reductions of 'imaginations' to 'imaginative' and 'occasional' to 'occasionally' – a shift that begins with a concrete noun and ends with an adverbial airy nothing – and suggests that readers can neither identify nor respond to the poet's hypothetical labour. By poking fun of Wordsworth's seeming simplicity and 'pure unlaboured style', Reynolds undercuts Wordsworth's assertions about the value of his labour and classes Wordsworth as one among many 'labourers' in simplicity. Wordsworth's rhetorical labours appear inflated and prosaic when investigated through Reynolds's reconfigurations, which shatter Wordsworth's paradoxical efforts to foreground his poetic labour in the public eye and to position that labour beyond public reproach. Although the 1814 preface to *The Excursion* and the essays book-ending volume 1 of his 1815 *Poems* present the value of Wordsworth's labour as a guarantee of the quality of his poetic productions, Reynolds's parody maintains that Wordsworth's labour and the hypothetical contract he offers his readers only benefit and bind Wordsworth.

Reynolds's mock-Wordsworth also sarcastically threatens that if readers give Wordsworth the chance, he will further replicate his labours – 'If I ever shall be surprised into a second edition of my whole Poems, I shall write an extra-supplementary Essay on the principles of simple Poetry'. Reynolds then ends his 'Supplementary Essay' with a quotation about fame and posterity from Wordsworth's own 'Essay Supplementary to the Preface' (1815):

> A sketch of my own notion of the Constitution of Fame has been given; and as far as concerns myself, I have cause to be satisfied, – The love, the admiration, the indifference, the slight, the aversion, and even the contempt, with which these Poems have been received, knowing, as I do, the source within my own mind, from which they have proceeded; and the *labour* and *pains* which, when *labour* and *pains* appeared needful, have been bestowed upon them, – must all, if I think consistently, be received as *pledges* and tokens, bearing the same general impression though widely different in *value*; – they are all *proofs* that for the present time I have not *laboured* in vain; and afford assurances, more or less authentic, that the *products* of my *industry* will endure.[26]

In this passage, Wordsworth's syntax confuses who is doing what and how. How are Wordsworth's readers related to the value of his labour? Kurt Heinzelman maintains that the ambivalent antecedent 'they' in 'knowing, as I do, the source within my own mind, from which *they* have proceeded' is the crux of this passage.[27] 'They' could refer back to 'these Poems', suggesting that the source of these poems has come from the poet's own mind, or it could refer to the myriad responses, both positive and negative, of Wordsworth's readers, suggesting that those responses have proceeded from his own mind. Heinzelman argues that

> the syntax implies that the poems and readers' responses to them bear the same general impression because the poet knows the source of both in *his* mind. The multiplicity of readers' responses comes to reflect the multiplicity of the poet's emotions, which went into the poems' composition in the first place.[28]

According to Heinzelman, Wordsworth becomes the reader of his readers' passions. However, Heinzelman overlooks how this section of the 'Essay Supplementary' further complicates Wordsworth's hypothetical contract between poet and readers. Reading the next clauses – 'and the labour and pains, which, when labour and pains appeared needful, have been bestowed upon them, must all, if I think consistently, be received as pledges and tokens' – in light of Heinzelman's account of the poet's labour and readers' responses confuses who is doing this labour. The 'labour and pains' that are 'bestowed' could be both the poet's and readers'. Wordsworth's rhetoric enacts and obfuscates a dual exchange between poet and readers in which readers should receive as a pledge the poet's labour, and the poet should receive as a pledge his readers' labours. Consequently, although Wordsworth may posit the source of his readers' responses in his own mind, the actual labour that readers engage in should solidify the future survival of Wordsworth's poems. Wordsworth, however, does not clearly differentiate between his labour and the labour of readers. Seemingly, for Wordsworth, the latter should imitate the former.

In the above passage, Wordsworth employs a chiasmic rhetoric similar to a passage in his 'Preface to *Lyrical Ballads*' (1802), which aligns, relates and substitutes the responses of Wordsworth's readers for the responses of the poet. In that preface, after describing the process of tempering the inspired creation of poetry – 'the spontaneous overflow of powerful feelings' – Wordsworth connects the mental processes behind composition to the mental processes that underpin reception. He suggests that readers must monitor their enthusiastic readings in the same manner that the poet reflects upon and tempers the inspired emotions that underpin a given poem. Moving from the pronoun 'I' to 'we', he describes how to strengthen the human mind by modifying the 'continued influxes of our feeling' – a process of reflecting on and comparing those feelings with thoughts of past feelings. He then equates poetic creation with reception and aligns the 'habits of mind' created by such mental exercise with the poet and with readers, whose understandings 'must necessarily be in some degree enlightened, and [whose affections [will be] strengthened and purified'.[29] However, in contrast to this passage from the 1802 'Preface', in this section of the 'Essay Supplementary to the Preface' Wordsworth does not overtly move from 'I' to 'we' to 'reader'. Instead he elides and confuses the gap between 'I' and 'reader'.

Furthermore, unlike Reynolds's reappropriation of this passage, this section of Wordsworth's 'Essay Supplementary' does not deal concertedly with the labour of his detractors. Outside the context of Wordsworth's 'Essay Supplementary' and reinserted into the context of the mock 'Peter Bell', Reynolds turns the confusing syntax of Wordsworth's passage against itself. Would Wordsworth accept Reynolds's parodic labour as a pledge? Is satirical parody a part of the labour bestowed to which Wordsworth refers?[30] In finishing his parody with this quotation, Reynolds reframes Wordsworth's double bind, which dismisses contemporary responses as largely irrelevant while also elevating those responses as pledges that authenticate the future fame of his poetry. What stands out as most problematic in Reynolds's reconfiguration is what mediates between the poet's contemporary critical reception and his future fame – labour. Although Wordsworth's referent 'they' ambiguously refers to either his poems or to his readers, he qualifies his statement regarding the negative reception of his work with the labour and pains bestowed on his works. Again, the passage hinges on who bestows labour and pains. In Wordsworth's 'Essay Supplementary' this passage anticipates his description of the contract that he maintains should connect the poet and his readers, and the passage closes a skewed, literary history that ends with his judgement that only posterity and the 'People, philosophically characterized' can judge the fame of a poet. Wordsworth's self-serving retrospective suggests that any poet who is popular amongst contemporary readers is doomed to be appreciated only by those contemporaries. The value of contemporary readers' labours seemingly must be deferred.

By concluding 'Peter Bell' with this reconfigured excerpt from Wordsworth's 'Essay Supplementary', Reynolds exacerbates Wordsworth's reception problem, suggests that Wordsworth is obsessed with his own contemporary fame and foregrounds Wordsworth in the act of building his own reputation. Reynolds bases Wordsworth's 'sketch of [his] notion of the Constitution of Fame' on his constant chatter about his poems and aggrandizement of his own labour, and not on his readers' responses. Furthermore, Reynolds's repetition of Wordsworth's 'labour', which mediates and underpins Wordsworth's concept of whether his poetry will endure, makes Wordsworth's argument appear circular. If Wordsworth can neither embrace nor completely dismiss public opinion, can he measure the value of his own labour? If his readers are unable to fulfil the kind of labour that he calls for, what is Wordsworth's labour worth? Reynolds's parody mocks Wordsworth's hypothetical contract, which posits a necessary, but uncertain and ill-defined place for readers. And, given the contingent nature of such a contract, one might assume that Wordsworth would reject Reynolds's parodic labour. However, Wordsworth's response to Reynolds's 'Peter Bell' and several other detractors shows how Wordsworth was capable and willing to absorb and reframe parody within the confines of his collected works.

Wordsworth's Parodic Response

Wordsworth's sonnet 'On the Detraction which Followed the Publication of a Certain Poem'[31] – a response to reviews of his 'Peter Bell', including Reynolds's pre-emptive strike – underscores the value of his poetic labour by measuring that labour against the pledges of his contemporaries. This sonnet reveals Wordsworth's complex engagement with the review culture and the reading public, as well as his definition of what constitutes valuable English literature. 'On the Detraction' parodies the language, subject matter, and form of Milton's twin sonnets 11 and 12 in order to engage contemporary reviewers and the reading public in a historical, self-reflexive and ironic inquiry into what defines the form and nature of England's literary tradition. Furthermore, it demonstrates his acute awareness of the conventions of parody and the shaping power of supplementary writing:

> ON THE DETRACTION WHICH FOLLOWED THE
> PUBLICATION OF A CERTAIN POEM
> See Milton's Sonnet, beginning, 'A Book was
> writ of late called 'Tetrachordon'
> A BOOK came forth of late, called PETER BELL;
> Not negligent the style; – the matter? – good
> As aught the song records of Robin Hood;
> Or Roy, renowned through many a Scottish dell;
> But some (who brook those hackneyed themes full well,
> Nor heat, at Tam o'Shanter's name, their blood)
> Waxed wroth, and with foul claws, a harpy brood,
> On Bard and Hero clamorously fell.
> Heed not, wild Rover once through heath and glen,
> Who mad'st at length the better life thy choice,
> Heed not such onset! Nay, if praise of men
> To thee appear not an unmeaning voice,
> Lift up that grey-haired forehead and rejoice
> In the just tribute of thy Poet's pen!

Before reading Wordsworth's poem, readers are directed to 'See' Milton's sonnet 12:

A book was writt of late call'd *Tetrachordon*,
　　And wov'n close both matter, form, and stile,
　　The subject new; it walk'd the town a while,
　　Numbring good intellects; now seldom por'd on.
Cries the stall-reader, bless us! what a word on
　　A title page is this! and som in file
　　Stand spelling fals, while one might walk to Mile-
End Green. Why is it harder, Sirs, then Gordon,
Colkitto, or Macdonnell, or Galasp?
　　Those rugged names to our like mouths grow sleek
　　That would have made *Quintilian* stare and gasp.
Thy age, like ours, O Soul of Sir *John Cheek*,
　　Hated not learning wors then toad or Asp,
　　When thou taught'st *Cambridge*, and King *Edward* Greek.[32]

Wordsworth's sonnet begins with an epigraph that directs readers to: 'See Milton's Sonnet, beginning 'A Book was writ of late called "Tetrachordon"'. Instead of merely answering his detractors with a prose attack, like his 'Essay Supplementary to the Preface', or even another ballad like 'Peter Bell', Wordsworth answered with a complex double-edged satire in a parodic sonnet that directs his readers' attention to Milton's sonnet 12 – a complex satiric response to detractors of Milton's *Tetrachordon*.[33] Furthermore, *Tetrachordon* was a response to detractors of Milton's *Doctrine and Discipline of Divorce*. Wordsworth draws upon a Milton sonnet that was distinctly representative of and officiously embedded in a complex intertextual and public controversy about the legality and ethics of divorce.

Wordsworth situates his public response to contemporary reviewers and parodists within the discourse of Milton's response to his critics and within the literary tradition of the sonnet. If Reynolds had satirically lambasted Wordsworth for writing in 'that pure unlaboured style, which can only be met with among labourers',[34] Wordsworth answered by explicitly naming a fellow labourer (Milton) and by writing in a self-consciously intricate form (the sonnet). Wordsworth appears to circumvent responses – like Reynolds's parodic appeals to contemporary writers and readers – by countering with a poetic appeal that only seemingly dismisses contemporary responses to his poetry. Wordsworth's epigraph enjoins contemporary readers to read his rejoinder within the context of Milton's battles with his critics.

In order for readers to acquire the competence to read Wordsworth's sonnet, the epigraph suggests, they first must grapple with the complex relationship between author, text and critics described in Milton's sonnet. Wordsworth may have chosen to refer his readers to Milton's twelfth sonnet for several reasons. First, Milton's sonnet responds to readers who misunderstood *Tetrachordon* and his divorce tracts as well as to readers who neglected to read *Tetrachordon*. Consequently, Milton's sonnet deals explicitly with the reception history of his works. Second, the sonnet satirizes the responses of contemporaries who happen across *Tetrachordon* in the marketplace of St Paul's: 'Cries the stall-reader, bless us! what a word on / A title page is this!' (ll. 5–6). These stall readers cannot grasp the meaning of Milton's Greek title – even though they mimic the sound of it, 'what a word on' – and they complain, 'Why is it harder Sirs then Gordon, / Colkitto, or Macdonnel, or Galasp' (ll. 8–9). An explicit commentary on learning in his age, these lines begin to suggest why Milton's readers were so bewildered by his Greek title. However, the fact that these stall readers mock the title by mimicking it also implies that Milton's work has gained a degree of currency among such readers.

Wordsworth's 'Peter Bell' also experienced a degree of currency and even popularity as a function of his detractors. His 'Peter Bell' sold more copies than any of his previous books of poetry, largely due to the popularity of Reynolds's parody, which was written only with the knowledge of Wordsworth's title. Although the meaning of Wordsworth's title is misrepresented and even misunderstood in such a context, Reynolds's parody also brought Wordsworth's name and work to a new level of public attention. Somewhat ironically, Wordsworth invites such attention to his title with the epigraph to his other spring 1819 publication *The Waggoner*: '"What's in a *Name*? Brutus will start a Spirit as soon as Caesar!"'. Widely commented on and ridiculed, Wordsworth's epigraph calls direct attention to his titles. Wordsworth's reference to Milton's sonnet also suggests that Wordsworth's contemporaries have not grasped the meaning of the title 'Peter Bell' any more than Milton's contemporaries could grasp his Greek title. In Wordsworth's '"Peter Bell" – A *Pons Asinorum* for Critics', G. H. Durrant maintains, through his discussion of Wordsworth's allusions to Midas and his ass ears, that Wordsworth was acutely concerned with encouraging his readers to consider the possible meanings of Peter Bell's name. Arguing that the prologue of 'Peter Bell' is meant 'to be humorously allusive, a challenge to the reader's intelligence',[35] Durrant points out that throughout the poem Wordsworth continually highlights the hardness of Peter Bell by suggesting Peter to mean stone and Bell to mean iron, substituting iron for Midas's golden touch. Peter seemingly turns all that he touches and perceives into rock-hard iron.

Wordsworth's epigraph to his sonnet, which refers readers to Milton's sonnet, implies that his critics have misread or overlooked the central importance of his character's name for the trajectory of the tale and the main character's reformation.[36] Instead of merely denigrating attacks on 'Peter Bell' from 'a harpy brood' (l. 7),[37] Wordsworth enables his sonnet, by way of Milton's sonnet 12, to comment indirectly on readers and learning in his own age. Wordsworth suggests that his critics, like Milton's critics, misunderstand his title and, therefore, cannot properly engage with his poem. Furthermore, what Wordsworth chooses not to say directly, Milton says for Wordsworth.

In 'Resembling Unlikeness: A Reading of Milton's *Tetrachordon* Sonnet', Patrick Cook draws attention to the subtle complexities of the speaker's tone, which connect contemporary readers (and learning) to Milton.[38] Cook argues that, although sonnet 12 satirizes a lack in contemporary learning, the speaker also implicates himself in the age that he critiques with the repeated use of 'our' in 'Those rugged names to our like mouths grow sleek' (l. 10) and 'ours' in 'Thy age, like ours, O Soul of Sir John Cheek, / Hated not Learning worse then Toad or Asp' (ll. 12–13). Cook maintains that '[t]he apparently unlike stall-readers are in fact most resembling – resembling both Milton and the earlier age he praises in both the poem and [*Tetrachordon*]'.[39] Although the sonnet foregrounds the differences between poet and readers, it collapses that difference in the sestet with the use of 'our'. Furthermore, Cook asserts that in line 10, '[j]ust as spelling the title brings the vulgar closer to Milton, so do considering, imitating, indeed even quoting the vulgar bring Milton closer to them'.[40]

In his sonnet, Wordsworth also seems to quote 'the vulgar' that seemingly have misunderstood and mocked his 'Peter Bell'.[41] He refers to Robin Hood and Rob Roy – references perhaps to Reynolds's sonnets about Robin Hood as well to Wordsworth's own poems and comments about the best-selling works of Sir Walter Scott. He also places his 'Peter Bell' in line with Robert Burns's popular Tam O'Shanter. Wordsworth mimics contemporary complaints against his work, echoes his own complaints against contemporaries and brings these voices together in the octave of his sonnet. Wordsworth also imitates and quotes Milton's speaker and, consequently, brings himself and his poem closer to the tone of Milton's sonnet. Against 'A book was writt of late call'd *Tetrachordon*, / And wov'n close both matter, form, and stile', Wordsworth writes, 'A BOOK came forth of late, called PETER BELL; / Not negligent the style; – the matter? – good'. Wordsworth too, these lines suggest, can parody another's work as well as any parodist can imitate his. Wordsworth can speak the language of his detractors and of Milton.

Curiously, Wordsworth's rendition of this second Miltonic line only deals with style and matter. Wordsworth has left out how the form is 'wov'n close', and the dashes elide this point. What Wordsworth seemingly has passed over is what his sonnet asks readers to weave together. This elision might be explained by Wordsworth's reference to Milton's title *Tetrachordon*. The title – suggestive of four disparate musical strings tuned together, which Milton metaphorically applies to his weaving together of four pieces of scripture – draws together Milton's attempts to bring into accord his age's views about marriage and divorce. For Wordsworth's readers, such weaving also turns on their recognition of how Wordsworth's sonnet responds to Milton's sonnet 12 and how it positions itself in relation to Milton's sonnet 11, sonnet 12's twin poem:

I did but prompt the age to quit thir clogs
    By the known rules of ancient liberty,
    When strait a barbarous noise environs me
Of Owls and cuckoos, asses, apes, and dogs.
As when those hinds that were transform'd to frogs
    Rail'd at *Latona's* twin born progeny
    Which after held the Sun and Moon in Fee.
    But this is got by casting pearl to hogs;
That bawl for freedom in thir senseless mood,
    And still revolt when Truth would set them free.
    Licence they mean, when they cry liberty,
For who loves that, must first be wise, and good;
    But from that mark how farr they roav, we see
    For all this wast of wealth, and loss of blood.

Wordsworth's sonnet alludes to two aspects of Milton's sonnet 11 through its characterization of critics and use of the word 'rover'. First, the last two lines of the octave in Wordsworth's sonnet declare that his detractors, 'Waxed wroth, and with foul claws, a harpy brood / On Bard and Hero clamorously fell', and evoke the Dionysian elements of Milton's sonnet 11. The speaker in Milton's sonnet, who prompts his contemporaries towards liberty with the argument of his twin treatises *Tetrachordon* and *Colasterion*, finds himself beset with 'a barbarous noise' of detractors, attempting to tear him apart. Cook points out,

> [t]hreatened by a relatively mild version of the Bacchanalian violence about which he repeatedly expresses anxiety, most recently in *Tetrachordon's* Pentheus allusion, Milton also suffers the fate of Latona, who was refused a place on earth to bear her children and persecuted by Lycian rustics.[42]

While Wordsworth follows Milton's depiction of a ravenous community of critics, the Lake poet chooses a different figuration of his detractors. Instead of Milton's lecherous detractors, 'Owls and cuckoos, asses, apes and dogs', Wordsworth describes a 'harpy brood' that attacks both 'Bard and Hero'. While Milton equates himself with the persecuted Latona who gave birth to Apollo and Diana, twin gods that suggest his twin treatises, Wordsworth describes his critics as a 'harpy brood' that are half predator-bird and half woman.

With such an image, Wordsworth implies that he, as a 'Bard', is in a position like Phineus from an episode in the Quest for the Golden Fleece. Given the gift of prophecy by Apollo and cursed for using this gift by Zeus, Phineus was beset, every time he attempted to eat, by harpies that defiled his food, leaving it so foul that no mortal would eat it. Like Milton's self-portrayal in sonnet 11 of a poet who attempts to provide truth and liberty, Wordsworth fashions himself as a seer, capable of prophesying truth that leads to liberty. Wordsworth also places his readers in a position to consider how he, like Milton's speaker in sonnet

11, prophesies the truth. This comparative image also has an economic significance. Beset by harpies that befoul his reputation, poetic characters and poems, Wordsworth's depiction suggests not only that these detractors plague his career, but also that parodists and critics render his works unfit for public consumption because they tamper with those works before they can be consumed. The image also suggests how critics tamper with the economics of his poetry, potentially ruining his capital gains from the sale of his works. These harpies seem to stand in the way of the poet reaping the benefits of his poetic truths. Ironically, however, in the case of 'Peter Bell', Wordsworth could attribute sales to that 'harpy brood'. To remain prominent in the public eye, Wordsworth needed the 'harpy brood' that his sonnet denigrates.

The second allusion to Milton's sonnet occurs when Wordsworth describes his hero Peter Bell as a 'Rover'. Besides using the proper name 'Rover', Wordsworth echoes the word 'roav', both from his own 'Peter Bell' and from Milton's sonnet 11: 'But from that mark how farr they roav, we see / For all this wast of wealth and loss of blood' (ll. 13–14). Milton chastises critics who 'still revolt when Truth would set them free' (l. 10), and choose 'License' instead of 'liberty', by, as John Shawcross points out, likening 'the people who think they aim at liberty by means of Civil War to wasteful archers whose arrows (rovers) miss their mark and merely wound their prey'.[43] Similar to Milton, Wordsworth suggests that his detractors have missed the mark with their criticisms of him and his characters. Correspondingly, Wordsworth's sestet begins, 'Heed not, wild Rover once through heath and glen, / Who mad'st the better life thy choice'. At the volta in his sonnet, he turns to address his 'Hero' Peter Bell directly and shifts the setting of the sonnet from the public responses of his critics to the seemingly private world of the poem 'Peter Bell'. Wordsworth's speaker urges his hero to ignore this brood of harpies and focuses instead on where Peter Bell has gone and will go.

Tellingly, the syntax of line 8 renders the meaning of the word 'once' slightly ambiguous. The word seems to imply that Peter Bell has already passed once through heath and glen; however, it also suggests a process, meaning that when he makes it through the heath, he should 'Heed not' this harpy brood. As a Rover, who has wandered and been once through an experience that has transformed him from a rogue to a more virtuous man, and as a character, who continues to grow as a portion of Wordsworth's larger poetic oeuvre, Peter Bell offers a character model for Wordsworth's readers – a model of progressive learning that would be undercut by only listening to Wordsworth's detractors. Like Peter Bell, Wordsworth suggests that his readers must pass 'once through heath and glen', make 'the better life [their] choice', and, once through, heed not the harpy brood. In this way, readers can progress forward into Wordsworth's poetic oeuvre.

Wordsworth's 'Rover' serves as a corrective surrogate for the roving license of his readers who have denigrated the type of moral and hermeneutic liberty that Wordsworth ascribes to this character's conversion and suggests is available through his poetic works.[44] Although Wordsworth creates a distinction between his detractors (in the octave) and his own private world of poetry (in the sestet), his sestet also suggests the manner in which his readers can become a part of this world, by following a path, like Peter Bell, through the heath and glen of his collected poems. Then, like Peter Bell, these readers will 'rejoice / In the just tribute of thy Poet's pen!' (ll. 13–14). Furthermore, like Milton and Sir John Cheek in sonnet 12, Wordsworth positions himself as a figure who introduces new learning into the land. Acutely aware that such learning is often responded to with hostility, Wordsworth offers a way for readers to identify with his work, through Peter Bell's conversion, and to evaluate his poetry against contemporary detractions of his poetry. Wordsworth's sonnet demonstrates the necessity of conjoining supplementary discourses about his poetry – like this sonnet – with contemporary discourses about the value of literature. By intermixing and juxtaposing his words with the language of his detractors, Wordsworth asserts the capacity his poetry has to absorb critics while also fostering a community of sympathetic readers. Such a hypothetical community, Wordsworth suggests, will come to appreciate why he finishes this sonnet, 'Lift up that grey-haired forehead, and rejoice, / In the just tribute of thy Poet's pen!'. They will grasp the reference to Peter's ass ears and rejoice with the poet who pens the often over-looked significance of Peter's transformation.

While Wordsworth's use of Milton's sonnets 11 and 12 offers his readers a dual perspective that sympathizes with and rejects contemporary readers, attentive readers might also recognize that Wordsworth's epigraph has drawn them towards the middle of Milton's sonnet sequence of twenty-three poems and invited them to look backwards and forwards. As Patrick Cook points out, '[m] odern criticism has increasingly discerned ordering patterns [in Milton's twenty-three sonnets], and there is growing acceptance of the idea that the sonnets constitute at least some kind of "intentional unit", if not a sequence planned from the start'.[45] For Wordsworth – an avid reader and imitator of Milton's sonnets, an expert sonneteer and a poet concerned with the arrangement of his poems – referring readers to the middle of Milton's sonnet sequence was no accident.[46] Wordsworth asks his readers to consider the placement of both Milton sonnets that he alludes to in the context of all twenty-three of Milton's sonnets, which trace Milton's youthful follies and ambitions, political involvements, subsequent blindness and continued sense of public duty.

Beyond prompting attentive readers to consider the relationship between Milton's twin sonnets and his series of sonnets, Wordsworth suggests that his own sonnet and the 'Miscellaneous Sonnets' in which it is grouped in 1820 are connected to the same tradition. Wordsworth did not publish 'On the Detraction' as a single piece. Instead, he organized the sonnet first within his 1820 *The River*

Duddon volume and then, a few months later, within the larger context of his 'Miscellaneous Sonnets', an ever-growing category that he first included as a section in his 1807 *Poems*. In Wordsworth's 1820 four-volume *Miscellaneous Poems*, 'On the detraction' is a part of a larger group of sonnets, which are, in turn, a portion of Wordsworth's larger poetic oeuvre. In the 1820 'Miscellaneous Sonnets', 'On the Detraction' appears eleven sonnets after 'To the Poet, John Dyer' – a tribute to the neglected genius of the 'Bard of the Fleece', a myth that Wordsworth aligns himself with, through his allusion to Phineas, in his sonnet to Dyer:

> Yet pure and powerful minds, hearts meek and still,
> A grateful few, shall love thy modest Lay,
> Long as the shepherd's bleating flock shall stray
> O'er naked Snowden's wide aerial waste;
> Long as the thrush shall pipe in Grongar Hill! (ll. 10–14)

Here, Wordsworth not only sets himself up as one of those 'grateful few' with a heart 'meek and still' who appreciates Dyer; he also, in relation to 'On the Detraction' sets himself up as a poet like Dyer, who seeks such a reception from a 'grateful few'.

More broadly, the sonnet form functions as a metaphor for Wordsworth's entire poetic works. At one point, Wordsworth conceived of modelling *The Prelude* according to the Petrarchan sonnet with fourteen books and a significant turn after book 8.[47] An astute practitioner and renovator of the sonnet tradition, Wordsworth's interest in the sonnet sheds light on how he organized his poems, how he opened his poems up to his readers, and how he attempted to revitalize and reform English literature. In answering Reynolds's 'Peter Bell' with a sonnet – embedded within his other sonnets, which are further embedded within the Miltonic tradition of sonneteering – Wordsworth demonstrates that the sonnet's 'scanty plot of ground' functions as an appropriate genre for engaging criticism. Wordsworth further suggests that his sonnet provides a fit space for a community of readers to join together, invest themselves in Wordsworth's larger poetic project and continue the labour needed to expand and connect together the parts of his poetic oeuvre. However, Wordsworth also would continue to guide that labour with the supplementary prose surrounding and within his poetic collections.[48]

In 'Peter Bell' Reynolds catches Wordsworth in the midst of his attempts to control the reception of his poetry. Besides showing his familiarity with reviewers' criticisms of Wordsworth's poetry, Reynolds's parody demonstrates his awareness of how Wordsworth employed his supplementary writings to manipulate the market. Wordsworth's poetic project proves itself vulnerable to parodic responses like Reynolds's because in the literary market readers – and not Wordsworth – must judge the validity of his supplementary statements about his unadulterated imagination, unlaboured labour and poetic simplicity in relation to the poems in his expanding collections. Perhaps even more than Reynolds's parody, Wordsworth's sonnet response to his detractors reveals how the success of his poetic collections turn on his ability to amalgamate his guiding prose discourse and network of poetry with reader's roving evaluations of what constitutes monumental literature. However, to prove the hypothetical power and lasting cultural value of his collected works, Wordsworth would need to convince readers that his poetic collections could reflect, absorb and participate meaningfully in shaping the tastes of the nation; and, as he laments in his 'Essay Supplementary', '*there* lies the true difficulty'.[49]

7 *THE RIVER DUDDON* VOLUME AND WORDSWORTH'S CANONICAL ASCENT

He has raised to himself a deathless monument of glory; he has fixed it as the land-mark of future ages, to show where the spirit of poesy remains enshrined, and the sensibilities of nature are consecrated; and while in his voyage down the stream of life toward the regions of immortality, his genius gathers glory as it proceeds, the bards of other times, who have so often been the themes of his praise and the subjects of his adoration, shall welcome him home to the everlasting temple of fame, as the brightest and the purest offering of Time to Eternity.[1]

1820 was a good year for Wordsworth's literary reputation.[2] He published the single volume *The River Duddon, a Series of Sonnets: Vaudracour and Julia and Other Poems. To which is Annexed, a Topographical Description of the Country of the Lakes, in the North of England*, the four-volume *Miscellaneous Poems of William Wordsworth* and a second edition of *The Excursion*.[3] Wordsworth's books of poetry were selling better than ever,[4] and, as Jeffrey Cox maintains, these publications came at a time when broad conceptions about a 'pantheon of living poets' were giving way to periodical debates and public lectures about canonizing a more select body of writers who defined the age.[5] Wordsworth's single-volume *The River Duddon* would solidify his place in that canon.

The River Duddon played a significant role in Wordsworth's designs to col-lect together all of his works and build his readership. Following the volume's title page, an internal 'Advertisement' printed on a half-title page announces: 'This Publication, together with the "Thanksgiving Ode", June 18, 1816, "The Tale of Peter Bell", and "The Waggoner", completes the third and last volume of the Author's Miscellaneous Poems'. According to this notice, *The River Duddon* rounds out Wordsworth's two-volume 1815 *Poems* and links together the three single-volume publications mentioned here with the 1815 *Poems*.[6] Furthermore, a few months after *The River Duddon* was published in late April 1820, its poems were absorbed into Wordsworth's expanded four-volume collection, which car-ries out the classification system from the 1815 *Poems*. It is partially because of this transitional publication history that *The River Duddon* has been so often overlooked by Wordsworth scholars.[7]

By contrast, Wordsworth's contemporary reviewers singled the volume out for particular praise, judging it to be the site of his aesthetic resurrection and the mark of his ascent towards lasting, literary prominence. The ultra-Tory *Blackwood's Edinburgh Magazine* led the way in styling Wordsworth as an essential, national poet for post-Waterloo Britain. In its May 1820 review of *The River Duddon*, *Blackwood's* John Wilson celebrates Wordsworth's Lake District genius, historical groundings, morality and political leanings. However, that May issue also recalls – in a separate parody featuring Wordsworth as a would-be contributor – his ironic dependence on *Blackwood's* as the pre-eminent reviewing engine responsible for positively altering his literary reputation and giving him access to the readership he had so long desired.

Alongside *Blackwood's* touting of Wordsworth, the miscellaneous arrangement of *The River Duddon* set the tone and trajectory for many positive reviews in the spring and summer of 1820. The volume begins with thirty-three sonnets – a form for which Wordsworth had often been praised since his 1807 grouping 'Sonnets Dedicated to Liberty' – followed by nearly twenty-eight pages of prose notes commenting on the sonnets. Those notes precede thirty-one narrative and lyric poems that lead to a lengthy, concluding prose 'Topographical Description of the Country of the Lakes'. Through its vacillating poetry and prose, the volume positions itself as a cultural treasure to be revered because of Wordsworth's uniquely situated and longstanding place in the Lake District. Particularly through his Duddon sonnets and extensive notes, Wordsworth maps Britain's heritage in the Lake District, juxtaposes the national significance of the Duddon with the Thames and prompts readers to trace the origin, progress and end of the Duddon from the mountains of the Lake District to the Irish Sea.

Reciprocally, the concluding 'Topographical Description' begins by situating readers in the Lake District, half-way between the peaks of Great Gavel and Scawfell mountains at the centre of an 'imaginary wheel' that encircles 'not fewer than nine' valleys, which radiate outward in all directions 'like the spokes from the nave of a wheel'.[8] This prose guide oversees the retrospective progress readers have made through Wordsworth's Duddon sonnets and reminds readers of how the connective, radiating 'spokes' of his miscellaneous volume can lead them to recover Britain's natural history. Through its forward and backward-looking poetry/prose form, the volume asserts the Lake District as the literary and moral seat of Britain, and identifies Wordsworth's collected works as the central prospect from which to view the nation's character. The four pages of advertisements that conclude the volume further invite readers to consider the significance of its interlocking poetic, geographic, historic, scientific and moral discourses. Although *The River Duddon* might seem an insular textual bridge, these advertisements link Wordsworth's collection with Britain's cultural viability as a treasury of traditional and naturally progressive knowledge that can bind together the nation.

Wordsworth's Periodical Value

The River Duddon was published less than four months after the government instituted six acts to quash journalistic and literary calls for political reform,[9] and in the midst of worries about socio-economic problems plaguing Britain's major industrial cities. Most notably, the nation was still reeling from the 'Peterloo Massacre' on 16 August 1819.[10] In the late summer and autumn of 1819, many British newspapers, magazines and periodicals condemned the police's bloody actions as one of the most horrific and shameful atrocities in England's history. Furthermore, as James Chandler notes, the Peterloo Massacre was reconstructed from these journalistic accounts 'in works like Shelley's *The Mask of Anarchy* and William Hone's *The Political House that Jack Built*, the latter alleged to have sold 100,000 copies by the end of the year (though this is almost certainly an inflated figure)'.[11] Even if this last number is a bit inflated, such high sales figures in such a short time reveal how deeply the Peterloo Massacre saturated the literary consciousness of writers and readers.

Chandler connects the historical self-consciousness of many literary writings about the Peterloo Massacre to his contention that

> English writing from 1819 is aware of its place in and as history. Much literary work *of* England in 1819, in other words, seems concerned with its place *in* England in 1819 – concerned that is with a national operation of self-dating, or – redating, that is meant to count as a national self-making, or – remaking.[12]

Chandler also argues that this 'intensely "hot" period in literary and political activity' was short-lived and led to a 'political reversal in 1820', articulated by politicians such as the newly elected George Canning who in a speech to his constituents on 18 March 1820 maintained that 'November 1819 and March 1820 effectively belonged to different "epochs" in the nation's history'.[13] Such a clear demarcation of historical difference in such a short period of time might seem hyperbolic, but the death of George III on 29 January 1820, coupled with the government crackdown at the end of 1819 and beginning of 1820, would have lent credence to Canning's bold statement.[14]

Curiously, the dramatic shift in the critical reception of *The River Duddon* versus Wordsworth's 1819 'Peter Bell' and 'The Waggoner' nearly mimics the abrupt sea change in British political history that George Canning posits. According to several reviews *The River Duddon* signals a new beginning, 'a poetical repentance', an 'ample atonement' that 'bursts upon us' not only as a new epoch in the history of his poetry, but as a new epoch in literary history.[15] The *European Magazine*'s assertion that the 'present volume is a welcome addition to [Wordsworth's] former productions', and the *Literary Chronicle*'s certainty – that 'the present volume possesses all the beauties and very few of the defects of this writer. We think it by far his best production' – signalled a wholesale reassessment of Wordsworth's reputation.[16] *Blackwood's* proclaimed, 'this author is a genuine English classic ... a pure and reverent worshipper of the true majesty of the English Muse', while the *British Review* maintained, 'we do really think that there is enough in the collection before us to fix the wreath upon his brows'.[17]

These reviews reveal a sometimes awkward, but resounding, transition between well-established critical jeers at the simple Wordsworth – enthralled by a wrong-headed system of poetry – and a growing certainty, expressed most dramatically in Joyce Gold's *London Magazine*:

> the native genius of Wordsworth. His palace is the edifice that was built on the rock; the winds came, and the floods descended, but it stirred not, for its foundation was of adamant. He has raised to himself a deathless monument of glory; he has fixed it as the landmark of future ages.[18]

Many other reviewers concurred with this assessment of Wordsworth's 'native genius', remarked on the unshakeable foundations of his poetry and declared that his work would endure to enrich future ages. While *Blackwood's* celebrated 'the solid and reposing grandeur of the main structure of [Wordsworth's] poetry', the *European Magazine* asserted that 'his poetry must, and will live; for it has an enduring principle of vitality within itself, which proclaims its origin, and will ultimately perfect its praise'.[19] Gold's *London Magazine* further declared that a 'code of morality ... [can be] read in the endless volume of external nature' described in his poetry. Origins and ends, vitality and endurance, morality and grandeur, self-reliance and perseverance, landmark and monument, the structure of his works and the literary canon – all coalesce in a series of reviews that echo many of Wordsworth's prose statements between 1814 and 1820 about the value of his collected works.

Wordsworth's ascent within the literary scene in 1820 was also noted in a fashionable magazine for women, the *Ladies Monthly Museum*, which showered praise on the 'brilliancy and pathos ... grandeur and a true simplicity' of the volume, celebrated Wordsworth's genius, which 'bursts upon us', and honoured him with the appellation 'the poet of nature'.[20] Speaking in superlatives, the conservative *European Magazine* went even further and heralded Wordsworth as 'beyond all comparison the most truly sublime, the most touchingly pathetic, the most delightfully simple, the most profoundly philosophical, of the poetical spirits of the age'.[21] Moreover, as noted above, conservative-leaning journals and magazines were not the only reviewing engines to proclaim Wordsworth's literary rise. The liberal-leaning *Monthly Review*, *Eclectic Review* and the year-old *Literary Chronicle and Weekly Review* all praised Wordsworth's volume.[22]

This widespread reappraisal of Wordsworth's reputation, genius and place in the literary canon also featured two pointed attacks on Wordsworth's most outspoken and long-standing critic, Francis Jeffrey of the *Edinburgh Review*.[23] Set up in large part as a political counter to the *Edinburgh*, *Blackwood's* in Wilson's May review roundly condemned Jeffrey's attacks and denounced 'the pertinacity of the wicked zeal with which [Wordsworth] has been persecuted'.[24] A month later, the more liberal-leaning Gold's *London Magazine* published its first review of Wordsworth's poetry and praised his 'humility' and fortitude while lambasting 'those aristocrats of literature, the Edinburgh Reviewers', who had attacked Wordsworth 'with all the bigotry of criticism'.[25] Each of these reviews challenges the *Edinburgh*'s long-standing influence on political and literary opinions, and Wordsworth's well-established position as the *Edinburgh*'s whipping boy made him the perfect vehicle from which to launch both of these partisan attacks.

Blackwood's support of Wordsworth and condemnation of Jeffrey's *Edinburgh* was of a piece with their already developed strategy in 1818 and 1819 for promoting their new periodical's pre-eminence and national value. As David Higgins shows in '*Blackwood's Edinburgh Magazine* and the Construction of Wordsworth's Genius', between 1818 and 1822 John Wilson's essays in *Blackwood's* frequently attack Jeffrey's *Edinburgh* and laud Wordsworth as a misunderstood genius whose reputation had been marred by prejudiced, partisan reviewers.[26] Though Wilson had criticized Wordsworth in two of his three articles about the poet in 1817, between 1818 and 1820 both Wilson and *Blackwood's* actively sought to correct negative assessments and redirect parodic responses about Wordsworth's egotism, simplicity and Lake District isolation.[27] *Blackwood's* contention that Wordsworth's particular genius had yet to receive its proper due gave them a new literary historical platform from which to tout the genius of their reviewing practices while denigrating other periodicals.[28]

In the May 1820 issue, Wilson (*aka* Christopher North) also included a parody that foregrounds *Blackwood's* capacity to play out Wordsworth's ambition to alter his reputation/readership. Wilson's review of *The River Duddon* follows a series of public elegies or '"Luctus" on the death of Sir Daniel Donnelly' (a popular Irish boxer allegedly knighted by George IV) submitted by contemporary authors including Byron, Scott and Wordsworth. These 'Luctus' are actually parodies manufactured by *Blackwood's* cohort of writers.[29] Wilson heads his two mock-Wordsworth poems – 'Extract from my Great Auto-Biographical Poem' and 'Sir Daniel Donnelly, a Ballad' – with a fictitious 'Letter from W. W. to Mr. Christopher North' that solicits publication in *Blackwood's*. In this letter Wordsworth disingenuously avows himself 'unapprised' of how periodicals influence the reading public, and he opportunistically offers his poems to

Blackwood's, seemingly unabashed at associating *The Prelude* – his long withheld autobiographical poem – with poetry about a celebrated Irish boxer:

> I therefore send you first, an Extract from my Great Poem on my Own Life, and it is a passage which I have greatly elaborated; – and, second, Sir Daniel Donnelly, a Ballad, which in the next edition of my works, must be included under the general class of 'Poems of the Imagination and the Affections'.[30]

North's Wordsworth follows this egotistical description of how he has absorbed Donnelly's recent public notice into his poetic collections by acknowledging

> that in seasons prior to this, I have transmitted to the Editors of divers periodical Miscellanies, small portions of large works, and even small works perfect in themselves; nor, would it be altogether inconsistent with those benign feelings which I am disposed to cherish towards your Miscellany, as a Periodical that occasionally aimeth at excellence.[31]

North charges that, given the opportunity, Wordsworth has, will and must rely on the very culture of periodical 'Miscellanies' that he has so often condemned in his supplementary prose.[32] Accordingly, much of the letter unfolds his mock-Wordsworth's convoluted praise of *Blackwood's* as a singular magazine that has often commended and only occasionally criticized his poetry and prose.

The letter also implies that *Blackwood's* periodical form and the form of Wordsworth's emerging collections have more in common than the 'real' Wordsworth might readily admit. North's Wordsworth asserts that *Blackwood's* should not be judged according to its individual monthly issues, which often feature multiple, serialized essays. Instead, 'to form a philosophical, that is, a true character of a work published periodically, it behoveth a man to peruse the whole series of the above-mentioned work seriatim, that is, in continuous and uninterrupted succession'.[33] This section of the letter pokes fun at Wordsworth's supposed concern about how readers will reconcile *Blackwood's* positive review essays about him with its occasional essays that criticize him. North's Wordsworth attempts to square these diverse voices of 'many shades' by stipulating that readers should evaluate *Blackwood's* comprehensively as a developing structure that requires extended, connective reading over its many issues. Any judgement based on abbreviated reading will 'greatly err' – a claim that North's Wordsworth awkwardly extends to erroneous judgements based on a limited 'knowledge of any work'. However, North's Wordsworth then quickly qualifies this generalization: '(that is, a periodical work, for indeed it is of such only that it can be so predicated,)'.[34] This parenthetical turn portrays Wordsworth as checking himself before fully revealing his thinly veiled defence of *Blackwood's* as a defence of how to read his own accumulating poetic collections. In other words, judging *Blackwood's* solely by one of its reviews of Wordsworth is as erroneous as judging Wordsworth's poetry by 'small portions of [his] large works'.[35] This tongue-in-cheek attack on Wordsworth's egotism also suggests that Wordsworth must acknowledge, however begrudgingly, that *Blackwood's* miscellaneous form and diversity of voices extend, validate and actualize the connective designs and habitual reading practices promoted in Wordsworth's aggregated collections.

Blackwood's parodic engagement with Wordsworth was not limited to its periodical pages. A year earlier in late June 1819, John Gibson Lockhart published an anonymous, single-volume ninety-six-page parody titled *Benjamin the Waggoner*.[36] Much like Reynolds's pre-emptive 'Peter Bell', Lockhart's parody responds to an advertisement in the *London Literary Gazette* on 22 May 1819 for Wordsworth's forthcoming *Benjamin the Waggoner*. Lockhart's *Benjamin the Waggoner* is much less a treatment of Wordsworth's *Waggoner* volume (published three weeks previously) than an extension of Reynolds's, Wordsworth's and the review culture's attention to multiple 'Peters' that spring.[37] Lockhart's extensive introduction and voluminous endnotes book-ending his 'Benjamin the Waggoner' poem present Wordsworth as completely obsessed with those very reviews and parodies.

Purportedly written by a young literary enthusiast, Lockhart's introduction unfolds an extensive conversation between his narrator and an unnamed Wordsworth who happens to sit across from him while travelling south by coach from Penrith towards London. Over the course of stopping at an inn and changing horses, they exchange sympathetic opinions about the worthlessness of 'malignant, malevolent, malicious critics' and the difficulties of reconciling personal and national politics.[38] In the midst of these discussions poking fun at Wordsworth's overblown self-assurance and rampant insecurity, Wordsworth reads aloud from his well-perused copy of Jeffrey's *Edinburgh*, which savages Wordsworth's 1807 *Poems*. Following this critical redaction, Wordsworth receives a package from his booksellers that includes a copy of Reynolds's 'Peter Bell' and informs him that the parody has amused the public, positively influenced sales of 'Peter Bell' and rendered the original 'Peter Bell' publicly indistinguishable from its parody. When initially looking over Reynolds's parody, Wordsworth appears unable to suppress 'a smile', but that bemused smile turns to rage as he reads to the end where he is killed off with the following promise: '"Never more will trouble you, trouble you"' (l. 227).[39] Wordsworth reacts to this parodic attack, identity theft and his figurative death in the literary market by vowing to inform the public of the truth. After declaring, 'the object of my journey [to London] is fruitless for the present', he quickly hires a post-chaise so that he can return to the Lake District and 'strike out something new' (l. 227). Before leaving, however, he throws his London-bound *Benjamin the Waggoner* manuscript into a fireplace. The narrator, who rescues this partially burned manuscript, first entertains publishing it as his own before finally deciding to publish it with the foregoing

'Introduction'. With such a counterfeit, Lockhart wryly announces his ensuing poem as Wordsworth's rejected work.

The capacious notes that follow Lockhart's poem further portray Wordsworth as a chatty editor and critic who obsequiously pays homage to *Blackwood's* writers for their positive reviews and sustained defences against the negative press besetting his publications.[40] If *Blackwood's* appears as his 'friend' and literary champion, Wordsworth shows himself to be its most ardent supporter and promoter – 'all hail!'. Lockhart's Wordsworth is preoccupied with his imminent fame and *Blackwood's* capacity to bring his poetry to a new public understanding and market share: 'N. B. Blackwood's Magazine contains the only true criticism of Peter Bell and all my works'.[41] Reciprocally, Lockhart's Wordsworth thanks the 'Gentleman' of the *Edinburgh* 'for [their] hostility' because their criticisms have played a significant part in turning *Blackwood's* into his champion. He also thanks *Blackwood's* for creating a medium through which readers can access and understand his poetry. On two occasions he gratefully defers to *Blackwood's* explanatory power. In reference to lines from 'Peter Bell' about the 'countenance' of 'mosques and spires', Wordsworth admits: 'I hardly know what to say about this. – I had best leave it to Blackwood, who will try and explain it in his next. – I confess I am at a loss'. A page later, he submits that if 'any doubt should exist about the meaning of any other line on my work, a note addressed to Mr. Blackwood will be sure to be attended to, and will meet with an explanation *of some sort*'.[42]

In 'The Dead Asses: A Lyrical Ballad' (published in early August 1819), J. H. Reynolds continues Lockhart's mock assurances of Wordsworth's reliance on the press and intimacy with the reading public by foregrounding a newspaper advertisement from which his parodic Wordsworth has developed another sequel to 'Peter Bell'.[43] Reynolds's Wordsworth assures readers that the following newspaper extract 'relates a simple fact, and it will acquaint [them] that my Poem has for its argument, (as a Writer, scarcely my inferior, hath it,) "an ower true tale"'. Wordsworth all too favourably compares his new work to the market value of the wildly successful novelist/poet Sir Walter Scott while publicly congratulating himself over the fact that he has grounded his poem on a current event, which he thinks will immediately interest readers:

> On Friday last two Donkies were found in Joiner's Woods, tied with chaise-reins to the shrubs, completely starved to death, having devoured every edible substance within reach. It is supposed that they were stolen, and fixed by some villains, who have since apprehended, and consequently left the wretched animals to perish thus miserably'.
> *New Times*, Wednesday, July 21, 1819.[44]

Beyond the grotesque and laughable subject matter in Reynolds's poem, which mocks the donkey in Wordsworth's 'Peter Bell' as well as Coleridge's and Wordsworth's literary relationship, this parody maintains that Wordsworth –

the poet who avowed himself uninterested in pleasing the 'Public' in his 1815 'Essay Supplementary' – will capitalize on any means to bring his poetry within the notice of the broader reading public. Reynolds also relates his Wordsworth's obsession with becoming popular with the poet's continual (asinine) efforts to market his poetry through touristic appeals to the Lake District. Accordingly, he includes a footnote to the following lines which situate the donkey of his tale, 'pacing on the green, / Which skirts the road that leads you down / From Ambleside to Keswick-town' (stanza 23). Reynolds's footnote reconfigures Wordsworth's footnote from the 1800 *Lyrical Ballads*: 'At no great distance from this very spot, rises Great How, a single and conspicuous hill, and the scene of an elegant ballad called "Rural Architecture"'.[45] Likened at the end of the poem to one of these dead asses, Reynolds's Wordsworth has completely consumed the Lake District to which he has so long been tied; having long since emptied the region of its poetic resources, this 'Recluse' has starved (stanza 33).[46]

In direct contrast to Reynolds's ridiculing of Wordsworth's past and present Lake District marketeering, in *Blackwood's* November 1819 issue the Irish poet William Maginn lauds Wordsworth's insistence on historical continuity. Instead of satirically attacking Wordsworth's poetry, *Blackwood's* arch-satirist Maginn uses Wordsworth's poem 'Yarrow Unvisited' as a parodic vehicle. Maggin juxtaposes Wordsworth's 'Yarrow Unvisited' – printed on the left side of the page – with his own 'Don Juan Unvisited' – printed on the right side of the page.[47] A preliminary note to the editor also imitates Coleridge's preface 'Of the Fragment of Kubla Khan' as a means to poke fun at the *Quarterly Review*, which has put the anonymous author to sleep, awoken him when he dropped one of its issues on his foot, and seemingly inspired him to create the ensuing dialogue with 'Yarrow Unvisited'. Maginn's work appropriates Wordsworth's poem, first published in his 1807 *Poems*, and redirects the parodic energy surrounding Wordsworth's twelve-year-old volumes towards a new end in a periodical age headed by *Blackwood's*.

'Don Juan Unvisited' excoriates radical and Whig authors, publishers and politicians. Maginn carries out these attacks on corrupting political and literary figures through a broad condemnation of Byron's proposed serialization at the end of canto 2 of *Don Juan* (1819, stanza 216). Against these satirical targets, Maginn implies *Blackwood's* serial integrity and continual affirmations of Britain's character and historical continuity. Maginn's split-page charges that Byron's new serialization will be detrimental to the reading public's moral character; 'Be Juan then unseen, unknown!'. 'Don Juan Unread' also catalogues the popular works that Byron had published previous to *Don Juan* and admits *Blackwood's* previous mistaken judgements: 'we followed cloven-foot / As faithfully as any' (ll. 5-6). In contrast to this evil, 'cloven foot' depiction of Byron and his forthcoming cantos, the left side of the page suggests that Wordsworth's accumulating collections, mediated by *Blackwood's*, can facilitate the connective workings of the national mind.[48] Maginn's use of Wordsworth's poem recalls how Wordsworth serially extended 'Yarrow Unvisited' in his 1815 *Poems* by following it with 'Yarrow Visited', a poem which recounts Wordsworth's tour of the Scottish river in 1814 with *Blackwood's* emerging 'Ettrick Shepherd James Hogg'.[49] Much like the 'silvery current [which] flows / With uncontrolled meanderings' (ll. 9–10) but which keeps 'a course of lively pleasure' (l. 78) in 'Yarrow Visited', Wordsworth's poetic designs manifest a natural, guiding integrity for *Blackwood's* that falls outside of London politics and publishing and which stations readers in a healthy process of serial reading that intertwines the past and the present.

Gazing Back Over *The River Duddon*

From Wordsworth's perspective, such parodic attention was not unwelcome. As early as 1817, Wordsworth had begun to draw courage from the review culture's continued attention to his poetic reputation. In a letter to the poet Samuel Rogers in 1817, he playfully advises, 'Why don't you hire somebody out to abuse you? ... For myself, I begin to fear that I should soon be forgotten if it were not for my enemies.'[50] In *The River Duddon* volume, Wordsworth sharpens his engagements with such 'enemies' in several poems that play on the press surrounding his recent publications. The sonnet 'On the Detraction which Followed the Publication of a Certain Poem', which Wordsworth placed near the middle of the volume, and the following sonnet, 'On Seeing a Tuft of Snowdrops in a Storm', maintain Wordsworth's humility and perseverance in the face of his critics. Furthermore, as Jalal Khan argues, 'The Pilgrim's Dream, or the Star and the Glow-Worm', which appears six poems earlier, lauds the Lake District and plays out an 'allegory of the relationship between Wordsworth and his critics such as Byron, Jeffrey, and Wilson'.[51] In these poems, Wordsworth invites readers to weigh the opinions of his critics against the poet's perseverance and poetic beauties enfolding those opinions. Wordsworth's sustained attention to these detractors also recalls how their criticisms of his poetry have ironically contributed to his recent market success and, potentially, to the broader success of *The River Duddon* volume.

The volume's opening sonnet sequence and concluding prose guide set the terms for how to celebrate Wordsworth's imminent cultural ascent. Particularly in the guide, Wordsworth's vision appears all-encompassing as he stations himself high up in the mountains of the Lake District overlooking the topographical beauties and natural treasures that the landscape has to offer. Through his meticulous attention in the guide to the numerous paths by which tourists can travel into the region, Wordsworth suggests that all roads lead to the Lake District. To illustrate that point, Wordsworth imaginatively joins readers with him on a cloud half a mile above the mid-point between the Great Gavel and Scawfell mountains. Floating above this 'central point', Wordsworth maintains that he and his readers will be able to consider virtually any path for exploration. As he looks out towards the Irish Sea, where the last river Duddon sonnet concludes, and over the surrounding 'plain country', Wordsworth remarks:

> there is – in the several ridges that enclose these vales, and divide them from each other, I mean in the forms and surfaces, first of the swelling grounds, next of the hills and rocks, and lastly of the mountains, an ascent of almost regular gradation, from elegance and richness, to their highest point of grandeur and sublimity.[52]

This ascent from 'swelling grounds' to 'hills and rocks' and 'mountains' telescopes the journey that Wordsworth asks readers to imagine as they pass from beautiful outlying areas, through picturesque ridges, to the sublime grandeur of the highest mountains in the Lake District. That sublime prospect also recalls the progress of Wordsworth's readers who have traversed the *Duddon* volume and poetically traced the origins and ends of his Lake District poetry.

On the half-title page preceding the guide, Wordsworth explicitly describes the retrospective relationship between prose and poetry that animates the volume:

> This Essay, which was published several years ago as an Introduction to some Views of the Lakes, by the Rev. Joseph Wilkinson, (an expensive work, and necessarily of limited circulation,) is now, with emendations and additions, attached to these volumes; from a consciousness of its having been written in the same spirit which dictated several of the poems, and from a belief that it will tend materially to illustrate them'.[53]

As the note points out, the guide 'illustrates' much of the geographical, botanical and historical information informing the volume's poetry, but none more so than the opening thirty-three sonnets. The guide looks back on these sonnets and evokes the collection's poetic and topographical beginnings in the mountains of the Lake District. Furthermore, instead of asking readers to intermittently read prose notes about individual poems, Wordsworth leads readers from a sonnet series originating in and gazing back on the Lake District towards a comprehensive prose guide about the Lake District.[54] In fact, given the amount of prose in the volume, it is difficult to tell which has more authority or significance, the poetry or prose.[55]

Much like the guide, Wordsworth begins the Duddon sonnets from an imagined mountain prospect, which an introductory prose note on the half-title page connects to the origin of the river Duddon 'rising upon Wrynose Fell' in the mountains of Cumberland, Westmoreland, and Lancashire.[56] Reviewers widely admired Wordsworth's multi-faceted treatment of the Lake District and particularly lavished praise on the volume's 'gem ... a set of Sonnets on the River Duddon'.[57] This sonnet series provided Wordsworth and his reviewers with a place, form and style through which they could proclaim the excellence of his poetry and pronounce his ascendance as a national treasure. The sonnets chart Wordsworth's fictional day-long journey from the origin of the river in the mountains of Cumberland to its end, the Irish Sea, while also – as Stewart Wilcox maintains – presenting the Duddon 'as a humble English river, signifying the life-span of an ordinary Englishman'.[58] In these sonnets Wordsworth traces the descent of the river and aligns its twists and turns with his own life, poetic journey, recovered histories of the region and efforts to educate his readers. During his excursion, which details geographic changes and prospect views that mark the poet's descent from the mountains, Wordsworth pays deference to the tradition of topographical river poetry, probes the mythological and geological place of the Duddon in Britain's past, relates his own life to the life of an ordinary Englishman and ties the significance of his pilgrimage to the continued health of the nation. The sonnets and their notes provide readers with the historical, philosophical, economic, geologic and mythological justifications for understanding the region not just as a tourist destination, but as a monument that grounds the nation's shared character.[59]

The sequence can be divided loosely into three groups of eleven sonnets with two injunctions which create a turn from one group to the next: 'On, Loitering Muse!' (sonnet 12); and 'Sad Thoughts, Avaunt!' (sonnet 13).[60] The first sonnet pays tribute to and separates the geographic and literary origins of Wordsworth's river sequence from Horace's 'rocky spring / Bandusia' in Rome, 'the moist marge of Persian fountains', and more recent eighteenth-century treatments of 'Alpine torrents thundering' (ll. 2, 6, 7). While sonnet 3 features the poet fancifully pondering, 'How shall I paint thee', in sonnet 2 he muses on a pre-history for the region when giant deer called the Leigh once roamed near the river. This vacillation between present contemplation and distant conjectures about the region's past animates the first group of eleven sonnets as the poet encounters shifting, natural forms and reflects on the human activities that have marked and been erased by the river's course. Although in sonnet 2 the Duddon appears as an entity apart from human activity – 'remote from every taint / Of sordid industry' (ll. 1–2) – in sonnet 5 the river shows itself to distinctly influence the lives of the rural inhabitants around it. As the poet descends from the mountains along the river's twisting path and relates his present observations, fancies, mythical projections and reflections on human life, love and mortality, he describes the river as less a clear record of history and more 'a soft record' that 'function[s] to heal and restore / To soothe and cleanse, not madden and pollute' (sonnet 8, ll. 13–14). In this first section of the sequence, Wordsworth aligns his poetry with that healing power and describes his poems as a necessary supplement that serves as a 'speaking monument' for all that has been erased or gone unrecorded in the region (sonnet 3, l. 3).

The next sonnet grouping (sonnets 12–22) explores the open prospects (sonnet 13) that reveal themselves to the poet's mind after the river disappears from sight into a 'wilderness' (sonnet 14, l. 12). Wordsworth's mind ranges from conjectures about a 'Statue' placed in a 'deep chasm' (sonnet 15) to Native

American myth-making about the deluge (sonnet 16) to fancies about a Danish raven, a Roman eagle and Druids (sonnet 17). In the midst of these historical imaginings, he considers what remains in the face of change and celebrates how a guide such as the river Duddon commingles with tributaries and still retains its independent character. Although the Duddon changes its 'temper' as it flows on (sonnet 20, l. 11), the river remains connected with its origins just as Wordsworth's childhood memories of the Duddon have stayed with him (sonnet 21). Wordsworth centres this developmental creed on sonnet 18, 'Seathwaite Chapel', and its accompanying fifteen-page end-of-series note about the Reverend George Robert Walker who died at ninety-three in 1802. In this elegiac 'Memoir', Wordsworth celebrates Walker's exemplary moral, religious and economic roles in Seathwaite and holds him up as the kind of ideal national character that permeates his collection.

Wordsworth also demonstrates how his poetry, much like the river Duddon in sonnet 19, has absorbed and been absorbed by other tributaries. The 'Postscript' following the Duddon sonnets renders this theme explicit by acknowledging Wordsworth's debt to Coleridge's unwritten 'rural poem, titled "The Brook"' as the chief source for his Duddon sonnets. Reciprocally, Wordsworth enjoins Coleridge to write 'The Brook' in response to his sonnets. The postscript also points out that the Duddon sonnets trace and connect together Wordsworth's own poetic tributaries:

> the above series of Sonnets was the growth of many years; – the one which stands the 14ᵗʰ was the first produced; and others were added upon occasional visits to the Stream, or as recollections of the scenes upon its banks awakened a wish to describe them.[61]

Wordsworth's explanation of why he placed the first sonnet he composed near the middle of the series reminds readers of how his careful poetic designs set up a progressive narrative that intermingles memory, imagination, identity, form and continual return to this region.

The closing section (sonnets 23–33) details the river's final movements towards the Irish Sea, and sonnets 31 and 32 juxtapose the Duddon and the Lake District with the national significance of the River Thames. Thematically, these eleven sonnets are concerned with liberty and freedom, forgiveness and thanks, progress and ends through the bonds that 'loosely' and joyfully tie the poet to the Duddon (sonnet 29, l. 9). The final poem, titled 'Conclusion' and later renamed 'Afterthought', particularly encourages readers to look forwards and backwards through Wordsworth's volume in order to retrace his geographical, literary and historical descent from the mountains of Cumberland to the Irish Sea. 'Conclusion' also prompts readers to connect the poet's expansive gaze to the continued progress and health of the British nation:

I THOUGHT of Thee, my partner and my guide,
As being passed away. – Vain sympathies!
For *backward*, Duddon! as I cast my eyes,
I see what was, and is, and will abide;
Still glides the Stream, and shall for ever glide;
The form remains, the Function never dies;
While *we*, the brave, the mighty, and the wise,
We Men, who in our morn of youth defied
The elements must vanish; – be it so!
Enough, if something from our hands have power
To live, and act, and serve the future hour;
And if, as tow'rd the silent tomb we go,
Thro' love, thro' hope, and faith's transcendent dower,
We feel that we are greater than we know.

'Conclusion' has been read by several twentieth-century scholars as an intimation of the poet's immortality and as a hope that his poetry – 'something from our hands' – will survive his death.[62] More recently, Benjamin Kim and James Garrett each have argued that the poem articulates Wordsworth's conception of nationhood through his figurations of the local.[63] Wordsworth's 'backward' gaze in line three aligns the bibliographic layout and miscellaneous form of the volume with the projected national significance of his collection.

In the first two lines the poet tracks the river west as it empties into the Irish Sea. As it does so, it becomes a part of a large body of water composed of many other tributaries. While that emptying provides the poet with an intimation of his immortality, it also suggests his view of how the Duddon sonnets and, by extension, his entire volume progress from his watchful eye into the print market. These two lines enable the poet to station himself and meditate on the reception of his volume. Then, in line three he turns his head and gazes back over the river, through space and time, towards its origins in the mountains of the Lake District. Bibliographically, that backward gaze moves in two directions. First, the poet looks back over the thirty-two preceding sonnets towards the origins of the river and of his poetry in the mountains of sonnet 1. That backward look over his sonnets, however, is also a forward look towards the imagined mountain prospect at the end of the volume which oversees the concluding prose guide. While Wordsworth uses this dual textual gaze to link together the beginning and end of his collection, that backward and forward look further invites readers to associate his work with other publications that seek to advance the reading public's knowledge of Britain's natural and – from his perspective – most significant and enduring cultural heritage.

Wordsworth articulates that web of connections in three interrelated ways. The first involves the history of his publications, the second his antipathy to London's cultural domination and the third his efforts to advertise his poetic collections as a multiform national treasure. Wordsworth repeatedly associates the concept of reading backward and forward in *The River Duddon* volume with a return to his earlier publications in verse and prose – a connective narrative movement that the anonymous author of 'The Nose-Drop' (1821) tried to flatten. 'The Nose Drop: A Physiological Ballad by the Late W. W.' was published in the *Academic*, a Liverpool-based periodical. Its parodic 'Preface by the Author' and eighty-two-line poem look back on *Lyrical Ballads* as the beginning of a calculated and ridiculous pastoral fiction and not as the treasured geographic origin of Wordsworth's poetic ascent toward lasting fame.[64] Together, the preface and poem tie Wordsworth's views of the Lake District in his 'Preface to Lyrical Ballads' (1800) to *The River Duddon* volume.[65] One footnote in the poem further plays on that textual relationship by poking fun at Wordsworth's note which precedes the Duddon sonnets: 'Wrynose Moor is situate on the confines of Cumberland, Westmoreland, and Lancashire: the RIVER DUDDON, "of which I sung one song that will not die", rises upon it.'[66] This parodic echo jeers at Wordsworth's efforts to equate the topographical origins of the River Duddon with the origins of his own poetic power.[67] Both the poetry and prose of 'The Nose Drop' mock Wordsworth's claims of geographic and moral preeminence and scoff at his efforts from his preface to *Lyrical Ballads* to *The River Duddon* to philosophize about and evaluate British culture by way of his seemingly idiosyncratic experiences in the Lake District. This parody broadly imitates Wordsworth's efforts in his opening sonnet series and concluding prose guide to contiguously align his twenty-year-old Lake District vision.

Moreover, through the preface's focus on Wordsworth's Lake District obsession and denigration of London city life, 'The Nose Drop' recalls Wordsworth's endeavours to dissociate *The River Duddon* and his previous publications from books concerned with London and the nation's urban culture. In his 1820 volume the two Duddon sonnets preceding the 'Conclusion' portray London's river Thames as culturally and morally suspect in comparison with the Duddon's humble history, geography and poetic value.[68] The turn between the last line of sonnet 31 about the Thames – 'With Commerce freighted or triumphant war' – and the first four lines of sonnet 32 particularly juxtapose the Thames's unsettling political and economic history with the 'radiant progress' of the Duddon:

> But here [on the Duddon], no cannon thunders to the gale;
> Upon the wave no haughty pendants cast
> A crimson color; lowly is the mast
> That rises here, and humbly spread the sail;

This comparison, however, reveals points of connection as well as departure. The end of sonnet 31 portrays the Duddon with 'sovereign Thames allied' (l. 12). Sonnet 32 styles this alliance of rivers as an absorptive process in which the Thames's history intermingles with the Duddon and the poet as they leave behind

> ... each tumultuous working ...
> At seemly distance, to advance ...
> Prepared in peace of heart, in calm of mind
> And soul ... (sonnet 32, ll. 11–14).

Carried into the final sonnet, the nation's vast historical freight appears 'to mingle' and 'advance' with the poet's reflections on 'Eternity' (sonnet 32, l. 14). As his 'partner and [his] guide', which he contends can never pass away, the Duddon provides a 'Form' that remains in memory (ll. 1, 6) and which continues to function in the historical present through '*we*, the brave, the mighty, and the wise' – a series of modifiers translated from Moschus's 'Lament for Bion' that Benjamin Kim convincingly glosses as 'the brotherhood of men who are properly guided by the love of national independence'.[69]

The four pages of advertisements at the end of the volume broaden Wordsworth's imaging of a shared national heritage and consciousness defined outside the parameters of London's river Thames. Wordsworth joins his volume to thirty-eight advertised books marketed to provide the public with a general education that will develop their capacities to appreciate, evaluate, classify and cultivate the most salient parts of Britain's rural character. These advertisements broaden the geographic and intellectual scope of Wordsworth's collection by linking it with the current dissemination of knowledge about Britain's natural treasures.[70] As the title to these advertised books declares – 'New Works on Botany, Gardening, Agriculture, Geology, Minerology, Philosophy, &c' – the books encompass all of these subjects, and several also deal with tourism, entomology, natural history and pharmacology.[71] The books are all publicized as introductions to or primers on a given subject, and each title is followed by a one or two sentence description. For example, after the first title in the list – *An Introduction to the Study of Physiological and Systematical Botany* – the description reads:

> The Plan of this Work is to render the Science of Botanical Arrangement as well as the general Structure of the Anatomy of Plants accessible, and in every Point eligible for young Persons of either Sex, who may be desirous of making this elegant and useful Science a Part of their Education or Amusement.[72]

Whether a treatise on botany, a book about geology that explains 'the easiest Methods of discriminating Minerals, and the Earthy Substances, commonly called Rocks',[73] or a primer on animals, 'comprising the Characters of the whole Genera, and of the most remarkable Species, particularly those that are Natives of Britain; with the principal circumstances of their History and Manners'[74] – these books are devoted to the education of the public and focus on the historical recovery, scientific analysis, moral appreciation and cultivation of the natural world in Britain.

Unsurprisingly, some of the most common words in these advertisements are 'arrangement', 'structure', 'class', 'anatomy', 'methods', 'branches', 'collecting', 'delineations', 'observations', 'discriminating', 'system', 'cataloguing', 'index', 'principles' and 'classification'. In the midst of this nomenclature, references to Carl Linnaeus's classification system of the natural world and to the Linnaean Society in England appear several times. The book list is also divided into its own Linnaean classification system, which separates scientific knowledge into closely related branches and, on several occasions, links those branches to the arts. Such connections are made explicit in the book *A Familiar Introduction to the Arts and Sciences*, rendered poetic in *A Geological Primer in Verse*, and played out in several other book descriptions where scientific knowledge is associated with the reading public's general education, amusement, historical awareness and capacity to collect together and cultivate Britain's natural treasures. The description of *The Naturalist's Pocket Book; or Tourist's Companion*, for instance, announces the book as 'a brief Introduction to the different Branches of Natural History, with approved Methods for collecting and preserving the various Productions of Nature'.[75] These advertised works suggest that British culture can be discovered, appreciated and propagated by applying the principles and classification systems in these books to first-hand observations of its countryside.

Although these thirty-eight books were published by Longman, they need not have been advertised with Wordsworth's volume. Their inclusion at the end of the volume, however, suggests that Wordsworth's collection can be classed in relation to these books. How exactly is not stated, but *The River Duddon* features many of the general principles that unite these books: the recovery, classification and dissemination of knowledge; the collection and appreciation of Britain's natural heritage; the education of the public; and the preservation and advancement of culture.

The anonymous review of *The River Duddon* in Gold's *London Magazine* figures a similar, radial scope for Wordsworth's volume. The review begins with a brief sketch of three different schools or 'systems' of poetry, canonized in the previous two centuries by the shifting market tastes of the reading public. This reviewer describes Wordsworth as 'the great founder' and 'literary sovereign' of the fourth school, who has 'hand[ed] us the intellectual telescope, and in bidding us behold the far-off glories of the country that were before seen darkly through the vista of the fancy, he stands alone, unapproachable and unrivaled'.[76] According to this reviewer, Wordsworth's poetry has a descriptive and figurative power that enables readers to see a great distance. His poetry brings distant objects in the 'country' into focus and activates readers' imaginative capacity to see anew the 'far-off glories of the country'. From this perspective, Wordsworth's volume signals a new beginning not only for Wordsworth – 'who stands alone' – but for 'us' – a beginning that necessitates considering how Wordsworth's poetic system, though still, as this reviewer maintains, 'in embryo' – meaning the initial plant contained in the seed – will gradually cultivate and be cultivated by readers who nurture that embryo into a garden that will 'diffuse [its] fragrance around'.[77]

This backward- and forward-looking, quasi-scientific and quasi-organic evaluation of the effects that Wordsworth's genius will have on present and future readers plays on Wordsworth's own articulations about the role of poetry, the Lake District and British history in *The River Duddon* volume. Measured against the political, economic and social eruptions marking post-Waterloo Britain, Wordsworth's miscellaneous volume offers a composed prospect and a historical continuum on which to centre Britain's past, present and future identity. For Wordsworth, the prospects in and of *The River Duddon* represent the prospects of the nation.

Postscript

Following the publication of *The River Duddon* and his *Ecclesiastical Sonnets* (1822), Wordsworth's reviewing critics and general poetry readers widely began to consider him as a moral, religious and philosophical educator whose poetry acts as a guide for how to live, learn and grow. By the mid-1820s Wordsworth began to receive numerous solicitations to include his poetry in publications that were previously unavailable, such as the literary *Keepsake*, which published a few of his poems in 1829. By 1831, his collections also were adapted into *Selections from the Poems of William Wordsworth, Esq. Chiefly for the Use of Schools and Young Persons*.[78] Before any of these successful market miscellanies, however, the prolific chapbook publisher James Kendrew published *The Little Maid and the Gentleman; or, We are Seven. Embellished with Engravings* (1820). The appearance of this chapbook suggests a great deal about Wordsworth's new mass cultural value for children and adults.[79]

Nearly four inches high and just over two inches wide, this chapbook, with eleven woodcut engravings, devotes one image per page to Wordsworth's 1798 *Lyrical Ballads*' poem. The final page features the last lines of 'We are Seven' recounted by the adult – 'The little Maid would have her will, / And said, "Nay, we are seven!"' – and provides an image of a man walking by himself in nature while reading a book. This man appears to represent the adult speaker in the poem, who has ended his conversation frustrated by the little girl because she seemingly cannot or will not grasp how death separates the living from the dead. However, the end of this dialogue, which foregrounds the man's aggravation and inability to understand the girl's continued intimacy with her dead siblings, is offset by his solitary walk with a book. Perhaps, he carries one of Wordsworth's books, and perhaps he contemplates the last lines of his own story. If so, as the man walks in nature, reading about the nature of human beings, he takes with him the parodic mark of his interaction with the child and the weight of his own thoughts. This story, his story, suggests that anyone can find a place in Wordsworth's multi-voiced and multivalent poetry – somewhere between the little man and the little girl, between life and death, materialism and idealism, high sincerity and parody. This chapbook plays out a new beginning for Wordsworth's poetry in 1820 – one in which his poetry would be collected as an educational tool for children and adults. Correspondingly, Wordsworth would come to be regarded as a national icon whose works centre a connective wheel of self-knowledge that radiates outwards from his Lake District home and guides the progress of the nation.[80]

NOTES

Introduction

1. I use the word 'poetic' to suggest that Wordsworth's collections involve readers in exploring recursive and progressive depths to his poems, created through interactions and overlaps between verse and prose.
2. The next section of the introduction details these three contexts.
3. See G. Genette's *Seuils*, translated in English as *Paratexts: Thresholds of Interpretation* (Lincoln, NE: University of Nebraska Press, 1997), which refers to any text outside of but also attached to the text proper – whether a title, dedication, preface, epigraph, footnote, endnote, advertisement, appendix or glossary. Genette broadly describes a paratext as any text outside of but also attached to the text proper. Although I alternately use the words paratext and supplement, the latter was the term used by Romantic period writers.
4. See J. Cox, 'The Living Pantheon of Poets in 1820', in J. Chandler and M. N. McLane (eds), *Cambridge Companion to British Romantic Poetry* (New York: Cambridge University Press, 2008), pp. 10–34.
5. Though I will have occasion to mention Wordsworth's single-volume *The White Doe of Rylstone* (1815), *Thanksgiving Ode, January 18, 1816 with Other Short Pieces* (1816), *Peter Bell: A Tale in Verse* (1819), and *The Waggoner; A Poem to which are Added Sonnets* (1819), I will not examine their contents and organization closely in this study.
6. In *Wordsworth and the Worth of Words*, ed. J. Kerrigan and J. Wordsworth (Cambridge: Cambridge University Press, 1987), Hugh Sykes Davies argues that Wordsworth's repetition of words not only defines his poetic style; 'it involved his whole future development as a writer ... the effects of repetition and apparent tautology were not by any means necessarily confined to particular poems, or to short passages in the longer poems. On the contrary, they naturally tended to extend their influence from poem to poem, over the whole range of his writing – even to his prose', p. 46.
7. P. Magnuson, *Reading Public Romanticism* (Princeton, NJ: Princeton University Press, 1998).
8. In Clifford Siskin's terms in *The Historicity of Romantic Discourse* (New York: Oxford University Press, 1988), Wordsworth asks his readers to be receptive to the concept of a projected whole Wordsworthian oeuvre based on its 'origin in the poet's mind and the other tendency in his completed work. Their co-relativity lies in their extra-Textuality, the text they both comment on being the Poem that is Wordsworth's completed oeuvre', p. 114.

9. Chapter one in *The Historicity of Romantic Discourse* points out how influential this revisionary aesthetic has been on our contemporary conceptions of genius and developmental tales of growth. One could argue that to study Wordsworth's poetic development is to study the concept of revision. In 'Revision as Making: *The Prelude* and Its Peers', in R. Brinkley and J. Hanley (eds), *Romantic Revisions* (Cambridge: Cambridge University Press, 1992), pp. 19–42, J. Wordsworth maintains that for Wordsworth '[r]evision was responsibility', p. 21. T. Kelley's *Wordsworth's Revisionary Aesthetics* (New York: Cambridge University Press, 1988) deals at length with Wordsworth's conception of revision as an excavation of the beautiful and the sublime, which Kelley traces through several of Wordsworth's prose pieces about landscapes and aesthetics.

10. Figure 1.1 in J. Raven's *The Business of Books: Booksellers and the English Book Trade, 1450–1850* (New Haven, CT: Yale University Press, 2007), p. 8, illustrates this publishing spike in Britain, which in 1800 nearly doubled the titles published in 1775. Furthermore, as A. Piper maintains in *Dreaming in Books: The Making of the Bibliographic Imagination in the Romantic Age* (Chicago, IL: University of Chicago Press, 2009), this increase in books and bookish forms – in poetry and prose – correlates closely with 'the rising social prominence of a number of bibliographically oriented individuals: not just authors, but also editors, translators, booksellers, printers, librarians, critics, and bibliographers all assumed an elevated professional status', p. 8. J. Klancher's '"Wild Bibliography": The Rise and Fall of Book History in Nineteenth-Century Britain', in I. Ferris and P. Keen (eds), *Bookish Histories: Books, Literature and Commercial Modernity, 1700–1900* (New York: Palgrave Macmillan, 2009), pp. 19–40, draws attention to a 'new bibliographical book history' emerging around 1800 that involved British readers in considering 'title pages, editions, publication dates, or lurid tales of violent Bibliomaniacal collecting passions in weekly or monthly magazines, [and] encouraged [readers] to *study* the bibliographical realm as a mode of public and … modern knowledge', p. 22. On the subject of how new bibliographic presentations of authorship in the second half of the eighteenth century 'ensured that readers understood the idea of "the author" in newly intimate and rarified ways', p. 46, see P. Keen, "Uncommon Animals: Making Virtue of Necessity in the Age of Authors', in Ferris and Keen's (eds), *Bookish Histories*, pp. 41–60.

11. See D. Wu, *Wordsworth's Reading, 1770–1799* (Cambridge: Cambridge University Press, 1993).

12. Arguably the heated critical responses, in the last third of the eighteenth century, to J. Macpherson's *Ossian* poems and T. Chatterton's 'Rowley' poems inaugurated these close, often sceptical, inquiries into how poetry collections are made. However, around the turn of the century, such questions about the nature and validity of poetic making were more often couched within political terms, exemplified in the recurring 'Arts' or poetry section of the government watchdog the *Anti-Jacobin; or Weekly Examiner*, a weekly publication that ran from November 1797 to July 1798. Such arguments about the national role of poetry were also couched within broader claims about the value of 'literature' and the material book in a revolutionary era of writing and reading. The essays in I. Ferris's volume 'Romantic Libraries', Romantic Circles Praxis Series (February 2004), at <http://www.rc.umd.edu/praxis/libraries/> [accessed 1 August 2011], detail many of these concerns with reading habits and the physical standing of books, and P. Keen's collection of primary texts in *Revolutions in Romantic Literature: An Anthology of Print Culture, 1780–1832* (Peterborough, Ontario: Broadview Press, 2004) demonstrates how often the meaning of 'literature' was publicly debated during this period and how many writ-

ers self-identified this age as one unparalleled in mass publishing, reading, writing and reviewing. See in particular I. D'Israeli, 'Preface to *An Essay on the Manners and Genius of Literary Character*' (1795), in Keen (ed.), *Revolutions*, pp. 110–12, and the anonymous essay 'On the Characteristics of Poetry' in the *Monthly Review* (1797), pp. 179–81.

13. As P. Garside and A. Mandell show in their Poetry vs Fiction, 1780–1829 graph in 'Producing Fiction in Britain, 1800–1829', *Romantic Textualities: Literature and Print Culture*, 1 (August 1997), available online at <http://www.romtext.cf.ac.uk//articles/cc01_n01.html> [accessed 5 July 2011], fiction output was on the rise in the Romantic period, though poetry output continued to exceed fiction until the late 1820s. In 'Romantic Poetry: Why and Wherefore?', in S. Curran (ed.), *Cambridge Companion to British Romanticism* (New York: Cambridge University Press, 1993), Curran suggests an intriguing, empirical connection between the approximately five thousand books of original verse published between 1789 and 1824 and his contention that poetry 'mattered to this age in a way that it has never mattered since' (p. 218). In the more recent *Cambridge Companion to British Romantic Poetry*, Cox broadens Curran's evaluative scope to 1770–1835 and points out that 'there were more than 4,000 writers producing poetry' (Cox, 'The Living Pantheon of Poets in 1820', p. 14). Curran and Cox both draw on statistics from J. R. de Jackson (ed.), *Annals of English Verse 1770–1835: A Preliminary Survey of the Volumes Published* (New York: Garland, 1985). Garside and Mandell compare these poetry statistics with A. Block's *The English Novel 1740–1850* (1939, rev. 1961; London: Dawson, 1968), which they take issue with and Garside revises in his two-volume *English Novels 1770–1830: A Bibliographical Survey of Prose Fiction Published in the British Isles* (Oxford: Oxford University Press, 2000).

14. I draw on J. McGann's *The Textual Condition* (Princeton, NJ: Princeton University Press, 1991), which describes 'textuality' as a 'laced network' of bibliographic 'typefaces, bindings, book prices, page format, and all those textual phenomena usually regarded as (at best) "peripheral" to poetry, linguistic texts, and paratexts', p. 13.

15. For Ravens's disagreements with the emphasis St Clair places on this 'watershed' moment, see Raven, *The Business of Books*, pp. 231–2.

16. See also M. Rose, 'Literary Property Determined', in D. Finkenstein and A. McCleary (eds), *The Book History Reader* (New York: Routledge, 2002), pp. 231–40, reprinted from *Authors and Owners: The Invention of Copyright* (Cambridge, MA: Harvard University Press, 1993).

17. By contrast, new single-author books of poetry became more expensive after 1774. See L. Erickson, 'The Poet's Corner', in *The Economy of Literary Form* (Baltimore, MD: Johns Hopkins University Press, 1996), pp. 19–48 and W. St Clair, 'Selling, Prices, and Access', in W. St Clair, *The Reading Nation in the Romantic Period* (Cambridge: Cambridge University Press, 2004), pp. 186–209.

18. St Clair, *The Reading Nation*, pp. 128, 486, 138. This 'Old Canon' of poetry consisted 'alphabetically, of Samuel Butler, some works of Chaucer, Collins, Cowper, Dryden, Falconer, Gay, Goldsmith, Gray, Milton, Pope, Shakespeare, Spenser, Thomson, and Young' (p. 128). These authors' poems became widely available just before the Donaldson decision through Hugh Blair's forty-three volume *The British Poets* (1773) published by Kincaid in Edinburgh. Then, following John Bell's one-hundred plus volume edition of *The Poets of Great Britain* (begun in 1778 and published in Edinburgh), London publishers countered with Samuel Johnson's *The Lives of the Most Eminent English Poets* (1779). In *The English Common Reader*, 2nd edn (Columbus, OH: Ohio State University Press, 1998), R. Altick singles out John Cook and John Harrison's editions of

British poets as the cheapest and most widely read at the end of the eighteenth century. For more information on this process of anthologizing and canonization, see chapter 7 in St Clair's *The Reading Nation*, pp. 122–39. Notably, although the 'Old Canon' was published frequently and cheaply until 1808 when copyright was extended to twenty-eight years, making such publications more expensive, St Clair argues that this canon of poets continued to predominate until the middle of the nineteenth century when the works of many Romantic poets came out of copyright restrictions and a new process of canonization began.

19. On Wordsworth's shifting concerns with literary property and copyright, see P. M. Zaul, 'Wordsworth and the Copyright Act of 1842', *PMLA*, 70 (1955), pp. 132–44, S. Eilenberg, *Strange Power of Speech: Wordsworth, Coleridge, and Literary Possession* (New York: Oxford University Press, 1992) and L. Erickson's chapter 'The Egoism of Authorship', in *The Economy of Literary Form*, pp. 49–69. Wordsworth was one of the few writers during this period who retained his copyrights, so he and his family stood to benefit from the 1842 act, which extended copyright to forty-two years or the life of the author plus seven years. More recently, T. Owens's 'Wordsworth, Galignani, and the Aesthetics of Piracy', *Library*, 12:1 (2011), pp. 23–36, examines Wordsworth's anxieties about pirated French editions of his 1828 *Poetical Works*, which he thought undercut his sales in Britain. Owens argues that Wordsworth responded to Galignani's single-volume editions of his *Poetical Works* with his own single-volume edition in 1845, which mimicked and attempted to improve on the French publisher's less expensive, double-column format in order to appeal to a broad readership for his poetry created by those very pirated editions.

20. W. J. B Owen's 'Costs, Sales, and Profits of Longman's Editions of Wordsworth', *Library*, 12 (1957), pp. 93–107, details the print runs, sales, costs and profits of Wordsworth's publications from the 1798 *Lyrical Ballads* to his 1835 *Guide Through the District of the Lakes*. Wordsworth was often frustrated by the process of marketing and selling his books of poetry, particularly when his print runs did not sell out.

21. W. Wordsworth, *Lyrical Ballads*, ed. R. L. Brett and A. R. Jones, 2nd edn (New York: Routledge, 1991), pp. 7, 243.

22. Percy was one of only a few editors given permission under the 'high monopoly Period' (1710–74) to produce a collection of reprinted ballads (St Clair, *The Reading Nation*, p. 345).

23. The endnote has a more extensive history than the footnote, which A. Grafton in *The Footnote: A Curious History* (Cambridge, MA: Harvard University Press, 1997) traces back to the English Catholic Richard White of Basingstoke's *Historiarum libri ... cum notis antiquitatum Britannicarum* (1597–1607). At the end of the seventeenth century, scholars began to cross-reference multiple printed versions of classical texts in order to check their textual integrity and historical validity. Such methods of textual scholarship necessitated a new kind of paratext that could clearly divide source text from editorial commentary while at the same time placing that text and its commentary in closer dialogue than an endnote could. For a seminal, albeit teleological discussion, see E. Eisenstein, *The Printing Press as an Agent of Change*, 2 vols (New York: Cambridge University Press, 1979), vol. 1, pp. 72–3.

24. In the first few decades of the eighteenth century, the uses for and prevalence of the footnote expanded dramatically as classical and then vernacular textual authority was debated in relation to England's literary heritage. Previously in England, prose notation, which commented on a host text, was predominantly limited to Anglican exegesis of the

bible or to glossators writing in the margins of culturally note-worthy texts. Of course, annotation to vernacular texts did exist before this period. The headnotes to individual poems in R. Tottel's *Songes and Sonettes* (London, 1557) reveal a distinctive editorial presence organizing the reception of this grouping of poems. A prime example of sixteenth-century marginal annotation appears in E. K.'s glosses in E. Spenser's *Shepheardes Calendar* (London, 1579).

25. In Milton's *Paradise Lost. A New Edition, by R. Bentley D.D.* (London: Printed for Jacob Tonson, 1732), Bentley's elaborate footnotes 'correct' numerous aspects of Milton's poem – errors that in his preface Bentley falsely attributes to the faulty work of a previous editor. For an extended discussion of Bentley's editorial practice in relation to other editing practices in the eighteenth century, see M. Walsh, *Shakespeare, Milton, and Eighteenth-Century Literary Editing* (Cambridge: Cambridge University Press, 1997).

26. A. Pope, *The Dunciad. In Four Books, Printed according to the Complete Copy Found in the Year 1742, with the Prolegomena of Scriblerus, and the Notes Variorum* (London: Printed for M. Cooper at the Globe in Pater-noster-row, 1743).

27. E. Young's *Conjectures on Original Composition* (London, 1759) is arguably the earliest treatise on this subject. For an astute engagement with constructions of creative genius in relation to the explosion of professional and 'hack' writers in the second half of the eighteenth century, see J. Brewer, *The Pleasures of the Imagination* (New York: Farrar Straus Giroux, 1997).

28. In their introduction to *The Poems of Ossian and Related Works* (Edinburgh: Edinburgh University Press, 1996), F. Stafford and H. Gaskill point out that – even though Macpherson's *Fragments of Ancient Poetry* was published in June 1760, *Fingal* was published in December 1761, reissued in a second edition one month later and followed by *Temora* in March 1763 – it was only in 1765 that the two-volume *Works of Ossian, The Son of Fingal* appeared in an affordable octavo edition, pp. v–xxvi.

29. See T. Chatterton, *Poems, Supposed to have been Written at Bristol, by Thomas Rowley, and Others, in the Fifteenth Century; the Greatest Part Now First Published from the Most Authentic Copies, with an Engraved Specimen of One of the Mss* (London: Printed for T. Payne & Son, at the Mews-Gate, 1777).

30. This line of argumentation draws on M. Levinson's 'Background' chapter in *The Romantic Fragment Poem: A Critique of Form* (Chapel Hill, NC: University of North Carolina Press, 1986), pp. 28–59, and A. Ferry's claims and material inquiries in *Tradition and the Individual Poem: An Inquiry into Anthologies* (Stanford, CA: Stanford University Press, 2001). For a list of public documents circulated in various attempts to denounce or validate Macpherson's and Chatterton's works, see Levinson's note number 14, pp. 237–8.

31. Levinson, *The Romantic Fragment Poem*, p. 37.

32. In his revised 1773 edition, Macpherson complicated these authorial issues by drawing further attention to his role as an author-editor who has significantly reorganized the poems into a history and expanded the textual apparatus surrounding 'Ossian's' translated texts (Gaskill (ed.), *The Poems of Ossian*, pp. xxii).

33. M. Russett, *Fictions and Fakes: Forging Romantic Authenticity, 1760–1845* (Cambridge: Cambridge University Press, 2006), p. 37.

34. In *The Making of Percy's Reliques* (Oxford: Oxford University Press, 1999), N. Groom contends that Percy 'restored the ballad its dignity by placing it in the evolving canon of English literature. He gave minstrels a voice, ballads a pedigree, and English literature a heritage', pp. 104. For more on Percy's literary relationship with Macpherson, see Groom's chapter 5, pp. 61–105.

35. Quoted from T. Percy, *Reliques of Ancient English Poetry Consisting of Old Heroic Ballads, Songs, and Other Pieces of our Earlier Poets (Chiefly of the LYRIC kind.) Together with Some Few of Later Date* (London: Printed for J. Dodsley in Pall-Mall, 1765).

36. Quoted from T. Percy, *Reliques of Ancient English Poetry*, 4th edn (London, 1794), I., pp. xvii.

37. Notably, in the 1800 'Preface' Wordsworth uses Percy's edited version of 'The Children in the Wood' to ground his argument about 'a mode of false criticism' that has produced wrong-headed parodies of simple language.

38. Wordsworth's interest in Percy's apparatus should be weighed against P. Murphy's broader contention in *Poetry as an Occupation and an Art in Britain, 1760–1830* (New York: Cambridge University Press, 1993), that '[a]lmost every Romantic collection of ballads contains a preface that works out a literary history which begins with the romance', p. 147.

39. I reference the following editions in the remainder of this section: C. Smith, *Elegiac Sonnets, and Other Essays. By Charlotte Smith of Bignor Park, in Sussex*, 2nd edn (Chichester: Printed by Dennett Jacques, and sold by Dodsley, Gardner, Galdwin, and Bew, London, 1784); C. Smith, *Elegiac Sonnets, and Other Poems, by Charlotte Smith*, 9th edn (London: Printed For T. Cadell, Jun. and W. Davies in the Strand, 1800); C. Smith, *Beachy Head: With Other Poems, by Charlotte Smith* (London: Printed for the Author: and sold by J. Johnson, St Paul's Church-Year, 1807); R. Burns, *Poems, Chiefly in the Scottish Dialect by Robert Burns* (Kilmarnock: Printed By John Wilson, 1786); R. Burns, *Poems, Chiefly in the Scottish Dialect, by Robert Burns, In Two Volumes, A New Edition, Considerably Enlarged* (Edinburgh: Printed for T. Cadell, London, and William Creech, Edinburgh, 1794); E. Darwin, *The Botanic Garden; A Poem in Two Parts, Part I. Containing the Economy of Vegetation. Part II. The Loves of the Plants. With Philosophical Notes* (London: Printed for J. Johnson, St Paul's Church-Yard, 1791); S. T. Coleridge, *Poems on Various Subjects, by S. T. Coleridge, Late of Jesus College, Cambridge* (London: Printed for G. G. and J. Robinsons, and J. Cottle, Bookseller, Bristol, 1796); S. T . Coleridge, *Poems by S. T. Coleridge, Second Edition. To Which are Now Added Poems by Charles Lamb, and Charles Lloyd* (Printed by N. Biggs, for J. Cottle, Bristol, and Messrs. Robinsons, London, 1797); R. Southey, *Joan of Arc. An Epic Poem* (Printed by Bulgin and Rosser, for Joseph Cottle, 1796); R. Southey, *Poems by Robert Southey* (Printed by N. Biggs, for Joseph Cottle, Bristol, and G. G. and J. Robinsons, London, 1797); R. Southey, *Poems by Robert Southey, the Second Volume* (London: Printed for Biggs and Cottle, for T. N. Longman and O. Rees, Paternoster-Row, 1799); W. Scott, *Minstrelsy of the Scottish Border, Consisting of Historical and Romantic Ballads Collected in the Southern Counties of Scotland*, 2nd edn, 2 vols (Edinburgh: Printed by James Ballantyne, for Longman and Rees, Paternoster-Row, 1803); *The Lay of the Last Minstrel, A Poem: The Eighth Edition With Ballads And Lyrical Pieces* (London: Printed for Longman, Hurst, Rees, and Orme, Paternoster-Row, and A. Constable & Co. Edinburgh; by James Ballantyne & Co. Edinburgh, 1810); T. Moore, *Corruption And Intolerance: Two Poems with Notes, Addressed to an Englishman by an Irishman* (London: Printed for J. Carpenter, Bond-Street, 1809).

40. M. Butler, 'Culture's Medium: The Role of the Review', in Chandler and McLane (eds), *The Cambridge Companion to Romanticism*, pp. 120–47, on p. 129. In this essay, Butler also contends that many of Darwin's readers 'would begin to read the upstaged poem ['The Economy of Vegetation'] for its footnotes, rather than the other way around – a reader-response Darwin presumably hoped for', p. 129.

41. Quoted from *Collected Letters of Samuel Taylor Coleridge*, ed. E. L. Griggs, 6 vols (Oxford: Clarendon Press, 1956–71), vol. 1, p. 412. For more on typography in the 1798 *Lyrical Ballads*, see A. Boehm, 'The 1798 *Lyrical Ballads* and the Poetics of Late Eighteenth-Century Book Production', *ELH*, 63:2 (Summer 1996), pp. 453–87.

42. Furthermore, as Klancher maintains, Coleridge's typographical requests and bibliographic enthusiasm tell of a more widespread late eighteenth-century exuberance that 'extended to the physical form of the book, the history of printing, the accrediting of its invention, its development and dispersion' ('"Wild Bibliography"'), p. 26.

43. Coleridge did not attach prose supplements to the sections featuring poetry by Lloyd and Lamb.

44. In his 'Introduction to the Sonnet' section, Coleridge traces the lineage of his 1796 effusions, repackaged as sonnets, to 'Charlotte Smith and William Bowles who first made the sonnet popular among the present English: I am justified therefore by analogy in deducing its laws from *their* compositions' (p. 71). His subsequent 'deductions' about Smith's and Bowles's sonnet forms, tones, subject matter and popularity arise as much from their accumulating prose supplements, as from their expanding sonnet collections.

45. Coleridge, *Poems on Various Subjects*, p. 244.

46. Ibid., pp. 185–6.

47. On at least one occasion, this note directly led to someone purchasing Wordsworth's 1793 publications. In a letter to Reverend H. F. Cary, Anna Seward confesses that Coleridge's 'assertion, in a note, page, 88, of the unrivalled powers, among the poets of the present day, of Wordsworth's muse in poetic essentialities, induced me instantly to send for his poems ... [Wordsworth's] was a name that I had not heard of ... This superiority which Coleridge assigns to [his poetry], is just as founded as the asserted superiority of Schiller and Shakespeare' (*Letters of Anna Seward*, ed. W. Scott, 6 vols (Edinburgh, 1811), vol. 6, p. 2).

48. 'Preface' to *Joan of Arc. An Epic Poem* (Bristol: Printed by Bulgin and Rosser, for Joseph Cottle, 1796), p. vi.

49. Coleridge, *Poems on Various Subjects*, p. xi.

50. Southey, *Poems by Robert Southey* (1797), p. 145.

51. Murphy, *Poetry as an Occupation and an Art in Britain*, p. 142.

52. S. T. Coleridge, *Coleridge: The Critical Heritage*, ed. J. R. de Jackson (New York: Barnes & Noble, 1970), p. 112.

53. For an informative discussion of the relationship between writer and reader in the Romantic prose preface, see J. Nabholtz, *'My Reader, My Fellow Laborer': A Study of English Romantic Prose* (Columbia, MI: University of Missouri Press, 1986).

54. Few Romantic period scholars have attempted to describe how the supplementary writings interspersed throughout Wordsworth's collections shape and publicize the process of reading his poetry. D. Duff offers a rare example of a scholar who deals expressly with a series of Wordsworth's paratexts in 'Paratextual Dilemmas: Wordsworth's "The Brothers" and the Problem of Generic Labeling', *Romanticism*, 6:2 (2000), pp. 234–52. Magnuson's *Reading Public Romanticism* is the only book-length study that I have come across about a variety of Romantic paratexts, including several of Wordsworth's supplements.

55. See A. Franta, 'Wordsworth's Audience Problem', in A. Franta, *Romanticism and the Rise of the Mass Public* (New York: Cambridge University Press, 2007), pp. 55–75, Franta reads Wordsworth's 1802 'Preface to *Lyrical Ballads*' and 1815 'Essay Supplementary to the Preface' together in order to demonstrate how Wordsworth, by 1815, had begrudgingly changed the reciprocal terms of his *Lyrical Ballads* engagement between poet and

readers by acknowledging the growing, unaccountable, and yet necessary power readers had over the immediate and long-term reception of poetic publications.

56. J. Heffernan's contention in 'Mutilated Autobiography: Wordsworth's *Poems* of 1815', *Wordsworth Circle*, 10:1 (Winter 1979), pp. 107–12 that 'Wordsworth himself *was* finished in 1814', typifies this evaluation, p. 110.

57. Even though Wordsworth wrote more poetry after his 1807 *Poems* than before, most critics (Romantic, Victorian and twentieth century) have argued that after 1807 Wordsworth's poetry was damaged by his roles as critic and editor of his poetry collections. In 'Peter Bell The Third', Percy Shelley portrays this shift as a change from a liberally, imaginative poet to a Tory and Anglican sympathizer, and Matthew Arnold, in his essay on 'Wordsworth' from his preface to *The Poems of Wordsworth* (1879), describes it as growing 'poetic baggage' (*Matthew Arnold's Essays in Criticism*, ed. K. Allott (New York: J. M. Dent & Sons, 1964), p. 299). Many twentieth-century critics have followed suit, including H. W. Garrod in *Wordsworth: Lectures and Essays*, 2nd edn (Oxford: Clarendon Press, 1927); W. L. Sperry in *Wordsworth's Anti-Climax* (Cambridge, MA,: Harvard University Press, 1935); C. C. Hamilton in *Wordsworth's Decline in Poetic Power: Prophet into High Priest* (New York: Exposition, 1963); and G. Hartman in *Wordsworth's Poetry, 1787–1814* (Cambridge, MA: Harvard University Press, 1964). Hartman takes an interest in Wordsworth's later career in *The Unremarkable Wordsworth* (Minneapolis, MI: University of Minnesota Press, 1987), and P. J. Manning in *Reading Romantics: Texts and Contexts* (New York: Oxford University Press, 1990) has headed a renewed scholarly interest in the poetry and poetic collections of the later Wordsworth. Most recently, in *Wordsworth and the Writing of the Nation* (Burlington, VT: Ashgate, 2008), J. Garrett examines how Wordsworth's classification system and construction of his collections from 1815 to 1820 relate to the English census, map-making and museum culture.

58. Most prominently, critics have remarked on the disjunction between the poetic theories articulated in the 'Preface to *Lyrical Ballads*' (1800/2) and the poems that follow it. In *The Hidden Wordsworth* (New York: W. W. Norton, 2000), pp. 532–4, K. Johnston provides a brief but concise summary of what critics have understood to be the purposes, challenges, and failings of the 'Preface'.

59. In Chapter 4 I will closely examine one such instance from F. Hodgson's review of the 1815 *Poems* in the *Monthly Review*. Hodgson interrupts his own remarks on Wordsworth's 'Essay Supplementary to the Preface' with this readerly appeal: 'We beg permission to subjoin to this extraordinary passage, as we cannot help considering it, the following still more extraordinary quotation and note ... That note we also subjoin: it alludes to "The Horn of Egremont Castle" and the well known "Goody Blake and Harry Gill"', quoted in Woof (ed.), *William Wordsworth: The Critical Heritage, Vol. 1: 1793–1830*, pp. 458–9.

60. A. Bennett, *Wordsworth Writing* (Cambridge: Cambridge University Press, 2007), p. 4. The *Cornell Wordsworth* series of Wordsworth's poetic productions reveals more about Wordsworth's writing process than ever before by providing detailed histories and facsimile copies of Wordsworth's manuscript revisions and published poetry from his earliest poems to his last.

61. Magnuson, *Reading Public Romanticism*, p. 6.

62. N. Fraistat's chapter, which maps out the 'Field' of the 1798 *Lyrical Ballads*, in *The Poem and the Book* (Chapel Hill, NC: North Carolina University Press, 1985), offers a rare example of this kind of attention to Wordsworth's poetic collections.

63. N. Trott's 'Wordsworth and the Parodic School of Criticism', in S. Jones (ed.), *The Satiric Eye* (New York: Palgrave Macmillan, 2003), pp. 71–98, is a pointed and notable exception. Referring to the year 1819, Trott even quips, 'It is as though the whole frame of Wordsworth's reception has become parodic', p. 90.

64. While in their introduction to *Romantic Parodies, 1797–1831* (London: Farleigh Dickinson University Press, 1992), D. Kent and D. R. Ewen contend that 'Wordsworth was the Romantic poet most widely parodied by his contemporaries', p. 17, J. Strachan maintains in his introduction to *Parodies of the Romantic Age*, 5 vols (London: Pickering & Chatto, 1999), vol. 2, that, according to 'our bibliographical researches, the most parodied authors of the Romantic period would appear to be Byron, Scott and Wordsworth', p. xiv.

65. G. Stones, 'The "Vile Art" of Romantic Parody', *Wordsworth Circle*, 27:2 (Spring 1996), pp. 87–95, on p. 88. In a previous essay, 'Parody and the *Anti-Jacobin*', *Wordsworth Circle*, 24:3 (Summer 1993), pp. 162–6, Stones also echoes Kent and Ewen's explanation in their introduction to *Romantic Parodies*: 'Generally, critics of Romanticism have continued to ignore the swarms of imitative poets and poems populating the period, in part because the traditional assessment of parody as a low, insignificant literary form does persist, but also because – and it is a corollary to the first reason – parody is still seen as a parasite on the host of creative literature', pp. 14, 162.

66. M. Gaull's 'Romantic Humor: The Horse of Knowledge and the Learned Pig', *Mosaic*, 9 (1976), pp. 43–64, arguably drew the earliest close attention in the twentieth century to the significance of parody in the Romantic period.

67. G. Dyer's *British Politics and the Politics of Style, 1789–1832* (Cambridge: Cambridge University Press, 1997) has led the way in reconsidering the significance of satiric subgenres during the Romantic period, including parodic satire. See particularly chapter 1, 'The Scope of Satire, 1789–1832', pp. 8–38.

68. The three most influential studies of reading, reception, publishing and authorship during the Romantic period – Altick's *The English Common Reader*, J. Klancher's *The Making of English Reading Audiences, 1790–1832* (Madison, WI: University of Wisconsin Press, 1987) and St Clair's *The Reading Nation* – do not provide extensive analyses of the forms and impact of parody on writers and readers. The same also holds true for T. Rajan's *The Supplement of Reading* (Ithaca, NY: Cornell University Press, 1990), which is concerned with the spaces carved out for readers in Romantic poems, and studies about the lingering after-presence of the author, such as A. Bennett, *Romantic Poets and the Culture of Posterity* (Cambridge: Cambridge University Press, 1999). In *Reading, Writing, and Romanticism: The Anxiety of Reception* (Cambridge: Cambridge University Press, 2000), L. Newlyn does devote several pages to parody, though parody plays only a small part in her larger argument about the Romantic period as a particularly troubled time for writers, which prompted many of them to develop defensive and offensive rhetorical strategies to engage with an unpredictable reading public. However, Newlyn's chapter on 'Wordsworth', pp. 91–133, and the section 'Poetry-Prose Dialogue and Parody', pp. 186–93, have greatly influenced the arguments in this book. More recently, in *Romanticism and the Rise of the Mass Public*, Franta contends that this collective anxiety in the Romantic period 'announces the advent of an era' – a regime of publicity that prompted poets, in particular, to 'consider literature's importance for creating groups that cannot readily be identified in terms of shared interests or identities', pp. 2, 15.

69. In *Wordsworth's Profession: Form, Class, and the Logic of Early Romantic Cultural Production* (Stanford, CA: Stanford University Press, 1997) T. Pfau brings many of the

concerns articulated in the note above about Romantic period authors and readers to bear on Wordsworth's struggles with a shifting, and largely unknowable, reading public. He particularly cites *Lyrical Ballads* as a new paradigm of literary experience that focuses on a plausible demographic community and a worthy audience of readers, stimulated 'to a degree of hermeneutic vigilance almost unprecedented in English Literature, with the possible exception of Milton and Blake', p. 182. M. Schoenfield's *The Professional Wordsworth: Law, Labor, and the Poet's Contract* (Athens, GA: University of Georgia Press, 1996) adds to this analysis of Wordsworth's potential readers by fleshing out his position as a '*professional* poet who found himself competing with other professional producers of ideology for the ability to shape the marketplace of ideas', p. 7. In *Wordsworth and the Writing of the Nation*, Garrett argues that Wordsworth's poetic collections after 1815 reflect his conflicted desires about how to preserve, account and speak for the nation.

70. In the last few decades, several Romantic period scholars have examined the dialogic nature of Wordsworth's poetry and his attempts to construct the role of his readers. See particularly D. Bialostosky, *Making Tales: The Poetics of Wordsworth's Narrative Experiments* (Chicago, IL: University of Chicago Press, 1984); Klancher, *The Making of English Reading Audiences*, ch. 5, pp. 135–71; M. Macovski, *Dialogue and Literature: Apostrophes, Auditors, and the Collapse Of Romantic Discourse* (New York: Oxford University Press, 1994); G. K. Thomas, 'The Lyrical Ballads Ode: "Dialogized Heteroglossia"', *Wordsworth Circle*, 20:2 (1989), pp. 102–6; Newlyn, *Reading, Writing, and Romanticism*, 'Wordsworth' chapter, pp. 91–133; and M. Baron, *Language and Relationship in Wordsworth's Poetry* (New York: Longman Group, 1995). Notions of Romantic irony and 'doubleness' also inform H. Glen's *Vision and Disenchantment: Blake's Songs and Wordsworth's Lyrical Ballads* (New York: Cambridge University Press, 1983) while in *Wordsworth's Bardic Vocation* (London: Palgrave Macmillan, 2003), R. Gravil probes potentially, parodic narratives and tonal turns directed at readers of *Lyrical Ballads*.

71. M. Jones, 'Parody and Its Containments: The Case of Wordsworth', *Representations*, 54 (Spring 1996), pp. 57–79, on p. 72. For example, in his letter to Francis Wrangham on 7 November 1806, Wordsworth declines to contribute to Wrangham's 'proposed [satirical] publication', expresses a desire that Wrangham destroy some of Wordsworth's earlier manuscript attempts at satire, and declares, 'I have long since come to a fixed resolution to steer clear of personal satire; in fact, I never will have anything to do with it as far as concerns the *private* vices of individuals on any account; with respect to public delinquents or offenders I will not say the same; though I would be slow to meddle even with these' (*The Letters of William and Dorothy Wordsworth, 1806–1811*, ed. E. de Selincourt, rev. M. Moorman, 8 vols (Oxford: Clarendon Press, 1969), vol. 2, p. 89. See also Wordsworth's third 'Essay on Epitaphs' as well as his low ranking of satire amidst the poetic kinds described in his 1815 'Preface'.

72. S. Simpkins's assessment of Wordsworth's *Fenwick Notes* in 'Telling the Reader What to Do: Wordsworth and the Fenwick Notes', *Reader*, 26 (1991), pp. 39–64, offers a good example of critics who describe his prose as a controlling and defensive endeavour, while H. Bloom's version of Wordsworth in *The Visionary Company* (Ithaca, NY: Cornell University Press, 1971) manifests a still often used rhetoric about Wordsworth's unified, bardic voice (section 2, pp. 124–98).

73. On these broad contexts, see M. Schoenfield, *British Periodicals and Romantic Identity: 'The Literary Lower Empire'* (New York: Palgrave Macmillan, 2009), ch. 1, 'Skirmishes in

the Lower Empire', pp. 13–48; and ch. 3, 'Proliferating Voices: Founding *The Quarterly Review* and Maga', pp. 79–108.

74. N. Trott, 'Wordsworth in the Nursery: The Parodic School of Criticism', *Wordsworth Circle*, 32:2 (Spring 2001), pp. 66–77.

75. S. Jones also published *Satire and Romanticism* (New York: St Martin's Press, 2000). For collections of Romantic parodies, see Strachan's five-volume *Parodies of the Romantic Age* and Kent and Ewen's one-volume *Romantic Parodies*. Dyer's *British Satire and the Politics of Style* deals widely with radicalism and the politics of satire in the Romantic period while in *Radical Satire and Print Culture 1790–1822* (Oxford: Oxford University Press, 1994), M. Wood closely examines popular modes of eighteenth-century parody and the radical free press.

76. W. Christie details this intimate relationship between periodical reviews and satire in '"Running with the English Hares and Hunting with the Scotch Blood-hounds": Jeffrey and Byron', in *The Edinburgh Review in the Literary Culture of Romantic Britain* (London: Pickering & Chatto, 2009), pp. 123–46.

77. See Trott, 'Wordsworth and the Parodic School of Criticism'. Jones's *Satire and Romanticism* also has an intriguing chapter, 'Representing Rustics: Satire, Countersatire, and Emergent Romanticism', pp. 15–46, about Wordsworth's attempts to define himself in relation to predominating modes of satire.

78. Judging solely by the average print runs and moderate sales of Wordsworth's books of poetry, his poetic collections did little to influence the reading public's views on poetry. In the first two decades of the nineteenth century, Wordsworth's material currency paled in comparison to the larger print runs, sales and subsequent vogue for the poetry of Scott and Byron. Wordsworth's collections of poetry were also circulated, bought and seemingly read much less than the publications of other contemporary poets such as Robert Bloomfield, James Montgomery, Samuel Rogers, Thomas Moore and James Campbell. Owen's 'Costs, Sales, and Profits of Longman's Editions of Wordsworth' demonstrates that most print runs of Wordsworth's publications were in 500 or 750 copy runs, which rarely sold out, partially because most of Wordsworth's volumes were expensive. For detailed publishing histories about the prices, print runs and sales of a variety of Romantic period authors, see St Clair's 'Appendix 9' in *The Reading Nation*, pp. 578–664.

79. In *Romanticism and the Gothic* (New York: Cambridge University Press, 2000), M. Gamer's analysis of how Gothic literature was received – both critically and popularly – after 1795 is particularly relevant here. Gamer contends that while H. Jauss's tripartite model of readership – reader/writers, reader/critics, reader/consumers – is empirically an inaccurate method for categorizing actual readers or reading practices, it does have an 'uncanny resemblance ... to the similarly imprecise ideas that late-eighteenth-century British writers and reviewers held about the makeup of their own readership', p. 32.

80. The 1815 preface is a good example of Wordsworth's readerly prescriptions giving way to readerly prerogative.

81. Wordsworth, *Lyrical Ballads*, ed. Brett and Jones, p. 268.

82. In '"Tis Three Feet Long, and Two Feet Wide": Wordsworth's "Thorn" and the Politics of Bathos', *Wordsworth Circle*, 22:2 (Spring 1991), pp. 92–100, P. Sheats astutely demonstrates how certain bathetic lines in 'The Thorn' ironically confront readers' expectations and play out 'deliberate acts of indirection', that initially offend 'the reader [while looking] forward to a central purpose in the poem as a whole, which is to present these 'extraordinary incidents' in such a way as to call forth what Wordsworth conceived of as the 'nobler powers of the mind', pp. 99, 93. Against the 'indeterminacy of the voice

within the poem', Sheats maintains that the 'Note to The Thorn' creates a kind of 'over-specification' that 'stands in stark and (to some readers) comic contrast', p. 94.

83. Franta's remark in his chapter 'Wordsworth's Audience Problem' that 'the poet who works to create the taste by which he will be enjoyed might discover, after the fact and in opposition to his intentions, that he has created the taste by which he is to be ignored, neglected, and abhorred' (p. 74) is particularly apt here.

1 Reframing *Lyrical Ballads* (1800/1798)

1. For the print run, see Owen, 'Costs, Sales, and Profits of Longman's Editions of Wordsworth'. In their introduction to *Lyrical Ballads and Other Poems, 1797–1800*, J. Butler and K. Green describe Cottle's gift of copyright to Wordsworth, but this gifting seems debatable given Wordsworth's anxious comments in a letter to Longman sent a few weeks before the publication of the 1800 *Lyrical Ballads* (*Lyrical Ballads and Other Poems, 1797–1800*, ed. J. Butler and K. Green (Ithaca, NY: Cornell University Press, 1992), p. 23; *The Letters of William and Dorothy Wordsworth*, ed. De Selincourt, rev. Shaver, vol. 1, p. 310. Cottle had sold all of his publishing rights to Longman in 1799. Though all of the reviews I quote from can be found in D. H. Reiman's ten-volume *Romantics Reviewed; Contemporary Reviews of British Romantic Writers* (New York: Garland, 1972) and many of them are now digitized in electronic sources as well, unless otherwise noted, I quote from, R. Woof (ed.), *William Wordsworth: The Critical Heritage, Vol. 1: 1793–1820* (New York: Routledge, 2001). For Woof's collection of *Lyrical Ballads'* reviews, see pp. 65–86.

2. Although Wordsworth states in a letter to Longman on 18 December 1800 that he had contracted for an 1800 edition that would be followed by another edition of 1,000 copies of each volume, Longman ended up splitting those 1,000 copies between the 1802 and 1805 editions of *Lyrical Ballads*. See *The Letters of William and Dorothy Wordsworth*, ed. De Selincourt, rev. Shaver, vol. 1, pp. 310.

3. See *Lyrical Ballads and Other Poems, 1797–1800*, ed. Butler and Green, pp. 21–4.

4. *The Letters of William and Dorothy Wordsworth*, ed. De Selincourt, rev. Shaver, vol. 1, pp. 285–8. The letters from July to December, which detail all of Wordsworth's requests about the 1800 edition, can be found in C. Shaver's second edition of E. de Selincourt's *The Letters of William and Dorothy Wordsworth*, vol. 1, pp. 285–312.

5. Wordsworth had largely finished the preface to the first volume by the end of September and then began writing a preface for the second volume, which was still unfinished in December and, thus, not published. In October Wordsworth rejected Coleridge's 'Christabel' from its place in the second volume and began working on 'Michael' as a substitute that seemingly better-suited his 1800 edition.

6. *Lyrical Ballads and Other Poems, 1797–1800*, ed. Butler and Green, pp. 26–31.

7. *The Letters of William and Dorothy Wordsworth*, ed. De Selincourt, rev. Shaver, vol. 1, p. 323.

8. As Butler and Green point out, several hundred nonverbal variants in this January publication differ from the 'MS 1800', which was the manuscript that Wordsworth and his circle of friends prepared for publication, *Lyrical Ballads and Other Poems, 1797–1800*, pp. 126–9. Of particular note for my argument, nearly all of the supplementary prose writings that Wordsworth attached to the first and second volumes appeared in the forms and textual spaces that he intended for them.

9. See S. Eilenberg, 'The Propriety of the *Lyrical Ballads*', in Eilenberg, *Strange Power of Speech*, pp. pp. 3–30.

10. While Bialostosky has opened the door for examinations of multiple voices in the poetry of *Lyrical Ballads*, and E. Fay has provided the most extended psycho-social treatment of Wordsworthian branding and multiple performances of self, K. Johnston has singled out most acutely the central issue defining the second edition of *Lyrical Ballads*: 'Many of the problems posed by the new poems of 1800 have as much to do with Wordsworth's ongoing process of self-creation as with the more narrowly focused issues raised in the famous "Preface"', p. 95. Bialostosky's *Making Tales: The Poetics of Wordsworth's Narrative Experiments* probes Wordsworth's longer, narrative poems while E. Fay's *Becoming Wordsworthian* (Amherst, MA: University of Massachusetts Press, 1995) describes Wordsworth's career as 'at once a performance of himself and two enacting selves: William and Dorothy combined', p. 3. Johnston's essay, 'Wordsworth's Self-Creation and the 1800 *Lyrical Ballads*', in N. Trott and S. Perry (eds), *1800: The New Lyrical Ballads* (London: Palgrave Macmillan, 2001), pp. 95–121, distinguishes Wordsworth's rationale for the 1798 *Lyrical Ballads* from his hopes and frustrations about the next edition.

11. *The Letters of William and Dorothy Wordsworth*, ed. De Selincourt, rev. Shaver, vol. 1, p. 307. Wordsworth's request was not carried out, perhaps because it was made so late in the printing process amidst so many other detailed instructions.

12. N. Mason's article 'Building Brand Byron: Early Nineteenth-Century Advertising and the Marketing of *Child Harold's Pilgrimage*', *Modern Language Quarterly*, 63:4 (2002), pp. 411–40, points out the manner in which increasingly after the 1760s branding of products such as medicine, blacking (shoe polish) and even shaving cream became normalized. Also, see N. McKendrick, J. Brewer, and J. H. Plumb (eds), *The Birth of a Consumer Society: The Commercialization of Eighteenth-Century England* (Bloomington, IN: Indiana University Press, 1982), Brewer, *The Pleasures of the Imagination*, and C. Rzepka, 'A Gift that Complicates Employ: Poetry and Poverty in 'Resolution and Independence'', *Studies in Romanticism*, 28:2 (1989), pp. 225–47.

13. *The Letters of William and Dorothy Wordsworth*, ed. De Selincourt, rev. Shaver, vol. 1, p. 303.

14. Ibid., vol. 1, p. 308. Wordsworth repeated this request to Longman in a letter sent one day later: 'It is my particular request that no Books be advertised at the end of the volumes. If you have given any directions to Mr Biggs that such advertisements should be printed pray let such orders be countermanded, or, if he is likely to do it without such orders from you pray, request him not. This I shall regard as a particular favor', p. 310.

15. Ibid., vol. 1, pp. 297–8.

16. On the last page of *Lyrical Tales by Mrs. Mary Robinson* (London: Printed for T. N. Longman & O. Rees, Paternoster Row, by Biggs & Co., Bristol, 1800), Longman includes nineteen advertisements for other works, printed for T. N. Longman & O. Rees, No. 39, Paternoster Row, London. These titles suggest the kinds of advertisements that might have been included with Wordsworth's 1800 *Lyrical Ballads*. The first two advertisements are for novels by Robinson, *The Natural Daughter* and *The False Friend*. The next five advertisements are for poems, letters and the *Annual Anthology*, edited by Robert Southey. Following Southey's works, Longman includes four selections from poetry by Joseph Cottle and his translation of *Icelandic Poetry, or The Edda of Saemund*. Number eleven on the list is *Lyrical Ballads, in 2 Vols. by W. Wordsworth*, followed by an advertisement for the second edition of Coleridge's poems, including poems by Lloyd and Lamb. Next, three works are listed by Mrs West, *The Pleasures of Hope* by T. Camp-

bell, *Poems* by A. Bannerman and finally *Poems of Achmed Ardebeili, a Persian Exile, with Notes*, by C. Fox. Conspicuously, *Lyrical Ballads* is the only advertisement that appears without its price. Did Longman not publish the price because it had not been decided definitively, or did Wordsworth ask him not to publish it?

17. See Erickson, *The Economy of Literary Form* and B. Colbert, 'Popular Romanticism? Publishing, Readership and the Making of Literary History', in E. J. Clery, C. Franklin and P. Garside (eds), *Authorship, Commerce and the Public Scenes of Writing* (London: Palgrave Macmillan, 2002), pp. 153–68. Colbert argues that despite the commentaries of many critics who have argued for the popularity of *Lyrical Ballads* during its time, *Lyrical Ballads* was largely unpopular.

18. Wordsworth's market competition was complex, but his immediate concern was probably with separating his brand of poetry from the circle of poets who published under J. Cottle – including Southey, Lamb, Coleridge and Cottle – and who Longman took over publishing in 1799. Wordsworth's engagement with earlier eighteenth-century poets should also be considered here. Throughout the 1800 volumes, he aligns himself with a pastoral tradition of English poetry that conjures up poetry by S. Duck, O. Goldsmith, A. Yearsley, G. Crabbe and Burns, but Wordsworth's ballad forms also reconfigure that tradition and draw on late eighteenth-century periodical/magazine publications and anthologies. Wordsworth was trying to find a generic ground for his poems to stand on – a ground that had not been criticized and/or usurped by someone such as Southey. As C. Smith demonstrates in 'Robert Southey and the Emergence of *Lyrical Ballads*', *RAVON*, 9 (1998), 37 par., http://www.erudit.org/revue/ron/1998/v/n9/005792ar. html [accessed 5 February 2009], Southey and Wordsworth frequently borrowed from each other in the period between 1797 and 1800.

19. *The Progress of Satire: An Essay in Verse with Notes, Containing Remarks on the 'Pursuits of Literature'*, 2nd edn (London: Printed for J. Bell, No. 148, Oxford Street, 1798) was one of several exasperated responses that charged the author of *The Pursuits of Literature* with libel and in which the anonymous author complains about the reality of such a threat: 'Does every man who publishes a book expose *thereby* all his private life to sarcastic observation and obloquy?', p. vi. In the second footnote to the poem, this complainant further derides the 'practice of ridiculing individuals by *name* in a satirical poem, and concealing that of the author who attacks them', p. 1.

20. T. J. Mathias, 'Advertisement to the Fourth and Last Part of The Pursuits of Literature', in *The Pursuits of Literature*, 5th edn (London, 1797), pp. i–xxx, on p. xxvii.

21. Mathias, 'Introductory Letter to a Friend', in *The Pursuits of Literature*, pp. 2, 13.

22. Ibid., p. 7.

23. Ibid., p. 12.

24. Mathias, *The Pursuits of Literature*, p. 281.

25. Gamer's explanation of Gifford's attacks in 'The Baviad' on Della Cruscan poetry as a function of his disdain for J. Bell's anthology of their poetry *The British Album* (1790) analyses an interesting precursor to Mathias's bibliographic focus. Gamer maintains that Gifford was incensed by how Bell's anthology, published in the same typography as Bell's numerous other volumes of British poetry, upset established literary hierarchies, critical prerogatives, editorial responsibilities, bookselling practices and the ephemeral nature of newspaper poetry. See M. Gamer, '"Bell's Poetics": *The Baviad*, the Della Cruscans, and the book of *The World*', in Jones (ed.), *The Satiric Eye*, pp. 31–53.

26. Mathias, *The Pursuit of Literature*, p. 49, l. 92.

27. On the extensive influence of Mathias's notes on Romantic writers, see A. Watson, 'Dark Assassin: Thomas James Mathias' Notes for The Pursuits Of Literature', in D. Lewes (ed.), *Double Vision: Literary Palimpsests of the Eighteenth and Nineteenth Centuries* (Lanham, MD: Lexington Books, 2008), pp. 37–51.

28. Edited by W. Gifford, the *Anti-Jacobin* was published every Monday in direct correspondence with the parliamentary session from 20 November 1797 to 9 July 1798. Its primary writers were Gifford, G. Canning, J. H. Frere and G. Ellis. For more on their political purposes, the *Anti-Jacobin's* multifaceted form and its popularity, see J. Halliwell, 'Loyalist Satire, Parody; and the *Anti-Jacobin*', in S. Hull (ed.), *The British Periodical Text, 1797–1835* [electronic resource] (Penrith: Humanities eBooks, 2008), pp. 36–67, and C.C. Barfoot, 'Parody and the Classic Art of Political Partisanship in *The Anti-Jacobin*', in C. C. Barfoot and T. D'Haen (eds), *Tropes of Revolution: Writer's Reactions to Real and Imagined Revolutions, 1789–1989* (Amsterdam: Rodopi, 1991), pp. 127–93.

29. *Anti-Jacobin*, 1:1 (20 November 1797), p. 8.

30. Mathias, *The Pursuits of Literature*, pp. 9–10.

31. Ibid., p. 8.

32. 'Introduction to the Poetry of the *Anti-Jacobin*', *Anti-Jacobin*, 1:1 (20 November 1797), p. 33.

33. Ibid., p. 32. Though many of these weekly poetry sections feature introductory prose, a few do not, and other weekly sections have footnotes or interlacing prose remarks that interrupt the *Anti-Jacobin's* parodies or the Jacobin poetry quoted.

34. Ibid., p. 33.

35. *Anti-Jacobin*, 36 (9 July 1798), pp. 36, 2, 38, quoted from the *Anti-Jocibin or Weekly Examiner, in Two Volumes*, 4th edn, revised and corrected (London: Printed for J. Wright, Piccadilly, 1799). Intriguingly, in 'Romantic Anti-Jacobins or Anti-Jacobin Romantics', *RAVON*, 15 (August 1999), p. 36 par., http://www.erudit.org/revue/ron/1999/v/n15/005862ar.html [accessed 10 July 2011], K. Johnston reads the following passage as a veiled call to Wordsworth:

>   – for who can tell
> What bashful Genius, in some rural cell,
> As year to year, and day succeeds to day,
> In joyless leisure wastes his life away?
> In him the flame of early Fancy shone;
> His genuine worth his old Companions own;
> In childhood and in youth their Chief confess'd,
> His Master's pride, his pattern to the rest.
> Now, far aloof retiring from the strife
> Of busy talents, and of active life,
> As, from the loop-holes of retreat, he views
> Our Stage, Verse, Pamphlets, Politics, and News,
> He loaths the world, – or with reflection sad
> Concludes it irrevocably mad;
> ...
> Awake! for shame! or e'er thy nobler sense
> Sink in the oblivious pool of Indolence!
> ...
>   – With unsparing hand
> Oh, lash the vile impostures from the land! (ll. 55–68, 71–2, 87–8)

Johnston also conjectures that the final missing name – filled by 'Co.' – in a list of five chastised poets towards the end of the poem is Wordsworth: 'And ye five other wandering Bards that move / In sweet accord of harmony and love, / C—DGE and S—TH—Y, L—D, and L—BE and Co./ Tune all your mystic harps to praise LEPAUX.'

36. Wordsworth, *Lyrical Ballads*, ed. Brett and Jones, p. 7.
37. Southey's review seems to have set the tone for several subsequent reviews of the collection. See Wordsworth's angry letter to Cottle in the summer of 1799 about Southey's negative review and Wordsworth's subsequent claim, 'I care little for the praise of any other professional critic, but as it may help me to pudding', *The Letters of William and Dorothy Wordsworth*, ed. De Selincourt, rev. Shaver, vol. 1, p. 268.
38. Less than a month before his review, Southey wrote to W. Taylor – Burger's most recent translator – and told him that *Lyrical Ballads* was written by Coleridge and Wordsworth.
39. Woof (ed.), *William Wordsworth: The Critical Heritage, Vol. 1: 1793–1830*, p. 67. In 'Robert Southey and the Emergence of *Lyrical Ballads*', Smith maintains: 'This, then, is how Southey stands in regard to the experiment of Lyrical Ballads – not simply as a kind of precursor-poet, nor simply as piratical hack who shamelessly borrowed, but as an established commercial writer and social commentator eager to maintain his own growing literary reputation in the experimental cutting-edges of the poetry of the 1790s, a man inside the debate, not upon its periphery', par. 29.
40. Woof (ed.), *William Wordsworth: The Critical Heritage, Vol. 1: 1793–1830*, p. 67.
41. Wordsworth, *Lyrical Ballads*, ed. Brett and Jones, p. 8; Woof (ed.), *William Wordsworth: The Critical Heritage, Vol. 1: 1793–1830*, p. 66.
42. Woof (ed.), *William Wordsworth: The Critical Heritage, Vol. 1: 1793–1830*, p. 66.
43. Wordsworth, *Lyrical Ballads*, ed. Brett and Jones, pp. 287–8.
44. Ibid., p. 268.
45. Ibid., p. 267.
46. Ibid., pp. 241, 264.
47. Ibid., p. 271.
48. In 'Romantic Poetry and the Romantic Novel', in Chandler and McLane (eds), *Cambridge Companion to Romanticism*, pp. 53–75, A. W. Rowland contends that these genre redefinitions led to a new understanding of 'literature' as an imaginative category, which has since become 'our modern conception of "Literature"', p. 123.
49. Wordsworth, *Lyrical Ballads*, ed. Brett and Jones, p. 242.
50. Ibid., pp. 241–2.
51. Ibid., p. 268. For more on Wordsworth's preoccupation with limits in the 'Preface', see Murphy's 'William Wordsworth', in *Poetry as an Art and an Occupation in Britain*, pp. 182–228.
52. That 'contextural' interweaving also involves the supplementary prose that Wordsworth strategically placed throughout the volumes. For a discussion of 'contexture' as a connective and coherent interweaving of textual parts in a collection, as well as its metaphorical relationship to architecture, see chapter 1, 'Ideas of Poetic Order and Ordering', in *The Poem and the Book: Interpreting Collections of Romantic Poetry*, and for parallels with my argument, look to 'The "Field" of *Lyrical Ballads* (1798)' and Boehm's 'The 1798 *Lyrical Ballads* and the Poetics of Late Eighteenth-Century Book Production'. Coleridge's often cited letter to Cottle, which compares the 1798 *Lyrical Ballads* to the organic unity of an ode, may shed light on the relationship between the poems in the 1798 *Lyrical Ballads*, but it does not illustrate the ordering, connections between and generic appeal of the poems in the 1800 edition.

53. On Wordsworth's antipathy to publishing single poems in early nineteenth-century literary anthologies, see S. Bauer, 'Wordsworth and the Early Anthologies', *Library*, 27:1 (1972), pp. 37–45.
54. For a list of popular anthologies published in the eighteenth century, see B. Benedict, 'Chronological Listing of Early Anthologies' at the end of *Making the Modern Reader* (Princeton, NJ: Princeton University Press, 1996). For the anthologies that Wordsworth read, see Wu's *Wordsworth's Reading, 1770–1799*.
55. Wordsworth's comments in his 'Essay Supplementary' (1815) about Percy as the great renovator of poetry in Britain demonstrate his allegiance to Percy as a composer, collector and poet. The 'Essay Supplementary' should be read as a work supplementary not just to the 1815 'Preface' but also to the 'Preface to *Lyrical Ballads*', and Wordsworth's remarks about Percy suggest a great deal about the editorial principles behind many of his collections of poetry as well as those of several of his contemporaries. In *Poetry as an Occupation and an Art*, Murphy traces 'the Romantic method for editing ballads' back to Percy and usefully pairs Wordsworth and Sir Walter Scott together as 'card carrying members of [this] ballad revival', pp. 150, 182. Murphy particularly focuses on the editorial prose/poetry forms of *Minstrelsy of the Scottish Border*, *The Lay of the Last Minstrel* and Wordsworth's *Lyrical Ballads*.
56. Wordsworth purchased the fourth edition of Percy's *Reliques* (1794) while in Hamburg, Germany in the autumn of 1798, but he probably had read the original 1765 publication, as well as the third edition published in 1775. See Wu, *Wordsworth's Reading 1770–1799*, pp. 110–11)
57. Wordsworth supervised a similar process that resulted in Coleridge changing the archaic spellings of dozens of words in the 1798 'The Rime of the Ancyent Marinere', including words in the title.
58. *Relique of Ancient English Poetry*, 4th edn (London, 1794), p. xii.
59. In *Wordsworth's Reading 1770–1799*, Wu points out that a part of Wordsworth's education at Hawkshead Grammar School would have drawn on Knox's *Elegant Extracts* and that Wordsworth had further access to the 1789 Dublin edition, owned by his brother Christopher. This anthology contained extracts from 'Spenser, Shakespeare, and Milton, poems by Pope, Gray, Collins, Goldsmith, Elizabeth Carter, John and Anna Laetitia Akin, and virtually every other significant writer of the eighteenth century', p. 83. On Knox's influence, see P. M. Zaul, 'The Cool World of Samuel Taylor Coleridge: Vicesimus Knox, Elegant Activist', *Wordsworth Circle*, 10 (1979), pp. 345–7, and L. Price, *The Anthology and the Rise of the Novel* (Cambridge: Cambridge University Press, 2000), pp. 67–77.
60. V. Knox, *Elegant Extracts: or Useful and Entertaining Pieces of Poetry, Selected for the Improvement of Youth* (London: Printed for Charles Dilly, Poultry, 1784), p. iv.
61. Ibid., p. vi.
62. Ibid., p. iv.
63. Quoted from Keen (ed.), *Revolutions in Romantic Literature*, p. 114.
64. Ibid., p. 114.
65. Ibid., pp. 114–15.
66. Ibid., p. 115.
67. Wordsworth, 'Advertisement' (1798), in *Lyrical Ballads*, ed. Brett and Jones, p. 7.
68. Published over fifty years ago, R. Mayo's seminal article 'The Contemporaneity of the *Lyrical Ballads*' argues that the poetic genres and subject matter in the 1798 *Lyrical Ballads* would not, on the surface, have appeared to most of their contemporary readers

as original. After looking through magazine publications of poetry in the 1790s, Mayo asserts that the subject matter (nature or pastoral), the tone (love of nature and morality), and even the form (the ballad, the philosophical poem, and lyrical pieces describing rural scenes) of the poems in *Lyrical Ballads* were all very common and widely familiar to the magazine reading public, pp. 71. Despite this seeming lack of originality, Mayo contends that *Lyrical Ballads* was successful in differentiating itself from similar publications of poetry through the power of its poetic language. I refer to Mayo's 'The Contemporaneity of the *Lyrical Ballads*', in M. H. Abrams (ed.), *Wordsworth: A Collection of Critical Essays* (Englewood Cliffs, NJ: Prentice Hall, Inc., 1972), pp. 67–74. See also, *PMLA*, 69:3 (1954), pp. 486–522.

69. In *Wordsworth's Profession* Pfau argues that a part of the purpose of the 1800 volumes was to appeal to emerging middle-class values of vigilant self-monitoring.

70. For more on uses of the word 'perusal' in relation to anxieties around the turn of the century about superficial reading, abridgments, mercenary book makers, late eighteenth-century anthology creations and declining standards of authorial distinction, see P. Keen, *Crisis of Literature in the 1790s: Print Culture and the Public Sphere* (Cambridge: Cambridge University Press, 1999), pp. 109–15. Keen's concluding argument, pp. 236–54, about Wordsworth's 1802 'Preface' as a manifesto for re-establishing a mutually binding contract between poet and reader that does not tyrannize over the reader offers a politically charged analysis of these bibliographic contexts.

71. Wordsworth, *Lyrical Ballads*, ed. Brett and Jones, vol. 1, pp. 244–5, 247, 265.

72. Ibid., vol. 2, p. 135.

73. Likewise, the endnote to 'The Thorn' begins: 'This Poem ought to have been preceded by an introductory Poem, which I have been prevented from writing by never having felt myself in a mood when it was probable that I should write it well', pp. 287–8.

74. Eilenberg's *Strange Power of Speech* differentiates usefully between Wordsworth's and Coleridge's views about literary property, propriety, and possession. Also, see Fraistat's 'The Field of *Lyrical Ballads*'. Brett and Jones's edition of *Lyrical Ballads* conveniently provides the table of contents for both editions and notes the variant placements of poems in volume 1 of the 1800 edition.

75. In the 1800 edition, Wordsworth situates 'The Ancient Mariner' directly before 'Tintern Abbey', thereby engaging the two in a dialogue. He also places Coleridge's poem after 'The Mad Mother', which bookends Coleridge's 'Love' with Wordsworth's 'The Idiot Boy' and replaced 'The Convict' with Coleridge's poem 'Love.'

76. Wordsworth, *Lyrical Ballads* (1800), ed. Brett and Jones, p. 276.

77. Ibid.

78. Ibid., p. 248.

2 Textual Travelling in the 1800 *Lyrical Ballads*

1. William and Dorothy began living in Grasmere in late December 1799, and much of the poetry in the second volume reflects Wordsworth's explicit attention to the geography of the Lake District. Wordsworth also owned several popular prose travel guides to the Lake District published after 1770, of which Thomas West's *A Guide to the Lakes*, which went through ten editions between 1778–1810, was, probably, the most widely read by his contemporaries.

2. In *Wordsworth's Profession*, Pfau argues that *Lyrical Ballads* encourages readers to engage in reciprocating, self-creating activities, which enable them to 'project, elaborate, and revise

the general hermeneutic framework within which any given utterance ... would appear to operate', p. 182, and Schoenfield strikes a similar chord in *The Professional Wordsworth* by examining Wordsworth's position as a '*professional* poet who found himself competing with other professional producers of ideology for the ability to shape the marketplace of ideas', p. 7. Picking up from S. Hess's more recent claims about Wordsworth's vacillating acceptance and rejection of eighteenth-century print culture, but focusing more closely on the textual features of the 1800 *Lyrical Ballads*, my argument rests on Wordsworth's endeavours to style himself as a tour guide throughout the revised *Lyrical Ballads*. See S. Hess, '"My Office Upon Earth": William Wordsworth, Professionalism, and Poetic Identity', and 'Pedlars, Poets, and the Print Market: Wordsworth's Poetic Self-Representation', in his *Authoring the Self* (New York: Routledge, 2005), pp. 199–234, 235–74, as well as Erickson's 'The Egoism of Authorship: Wordsworth's Poetic Career', in his *The Economy of Literary Form*, pp. 49–70.

3. See S. Parrish, 'The Ballad as Pastoral', in *The Art of the Lyrical Ballads* (Cambridge, MA: Harvard University Press, 1973), pp. 149–87, and Duff, 'Paratextual Dilemmas'.

4. Perhaps the most compelling evidence is that Wordsworth changed the title of the 1802 edition from *Lyrical Ballads, with Other Poems* to *Lyrical Ballads, with Pastoral and Other Poems*. Wordsworth also had wanted to change the title of the 1800 edition as well, and one of Coleridge's letters to Southey describes Wordsworth's plan to publish 'a second Volume of Lyrical Ballads, & Pastorals'. See *Collected Letters of Samuel Taylor Coleridge*, ed. Griggs, vol. 1, p. 585.

5. See chapter 1 'Representing Rustics: Satire, Countersatire, and Emergent Romanticism' in Jones's *Satire and Romanticism*, pp. 15–45.

6. In the first section of his chapter 'Poetry, Language and Difference' in *Language and Relationship in Wordsworth's Writing*, pp. 11–52, Baron details Wordsworth's concern for writing in an accepted national language and for balancing local incident with national significance in relation to Anderson, Burns and Chatterton (pp. 11–36). More recently, in 'Framing Dialect in the 1800 *Lyrical Ballads*: Wordsworth, Regionalisms and Footnotes', *Language and Literature*, 19:3 (2010), pp. 249–63, A. Broadhead extends this line of inquiry by examining Wordsworth's selective use of regional dialect in the volumes and even more selective use of footnotes to gloss that dialect.

7. In the 1798 *Lyrical Ballads*, Wordsworth and Coleridge also employed a few footnotes to connect their poetry to the 'Old Canon' of English poetry. While a footnote to Coleridge's 'The Nightingale' explains the high sincerity associated with quoting a line of poetry from Milton, 'Most musical, most melancholy', another footnote to 'Lines Written Near Richmond' tags the words 'a later ditty' with this note: 'Collins's Ode on the death of Thomson, the last written, I believe, of the poems which were published during his life-time. This Ode is also alluded to in the next stanza.' Finally, a footnote in 'Tintern Abbey' traces the words 'half-create, / and what perceive' back to Edward Young: 'This line has a close resemblance to an admirable line of Young, the exact expression of which I cannot recollect'. To view these notes in all five *Lyrical Ballads* editions, go to *Romantic Circles* at <http://www.rc.umd.edu/editions/LB/> [accessed 10 June 2009].

8. In his chapter '"Gross and Violent Stimulants": Producing *Lyrical Ballads* 1798 and 1800', in his *Romanticism and the Gothic*, pp. 90–126, Gamer makes a compelling series of economic and aesthetic arguments about the character and purpose of Wordsworth's 1800 *Lyrical Ballads*. Gamer focuses on how and why Wordsworth distanced the 1800 volumes from the negatively reviewed Gothic ballads of the 1798 volume and, alternately, marked his revised, poetic collection with a distinctive pastoral identity (pp. 116–26).

9. In *Wordsworth's Style: Figures and Themes in the* Lyrical Ballads *of 1800* (Lincoln, NE: University of Nebraska Press, 1967), R. Murray's discussion of the 'web' of words in the 1800 *Lyrical Ballads* articulates a similar argument, pp. 5–7. He devotes an entire chapter to figures of repetition in the 1800 *Lyrical Ballads*, and his examination of how repeated objects – such as the word 'rock' in 'The Brothers' – serve as 'links' between the figurative and literal is particularly relevant, pp. 22, 38–42. Newlyn's reflections in *Reading, Writing, and Romanticism* on Wordsworth's methods for critiquing and containing reading strategies in the 1800 *Lyrical Ballads*, particularly through 'the symbolic laying of a stone' in 'Michael' are also relevant, p. 123.

10. While Wordsworth's juxtapositions of the country and the city have become a critical commonplace, my argument centres on his interest in detailing the Lake District as more than a fleeting curiosity or vacation site; instead, he describes it as a permanent place for appreciation – a place to be revered because, as D. Simpson points out throughout *Wordsworth and the Figurings of the Real* (Atlantic Highlands, NJ: Humanities Press, 1982), it has fewer people in it, fewer outrageous stimuli, fewer objects to apprehend, more abiding objects to contemplate, more space in which to contemplate and fewer incoherent significations than in the crowded city.

11. Wordsworth, 'Preface' to *Lyrical Ballads* (1800, vol. 2), ed. Brett and Jones, p. 249.

12. Wordsworth, *Lyrical Ballads* (1800, vol. 2), ed. Brett and Jones, p. 211.

13. These maneuverings extend Boehm's claim for the 1798 *Lyrical Ballads*: 'In publishing *Lyrical Ballads* in a small portable format – contemporary booksellers often called fools-cap octavo volumes "pocket editions" – Wordsworth and Coleridge adopted the pocket edition and reformulated the fashion for picturesque reading', 'The 1798 *Lyrical Ballads*', p. 461. Even more explicitly than the 1798 edition, volume 2 of the 1800 edition grounds itself in a place (the Lake District) and offers readers specific directions to and descriptions of picturesque locations in its notes. Wordsworth appears to have conceived of the 1800 edition, at least partially, as volumes that would be carried with (or perhaps more aptly that would carry) travellers into the Lake District or, as in the following example, into Coleridge's Somersetshire. Six stanzas from the end of 'Ruth', Wordsworth includes a footnote that describes the river and woods to which Ruth has retired as a means to endure her abandonment: 'The Tone is a River of Somersetshire at no great distance from the Quantock hills. These Hills, which are alluded to a few stanzas below, are extremely beautiful, and in most places richly covered with Coppice woods', p. 187.

14. Wordsworth, *Lyrical Ballads* (1800, vol. 2), ed. Brett and Jones, p. 227.

15. Ibid., p. 222.

16. In *Reading, Writing, and Romanticism*, Newlyn points out that many reviewers of poetry in the early nineteenth century voiced direct hostility toward authorial instructions in the form of footnotes to poems. One critic in particular, reviewing Percival Stockdale's *Lectures on the Truly Eminent English Poets* (1807) exclaims: 'Whatever truth there may be in the assertion, that none but a poet should criticize a poet, we are nevertheless extremely happy to meet now and then with dissertations on poetry in sober prose; for most of our modern bards, as if they were afraid that posterity would not take the trouble to be their commentators, have enshrined themselves in their own annotations (187). See *Edinburgh Review*, 12/23:4 (April 1808), p. 62.

17. Woof (ed.), *William Wordsworth: The Critical Heritage, Vol. 1: 1793–1830*, p. 139.

18. Wordsworth, *Lyrical Ballads* (1800, vol. 1), ed. Brett and Jones, p. 46.

19. Ibid., p. 113. Many contemporary critics have commented on where Wordsworth situates himself in the poem in relation to Tintern Abbey. C. Rzepka's 'Pictures of the Mind:

Iron and Charcoal, "Ouzy Tides, and 'Vagrant' Dwellers" at Tintern, 1798', *Studies in Romanticism*, 42:2 (Summer 2003), pp. 155–85, usefully summarizes the nature of these debates. My concern is with why Wordsworth chose to include this footnote and did not remove it from future publications of the poem.

20. I am not trying to politicize this prospect view in the ways that M. Levinson does in *Wordsworth's Great Period Poems* (Cambridge: Cambridge University Press, 1996). Instead, my contention is that Wordsworth encourages his readers to apply his concept of 'similitude in dissimilitude' and 'dissimilitude in similitude' to landscape aesthetics, language and poetic collections.

21. Quoted from *Lyrical Ballads with Other Poems in Two Volumes*, 2nd edn (London: Printed for T. N. Longman and O. Rees, Paternoster Row, by Biggs & Co. Bristol, 1800), pp. 215.

22. In *Wordsworth and the Enlightenment* (New Haven, CT: Yale University Press, 1989), A. Bewell argues that in this note, Wordsworth maintains that 'poetry and passion ... are born and develop within the interplay between "the deficiencies of language" and linguistic "repetition"', p. 170. My argument focuses on how readers are affected developmentally throughout *Lyrical Ballads* by what Bewell describes as this 'play of pleasure and insufficiency' that characterizes repetitive language, p. 174. I also echo Murray's contention in *Wordsworth's Style* that Wordsworthian repetition 'is not only a means of expressing passion; it is a ... means of bringing the actual and the ideal, the literal and the symbolic into a close relation', p. 7.

23. Wordsworth, *Lyrical Ballads* (1800, vol. 1), ed. Brett and Jones, p. 288.

24. Ibid., p. 289.

25. Ibid. (vol. 2), p. 127.

26. I will analyse this poem in more detail in the final section of the chapter. Notably, this headnote situates readers well north of London, within 50 miles of Wordsworth's home in Grasmere. As Brett and Jones note, William and Dorothy had covered this distance in a three-day journey in December 1799 from Sockburn to Grasmere, p. 299. Wordsworth's own note about 'Hart-Leap Well' in his *Fenwick Notes*, ed. J. Curtis (London: Bristol Classics Press, 1993), recounts how a peasant that they encountered along the way told them this story, p. 15.

27. Wordsworth, *Lyrical Ballads* (1800, vol. 2), ed. Brett and Jones, p. 226.

28. In a letter to Biggs and Cottle on 1 August 1800, Wordsworth asks that 'The Brothers' begin the second volume, but his instructions appear to have arrived too late to be implemented before printing began, *The Letters of William and Dorothy Wordsworth*, ed. De Selincourt, rev. Shaver, vol. 1, p. 290).

29. Wordsworth, *Lyrical Ballads* (1800, vol. 2), ed. Brett and Jones, p. 226.

30. Ibid., p. 222.

31. Ibid., 'Preface', p. 247.

32. Ibid., p. 217.

33. The manuscript that Wordsworth sent to his printers for final copy also capitalizes the word 'Interest', which perhaps best encapsulates the intense emotions that Wordsworth records and hopes to elicit in these poems.

34. While the 1800 edition seems aimed primarily at a London audience, Klancher also argues in *The Making of English Reading Audiences* that the 'poems of 1800 are not merely textual relays between two autonomous cultures. They compose the textual countermove against that vast social transformation that since Wordsworth's birth has been turning one (full) culture into another (empty) culture, as the peasants who speak "the

very language of men" become historically the future urban readers who, at further and further textual removes, can at best read only *about* such a language in the poems the poet offers them', p. 144.

35. In 'Sacrificial Sites, Place-Keeping, and "Pre-History" in Wordsworth's "Michael"', *ERR*, 15:2 (2004), pp. 205–13, C. Rzepka maintains that in writing *Lyrical Ballads*, Wordsworth 'became very interested in stones, which seem to litter the *Ballads* like glacial erratics', p. 205. In *The Linguistic Moment* (Princeton, NJ: Princeton University Press, 1985), J. H. Miller contends that 'stones play an important role in Wordsworth's poetry', pp. 81–2.

36. Wordsworth, *Lyrical Ballads* (1800, vol. 2), ed. Brett and Jones, p. 227.

37. A tremendous amount of scholarship has been devoted to Wordsworth's epitaphic/ cenotaphic mode of writing, usually related to his three *Essays on Epitaphs*. D. D. Devlin's *Wordsworth's Poetry of Epitaphs* (Totowa, NJ; Barnes & Noble, 1981) is the most representative example. My argument about this poem follows J. Viscomi's claims in 'Wordsworth's Dramatic Antipicturesque', in 'Scholarly Resources', *Romantic Circles*, at <http://www.rc.umd.edu/reference/> [accessed 15 December 2008], that this poem exemplifies Wordsworth's efforts to include his readers in his disdain of popular, picturesque tours.

38. For commentary on this poem, see particularly Hartman, *Wordsworth's Poetry 1787–1814*, pp. 141–2, Schoenfield, *The Professional Wordsworth*, p. 143, and Pfau, *Wordsworth's Profession*, pp. 220–7.

39. There are other poems in the volume that mention stones as well. See 'The Oak and the Broom', 'Lucy Gray', 'Nutting', 'The Pet-Lamb', 'A Fragment' and three of the 'Poems on the Naming of Places'. Wordsworth also uses the word 'rock' often in the second volume.

40. The next poem, 'A Poet's Epitaph', describes the type of reader/traveller that Wordsworth is attempting to call into being. Largely satirical, the poem condemns statesmen, clerics, lawyers, doctors, philosophers and moralists as unfit to approach the burial place of a poet. In their stead, he praises the soldier who puts aside his sword for a peasant's staff. Above all others, though, Wordsworth singles out the loiterer as a model to imitate. This poem describes the kind of reader/traveller that Wordsworth invites to his poetry and singles the poet out as the only kind of professional who can effectively link human beings together. As Schoenfield points out in *The Professional Wordsworth*, pp. 186–7, in the last two lines of the poem the poet offers the idler he praises a will of property: 'Here stretch thy body at full length; / Or build thy house upon this grave' (ll. 59–60). Such a final figuration offers the reader a potential place to build upon, a place to rest, and a place to return.

41. In his chapter 'Law, Labor, and the Shepherd's Household: "Michael"' in *The Professional Wordsworth*, pp. 31–60, Schoenfield makes a convincing case for the sheepfold as a poetic version of a traditional contract that reveals itself in the reciprocal labour of the reader and writer.

42. I follow Baron's claims in *Language and Relationship in Wordsworth's Writing* about Wordsworth's 'habitual supposition that reading and writing are psychologically very similar activities', p. 227.

3 Short-Circuiting Wordsworth's 1807 *Poems*: Richard Mant's *The Simpliciad*

1. *Records of Literature*, 1 (October 1807, pp. 468–9, on p. 468.
2. F. Jeffrey, *Edinburgh Review*, 11 (October 1807), pp. 214–31, on p. 231.
3. *The Letters of William and Dorothy Wordsworth*, ed. De Selincourt, rev. Moorman, vol. 2, p. 147.
4. Following the 1800 edition of *Lyrical Ballads*, Wordsworth published an expanded third edition in 1802, which includes several new poems, a substantial rearrangement of the 1800 poems, an extended section in the 'Preface' on the role of the poet, and a concluding 'Appendix on Poetic Diction'. Then, in 1805 he published the final edition of *Lyrical Ballads*, which is virtually identical to the third edition. In the autumn of 1806, Longman thought Wordsworth's *Lyrical Ballads* poetry popular enough to merit a 1,000 copy print run of the new *Poems in Two Volumes*. Initially, Wordsworth had conceived of a one-volume publication, the contents of which Curtis describes in two footnotes in his 'Introduction' to *Poems, in Two Volumes, and Other Poems, 1800–1807* (Ithaca, NY: Cornell University Press, 1983), pp. 17–18. Although Wordsworth was amenable to a two-volume publication, Curtis maintains that Longman probably suggested the two-volume plan. As Erickson points out, 'unlike *Lyrical Ballads*, this [1807] collection languished. Seven years later when Wordsworth was beginning to see proof for *The Excursion* and arranging for the publication of his *Poems* of 1815, 230 copies remained unsold' (*The Economy of Literary Form*, p. 51). See also Owen's 'Costs, Sales, and Profits of Longman's Editions of Wordsworth', and Erickson's 'The Egoism of Authorship: Wordsworth's Poetic Career' in *The Economy of Literary Form*. For a comparison of Wordsworth's success in relation to other contemporary poets, see Colbert, 'Popular Romanticism? Publishing, Readership and the Making of Literary History'.
5. Notably, before lambasting Wordsworth's 1807 *Poems*, Jeffrey acknowledges that the '*Lyrical Ballads* were unquestionably popular, and we have no hesitation in saying, deservedly popular', quoted in Woof (ed.), *William Wordsworth: The Critical Heritage, Vol. 1: 1793–1830*, p. 186.
6. On these high expectations, see Wordsworth's letter to Walter Scott on 10 November 1806, *The Letters of William and Dorothy Wordsworth*, ed. De Selincourt, rev. Moorman, vol. 2, p. 96, as well as Curtis's 'Introduction', pp. 5–39.
7. In preparing the 1807 volumes for press, Wordsworth wrote a short, prefatory 'Advertisement', which Longman cancelled from the final copy. In the manuscript of that advertisement, Wordsworth describes his new poems as a release from the work that he has been doing on *The Prelude*, though in *Wordsworth's Experiments with Tradition: The Lyric Poems of 1802* (Ithaca, NY: Cornell University Press, 1971), J. Curtis maintains that 'the typical short poem deals with the very same concerns that generated the large work', p. 13. That 'Preface', reproduced in Curtis's Cornell Wordsworth volume begins: 'The short Poems of which these Volumes consist, were chiefly composed to refresh my mind during the progress of a work of length and labor, in which I have for some time been engaged; and to furnish me with employment when I had not resolution to apply myself to that work, or hope that I should proceed with it successfully. Having already, in the Volumes entitled Lyrical Ballads, offered to the World a considerable collection of short poems, I did not wish to add these to the number, till after the completion and publication of my larger work; but, as I cannot even guess when this will be, and as several of these Poems have been circulated in manuscript, I thought it better to send them forth at

once. They were composed with much pleasure to my own mind, and I build upon that remembrance a hope that they may afford profitable pleasure to many readers', p. 527.

8.	Although Wordsworth's 'Preface' was widely criticized – from Jeffrey's 1802 review of Southey's *Thalaba* onward – reviewers continued to rely on that preface as a touchstone from which to judge the aesthetic and cultural value of his poetry. Even if critics disagreed with his 'Preface', they delighted in proving that Wordsworth's poetry did not adhere to his own poetic theories. In the hands of the Francis Jeffrey-led review culture, Wordsworth's 'Preface' was often turned into his poetry's worst enemy.

9.	The following anonymous review sums up the detrimental views of Wordsworth's supposed system: 'But Mr. Wordsworth is a System maker. He has formed an out of the way, incomprehensible system of poetry; and on the altar of that system he sacrifices melody, elegance, spirit, and even common sense. Whenever he deviates from his monstrous system he writes like a man of genius...It is to be hoped that he will see his error, and not persist in making murderous attacks upon his own literary reputation' (*Poetical Register*, vol. 6, 1811, pp. 540–1).

10.	The full title of the volumes – *Poems in Two Volumes, by William Wordsworth, Author of the Lyrical Ballads* – also encourages readers to make connections between his past and present poetic collection.

11.	Woof (ed.), *William Wordsworth: The Critical Heritage, Vol. 1: 1793–1830*, p. 231. Chapter 9 of S. Gill's biography *Wordsworth: A Life* (Oxford: Oxford University Press, 1990) provides a detailed exposition of the decision-making behind Wordsworth's publication of his 1807 *Poems* as well as the subsequent reception of those poems. Generally, the poems were scoffed at as childish and nonsensical productions, and his 'Intimations Ode' was even described as an incomprehensible attempt at sublimity.

12.	Mant's synthetic parody of Coleridge's poetry, Southey's poetry and Wordsworth's poems from *Lyrical Ballads* to his 1807 *Poems* does not possess the type of raucous humour (as in J. H. Reynolds's 'Peter Bell's dynamic Menippean satire) that later Regency parodies often exhibit. It also lacks the carnivalesque punch of *The Dunciad*, the form with which it closely aligns itself. Instead, *The Simpliciad* follows Gifford's scathing condemnation of the Della Cruscan School of poetry in 'The Baviad' and mimics the textual layout and cultural authority of Mathias's *The Pursuits of Literature*.

13.	In his chapter 'The Dedication of *Don Juan*', in *Reading Public Romanticism*, pp. 122–66, Magnuson illustrates this reviewer/poet relationship by detailing how much Byron incorporated journalistic language into canto 1 of *Don Juan*.

14.	On the American side, see R. Rose's poetry in *The Port Folio* (1804), reprinted in Strachan's *Parodies of the Romantic Age*, vol. 2.

15.	D. Chandler's '"Twisted in Persecution's Loving Ways": Peter Bayley Reviewed by Southey, Wordsworth, and Coleridge', *Wordsworth Circle*, 24:4 (1993), pp. 256–60, recounts Bayley's biography as well as reconstructing how Southey, Wordsworth and Coleridge collaborated to write the review. For an earlier and more painstaking effort to point out Bailey's plagiarisms from Wordsworth, see J. S. Martin, 'Peter Bayley and the *Lyrical Ballads*', *English Studies*, 48 (1968), pp. 533–7.

16.	R. Southey, *Annual Review* (1803), quoted in Woof (ed.), *William Wordsworth: The Critical Heritage, Vol. 1: 1793–1830*, p. 163.

17.	Quoted in ibid., p. 165.

18.	Southey's review also suggests his own guilt over plagiarizing from Wordsworth's poetry. Arguably, the review did more to solidify Southey, Coleridge and Wordsworth together as a 'New School' than to successfully defend Wordsworth's poetry.

19. *The Simpliciad* begins with a dedication to M-ssrs. W-ll-m W-rdsw-rth, R-b-rt S-th-y, and S.T. C-l-r-dg- and declares Mant's intention to construct a 'satiric' set of rules (loosely based on Horace's 'Art of Poetry') for what he terms the new 'ANTI-CLAS-SICAL SCHOOL' to 'hold up [this] new school to ridicule', pp. iv–v. The poem begins with a series of exchanges between the two about this 'new school', which leads to P's mock description of an 'Art of Poetry' for that 'new school', and the poem ends with an exchange between the two that results in a throwing up of hands over such new poets who must have their way: 'And when the fit's on, 'tis as well to kill, / As strive to cure a madman 'gainst his will', ll. 367–8.

20. Mant's textual bifurcation mimics the practices of many reviewing critics in the early nineteenth century who sought to reduce and control collections of poetry by poaching from and resituating selections of that poetry.

21. S. Curran's 'Multum in Parvo: Wordsworth's *Poems* in Two Volumes, of 1807', in Fraistat (ed.), *Poems in their Place: The Intertextuality and Order of Poetic Collections*, pp. 234–53, provides the closest examination of the field of the 1807 *Poems* that I have encountered. However, Curran focuses primarily on the sonnet sections. Davies's *Wordsworth and the Worth of Words* more closely examines the repetitive power and layers of meaning in Wordsworth's language.

22. Curtis argues that Wordsworth probably oversaw every page of the final proofs for the 1807 *Poems*, though his argument cannot be proven irrefutably since the proofs, unlike the first manuscript sent to the printer, have not been located (Curtis (ed.), *Poems, in Two Volumes*, pp. 51–3). One of Wordsworth's letters to Walter Scott particularly reveals Wordsworth's extended engagement with those proofs: 'the printing of my work which is now to be extended to two small Vols of 150 pages or so each has met with unexpected delays, and as the sheets are sent down to me for correction, and three are only yet gone through, it will be full three months before it is out; for we do not get on faster than at the rate of a sheet a week', *The Letters of William and Dorothy Wordsworth*, ed. De Selincourt, rev. Moorman, vol. 2, pp. 122–3. Beyond footnotes, endnotes and headnotes to individual poems, Wordsworth conceived of four section headings in volume 1 – 'The Orchard Pathway', 'Poems Composed During a Tour, Chiefly on Foot' and 'Sonnets' (subdivided into 'Part the First. Miscellaneous Sonnets' and 'Part the Second. Sonnets Dedicated to Liberty') – and four section headings in volume 2 – 'Poems Written during a Tour in Scotland', 'Moods of My Own Mind', 'The Blind Highland Boy; with Other Poems', and 'Ode'. During the final printing, the 'Orchard Pathway', along with its six line poem/motto and the preceding 'Advertisement' discussed above, were cancelled, probably to dispel confusion about the title of the volumes. This confusion arose because of several advertisements in February and March, which identified the forthcoming work as 'the Orchard Pathway, a collection of poems, with other Miscellaneous Poems.' That advertising error seems to have occurred because of the printers' or Longman's agent's misinterpretation of Wordsworth's manuscript section heading as the title for the collection (see Curtis (ed.), *Poems, in Two Volumes*, pp. 26–7).

23. Wordsworth's 21 May 1807 letter to Lady Beaumont spells out his conception of how the 1807 *Poems* should engage readers. Responding to S. Rogers's reading of his 1807 volumes, Wordsworth first describes Rogers as 'representative of a class' of readers and then singles out the section heading 'Sonnets Dedicated to Liberty' to illustrate his point: 'there is one thing that must strike you at once if you will only read these poems – that those to Liberty, at least, have a connection with, or a bearing upon, each other, and therefore, if individually they want weight, perhaps as a Body, they may not be so defi-

cient ... But dropping this, I would boldly say at once, that these Sonnets, while they each fix the attention upon some important sentiment separately considered, do at the same time collectively make a Poem on the subject of civil Liberty and national independence, which either for simplicity of style or grandeur of moral sentiment, is alas! Likely to have few parallels in the Poetry of the present day.' *The Letters of William and Dorothy Wordsworth*, ed. De Selincourt, rev. Moorman, vol. 2, p. 147.

24. See Wordsworth's letter to Walter Scott on the poem's similarities with Scott's poem 'Hellvellyn', *The Letters of William and Dorothy Wordsworth*, ed. De Selincourt, rev. Moorman, vol. 2, p. 96).

25. Wordsworth, *Poems, in Two Volumes, and Other Poems, 1800–1807*, ed. Curtis, p. 38.

26. Curran, 'Multum in Parvo', p. 236. While Wordsworth's 'Sonnets Dedicated to Liberty' address national liberty, heroism, duty and independence directly, his footnotes, headnotes and endnotes redouble attention to these themes. In the first volume, his footnote to 'Character of the Happy Warrior' claims that these 'Verses were written soon after tidings had been received of the Death of Lord Nelson', p. 36, while an endnote to 'The Horn of Egremont Castle' identifies this chivalric and martial tale as a 'Cumberland tradition' before the final endnote traces the last two lines of his sonnet 'Another year' to Lord Brooke's heroic 'Life of Sir Philip Sidney.' The headnote to the first poem in volume 2, 'Rob Roy's Grave', situates Wordsworth as a traveller who has come to pay homage to Scotland's national hero, and an endnote to the poem expounds on the extraordinary strength and length of Rob Roy's sword fighting arm. By far the longest prose supplements in the volumes, two endnotes to 'Song, at the Feast of Brougham Castle' relate an entire history of the martial exploits of Lord Clifford's family.

27. As Curtis points out, Wordsworth seems to have tacitly agreed to an ordering of the poems in 'Moods of My Own Mind', which did not completely reflect the order in which he placed the poems in the manuscript sent to the printers. Wordsworth appears to have sent three of these poems to the printer after most of the section already was printed; consequently, the printer made a few practical decisions about how to place the poems in this section heading, *Poems, in Two Volumes, and Other Poems, 1800–1807*, pp. 28–9.

28. See pp. 15–16 in J. Wordsworth's edition of *The Simpliciad* (New York: Woodstock Books, 1991) for Mant's reaction to the redbreast and butterfly. On cuckoos, see pp. 12, 25.

29. Trott, 'Wordsworth and the Parodic School of Criticism', p. 74. Trott also suggests that Mant's manoeuvring might appeal to Gifford, the editor of the *Quarterly Review* (1808), a Tory counter to the Whig *Edinburgh Review*, p. 72.

30. *Edinburgh Review* (October 1807), p. 169.

31. Ibid.

32. Ibid., p. 170. Wordsworth was criticized in *Lyrical Ballads* particularly for his poems announced by an advertisement in the second volume, 'Poems on the Naming of Places', and for publishing poetry addressed to a coterie circle. Wordsworth and Longman's decision to cancel the 1807 'Advertisement' and initial section heading 'The Orchard Pathway' might be attributed to similar fears about such criticism. Regardless, the 1807 volumes elicited further criticism on both scores.

33. *Edinburgh Review* (October 1807), pp. 170, 171.

34. Wordsworth, 'Note to The Thorn', in *Lyrical Ballads, with Others Poems, in Two Volumes* (London: Printed for T. N. Longman and O. Rees, Paternoster-Row, by Biggs & Co. Bristol, 1800), p. 213.
35. Ibid.
36. I wandered lonely as a cloud

    That floats on high o'er vales and hills,
    When all at once I saw a crowd,
    A host of *dancing daffodills.*
    * * * * * * *
    A Poet could not be but gay
    In such a *laughing* company.
    * * * * * * *
    And then my heart with pleasure fills,
    And dances with the daffodills.

    The whole poem, consisting of eighteen lines, is exquisite. This is all from Mant's *The Simpliciad* in a footnote on p. 14.

37. R. Mant, *The Simpliciad* (1808), ed. J. Wordsworth (New York: Woodstock Books, 1991), p. 14.
38. Ibid., p. 13.
39. In his note to 'The Thorn', when describing the character and language of his retired sea captain narrator, Wordsworth asserts his intention to adhere 'to the style in which such persons describe, to take care that words, which in their minds are impregnated with passion, should likewise convey passion to Readers who are not accustomed to sympathize with men feeling in that manner or using such language'. 'Note to The Thorn', in *Lyrical Ballads*, ed. Brett and Jones, p. 288.
40. Ibid., p. 213.
41. As P. Gilman points out in '"To Kill and Bury the Poor Thorn Forever": "The Thorn" and Mant's *Simpliciad*', *Wordsworth Circle*, 27:1 (1996), pp. 37–41, Mant equates Wordsworth with the narrator of 'The Thorn', suggesting that Wordsworth is just as fixated on the bizarre moods of his own mind as the odd sea captain. In much the same way as Gilman argues that Mant attempts to bury Wordsworth's 'poor thorn forever', Mant also seeks to bury the emotional power of the Lake poet's words through his figurations of Wordsworth as a son of Nonsense, 'prat[ing] in phrase so like her own', l. 154.
42. Mant, *The Simpliciad*, p. 27.
43. Ironically, the text-based dialogue between Mant's poetic couplets and footnotes enables a dialogic criticism that upstages the sparse conversation in the text proper between P and F. Mant heads every section of his footnotes with the title 'Authorities', referring to Wordsworth, Coleridge and Southey.
44. In his 'Dedication' Mant points out 'that in attempting to excite ridicule, I have employed no unfair exaggeration; that the school is incapable of caricature; and that if a smile be raised by my illustrations, it will be heightened by a perusal of the originals whence they are drawn', p. v. By employing the word 'illustrations', Mant posits *The Simpliciad* as a structure that sheds light on the original composition of the works that he sings directly above. *The Simpliciad* announces itself as a supplement, a textual picture or diagram that redoubles attention to key features of its host text.
45. In '"To Kill and Bury the Poor Thorn Forever,"' Gilman contends that 'The Thorn' is a satire on *The Simpliciad* (p. 40). She argues that through his attempts to identify the

simple Wordsworth of 'The Thorn', Mant ironically brings out the kind of reading that Wordsworth suggested in his note to 'The Thorn' – a reading that forces them to grapple with awkwardness and uncertainty.

46. Mant appeals to Gifford: 'Gifford, the dread of every sniveling fool, / That loves and rhimes by Della Cruscan rule' (ll. 64–5).

47. J. Hollander, *The Figure of Echo* (Berkeley, CA: California University Press, 1981), p. 11.

48. By contrast, several reviewers mentioned Wordsworth's two sonnet sections in the 1807 volumes, placing him squarely in the midst of discussions about the very public value of English poetry. Tellingly, Mant alludes to none of these sonnets and quotes, none of Wordsworth's extensive prose notes about heroic and martial duties.

49. Wordsworth, *Poems, in Two Volumes, by William Wordsworth, Author of Lyrical Ballads* (London: Paternoster Row, 1807), p. 163.

50. *The Letters of William and Dorothy Wordsworth*, ed. Selincourt, rev. Shaver and Moorman, vol. 2, p. 194.

51. Wordsworth, *Poems, in Two Volumes* (1807), p. 267.

52. Mant, *The Simpliciad*, pp. 17–18.

53. The passages that Mant quotes in the footnote continue this purposeful elision:

> I saw a man before me unawares,
> The oldest man he seemed, that ever wore gray hairs.
> * * *
> Motionless as a cloud the old man stood,
> That heareth not the loud winds when they call,
> And moveth altogether, if it move at all.
> At length himself, unsettling, he the pond
> Stirred with his staff, and fixedly did look
> Upon the muddy water, which he conn'd
> As if he had been reading in a book.
> * * *
> He with a smile did then his words repeat;
> And said that gathering leeches, far and wide
> He traveled, stirring thus about his feet
> The waters of the pond where they abide.
> Once I could meet with them on every side,
> But they have dwindled long by slow decay;
> Yet still I persevere, and find them where I may.
> * * *
> ----------when he ended,
> I could have laughed myself to scorn, to find
> In that decrepit man so firm a mind.
> 'God, said I, be my help and stay secure;
> I'll think of the leech-gatherer on the lonely moor.'

54. In *Wordsworth and the Enlightenment*, Bewell usefully describes the poet in 'Resolution and Independence' as engaged in 'word gathering', p. 269.

55. Wordsworth was acutely aware of differing types of readers. His revisions to the first version of this poem, 'The Leech Gatherer', which transformed it into 'Resolution and Independence', demonstrate the impact of his coterie circle's opinions. See G. Ruoff's two chapters 'Wordsworth's "The Leech Gathere"', pp. 104–37, and 'Wordsworth's

"Resolution and Independence"', pp. 138–66, in *Wordsworth and Coleridge: The Making of the Major Lyrics 1802–1804* (New Brunswick, NJ: Rutgers University Press, 1989). Wordsworth's letter to Lady Beaumont on 21 May 1807 also demonstrates his grasp of differing reader responses. And, his 1815 'Essay Supplementary to the Preface' further divides readers of poetry into three categories: (1) those people who in their youth loved poetry, like 'a passion', but then outgrew that passion to look on poetry as either an 'occasional recreation' or a 'luxurious amusement'; (2) those people 'in middle age', who 'resort to poetry, as to religion'; and (3) those people who 'cultivate general literature' and comprehend poetry 'as a study', *Shorter Poems, 1807–1820*, ed. C. Ketcham, pp. 643–5. Here, Wordsworth points out the errors that each group is prone to make, and he places his seeming trust in the third group of readers, whose opinions can suggest 'the destiny of a new work', p. 643.

56. Compare this type of reading to the reading he describes in his letter to Lady Beaumont about his 1807 sonnet 'With Ships the Sea was Sprinkled Far and Nigh'. Wordsworth not only details his movement from 'a pleasurable state of feeling' succeeded by 'listlessness or apathy', a state of 'remissness' to a redoubled act of attention that is 'awakened', 'fixed and aroused', he also remarks that his intention is to include his 'Reader' in this process, 'inviting him to rest his mind as mine is resting', *The Letters of William and Dorothy Wordsworth*, ed. De Selincourt, rev. Moorman, vol. 2, p. 149).

57. Wordsworth extensively revised this poem and excised nearly all of the leech gatherer's speech from an earlier version. These revisions were a response to S. Hutchinson and M. Wordsworth who criticized the leech gatherer's multiple speeches. See Curtis's chapter 'Toward the Language of Vision: Two Versions of "Resolution and Independence"', in *Wordsworth's Experiments with Tradition*, pp. 97–113.

58. Wordsworth, 'Resolution and Independence' line references.

59. Wordsworth's poems in volume 2, which provide a tour of Scotland and the Lake District, continue several of these themes and single out specific political, martial and literary figures as heroic symbols who point towards Britain's common heritage. That journey ends, as does the collection, with the poet, who, in the concluding 'Ode', announces his own place in this pantheon of sites and heroic figures – 'my head hath its coronal' (l. 40).

4 Wordsworth's 'Library of Babel': *The Excursion* and the 1815 *Poems*

1. This twist on Borges's story responds, in part, to the opening sentence of Heffernan's 'Mutilated Autobiography': 'Jorge Luis Borges has written that to arrange one's books is, in a modest way, to practice criticism' (p. 107). In the midst of this article, Heffernan 'frankly admit(s) that I have never read' the 1815 *Poems* (p. 108).

2. According to Owen in 'Costs, Sales, and Profits', Longman's figures show that 230 copies of his two-volume edition still remained from the initial 1,000 copy print run of the two-volumes (p. 96).

3. Between the 1807 *Poems* and the 1814 *The Excursion*, Wordsworth published his first *Essay upon Epitaphs* in Coleridge's the *Friend* (1810) as well as his essay 'The Convention of Cintra' (1809). Notably, Wordsworth withheld 'The White Doe of Rylstone' (1815), 'The Waggoner' (1819) and 'Peter Bell' (1819) until after he published *The Excursion* and the 1815 *Poems*. See Manning's chapter '*The White Doe of Rylstone, The Convention of Cintra*, and the History of a Career', in his *Reading Romantics*, for an explanation of the politics that influenced Wordsworth's reluctance to publish, pp. 165–94.

4.   P. Connell, 'Bibliomania: Book Collecting, Cultural Politics, and the Rise of Literary Heritage in Romantic Britain', *Representations*, 70 (Summer 2000), pp. 24–47, on p. 27.

5.   While my argument about Wordsworth's re-entrance into the print market relates to the number of publications (both poetry and prose) flooding the print market in the 1810s, further inquiry into this subject would need to closely take into account the production of poetry anthologies and miscellanies. These anthologies typically feature numerous poets, and they were often organized according to principles that would lead to their highest economic success. Consequently, popular poets, both contemporary and canonical, were featured in ways that were immediately pleasing and easily readable. As Ferry points out in *Tradition and the Individual Poem*, short lyric poems and even excerpted poems became the norm, allowing readers to skip from poem to poem at their leisure and whim. Wordsworth's endeavours, then, not only countered the growing economic stagnation of publishing individual poets, which comes to a head in the 1820s; they also seem to combat the type of reading that these anthologies set up as pleasurable for a growing middle-class readership.

6.   J. Gross's *The Rise and Fall of the Man of Letters: Aspects of English Literary Life Since 1800* (Ivan R. Dee: Chicago, 1969) provides a succinct history, as does M. Butler's 'The Rise of the Man of Letters: Coleridge', in her *Romantics, Rebels, and Reactionaries* (Oxford: Oxford University Press, 1981).

7.   During the first few decades of the nineteenth century, the concept of the 'man of letters' was undergoing a redefinition, perhaps, most acutely through Coleridge's *Biographia Literaria* (1817). In his article Connell focuses on the burgeoning role of this new 'man of letters' by analysing T. F. Dibdin's and I. D'Israeli's writings about bibliomania. In *The Bibliomania; or, Book Madness* (London, 1809), Dibdin calls for the creation of well-informed bibliographers to help transform the aristocratic bibliomaniac from a self-serving collector into a public benefactor interested in collecting together the nation's literary heritage. By contrast, in his *Curiosities of Literature* (London, 1817) and *The Literary Character* (London, 1822), D'Israeli appeals to a mass audience by establishing the 'man of letters' as a mediator who redirects the reading public's book cravings through an anecdotal method of writing. Connell maintains that D'Israeli's method was popular because it enabled diverse readers to 'aspire to a moment of cultural identification seemingly unconstrained by social class or narrowly institutionalized forms of knowledge', 'Bibliomania', p. 42.

8.   Connell, 'Bibliomania', p. 42.

9.   My argument about Wordsworth as a collector draws on a number of works about Wordsworth's classification system for his 1815 collection. See Arthur Beatty's *William Wordsworth: His Doctrine and Art in their Historical Relations* (Madison, WI: University of Wisconsin Press, 1962); James Scoggins's defence of Wordsworth's category of fancy and juxtaposition of it with imagination in *Imagination and Fancy: Complementary Modes of the Poetry of Wordsworth* (Lincoln, NE: University of Nebraska Press, 1966); and Francis Ferguson's *Wordsworth: Language as Counter-Spirit* (New Haven, CT: Yale University Press, 1977), which offers a sweeping analysis of four of Wordsworth's psychological categories as a developmental narrative. In the *Wordsworth Circle* a series of articles discuss Wordsworth's psychological categories, Wordsworth's role as editor, and his awareness of reader response. See G. Ruoff, 'Critical Implications of Wordsworth's 1815 Categorization, with Some Animadversions on Binaristic Commentary', 9 (1978), pp. 75–82, J. B. Herman, 'The Poet as Editor: Wordsworth's Edition of 1815', *Wordsworth Circle*, 9 (1978), pp. 82–7, Hefferman's 'Mutilated Autobiography' and D.

Ross Jr's 'Poems "Bound Each to Each" in the 1815 Edition of Wordsworth', 12 (1981), pp. 133–40. S. Meisenhelder's *Wordsworth's Informed Reader: Structures of Experience in his Poetry* (Nashville, TN: Vanderbilt University Press, 1988) offers a pointed examination of the experience of reading the 1815 Poems, and D. Duff's 'Wordsworth and the Language of Forms: The Collected *Poems* of 1815', *Wordsworth Circle*, 34:2 (2003), pp. 86–90, analyses Wordsworth's rhetorical genre difficulties and paradigm shifts in the 1815 'Preface'.

10. Unless otherwise noted, all passages from *The Excursion* are quoted from E. de Selincourt's *The Poetical Works of William Wordsworth*, 5 vols (Oxford: Clarendon Press, 1959).

11. Gill, *William Wordsworth: A Life*, p. 302.

12. Wordsworth uses the form of this sonnet to structure his anxiety about publication and the integrity of his work. Like several of Shakespeare's sonnets, this sonnet testifies to its monumental status as a complete whole and points metonymically to a larger whole. Wordsworth inverts the rhyme scheme of the final two lines from DE to ED, suggesting his ability to manipulate poems that only seem 'premature' within a coherent and contained structure.

13. 'Preface to the Edition of 1814', in *The Poetical Works of William Wordsworth*, ed. De Selincourt, vol. 2, p. 1.

14. Ibid., vol. 2, pp. 2–3.

15. Ibid., vol., 2, p. 2.

16. As K. Johnston shows in *Wordsworth and The Recluse* (New Haven, CT: Yale University Press, 1984), Wordsworth creates this chronology for his readers, though actual composition of *The Recluse* began before *The Prelude*.

17. 'Preface to the Edition of 1814', p. 1.

18. Quoted in Woof (ed.), *William Wordsworth: The Critical Heritage, Vol. 1: 1793–1830*, p. 385.

19. Quoted in ibid., p. 382.

20. Quoted in ibid.

21. Quoted in ibid., p. 383. For a brief history of how commonly reviewing critics in the Romantic period appropriated medical discourses to elevate their professional status and to position themselves as physicians diagnosing the perversity of seeming literary genius, see D. Felluga's chapter 'The Tropic Body and the Constitution of the Man of Letters', in his *The Perversity of Poetry: Romantic Ideology and the Popular Male Poet of Genius* (Albany, NY: State University of New York Press, 2005), pp. 13–32.

22. Quoted in Woof (ed.), *William Wordsworth: The Critical Heritage, Vol. 1: 1793–1830*, p. 383.

23. Quoted in ibid.

24. Quoted in ibid., p. 384.

25. Quoted in ibid., p. 382.

26. In 'Rhetorical Structure of the Prospectus to *The Recluse*', in his *Monumental Writing: Aspects of Rhetoric in Wordsworth's Poetry* (Lincoln, NE: University of Nebraska Press, 1988), J. D. Kneale unpacks the rhetoric of the 'Prospectus' by focusing on how Wordsworth vacillates between proposal and apostrophe and draws attention to the complex allusive nature of its Miltonic and Shakespearean design.

27. R. A. Foakes (ed.), 'Unassigned Lecture Notes: Milton and *Paradise Lost*', in *The Collected Works of Samuel Taylor Coleridge, Vol. 5: Lectures 1808–1819 on Literature*, ed.

K. Coburn (London: Routledge, Kegan Paul and Princeton University Press, 1987), pt 2, p. 428.

28. In *Palimpsests Literature in the Second Degree*, trans. C Newman and C. Doubinsky (Lincoln, NE: University of Nebraska Press, 1997) G. Genette's discussion of cyclical continuations offers several valuable insights for describing the reading and rewriting activities that Wordsworth's intertextual connections invite. I draw on the four types of hypertextual continuation that Genette describes as 'proleptic' (a text that finishes another text), 'analeptic' (a text that provides the events leading up to that text), 'elleptic' (a text that bridges two texts), and 'paralleptic' (a text providing contiguous present moments for another text).

29. T. McFarland, *Romanticism and the Forms of Ruin: Wordsworth, Coleridge, and Modalities of Fragmentation* (Princeton, NJ: Princeton University Press, 1981), p. 109.

30. Wordsworth, quoted in ibid., p. 2.

31. Wordsworth, quoted in ibid., p. 2.

32. In *Reading, Writing, and Romanticism*, Newlyn provides a useful parallel for considering Wordsworth's Gothic church metaphor. Describing Coleridge's spoof-letter from a friend in book 13 of the *Biographia Literaria*, Newlyn maintains that readers who gaze on this Gothic church and work through their initial frustration and/or dissatisfaction will move from resistance to awe, even becoming a part of the very Gothic structure that they contemplate (p. 82). In *The Professional Wordsworth*, Schoenfield draws even wider cultural implications from Wordsworth's Gothic church metaphor: 'Wordsworth uses the architectural metaphor of a gothic church, the social function of which overspills its confines into the courts, the shops, the farms, the day-to-day life of the town, and which, because its construction takes centuries, is used before completion and requires its occupants to complete it imaginatively' (p. 195).

33. W. J. B. Owen's *Wordsworth as Critic* (Toronto, Ontario: Toronto University Press, 1969) has, arguably, the most influential analysis of the 1815 essays.

34. The 1815 *Poems* were supposed to be published within a few months of the 1814 *The Excursion*. However, Wordsworth delayed publication until 1815 largely to write the 'Essay Supplementary to the Preface', which responds to scathing reviews of *The Excursion*. For a brief history of the categories in and construction of the 1815 volumes, see C. Ketcham's introduction to *Shorter Poems, 1807–1820* (NY: Cornell University Press, 1989), pp. 19–32. Ketcham also provides the published version and manuscripts of Wordsworth's 1815 *Poems*, though not in the order in which they were published.

35. This review appears in *Theatrical Inquisitor*, 6 (June 1815), pp. 445–50, quoted in Woof (ed.) *William Wordsworth: The Critical Heritage, Vol. 1: 1793–1830*, on p. 521.

36. Woof (ed.), *William Wordsworth: The Critical Heritage, Vol. 1: 1793–1830*, p. 521.

37. See Franta's recent discussion of this skewed history in his chapter 'Wordsworth's Audience Problem', in *Romanticism and the Rise of the Mass Public*, pp. 57–61.

38. *The Prose Works of William Wordsworth*, ed. W. J. B. Owen and J. W. Smyser, 3 vols (Oxford : Clarendon Press, 1974), vol. 2, p. 426.

39. Ibid., vol. 2, p. 430.

40. In the preface to *Wordsworth's Reading 1800–1815* (Cambridge: Cambridge University Press, 1995), Wu describes the development of Wordsworth's private library beginning with his move to Grasmere in 1799 up to the collection of his library after his move to Rydal Mount in 1812. Wu also points out the difficulties of identifying all of the books that Wordsworth collected at any one given period of time.

41. *The Prose Works of William Wordsworth*, ed. Owen and Smyser, vol. 2, p. 417.

42. Ibid.
43. Ibid., vol. 2, p. 425.
44. Ibid.
45. Ibid., vol. 2, p. 417.
46. Ibid. vol. 2, p. 416.
47. Ibid., vol. 2, p. 421.
48. Ibid., vol. 2, p. 422.
49. Ibid., vol. 2, pp. 424–5.
50. In 'Walter Scott, Antiquarianism and the Political Discourse of the *Edinburgh Review, 1802–1811*', in M. Demata and D. Wu (eds), *British Romanticism and the Edinburgh Review* (New York: Palgrave Macmillan, 2002), pp. 102–23, S. Manning describes several public discussions about the cultural importance of antiquarian collecting pursuits, both from a Whig perspective of progress (Jeffrey) and from an elegiac Tory perspective (Scott). Taking Percy's *Reliques* as a point of reference for collecting tendencies that Jeffrey praises, Manning remarks that it 'was chronologically arranged to display the "progress" of poetry from primitive expression towards (relatively) reflective refinement' (p. 113).
51. *The Prose Works of William Wordsworth*, ed. Owen and Smyser, vol. 2, p. 426.
52. Ibid., vol. 2, p. 429.
53. Ibid.
54. Ibid., vol. 2, p. 430.
55. Such a statement harkens forward to 'men of letters' who champion Wordsworth like J. S. Mill, Matthew Arnold, Thomas Carlyle and John Ruskin.
56. My claims counter Abrams's influential argument that Wordsworth's 'Essay Supplementary' demonstrates how Wordsworth turned his back on his audience and adopted an attitude towards poetry, perhaps best articulated by J. S. Mill in 'What is Poetry' (1833). My argument also differs from Newlyn's in *Reading, Writing, and Romanticism* as well as from Bennett's in *Romantic Poets and the Culture of Posterity* in that I do not understand Wordsworth to be limiting his audience to a coterie circle of close friends and family. Franta's argument in 'Wordsworth's Audience Problem', pp. 68–75, begins to suggest the position I develop here.
57. Connell provides an excellent discussion of D'Israeli's anecdotal method in his essays, which 'blended biographical anecdote with history, criticism, and sociology of literature gleaned from a bewildering variety of sources and ranging eclectically over time and place, polite and popular culture' ('Bibliomania', p. 40).
58. *The Prose Works of William Wordsworth*, ed. Owen and Smyser, vol. 2, p. 431.
59. Ibid., vol. 2, p. 432.
60. Ibid.
61. Ibid., vol. 2, pp. 432–3.
62. Ibid., vol. 2, p. 434.
63. Ibid.
64. Ibid.
65. Ibid., vol. 2, p. 435.
66. Connell, 'Bibliomania', p. 42.
67. Woof (ed.), *William Wordsworth: The Critical Heritage, Vol. 1: 1793–1830*, p. 558.
68. Ibid.
69. Ibid., p. 559.

70. Wordsworth previously related the word 'composition' to British nationalism in his categories 'Miscellaneous Sonnets' and 'Sonnets Dedicated to Liberty' in *Poems, in Two Volumes* (1807).

71. One of Wordsworth's 1815 poems in his section 'Epitaphs and Elegiac Poems' demonstrates how readers can inscribe themselves in Wordsworth's collected poems. In the headnote, 'written, november 13, 1814 on a blank leaf in a Copy of the Author's Poem *THE EXCURSION*, upon hearing of the death of the late Vicar of Kendal', Wordsworth writes:

> To public notice, with reluctance strong,
> Did I deliver this unfinished song,
> Yet for one happy issue;– and I look
> With self-congratulation on the Book
> Which pious MURFITT saw and read;–
> Upon my thoughts his saintly Spirit fed;
> He conn'd the new-born Lay with grateful heart;
> Foreboding not how soon he must depart,
> Unweeting that to him the joy was given
> Which good Men take with them from Earth to Heaven. (p. 336)

   Wordsworth inscribes an epitaph for a vicar within *The Excursion*, an epic poem that charts the life, death and times of early nineteenth-century Britain. The vicar's active reading and emotional investment in *The Excursion* situate Wordsworth's fragmented epic as a link between the living and the dead, and as a work to be looked back on and revered for what it can provide in the future. Murfitt, the vicar, becomes a monumental part of Wordsworth's fragmented poem. Like the 'Leech Gatherer', Wordsworth transforms 'pious Murfitt' into a poetic model to be revered and imitated; he joins Wordsworth's pages and cast of characters and monumentalizes *The Excursion* as a poem central to the nation's heritage and development.

72. Although S. Curran's chapter 'Composite Orders' in *Poetic Form and British Romanticism* (Cambridge: Cambridge University Press, 1986), pp. 180–203, deals with longer Romantic poems, his definitions provide a useful starting point for considering the construction of mixed genres in the Romantic period.

73. *The Prose Works of William Wordsworth*, ed. Owen and Smyser, vol. 2, p. 432.

74. Wordsworth, *Lyrical Ballads* (1800), quoted in *Lyrical Ballads and Other Poems, 1797–1800*, ed. Butler and Green, p. 116.

75. A. Patterson's 'Two Steps Forward, One Step Backwards: William Wordsworth's Revisionism', in her *Nobody's Perfect: A New Whig Interpretation of History* (New Haven, CT: Yale University Press, 2002), pp. 238–56, provides a fresh perspective on Wordsworth's purposeful return in his poetry to his youthful errancy. For a closer literary study of the poem, see Kelley's section on 'Tintern Abbey' in her chapter 'The Scene of Aesthetic Instruction', in *Wordsworth's Revisionary Aesthetics*, pp. 57–62.

76. 'Composed' also suggests a collective psychological calming or balancing, which might be aligned with E. Burke's political thought and a broader conservative movement in politics in 1815. However, Wordsworth's attempts in his 1815 *Poems* to unite a war-torn nation are far less programmatic and politically motivated than his overt declaration of patriotism in the 'Advertisement' to his *Thanksgiving Ode* volume (1816) – a tribute

to Waterloo and Britain's defeat of Napoleonic France. Garrett describes Wordsworth's patriotism in that 1816 volume in *Wordsworth and the Writing of the Nation*, pp. 81–9. On British Romantic nationalism and the Napoleonic Wars, see D. Simpson, *Romanticism, Nationalism and the Revolt Against Theory* (Chicago, IL: University of Chicago Press, 1993), pp. 40–3; M. Ross, 'Romancing the Nation-State: The Poetics of Romantic Nationalism', in J. Arac and J. Ritvo (eds), *Macropolitics of Nineteenth-Century Literature* (Durham, NC: Duke University Press, 1995), pp. 56–85; P. Shaw's edited collection *Romantic Wars: Studies in Culture and Conflict, 1793–1822* (Burlington, VT: Ashgate University Press, 2000) and his *Waterloo and the Romantic Imagination* (Basingstoke: Palgrave Macmillan, 2002); and J. R. Watson, *Romanticism and War* (Basingstoke: Palgrave Macmillan, 2003).

77. In 1815, 'Lines Composed' falls more clearly under the georgic than the pastoral. R. Crawford's *Poetry, Enclosure, and the Vernacular Landscape, 1700–1830* (Cambridge: Cambridge University Press, 2002), pp. 24–8, considers the georgic as a genre about nationhood that invites readers to participate. For the influence of Virgil's *Georgics* on Wordsworth's 1798 'Tintern Abbey', see J. Rieder, *Wordsworth's Counterrevolutionary Turn: Community, Virtue, and Vision in the 1790s* (Newark, DE: University of Delaware Press, 1997), pp. 206–11.

78. Levinson's *Wordsworth's Great Period Poems* still resounds as the most controversial attack on Wordsworth's political occlusions, though, K. Johnston's 'The Politics of "Tintern Abbey"', *Wordsworth Circle*, 14 (1983), pp. 6–14, sounds an earlier but less derisive inquiry into Wordsworthian politics. Building from J. McGann's wider critique of Romanticism in *The Romantic Ideology: A Critical Investigation* (Chicago, IL: Chicago University Press, 1983), Levinson's argument met with heated resistance in books like T. McFarland's *William Wordsworth: Intensity and Achievement* (Oxford: Oxford University Press, 1992) and in more pointed articles like M. H. Abrams's 'On Political Readings of "Tintern Abbey"', in K. Johnston (ed.) *Romantic Revolutions: Criticism and Theory* (Bloomington, IN: Indiana University Press, 1990), pp. 320–49. Abrams's counterargument also offers an intriguing return to his position on 'Tintern Abbey' as a greater Romantic lyric. Rzepka's article 'Pictures of the Mind' is the latest attempt to refute Levinson's argument and evidence while A. Liu's *Wordsworth: The Sense of History* (Palo Alto, CA: Stanford University Press, 1989) provides the widest-sweeping exploration of Wordsworth's poetic project and supposed 'bad faith'. For a slightly different political analysis, see W. Richey, 'The Politicized Landscape of "Tintern Abbey"', *Studies in Philology*, 95:2 (1998), pp. 197–219, which asserts that Wordsworth deliberatively engages the reading public with social and political issues in the poem.

79. 'No poem of mine was composed under circumstances more pleasant for me to remember than this: I began it upon leaving Tintern, after crossing the Wye, and concluded it just as I was entering Bristol in the evening, after a ramble of 4 or 5 days, with my sister. Not a line of it was altered, and not any part of it written down till I reached Bristol. It was published almost immediately after in the little volume of which so much has been said in these notes'. See *The Fenwick Notes*, ed. Curtis, p. 15).

80. As the poet of nature and a poet widely known to 'compose', recite and dictate his poetry out loud, Wordsworth is often described as a poet unconcerned with the textuality of his books of poetry. In the Winter 2003 issue of the *Wordsworth Circle* devoted to Wordsworth as a writer, see A. Bennett's 'Wordsworth Writing', *Wordsworth Circle*, 34:1 (2003), pp. 1–8, which focuses on the commonplace critical belief that Wordsworth

placed little stock in words, was a spontaneous, oral poet of nature, and actually wrote very little poetry, pp. 3–8. Bennett, however, maintains:

'As a glance at the surviving manuscripts amply demonstrates, the emphasis on Wordsworth's effusive, alfresco, extempore, spontaneous, perambulatory mode of composition focuses on just a part of his practice, which in fact involves writing, re-writing, deleting, scratching out and overwriting, murmuring, 'bumming and booing about', revising and dictating, in a variety of places and postures that include walking, sitting, lying down, standing still, riding a horse or sitting in a carriage as well as, finally, sitting at a table in a house, pen or pencil in hand, to write or write out words that – after revision and replacement, deletion, review, re-revision, alteration, correction and editing – become completed poems.' (p. 8)

Chapter 2, 'Tintern Abbey and the Nature of Writing', pp. 42–57, in Bennett's *Wordsworth Writing* offers a fresh interpretation of the title change from 'Lines Written' to 'Lines Composed'. He argues that the poem's multiple titles and structure laud speech and natural inspiration but also anxiously record how necessary Bristol and writing were for its creation and are for its reception.

81. In the 1850 *The Prelude*, it is part of book 11.

82. Book 5 explores the relationship between perishable, praiseworthy and detrimental books, as well as the seemingly imperishable character of nature. In book 5, 'The Boy of Winander' episode comes between the poet's dream and the episode of the drowned man.

83. In the 1815 'Preface', Wordsworth singles this poem out to represent 'one of the earliest processes of Nature in the development of [the imagination ... I have represented a commutation and transfer of internal feelings, co-operating with external accidents to plant, for immortality, images of sound and sight, in the celestial soil of the Imagination', p. 440.

84. The poem was actually written sometime between 1802 and 1803.

85. Wordsworth includes the following quotation to explain his editorial decision to include *An Evening Walk* and *Descriptive Sketches* in the 1815 collection:

> the sounding cataract
> Haunted me like a passion: the tall rock
> The mountain, and the deep and gloomy wood,
> Their colours and their forms were then to me
> An appetite, a feeling and a love,
> That had no need of remoter charm,
> By thought supplied, or any interest
> Unborrowed from the eye. (pp. 76–83)

86. A. Janowitz, 'Coleridge's 1816 Volume: Fragment and Ruin', *Studies in Romanticism*, 24:1 (1985), pp. 21–39, on p. 32.

87. K. Heinzelman explains how aspects of economics are created/produced linguistically and how economics are imaginatively used (In *The Economics of the Imagination* (Amherst, MA: University of Massachusetts Press, 1980); of particular use for my argument are chapters 5–7: 'The Art of Labor'; 'The Psychomachia of Labor'; and 'Wordsworth's Labor Theory: An Economics of Compensation'.

5 Opening up Chapter 13 of Coleridge's *Biographia Literaria*

1. Divided into two parts, the letter first offers a private testimony (quoted above) about the disturbing effects that reading this chapter has had on the 'Friend' and then outlines why the reading public would react negatively to such an inordinately long, obscurely written, intellectually vexing and economically taxing chapter.

2. I draw on J. Hogle's 'Introduction: The Gothic in Western Culture', in J. Hogle (ed.), *The Cambridge Companion to Gothic Fiction* (Cambridge: Cambridge University Press, 2002), pp. 1–20, about the Gothic counterfeit as a sign of textual instability. Generally, a Gothic counterfeit is a playful fakery of textual authenticity that often stands in the way of (and prompts) readers' engagement with an 'original' text. Following Horace Walpole's presentation of the first edition of *The Castle of Otranto* (1764) as a found and translated, medieval text, Gothic counterfeits became staples of Gothic romances in prose and poetry.

3. For a full discussion of these issues, see Gamer's introduction, 'Romanticism's 'Pageantry of Fear', in *Romanticism and the Gothic*, pp. 1–26.

4. B. Mudge, '"Excited by Trick": Coleridge and the Gothic Imagination', *Wordsworth Circle*, 22:3 (Summer 1991), pp. 179–184, on p. 182.

5. Coleridge's 1818 lectures delivered in Bristol on the 'General Character of the Gothic Mind in the Middle Ages' and the 'General Character of the Gothic Literature and Art' demonstrate how invested Coleridge was in sketching out the nation's political and aesthetic Gothic heritage. Notes taken by two members of Coleridge's Bristol audience, J. H. Green and W. Hammond, testify to Coleridge's unbounded praise for the independent, freedom loving character of the Goths in the '[n]orthern nations' and their architecture, which encourages 'submission, but with free choice', fills the viewer 'with devotion and awe', and transforms that viewer into 'a part of the work contemplated [because of] ... endless complexity and variety [which] are united into one whole, the plan of which is not distinct from the execution', pp. 95–6. Quoted from E. J. Clery and R. Miles (eds), *Gothic Documents A Sourcebook 1700–1820* (New York: Manchester University Press, 2000), which was quoted from *Coleridge's Miscellaneous Criticism*, ed. T. M. Raysor (London: Constable, 1936), pp. 6–8, 11–13.

6. Simpson, *Romanticism, Nationalism, and the Revolt Against Theory*, p. 62.

7. Ibid., p. 40. See volume 1 of the *Friend*, ed. B. E. Rooke, 2 vols (Princeton, NJ: Princeton University Press, 1969), pp. 421–3. Although Simpson only briefly deals with Coleridge's sense of nationalism, he provides a useful framework that describes the forms and effects of this triad of faculties: 'in Germany, idea, totality, and distinctness; in England, law discovered, selection, and clearness; and in France, theory invented, particularity and palpability. Finally, each of the three countries demonstrates a nationally specific attitude toward time. Germany is occupied with past and future, England with past and present, and France with the present', p. 40. I draw broadly on Simpson's exposition of the development, from the seventeenth through the early nineteenth century, of a national character, which he maintains was based heavily on 'British hostility toward theory and method', p. 30.

8. Coleridge's efforts to equate Britain's enduring literary character with a distinctly English character might also be understood as an attempt to rest power away from Jeffrey's *Edinburgh Review*, which Coleridge contends, throughout the *Biographia Literaria*, had dictated and largely perverted the tastes of the reading public. According to W. Christie in his chapter 'A Mortal Antipathy to Scotchmen', pp. 101–22, *Biographia Literaria*

plays out Coleridge's 'antipathy to Scotchmen' and denigrates Jeffrey's position as a Scottish 'pragmatist, associationist, consensualist, and sceptic; Whig reformist and agent and prophet of the middle-class hegemony' while celebrating Coleridge's portrait of his own English literary character and disinterested role as a reviewing critic, *The Edinburgh Review*, pp. 102, 122.

9. The works of most importance to my argument are: G. Spivak, 'The Letter As Cutting Edge', *Yale French Studies*, 55/56 (1977), pp. 208–26; J. Christensen, *Coleridge's Blessed Machine of Language* (Ithaca, NY: Cornell University Press, 1981); K. Wheeler, *Sources, Processes and Methods in Coleridge's Biographia Literaria* (Cambridge: Cambridge University Press, 1980); Johnston, *Wordsworth and The Recluse*; F. Burwick's edited collection, *Coleridge's Biographia Literaria Text and Meaning* (Columbus, OH: Ohio State University Press, 1989); S. Pricket, '*Biographia Literaria*: Chapter Thirteen' D. Coleman and P. Otto (eds), *Imagining Romanticism: Essays on English and Australian Romanticisms* (West Cornhall, CT: Locust Hill Press, 1992), pp. 3–24; S. Kearns, *Coleridge, Wordsworth, and Romantic Autobiography* (Madison, NJ: Farleigh Dickinson University Press, 1995); and A. Timar, 'Imagination Disconnected: On Chapter XIII of *Biographia Literaria*', *The AnaChronisT* (2002), pp. 79–111. Timar usefully divides recent criticism of the letter into two categories: critics either focus on the hermeneutic purpose of the letter, or they concentrate on identifying who the persona of the letter actually is (pp. 79–84).

10. Simpson, *Romanticism, Nationalism and the Revolt Against Theory*, pp. 42–3.

11. My argument draws on the intertextual references that Johnston identifies in his chapter '*The Recluse* and *Biographia Literaria*, 1814–1815', pp. 333–62. He argues that chapter 13 responds to Wordsworth's 'Preface to *The Excursion*' and supplementary prose published with his 1815 *Poems*, as well as to private correspondence that passed between the two concerning the failings of Wordsworth's *The Recluse* project. Some of the particular parallels that Johnston points out are: *Biographia Literaria* as equivalent to *The Excursion*, *Sibylline Leaves* as equivalent to Wordsworth's 1815 *Poems*, the letter in chapter 13 as equivalent to Wordsworth's 'Essay Supplementary', Coleridge's short definitions of the fancy and imagination as equivalent to Wordsworth's 'Prospectus to *The Excursion*'. Johnston also argues that the fictitious friend is really 'Coleridge ... writing to himself as he had written in a letter to Wordsworth [about *The Recluse*], and as if Wordsworth were now writing to him – albeit a Wordsworth, who speaks in playful Coleridgean ironies', p. 355. While this last claim reveals a great deal about Wordsworth and Coleridge's literary relationship, it does not adequately explain the many complex issues about reading, writing and reception that this letter plays out.

12. Through the 'Friend's' reading, Coleridge gathers together public opinion into a quasi-Wordsworthian prospectus, preface and essay supplementary that link together pieces of Coleridge's works.

13. In 'Romancing the Nation-State: The Poetics of Romantic Nationalism', in *Macropolitics*, Ross explains a related, but more politically conservative conception of nationhood: 'For a modern nation to progress, [Edmund Burke] claims, it must never lose touch with its past; for it to expand, it must never lose sight of its center ... Burke's state becomes a living body, an organic form that grows into itself by feeding on its origin', pp. 57–58.

14. I draw on the following definitions in the *Oxford English Dictionary*: 'Paper, parchment, or other writing material designed to be reusable...on which the original text has been effaced or partially erased, and then overwritten by another; a manuscript in which later writing has been superimposed on earlier (effaced) writing'; 'In extended use: a thing

likened to such a writing surface, esp. in having been reused or altered while still retaining traces of its earlier form; a multi-layered record ... or structure characterized by superimposed features produced at two or more distinct periods'.

15. On Coleridge's poetry in the 1790s, see N. Roe, *Wordsworth and Coleridge: The Radical Years* (Oxford: Oxford University Press, 1988), and on Coleridge's place in the Regency period, see R. Lapp, *Contest for Cultural Authority: Hazlitt, Coleridge and the Distresses of the Regency* (Detroit, MI: Wayne State University Press, 1999).

16. Coleridge went to great lengths to ensure that chapter 13 would remain in its textual place. See J. Engell and W. J. Bate's introduction to the *Biographia Literaria* (1817) (Princeton, NJ: Princeton University Press, 1983), pp. lviii–lxviii.

17. In *Britons* (New Haven, CT: Yale University Press, 1992), L. Colley maintains that in the late eighteenth and early nineteenth centuries, it was common for people – whether rich and educated or poor and uneducated – in the British isles to 'think in terms of dual nationalities, not a single national identity', p. 373. In other words, one could think of oneself as Scottish and British, though one identity might take priority over the other given the context. In the *Biographia Literaria* Coleridge seems intent on establishing his concept of England's literary character as a foundation on which Britain's shared, evolving cultural identity might rest.

18. Coleridge, *Biographia Literaria*, ed. Engell and Bate, p. 304.

19. Ibid., p. 306.

20. Many contemporary critics have explained away the fragments, gaps and unfinished pieces in Coleridge's works by asserting his inability to finish what he starts. I draw on Levinson's explanations of fragmentation as an aesthetic and cultural phenomenon in *The Romantic Fragment Poem*.

21. A few reviewing critics did understand chapter 13 as a joke on readers. In *Blackwood's Edinburgh Magazine* (October 1817), C. North enacts the practical-minded criticism that underpins the public objections described in the second half of the 'Friend's' letter. In trying to make sense of the disruption in chapter 13, North imagines Coleridge as if Coleridge was delivering a public lecture: '[Coleridge] has written a long chapter purposely to prepare our minds for the great discussion [of Fancy and Imagination]. The audience is assembled, the curtain is drawn up, and there, in his gown, cap, and wig is sitting Professor Coleridge. In comes a servant with a letter; the Professor gets up, and, with solemn voice, reads it to his audience. It is from an enlightened Friend; and its object is to shew, in no very courteous terms either to the Professor or his Spectators, that he may lecture, but that nobody will understand him. He accordingly makes his bow, and the curtain falls; but the worst of the joke is, that the Professor pockets the admittance-money, for what reason, his outwitted audience are left, the best way they can, to "fancy or imagine"'. See *Coleridge: The Critical Heritage*, ed. De Jackson, p. 348.

22. *The Rime* follows 'two school boy poems', 'a song modernized with some additions from one of our elder poets' and a list of 'Errata' (iii). These preliminary poems are titled 'Time, Real and Imaginary', 'The Raven' and 'Mutual Passion'.

23. In July 1817 Coleridge published his two-volume *Biographia Literaria* and his one-volume collected poems *Sibylline Leaves*. In the spring of 1815 when Coleridge began writing/dictating the *Biographia Literaria*, he described it as a preface to his collected poems and as a direct response to Wordsworth's 1814 *The Excursion* and 1815 two-volume *Poems*. For a history of how this initial conception was altered, see Jackson and Bate's introduction to *Biographia Literaria*, pp. xlv–li. The spring of 1815 marked the

beginning of an energetic time for Coleridge that resulted in his collecting together a great deal of his older poetry and writing of a large body of new prose. Beyond preparing *Sibylline Leaves*, in May 1816 'Christabel', 'Kubla Khan', and 'The Pains of Sleep' were published in a slim volume by John Murray. On the prose side, Coleridge published the *Statesman's Manual* (December 1816) and his second *Lay Sermon* (April 1817). He also prepared a three-volume edition of the *Friend* (November 1818).

24. This reference also calls attention to the poem's changing place and status in *Lyrical Ballads*. P. Fry's 'Wordsworth in the "Rime,"' in *The Rime of the Ancient Mariner: Complete, Authoritative Texts of the 1798 and 1817 Versions* (New York: Bedford St Martin's 1999), pp. 319–42, probes in detail the poetic allusions and philosophical disagreements between Wordsworth and Coleridge over the poem.

25. Coleridge, *Biographia Literaria*, ed. Engell and Bate, p. 231.

26. In *Coleridge and Textual Instability: The Multiple Versions of the Major Poems* (New York: Oxford University Press, 1992), J. Stillinger points out that as Coleridge 'kept revising his works, he also called attention to his revising in notes and prefaces to the poems. And he frequently changed his texts right before the reader's eyes (as it were) by means of printed errata lists, which both emphasize the fact that the revisions were made since the poems were set in type for the book and provide a second version of the printed poem to accompany and perhaps serve as a counterpoint to the first', p. 109. Stillinger refers to *Sibylline Leaves* to make his point: 'In *Sibylline Leaves*, where the errata revisions are the most extensive of all, the errata pages were (in most copies) placed prominently at the beginning rather than the end of the volume. Then there are the handwritten changes and revisions that Coleridge wrote in the margins and between the lines in copies of his works that he gave to his friends and acquaintances', p. 109.

27. Coleridge, *Biographia Literaria*, ed. Engell and Bate, p. 301.

28. As late as chapter 22 in the *Biographia Literaria*, Coleridge continues to encourage his readers to relate his philosophical arguments about poetry to *Sibylline Leaves*. At this point, he also expresses his wish that someone might give his poems in *Sibylline Leaves* the same critical attention that he has shown to Wordsworth's collected poems in the *Biographia*. Coleridge humbly requests, 'Even as I have done, so would I be done unto', p. 159.

29. For discussions of such a system-less system or encyclopedism, see D. Ferris, 'The Question of a Science: Encyclopedic Romanticism'; T. Rajan, 'Philosophy as Encyclopedia: Hegel, Schelling, and the Organization of Knowledge', *Wordsworth Circle*, 35:1 (Winter 2004), pp. 2–5; 6–11); and W. Moser, 'Translating Discourses: Inter-Discursive Mobility in the Early Romantic Encyclopedia', *The Eighteenth Century*, 22:1 (1981), pp. 3–20.

30. Quoted in *Coleridge: The Critical Heritage*, ed. De Jackson, pp. 388–9.

31. This critic does hazard a guess: 'the Sibylline books were preserved by Kings, had a College of Priests to take care of them, and were so esteemed by the people, that they were very seldom consulted; even so does Mr. Coleridge look to delight Monarchs, his book will be treasured by the Eleven Universities, and we venture to suppose that it will be treated by the public, quoad frequent perusal, pretty much in the same way with the ravings of his Archetypes', quoted in *Coleridge: The Critical Heritage*, ed. De Jackson, p. 389.

32. Coleridge, *Sibylline Leaves: A Collection of Poems* (London: Rest Fenner, 23, Paternoster-Row, 1817), p. i.

33. Coleridge does include subcategories in the volume, which readers encounter on half-title pages within the volume and which loosely divide his poems into sections: *The Rime of the Ancient Mariner. In Seven Parts*; *Poems Occasioned by Political Events or Feelings*

Connected with Them; *Fire, Famine, and Slaughter. A War-Eclogue with an Apologetic Preface*; *Love-Poems*; *Meditative Poems in Blank Verse*; *The Three Graves*; and *Odes and Miscellaneous Poems*. Unlike Wordsworth's intricate classification system in the 1815 *Poems* – a system with which the review culture had recently been preoccupied – where all might be said to fall under categories within the poet's mind, Coleridge's works very much resemble a collection of scattered leaves long out of their author's control.

34. *Coleridge: The Critical Heritage*, ed. De Jackson, p. 389.
35. Coleridge, *Sibylline Leaves*, pp. i–ii.
36. Ibid., p. ii.
37. Ibid.
38. 'The Destiny of Nations. A Vision', which concludes the volume, only furthers this aesthetic, not only because it is incomplete, but also because its last eleven pages are a series of fragments introduced by the following in-text note: '[The following fragments were intended to form part of the Poem when finished]', p. 293. Quoted from *Samuel Taylor Coleridge Sibylline Leaves* (Oxford and New York: Woodstock Facsimile, 1990), p. 293.
39. This backward movement to chapter 4 of the *Biographia Literaria* is also a reminder of the seeming ubiquity of Coleridge's name over the previous two decades because of these various controversies over prose and poetry. Coleridge's introduction to chapter 3 addresses this issue directly: 'To anonymous critics in reviews, magazines, and news-journals of various name and rank, and to satirists with or without a name, in verse or prose, or in verse-text aided by prose-comment, I do seriously believe...that I owe full two-thirds of whatever reputation and publicity I happen to profess. For when the name of an individual has occurred so frequently, in so many works, for so great a length of time, the readers of these works...cannot but be familiar with the name, without distinctly remembering whether it was introduced for an eulogy or for censure'. (pp. 49–50)
    Coleridge claims that without this constant attention through which 'year after year, quarter after quarter, month after month', he has been 'for at least 17 years consecutively dragged forth', his name would not have achieved such public notoriety (p. 50). Bate and Engell point out in a footnote to this passage that over ninety extant articles and reviews were published from 1798 to 1814 that deal with Coleridge or his works.
40. Coleridge, *Biographia Literaria*, ed. Engell and Bate, pp. 71–2.
41. Ibid., p. 72.
42. Ibid., pp. 72–3.
43. Ibid., pp. 69–70.
44. Wordsworth's 1815 *Poems* suggest a way to interpret the historical and intertextual scope of the 'Friend's' reference. His letter picks up where Wordsworth's 'Essay Supplementary to the Preface' leaves off. The 'Essay Supplementary' demonstrates through its skewed literary history from Shakespeare to the publication of *Lyrical Ballads* that Wordsworth's poems have been necessarily marginalized by the public. However, while Wordsworth's prose history highlights how his poems have been neglected, Coleridge's footnoted commentary maintains that the reading public and reviewers cannot leave his works alone.
45. Gamer, *Romanticism and the Gothic*, p. 47.
46. Coleridge, *Biographia Literaria*, ed. Engell and Bate, p. 303.
47. Coleridge prepares readers for such an 'intuitive' engagement with his three epigraphs to chapter 13. The first from book 5 (469–88) of *Paradise Lost* features Raphael's discussion with Adam about discursive and intuitive reason; the second from Leibniz concerns a higher formal principle above material things; and the third from Synesius is about 'some medial element that may not be distributed'.

48. Given the fact that Coleridge completed chapter 13 several months before he published *Christabel*, this allusion also acts as an advertisement for the poem.
49. This critical engagement began most prominently when Coleridge commenced his public lectures in 1808 and started his periodical publication the *Friend* (1809–11).
50. Coleridge, *Biographia Literaria*, ed. Engell and Bate, p. 301.
51. For many reviewing critics and general readers such an allusion in 1817 would point back to Coleridge's 1816 publication of *Christabel*. Like Wordsworth's publication of *The Excursion*, Coleridge's *Christabel* volume marked his re-entrance into the print market – Coleridge had not published a volume of poetry since 1803.
52. In *Strange Power of Speech*, Eilenberg describes how Wordsworth rejected 'Christabel' from the 1800 *Lyrical Ballads* in favour of Wordsworth's 'Michael'. Although 'Christabel' remained in manuscript form for over seventeen years, Coleridge was infamous for reciting the poem at social gatherings. The manuscript fame of 'Christabel' spread to the point where several people who had heard Coleridge recite the poem were able to recite large portions of it too. Walter Scott's 'The Lay of the Last Minstrel' was, Coleridge maintained, largely developed from the design of 'Christabel.' In chapter 24 of the *Biographia Literaria*, Coleridge reminds his readers of exactly how popular *Christabel* was throughout its long manuscript history versus the negative reception it received from the *Edinburgh Review*, following its 1816 publication, pp. 238–9.
53. In 1815, Coleridge sent a copy of 'Christabel' to Byron to help him solicit Murray as publisher. Byron's praise of the poem also appeared in advertisements for 'Christabel' and his remarks that 'Christabel' is 'a wild and singularly original poem' earned Byron derisive comments from reviewers such as Thomas Moore, who, in the *Edinburgh Review* in September 1816, questions Byron's critical judgement: 'some of his latest *publications* dispose us to distrust his authority, where the question is what ought to meet the public eye', *Coleridge: The Critical Heritage*, ed. De Jackson, p. 226.
54. *Christabel, &Cc, by S. T. Colerige, Esq.*, 3rd edn (London: Printed for John Murray, Albermarle Street, by William Bulmer & Co. Cleveland-Row, St James's, 1816), p. v. The reviewer particularly genders this currency female, as if to suggest its trendy, ephemeral, and insubstantial value: 'The artifice has succeeded so far as to force [the *Christabel* volume] into a second edition! For what woman of fashion would not purchase a book recommended by Lord Byron', *Coleridge: The Critical Heritage*, ed. De Jackson, p. 217.
55. S. T. Colerige, 'Preface', *Christabel* (1816), p. vi.
56. Coleridge, 'Preface', *Chistabel*, p. vi.
57. Gamer also relates Wordsworth's reluctance to publish 'Christabel' in the 1800 *Lyrical Ballads* to Wordsworth's anxiety about how critics might react to such a distinctly gothic poem (*Romanticism and the Gothic*, pp. 123–6). In her chapter 'From "Christabel" to *The Lay of the Last Minstrel*', in *Fictions and Fakes*, Russett suggests that Wordsworth's *The White Doe of Rylstone* (1815) might be understood as an imitation of the meter and mode of narration in 'Christabel' which borders on plagiarism, p. 83.
58. Coleridge, 'Preface', *Christabel*, p. vi.
59. Coleridge's authorial presence particularly disturbed Hazlitt. See Lapp's *Contest for Cultural Authority*, which deals primarily with Hazlitt's disdain for Coleridge's politics and Regency publications. I argue that Hazlitt also disapproved of Coleridge's authorial presentation. In a pre-emptive review on 8 September 1816 of Coleridge's the *Statesman's Manual* – a response to an advertisement for the first 'Lay Sermon' in the *Statesman's Manual* – Hazlitt rejects Coleridge's method of writing and self-presentation because Coleridge will not lay the full body of his texts down in public view. Hazlitt maintains

that the advertisement for the *Statesmen's Manual* is all that the public will ever see of the projected work: 'The ingenious author, in a preface, which is a master-piece in its kind, having neither beginning, middle, or end, apologizes for having published a work, not a line of which is written, or ever likely to be written', *Coleridge: The Critical Heritage*, ed. De Jackson, p. 248. Turning to Coleridge's the *Friend*, Hazlitt demands, 'What is his *Friend* itself but an enormous Title-page; the longest and most tiresome Prospectus that ever was written; an endless Preface to an imaginary work; a Table of Contents that fills the whole volume', *Coleridge: The Critical Heritage*, ed. De Jackson, 249. Hazlitt regards Coleridge as an authorial ghost who 'haunts the public imagination with obscure noises … and does not venture out in *propria persona* with his shroud and surplice on, the Cock-lane Ghost of mid-day, [so that] he may escape in a whole skin without being handled by the mob, or uncased by the critics', *Coleridge: The Critical Heritage*, ed. De Jackson, pp. 248–9.

60. Coleridge, *Biographia Literaria*, ed. Engell and Bate, p. 302. This quotation also comes before one of the most frequently noted moments in Coleridge's poem. Several reviewers of 'Christabel' remarked with disgust or wonder at the undressing scene in Christabel's room. In the 1816 version, those lines are printed with a dash that leaves out what is revealed: 'Her silken robe and inner vest / Dropt to her feet, and in full view / *Behold her bosom and half her side* – / A sight to dream of, not to tell!'. Hazlitt was so infuriated by this omission that in his *Examiner* review of the poem on 2 June 1816 he provides the line which follows the dashes in the manuscript version: 'Hideous, deformed, and pale of hue' and charges that Coleridge purposely has left the line out, which Hazlitt contends provides the 'keystone that makes up the arch', of the poem, *Coleridge: The Critical Heritage*, ed. De Jackson, p. 207.

61. Engell and Bate's footnote explains that Trophonius was an 'architect in Greek legend who … built the temple of Apollo at Delphi … Those consulting the oracle were dragged to the bottom of the cave and subjected to earthly noises and lurid lights and sudden glares before receiving their revelation', *Biographia Literaria*, p. 302.

62. Ibid.

63. This moment follows the 'Friend's' sublimely Gothic description of seeing all that he has previously known and understood turned upside down and inside out – a testimony that mimics Coleridge's method throughout the *Biographia Literaria* of tearing down long-worshipped intellectual figures and building up more obscure ones. He remarks, 'In short, what I had supposed substances were thinned away into shadows, while every where shadows were deepened into substances', and then he adds an illustrating quotation from book 2 of *Paradise Lost*: 'If substance may be call'd what shadow seem'd / For each seem'd either!', p. 301. In *Paradise Lost* having come to the gates of hell on his journey towards earth, Satan encounters Sin and their son Death. While Sin 'seem'd Woman to the waste, and fair / But ended foul in many a scaly fould', Death has no distinguishable form 'in member, joynt, or limb, / Or substance might be call'd that shadow seem'd, / For each seem'd either', ll. 650–1, 668–70.

64. At the end of chapter 1 in the *Biographia Literaria*, Coleridge uses a similar 'trick' when he explains in a footnote how he was told about an insulting epigram directed against 'The Ancient Mariner' that turned out to be Coleridge's own mocking criticism of the poem: 'Your poem must eternal be, / Dear sir! it cannot fail, / For 'tis incomprehensible / And without head or tail.' Bate and Engels note, however, that when Coleridge first published this epigram in 1797 in the *Morning Post*, it was addressed to the poet laureate Henry James Pye, and not titled, as it in the *Biographia* 'To the author of the Ancient

Mariner'. Concluding a chapter that features three of Coleridge's Nehemiah Higgen-bottom sonnets, which mock his own sonnets as well as the sonnets of several friends, Coleridge freely and laughingly uses this textual 'trick' to change the referent and context of his previously published epigram.

65. Written in response to Wordsworth's recital of *The Prelude* in 1807, 'To William Wordsworth' remained unpublished largely because Wordsworth was concerned that its publication would hurt the future reception of *The Prelude*.

66. In defining the words at issue in this paragraph, I have drawn heavily on S. Johnson's *A Dictionary of the English Language: In Two Volumes, The Fourth Edition, Revised by the Author* (London: Printed by W. Strahan, 1773).

67. Coleridge, *Biographia Literaria*, ed. Engell and Bate, p. 304.

68. Price, *The Anthology and the Rise of the Novel*, p. 98.

69. In *The Anthology and the Rise of the Novel*, pp. 93–9, Price describes several reviews that explicitly weigh the value of Radcliffe's poetic excerpts against her Gothic prose plots. Coleridge added his own opinion to this debate in his review of *The Mysteries of Udolpho*, which appeared in the *Critical Review* (August 1794), pp. 361–72. In that review, Coleridge quotes one of Radcliffe's embedded poems and, from Price's perspective, 'justifies the inclusion of the excerpt by the need to counteract readers' presumed preference for [plot] adventures to [poetic] beauties', p. 95.

70. See Gamer's *Romanticism and the Gothic* on the rise and fall of Radcliffe's critical popularity, pp. 69–73.

71. In his chapter 'Producing *Lyrical Ballads* 1798 and 1800', Gamer details Wordsworth's anxiety about how reviewing critics might receive the more Gothic poems in the second edition of *Lyrical Ballads*. He also explores the complex ways that Wordsworth and Coleridge put 'into practice the aesthetic ideologies of gothic reviewers' in the 'Preface', as well as creating poems for the first and second editions that encouraged readers to distance themselves from the overt Gothic elements in those poems while also reflecting on their potential moral value (*Romanticism and the Gothic*, p. 102).

6 J. H. Reynolds's 'Peter Bell' and the Wordsworthian Reputation

1. The quotation, 'bound each to each', is from 'My Heart Leaps Up' – the opening poem of Wordsworth's 1815 *Poems*.

2. See Chapter 7 for more on 'Benjamin the Waggoner' (1819), 'The Dead Asses: A Lyrical Ballad' (1819), and a few other parodic attacks on Wordsworth after 1815. Notably, the parodies 'Benjamin the Waggoner' and 'The Dead Asses' were reviewed alongside Wordsworth's 'Peter Bell'. Percy Shelley also wrote his own (unpublished) version of 'Peter Bell', which responds to Reynolds's and Wordsworth's versions of it. Shelley's 'Peter Bell' utterly condemns what he understood as Wordsworth's political flip-flopping and abandonment of the revolutionary, poetic principles in *Lyrical Ballads*.

3. In his infamous review, Jeffrey's exasperated commentary about Wordsworth's 'Preface to *The Excursion*' set the tone for much of the review culture's subsequent response to Wordsworth's newest publication. In the following passage, Jeffrey inverts the familiar part/whole Wordsworthian proposition to whole/part, weighing the new production (*The Excursion*) against the past whole of Wordsworth's poetry from *Lyrical Ballads* and his 1807 *Poems* up to Jeffrey's review: 'it is stated in the title – with something of an impudent candour – to be but "a portion" of a larger work; and in the preface, where an attempt is rather unsuccessfully made to explain the whole design, it is still more rashly

disclosed, that it is but "a part of the second part of a *long* and laborious work" – which is to consist of three parts", Woof (ed.), *William Wordsworth: The Critical Heritage, Vol. 1: 1793–1820*, p. 382.

4. The relationship between part and whole is a well-worn Romantic cliché by now. However, my exploration of parodic reactions to Wordsworth's system for organizing, collecting and collating together his poems underscores the type of contract between author and readers, implicit in Wordsworth's 'Preface' and 'Essay Supplementary to the Preface'. J. Hogg's satiric treatment of Wordsworth's titles and part/whole relationships in *The Poetic Mirror* (London: Printed for Longman, Hurst, Rees, Orme, and Brown; and John Ballantyne, Edinburgh, 1816) inaugurated these parodic engagements. For a historical analysis of 'system' as genre classification, see C. Siskin, 'The Year of the System', in R. Cronin (ed.), *1798: The Year of the* Lyrical Ballads (New York: St Martin's Press, 1998), pp. 9–31.

5. Responding to an advertisement for Wordsworth's forthcoming poem, Reynolds published his pre-emptive parody nearly two weeks before Wordsworth's 'Peter Bell'.

6. Coleridge not only helped Wordsworth prepare the 1798 *Lyrical Ballads* for press; he also played an integral part in figuring out the textual layout, including the length and size of prose notes for the 1800 *Lyrical Ballads*.

7. For Coleridge's response, see the *Collected Letters of Samuel Taylor Coleridge*, ed. Griggs, vol. 4, p. 934. Notably, Coleridge's reaction to the public appearance of Reynolds's 'Peter Bell' provides a parodic means for evaluating his impressions in the *Biographia Literaria* of Wordsworth's paratextual endeavours, and that reaction suggests a fundamental difference between how they each defended against and engaged public opinion. Furthermore, Coleridge's initial confusion over the advertisement that he read for 'Peter Bell, a Lyrical Ballad' reveals a great deal about his concern for how literary property should be treated differently in the public versus the private spheres. Coleridge willingly admits that all is 'FAIR' with Reynolds's pre-emptive treatment of Wordsworth's forthcoming publication. Although he dismisses Reynolds's poetry as 'but mimicry, buffoonery' and refers instead to his own *Biographia Literaria* as the first work of criticism to do justice to Wordsworth's poetry by pointing out its merits and defects, he twice praises the prose and notes accompanying Reynolds's poem. Coleridge recognizes that Reynolds has successfully infiltrated Wordsworth's mechanism for controlling the opinions of the review culture and the public. Perhaps more intriguing, Coleridge claims that he would have found the parody even more humorous had it focused on him instead of on Wordsworth.

8. Quoted from Reynolds's 'Peter Bell: A Lyrical Ballad', in D. Kent and D. R. Ewen (eds), *Romantic Parodies, 1797–1831* (London: Farleigh Dickinson University Press, 1992), pp. 173–84, on pp. 183–4.

9. All quotations or paraphrases from Wordsworth's footnotes are from *Poems by William Wordsworth: Including Lyrical Ballads, and the Miscellaneous Pieces of the Author. With Additional Poems, a New Preface, and a Supplementary Essay* (London: Paternoster Row, 1815) and *Poems, in Two Volumes, by William Wordsworth, Author of Lyrical Ballads* (London: Paternoster Row, 1807), p. 342.

10. Reynolds, 'Peter Bell', p. 174.

11. *Collected Letters of Samuel Taylor Coleridge*, ed. Griggs, vol. 3, pp. 277–8.

12. Reynolds, 'Peter Bell', p. 181.

13. G. J. Pyle, 'J. H. Reynolds's "Peter Bell"', *Notes and Queries*, 24 (1977), pp. 323–4.

14. Reynolds, 'Peter Bell', p. 177.

15. R. B. Sheridan, *The Critic*, I.ii.147. See R. B. Sheridan's *The School For Scandal and Other Plays*, ed. E. Rump (New York: Penguin Books, 1988).
16. Ibid., II.ii.172.
17. Ibid., I.ii.151.
18. Reynolds, 'Peter Bell', p. 176.
19. Ibid., p. 174.
20. Ibid., p. 178.
21. Wordsworth, *Poems by William Wordsworth* (1815), p. 239.
22. Reynolds, 'Peter Bell', p. 174.
23. Ibid.
24. See Schoenfield, *The Professional* Wordsworth, in ch. 5, pp. 109–38 and ch. 7, pp. 189–223. Schoenfield focuses on *Lyrical Ballads* and *The Excursion* and contextualizes conflicts between Wordsworth, his reviewers and the reading public within legal debates about contracts, property and law.
25. Reynolds, 'Peter Bell', p. 174.
26. Ibid., p. 184; emphasis added.
27. See Heinzelman, *The Economics of the Imagination*, ch. 5, 'The Art of Labor'; ch. 6, 'The Psychomachia of Labor'; ch. 7, 'Wordsworth's Labor Theory: An Economics of Compensation'.
28. Ibid., p. 211.
29. J. Stillinger (ed.), *William Wordsworth: Selected Poems and Prefaces* (Boston, MA: Houghton Mifflin, 1965), p. 448.
30. Franta sounds a similar note in *Romanticism and the Rise of the Mass Pubic* when he remarks in his chapter 'Wordsworth's Audience Problem' that 'Wordsworth is working to take seriously a whole range of emotions and judgments ... as possible responses to his poetry, and he is doing so in order to argue that getting a response – any response – is what counts in the long run', p. 70.
31. The poem first appeared in Wordsworth's 1820 *The River Duddon* volume and then a few months later in the section *Miscellaneous Sonnets* of Wordsworth's 1820 *Poems*. I quote from *The Poetical Works of William Wordsworth*, ed. De Selincourt, vol. 3, p. 11.
32. Quoted from *The Complete Poetry of John Milton*, ed. J. T. Shawcross (New York: Doubleday, 1971).
33. One anonymous review, probably by J. Conder, in the *Eclectic Review*, 2nd series, 14 (August 1820), pp. 170–84, was particularly vexed by how to read Wordsworth's sonnet because of its injunction to read Milton's 'A Book was Writ of Late Called Tetrachordon'. This reviewer describes Wordsworth as 'devoid of any talent for humour', and, consequently, contends that Wordsworth 'blundered in his serious imitation of a burlesque poem', Woof (ed.), *William Wordsworth: The Critical Heritage, Vol. 1: 1793–1830*, p. 772.
34. Reynolds, 'Peter Bell', p. 174.
35. G. H. Durrant, 'Wordsworth's "Peter Bell" – A *Pons Asinorum* for Critics', *Wascana Review of Contemporary Poetry and Short Fiction*, 1 (1996), pp. 26–43, on p. 32.
36. Notably, Milton's sonnet 13 also refers to Midas's ears. See A. Nardo, *Milton's Sonnets and the Ideal Community* (Lincoln, NE: University of Nebraska Press, 1979); S. K. Heninger, *The Subtext of Form in the English Renaissance* (University Park, PA: Pennsylvania State University Press, 1994); and B. Lewalski, *Paradise Lost and the Rhetoric of Literary Forms* (Princeton, NJ: Princeton University Press, 1985).

37. Quoted from Wordsworth's 'On the Detraction which Followed the Publication of a Certain Poem'.
38. P. J. Cook, 'Resembling Unlikeness: A Reading of Milton's *Tetrachordon* Sonnet', *Milton Quarterly*, 26.4 (1992), pp. 121–9.
39. Ibid, p. 123.
40. Ibid., p. 124.
41. One critic's plot summary of Wordsworth's 'Peter Bell' for the *Literary Gazette*, 1 May 1819, pp. 273–6, derisively explains what many other reviewing critics also recognized as another simplistic lyrical ballad: 'Peter Bell is a strange story written to shew that supernatural agency may be dispensed with ...The Hero, a low and abandoned vagrant ... roaming at night for pleasure or for plunder, finds a lean ass on the bank of a river, which he determines to steal ... and this ass will not stir at all, but bends ruefully over the water. In the water is the drowned body of its master, which it has watched, without tasting food, for four days and nights. The apparition of this corse terrifies the marauder; he drags it out, and mounts the ass in search of the friends of the deceased ... [until they] finally turn up a lane where the widow of the drowned owner presides.' This critic then expresses dismay over this conversion experience, which results in Peter Bell's transformation from a morally reprehensible and profligate man to a purportedly good and honest one.
42. Cook, 'Resembling Unlikeness', p. 122.
43. Shawcross's comment is an editorial gloss from *The Complete Poetry of John Milton*, p. 201.
44. For a parallel reading, see Murphy's contention in *Poetry as an Occupation and an Art* that Wordsworth's dedication, prologue and 'Peter Bell' poem suggest how the character Peter stands in for a certain type of 'susceptible ... deluded or bad reader', whose 'unenlightened sensibility' is targeted and redirected through the poem, p. 193.
45. Cook, 'Resembling Unlikeness', pp. 125–6.
46. As I argue in Chapter 4, in his 'Preface to *The Excursion*' (1814), Wordsworth alerts readers to the fact that they are being introduced to the centre point of his larger poetic project.
47. See L. Johnson, *Wordsworth and the Sonnet* (Copenhagen: Rosenkilde & Bagger, 1973), pp. 174–80.
48. In an 1845 letter to his publisher E. Moxon, Wordsworth declares, 'by all means', that his prose be printed uniform with his poetry for the upcoming collected edition. Prose and poetry should go hand in hand and be placed consistently next to each other for readers to grasp 'the grounds of arrangement'. Wordsworth's reluctance to remove his system of prose notation, even in 1845, demonstrates his continued understanding that his prose offers the only firm ground on which poet and readers can meet that can 'gratify' the public and demonstrate the 'merits' of his poetry, *The Letters of William and Dorothy Wordsworth*, ed. De Selincourt, rev. Shaver and Moorman, vol. 3, pp. 248–9. For more on the market implications for this edition, see T. Owens's article 'Wordsworth, Galignani, and the Aesthetics of Piracy'.
49. Wordsworth, 'Essay Supplementary to the Preface', in *Poems by William Wordsworth* (1815), p. 371; original emphasis.

7 *The River Duddon* Volume and Wordsworth's Canonical Ascent

1. Anonymous Review, *London Magazine*, 1 (June 1820), pp. 618–27.

2.   In 'Publication and Reception of Wordsworth's "The River Duddon" Volume', *Modern Language Studies*, 32:2 (2002), pp. 45–67, J. Khan contends that 1820 marked a decisive turn for Wordsworth's career, as does S. Gill in 'Wordsworth and *The River Duddon*', *Essays in Criticism*, 57:1 (2007), pp. 22–41, and Garrett in his chapter 'A Detailed Local Survey', in *Wordsworth and the Writing of the Nation*, pp. 125–48. By contrast, several earlier scholars single out later dates as benchmarks for evaluating Wordsworth's canonical ascent. R. Woof relates Wordsworth's growing popularity to his 1822 publications, *Ecclesiastical Sonnets* and *Memorial of a Tour of the Continent 1820*: Wordsworth 'had, with this least memorable of his poetry, found a rather drear coincidence of taste with the reviewers and the reading public'. In *English Literature 1815–1832* (Oxford: Clarendon Press, 1963), I. Jack singles out W. Hazlitt's *The Spirit of the Age* (1825) as the definitive marker from which to measure Wordsworth's ascent through Hazlitt's declaration of 'a large body of determined partisans' for Wordsworth, pp. 3–4. In 'Publication and Reception of Wordsworth's "The River Duddon" Volume', Khan makes a convincing case for the significance of 1820. After pointing out that Wordsworth's 1820 volume appealed to conservative and liberal critics alike, Khan details how Wordsworth's revised and elevated style, which includes a heavy reliance on classical allusions and myths, as well as a general divesting of 'metaphysical mysteries of common occurrences and fundamental human passions understood by the select few only', p. 54, led to widespread critical praise. I agree with Khan's assessment and build on Garrett's claim that in this volume 'Wordsworth embarks on a project of preservation, of a not-forgetting that seeks to locate the character of the nation in its ability to remember and to read the landscape marked with history, the landscape of memory', 126. I further contend that the volume appealed to reviewers as a poetic treasury and moral touchstone for a nation reeling from political, social, and economic crises.

3.   As Owen notes in 'Costs, Sales, and Profits', the 500 copy print run of the 1815 *Poems* was 'exhausted' by 1820, and in 1820 sales of the *Excursion* more than doubled from 11 copies in 1819 to 25 copies of the smaller and more affordable version in 1820 – perhaps also because of 'the expenditure of 4s.7d. on advertising; or the success of *Peter Bell*', 97. In any case, Longman felt that a second edition of the *Excursion* would sell, and the 221 copies sold in 1821 out of the 500 copy print run for this edition would seem to prove his intuition. Where about half the run of 500 copies for the 1814 *Excursion* had sold within a year, with some copies still being remaindered in 1834, the 1820 edition sold out by 1824'. The four-volume *Miscellaneous Poems* also sold 255 out of its 500 copies in 1821' and was sold out by 1826 (p. 101).

4.   In 'The Living Pantheon of Poets in 1820', Cox highlights the print runs and sales of Wordsworth's publications beginning with 'Peter Bell' (1819): '*Peter Bell* marked a turning point, with 1,000 copies (rather than the usual 500 copies for Wordsworth) being issued and with 700 being sold within about a month. *The River Duddon* sold 340 of its 500 copies' by the end of June 1820, p. 18. See also Owen's 'Costs, Sales, and Profits', p. 101. Beyond the 30 pounds Longman spent on advertising this work, which was fairly standard for Wordsworth's publications, its successful early sales might also be attributed to a glowing review/preview of the volume on 24 March in the Tory *Literary Gazette*, which came out over a month before the work was published. The review concludes by proclaiming it a 'volume conferring immortality, and ranking their author, even with those hitherto most sceptical of his powers, among the foremost bards of the age', Woof (ed.), *William Wordsworth: The Critical Heritage, Vol. 1: 1793–1830*, p. 754.

5. In her chapter 'Literary History, Periodicals, Lectures' in *Literary History Writing, 1770–1820* (London: Palgrave, 2010), A. London describes this period as 'the literary critical skirmishes of 1818–1819', p. 151. Hazlitt's *Lectures on the English Poets* (1818) were central to these 'skirmishes', which notably involved J. G. Lockhart's attacks on the Cockney School and J. Wilson's defences of Wordsworth and the Lake School in July and December 1818. However, on at least one point, Wilson and Hazlitt seem to agree. As Hazlitt maintains in his lecture 'On the Living Poets', Wordsworth is 'the most original poet living now.' Wilson identifies Wordsworth as one of the 'exemplary triumvirate' of contemporary poets, including Byron and Scott. See *Literary History Writing*, p. 146. This enthusiastic consensus from a liberal and conservative critic helped pave the way for the critical success of *The River Duddon* volume.

6. Several reviewers mention this 'Advertisement' in much the same manner that in November 1816 the *Dublin Examiner* recalls the internal announcement in Wordsworth's *Thanksgiving Ode* volume, which sets the volume up as 'a sequel to the Author's Sonnets, dedicated to Liberty; and therefore [is] printed uniformly with the two volumes of his Poems [1815], in which those Sonnets are collected, to admit of their being conveniently bound up together', Woof (ed.), *William Wordsworth: The Critical Heritage, Vol. 1: 1793–1830*, p. 630. Furthermore, as Gill usefully points out in *William Wordsworth: A Life*, *The River Duddon* volume was published with 'an alternative title-page ... so that the book could be bound up into a uniform set', which would include a 'second edition of [the soon to be published] *The Excursion*', p. 336.

7. In 'Wordsworth's "Third Volume" and the Collected Editions, 1815–1820', *Bibliographical Society of America*, 80:4 (1986), pp. 437–53, E. C. Walker provides a clear bibliographical history of this often misconstrued volume, as well as hypothesizing about when it was conceived, how it related to Wordsworth's collecting endeavours from 1815 and 1827, and why it was published before the 1820 four-volume edition.

8. In *Wordsworth's Revisionary Aesthetics*, Kelley singles out this passage and argues that Wordsworth transforms the language of maps to illustrate the relationship between his aesthetic and ideological conceptions of the sublime and the beautiful, pp. 15–17.

9. On 30 December 1819, Parliament passed six Acts reflecting growing fears that a revolution was imminent. These Acts sought to stop the organization of further radical activities and publications in Britain, and they effectively ended debates about reforming Parliament and extending the male franchise. These Acts were the 'Training Prevention Act', the 'Seizure of Arms Act', the 'Seditious Meetings Act', the 'Blasphemous and Seditious Libels Act', the 'Misdemeanors Act' and the 'Newspaper Stamp Duties Act'.

10. On that day the renowned orator, political radical and working-class advocate Henry Hunt delivered a highly publicized lecture at St Peter's Field in Manchester about the need to reform Parliament and extend the male franchise. This widely anticipated event led to a terrifying conflict between the local police, known as the 'Manchester Yeomanry', and a crowd of 60,000 people that gathered to listen to Hunt. As the yeomanry cavalry attempted to arrest Hunt and disperse the crowd, they entangled themselves in a mass of people and apparently panicked. Many of these officers drew their swords and attacked the crowd indiscriminately. At the end of the day, over 300 civilians were seriously injured and nearly a dozen were killed. The incident was quickly dubbed the 'Peterloo Massacre' in reference to the regiment of Waterloo veterans that backed up the Manchester Yeomenry and in ironic comparison to the Battle of Waterloo.

11. J. Chandler, *England in 1819* (Chicago, IL: University of Chicago Press, 1998), p. 17.

12. Ibid., p. 5.

13. Quoted in ibid., p. 22.
14. Chandler attributes this political reversal and shift in public opinion to the arrests of several key leaders in the radical movement, as well as to what he calls 'historical accident (the death of George III on January 29, 1820) and desperate radical plots [like] the Cato Street Conspiracy, discovered on February 23, 1820', which was a plan to murder the British Prime Minister and all of the cabinet ministers, which would be replaced by a provisional government to oversee a radical revolution in Britain similar to the one during the French Revolution', p. 22.
15. Woof (ed.), *William Wordsworth: The Critical Heritage, Vol. I., 1793–1820*, pp. 791, 776, 769.
16. Ibid., pp. 765, 768.
17. Ibid., pp. 756–7, 787.
18. Ibid., p. 763.
19. Ibid., p. 767.
20. Ibid., p. 769.
21. Ibid., p. 765.
22. Notably, the *Literary Chronicle* changed its position after the publication of Wordsworth's *Ecclesiastical Sonnets* (1822) and sided with the *Edinburgh Review's* charges against Wordsworth's 'admiration for and connections with the ministry'. Quoted from J. O. Hayden, *The Romantic Reviewers, 1802–1824* (Chicago, IL: University of Chicago Press, 1969), p. 101.
23. Curiously, the *Edinburgh Review* did not review Wordsworth's volume.
24. Woof (ed.), *William Wordsworth: The Critical Heritage, Vol. I., 1793–1820*, p. 755.
25. Ibid., pp. 760, 763, 761. This periodical, whose full title was the *London Magazine and Monthly Critical and Dramatic Review*, began in January 1820. According to Haydon, after changing names in February 1821 to *Gold's London Magazine and Theatrical Inquisitor*, it was 'almagamated' in July 1821 with Robert Baldwin's magazine, which possessed the same initial title, *The London Magazine*, p. 65. Baldwin's *London Magazine*, which often featured the writings of Lamb and Hazlitt, was edited by Wordsworth's acquaintance and frequent correspondent J. Scott, who published five sonnets by Wordsworth in 1816 in his newspaper the *Champion* as well as a glowing review of Wordsworth's 'Thanksgiving Ode' volume on 20 October, 1816. See Wordsworth's letter to R. P. Gilles on 9 April, 1816 in which, after describing the publication of a sonnet in Hunt's *Examiner*, he remarks: 'In the Champion, another weekly journal, have appeared not long since five sonnets of mine ... They will form part of a Publication [Thanksgiving Ode] which I sent to the Press three weeks ago', *The Letters of William and Dorothy Wordsworth*, ed. De Selincourt, rev. Moorman, vol. 2, p. 729.
26. D. Higgins, '*Blackwood's Edinburgh Magazine* and the Construction of Wordsworth's Genius', in K. Wheatley (ed.), *Romantic Periodicals and Print Culture* (Portland, OR: Frank Cass, 2003), pp. 122–36. Higgens also recalls that Wilson was a close friend of Wordsworth's and was briefly considered a devotee of the Lake poets (p. 128). For more on the form of periodicals, see Schoenfield's discussion of the heteroglossic 'confederacy between poetry ... and periodical culture' from his chapter 'Skirmishes in the Lower Empire', in *British Periodicals and Romantic Identity*, p. 34.
27. See Wilson's three essays about the Lake District and its poets, particularly Wordsworth, between 1818 and 1819.
28. The May review of *The River Duddon* expressly reminds readers of *Blackwood's* continual attention to Wordsworth's reception: 'The way in which the fame of this poet had been

attacked by the Edinburgh Reviewers, has already frequently induced us to speak of the philosophical spirit in which the more peculiar productions of his genius are conceived', p. 207.

29. This parody also could be read in relation to *Blackwood's* recurring *Boxianna* essays, a few of which equate literary figures with champion pugilists.

30. *Blackwood's Magazine*, 7 (May 1820), quoted from Strachen (ed.), *Parodies of the Romantic Age*, vol. 2, pp. 245, 246.

31. Ibid., p. 246.

32. *Blackwood's* was also trying to recruit Wordsworth to write for them. As a means to persuade Wordsworth, Wilson sent him the March 1819 issue of *Blackwood's*, which features Wilson's high praise of the poet in 'Letters from the Lakes: Written during the Summer of 1818', 4 (March 1819), pp. 735–44.

33. *Blackwood's Magazine*, 7 (May 1820), quoted in Strachen (ed.), *Parodies of the Romantic Age*, vol. 2, p. 245.

34. Ibid.

35. Ibid., p. 246.

36. *Benjamin The Waggoner, A Ryghte Merrie and Conceited Tale in Verse* was published on Paternoster Row in London and printed for Baldwin, Cradock, and Joy. Its authorship is debatable. While some scholars have conjectured J. H. Reynolds to be its author, I agree with J. B. Gohn's evidence claiming Lockhart as the author, presented in 'Who Wrote *Benjamin the Waggoner*?: An Inquiry', *Wordsworth Circle*, 8:1 (Winter 1977), pp. 69–74.

37. In the introduction to his Cornell edition of *Benjamin the Waggoner* (Ithaca, NY: Cornell University Press, 1981), P. Betz hypothesizes that Wordsworth changed the title from *Benjamin the Waggoner* to *The Waggoner* out of concern that, much like J. H. Reynolds did with 'Peter Bell', someone would write a parody of his *Benjamin* with the exact same title , p. 26.

38. Quoted in Strachen (ed.), *Parodies of the Romantic Age*, vol. 2, p. 218.

39. From Reynolds's, 'Peter Bell', quoted in Strachen (ed.), *Parodies in the Romantic Age*, vol. 2.

40. This mock Wordsworth maintains: 'All your review of me is excellent, but the following quotation I will select for the perusal of my reader, leaving him and recommending to him a perusal of the whole, in Blackwood's Magazine for June, price 2s. 6d.', quoted in Strachen (ed.), *Parodies of the Romantic Age*, vol. 2, p. 256.

41. Wordsworth, quoted in Strachen (ed.), *Parodies of the Romantic Age*, vol. 2, p. 255.

42. Ibid., p. 259. The parody also features an epigrammatic list of 'Elegant Extracts (For My Title Pages)', a descriptive list of 'Plates To Be Engraved For This Work', and forthcoming publications purportedly by Wordsworth. Lockhart's mock-Wordsworth maintains, 'The reader must long have since observed how my little daisies, my pansies, my cuckoos, my butterflies, and my donkies talk to me', p. 247.

43. In *Benjamin the Waggoner*, this feigned certainty of the reading public's familiarity with and abiding interest in Wordsworth's poetic collections is supported by singularly ridiculous lines that are spliced together from 'To a Butterfly', 'Moods of my own Mind', 'To a Daisy', 'Idiot Boy', and 'Peter Bell.' These notes also include an advertisement 'By the Same Author, And Shortly to be had of All the Booksellers, MY MOTHER'S DUCKLINGS, An Affecting Tale in Verse, and Founded Upon Fact', featuring a promise that 'Early next spring, the same author hopes to indulge the Public...with his long Poem of 'The Cat and the Fiddle', which will be compressed 'into as little space as possible, and the Author hopes to do it in two volumes quarto. A few volumes royal quarto, with numerous illustrative engravings, will be struck off for Subscribers only.' The advertise-

ment then announces the author's intention of publishing subsequent parts of 'Peter Bell' and concludes with a collective puff: 'The other favourite works of the Author – 'The Silent Cricket', 'The Thinking Pony', 'The Speaking Cuckoo', 'The Whispering Leaf', 'The Laughing Flowers', and 'The Scornful Boat', to be had of all the Booksellers in Christendom, having been translated into all the modern Languages', quoted in Strachen (ed.), *Parodies of the Romantic Age*, vol. 2, pp. 273–4.

44. Quoted from Kent and Ewen (eds), *Romantic Parodies*, p. 205. See Wordsworth's account, in Curtis's edition of *The Fenwick Notes*, of grounding the poem on 'an anecdote, which I read in a newspaper, of an ass being found hanging his head over a canal in a wretched posture', p. 17.

45. The quotation is from Reynolds's 'The Dead Asses'.

46. This parody also nods toward Wordsworth's Tory campaigning in the region. In a letter to Lord Londsdale on 18 January 1818, Wordsworth's makes the case that the forthcoming election in Westmorland is a microcosm of national politics. Wordsworth actively and, according to Gill, 'tirelessly', campaigned in support of the established Tory Lowthers against the liberal incumbent Henry Brougham in the elections of 1818 and 1820, *William Wordsworth: A Life*, p. 329. In his letter to Londsdale, Wordsworth maintains: 'I should not feel to the degree that I do upon this occasion, were I not assured that this attempt is no common affair of county Politics, but proceeds from dispositions and principles, which if not checked and discountenanced, would produce infinite mischief not to Westmoreland only, but to the whole kingdom', *The Letters of William and Dorothy Wordsworth*, ed. De Selincourt, rev. Shaver and Moorman, vol. 3, p. 411. Drawing on this personal and political investment, Wordsworth also published *Two Addresses to the Freeholders of Westmorland* in 1818, which outline his views against radical politicians, radical public movements and abuses of freedom of the press. In opposition to these radicalisms, Wordsworth asserts the necessity of social cohesion and the benefits for society that come with upholding the landed interests of Freemen.

47. This use of 'Yarrow Unvisited', perhaps, also ironically recalls Hogg's rejection of Wordsworth's 'Yarrow Visited' for his projected collection of contemporary poets. Hogg was an active and continual presence within *Blackwood's* essay writing and parodic engagements. After receiving very few submissions answering his solicitations, Hogg decided to publish a series of parodies of contemporary poets, including Wordsworth, in *The Poetic Mirror* (1816). Hogg apparently had mixed feelings about Wordsworth whom Hogg felt had insulted him in September 1814 when he, John Wilson, Charles Lloyd, and Thomas De Quincey met in the Lake District following one of Wordsworth's Scottish tours. For that account, see Douglas Mack's edition of Hogg's *Memoirs of the Author's Life* (Edinburgh: Scottish Academic Press, 1972), p. 70.

48. On this topic, see also Wilson's essay two months later, 'On the Analogy between the Growth of Individual and National Genius', in the Jan. 1820 issue of *Blackwood's*, pp. 375–81.

49. In 1831 he also published a collection of poems *Yarrow Revisited*.

50. Woof (ed.), *William Wordsworth: The Critical Heritage, Vol. 1: 1793–1830*, p. 6.

51. See J. Khan, 'Publication and Reception of Wordsworth's 'The River Duddon' Volume', *Modern Language Studies*, 32:2 (2002), pp. 45–67, on p. 51, as well as J. Khan, 'The Allegories of Wordsworth's 'The Pilgrim's Dream; or, The Star and the Glow-Worm', *Studies in Philology*, 4 (Fall 1997), pp. 508–22.

52. Wordsworth, *The River Duddon* (1820), p. 197.

53. Ibid., p. 214. In a letter to Lady Beaumont on 10 May 1821, Wordsworth explains that he published his prose guide with the Duddon Sonnets 'from a consciousness of its having been written in the same spirit which dictated several of the poems, and from a belief that it will tend naturally to illustrate them.'

54. This process of reading his prose notes as an after-thought, which M. Ponder describes in 'Echoing Poetry with History: Wordsworth's Duddon Sonnets and Their Notes', as the notes 'echo[ing] the poetry by calling up the places which were the loci of the poet's imagination in the sonnets', also applies to the concluding prose guide, which looks back on the opening sonnets (175). In Ponder's essay in *Genre*, 21 (Summer 1988), pp. 157–78, she argues that Wordsworth conceived of these sonnets and notes as 'a whole text' that responds 'to Coleridge's advocacy of poetry which excludes the biographical, historical, and, ultimately, the human elements necessary to move, and consequently, to educate the reader', p. 163.

55. As readers progress through the volume, they also encounter a few footnotes to poems, such as his note to 'Ode, Composed Upon an Evening of Extraordinary Splendor and Beauty.' This note relates Wordsworth's new poems to his past poetry and grounds his poetic images on the topographical beauties detailed in the concluding prose guide: 'The multiplication of mountain-ridges, described, at the commencement of the third stanza of this Ode, as a kind of Jacob's Ladder, leading to Heaven, is produced either by watery vapours, or sunny haze, – in the present instance by the latter cause. See the account of the Lakes at the end of this volume. The reader, who is acquainted with the Author's Ode, intitled, "Intimations of Immortality, &c." will recognize the allusion to it that pervades the last stanza of the foregoing poem.' Wordsworth's note likens the relationship between his prose guide, previously published 'Intimations Ode' and this footnoted ode to ascending mountain ridges in the Lake District – a kind of 'Jacob's Ladder' that seemingly reaches toward heaven. Wordsworth posits a metaphorical continuum between his past and present poetry, which encourages readers to remember and connect together his poems through their geographical locations as well as through the poet's metaphysical intimations.

56. In the first publication of the volume, 'Wrynose Fell' was misprinted as 'Wrynose Tell.'

57. Woof (ed.), *William Wordsworth: The Critical Heritage, Vol. 1: 1793–1830*, p. 810.

58. S. Wilcox, 'Wordsworth's *River Duddon* Sonnets', *PMLA*, 69:1 (1954), pp. 131–41, on p. 136. The Duddon sonnets also trace a theme of progressing from childhood to adulthood and immortality.

59. The relationship between the Duddon sonnets and the prose guide was noted by several reviewers. One reviewer declares: 'And this tempts us to suspect that Mr. Wordsworth is not so much to blame, after all, for the choice of many of his subjects, as for writing ballads and lyrical pieces about them, instead of throwing them into the honest form of prose', Woof (ed.), *William Wordsworth: The Critical Heritage, Vol. 1: 1793–1830*, p. 773. Another reviewer asserts that 'the Tour to the Lakes seems to us to be as topographically useful as it is *poetically picturesque*', Woof (ed.), *William Wordsworth: The Critical Heritage, Vol. 1: 1793–1830*, p. 794.

60. Most scholars describe this sonnet series as disjunctive and follow Wilcox's division of the sequence into three groups of eleven. By contrast, L. Johnson contends that the sequence can be divided into four groups. See his 'Origins of *The River Duddon*', in *Wordsworth and the Sonnet*, pp. 120–44.

61. Wordsworth, *The River Duddon*, p. 38.

62. See Hartman, *Wordsworth's Poetry*, pp. 335–7; J. Chandler, *Wordsworth's Second Nature* (Chicago, IL: Chicago University Press, 1984), pp. 170–1; De Mann, 'Time and History in Wordsworth', *Diacritics*, 17:4 (Winter 1987), pp. 4–17; J. Wyatt, *Wordsworth's Poems of Travel* (New York: St Martin's Press, 1999), p. 42. For a more recent engagement with Wordsworth's conception of the sonnet tradition and his sonnet practices, see D. Robinson, '"Still Glides the Stream": Form and Function in Wordsworth's *River Duddon* Sonnets', *European Romantic Review*, 13:4 (2002), pp. 449–64.

63. See B. Kim, 'Generating a National Sublime: Wordsworth's The *River Duddon* and *The Guide to the Lakes*', *Studies in Romanticism*, 45.1 (Spring 2006), pp. 49–75, and Garrett, 'A Detailed Local Survey: The *River Duddon* Sonnets and the Writing of the Nation', in *Wordsworth and the Writing of the Nation*, pp. 125–48. For a more regional perspective that '[l]ocal specificity, local pride, loving attention to the unsung and little known are the keynotes ... of the whole volume', p. 24, see Gill, 'Wordsworth and *The River Duddon*'.

64. R. Mortenson's '"The Nose-Drop": A Parody of Wordsworth', *Wordsworth Circle*, 2 (1971), pp. 91–100, provides the closest textual exploration of this parody and its allusions to Wordsworth's poems that I have found.

65. Wordsworth published that 'Preface' at the end of his two-volume 1815 *Poems* and at the end of his four-volume 1820 *Poems*. The mock preface here trades on how well-known many of the dictums within it were to readers familiar with his poetry and reviews of that poetry. Each time Wordsworth republished this 'Preface', he chose not to alter the substance of his previous emendations for the 1802 *Lyrical Ballads*. Furthermore, Wordsworth's twisted sentences and the satirical treatment his subject matter receives in this piece also suggest the reading public's long-standing familiarity with Wordsworth's supplementary prose by 1821. Aimed at Wordsworth's editorial compunction and obsessive revising, 'The Nose-Drop', which announces the death of the author, includes potential alterations for the poem that follows. Taken from 'among his papers', the parodist has found 'several small fragments, containing lines, or parts of lines, to be wrought at some future period of revision into the text', p. 251. Wordsworth appears as an obsessive revisionist, who looks to further propagate his *Lyrical Ballads* system through future publications while reminding readers of where he started with the 'The Preface to *Lyrical Ballads*.'

66. Quoted in Kent and Ewen (eds), *Romantic Parodies*, p. 253.

67. As his 'Fenwick Note' to these sonnets suggests, Wordsworth did partially fabricate the river's 'rise': 'In my own fancy I have fixed [the river's] rise near the noted Shire stones placed at the meeting point of the counties Westmoreland, Cumberland and Lancashire ... and it used to be a proud thing to say, that by touching them at the same time with feet and hands one had been in three counties at once', p. 99. Linking together three counties through the 'rise' of the Duddon, as well as his 'feet' and 'hands', Wordsworth unites a large portion of the Lake District through one geographically remarkable spot. Although probably unaware of Wordsworth's particular poetic liberties, the 'Nose-Drop's' echo of Wordsworth's prose note wryly calls attention to how Wordsworth, throughout his career, has overwritten the geography of this area with his own poetry: 'the RIVER DUDDON, 'of which I sung one song that will not die', rises upon it.' From this perspective, Wordsworth's sonnets – his song – not only rise out of this spot; they make up and supersede the river's connective topographical origins.

68. For more on this subject, see Garrett's comparison in his chapter 'A Detailed Local Survey' of Wordsworth's Duddon sonnets with J. Thomson's poetry about the Thames, in *Wordsworth and the Writing of the Nation*, pp. 129–33.

69. B. Kim, 'Generating a National Sublime: Wordsworth's The *River Duddon* and *The Guide to the Lakes*', *Studies in Romanticism*, 45:1 (Spring 2006), pp. 49–75, on p. 68.

70. Notably, only two of Wordsworth's dozen publications with Longman from 1800–1820 appeared with a list of advertisements for other author's works: his 1814 large quarto edition of *The Excursion* and his 1820 *River Duddon* octavo volume.

71. Such associations recall Wordsworth's declaration in his 1802 'Preface to *Lyrical Ballads*': 'If the labours of Men of science should ever create any material revolution, direct or indirect, in our condition, and in the impressions which we habitually receive, the Poet will sleep then no more than at present; he will be ready to follow the steps of the Man of science, not only in those general indirect, but he will be at his side, carrying sensations into the midst of the objects of the science itself. The remotest discoveries of the Chemist, the Botanist, or Minerologist, will be as proper objects of the Poet's art as any upon which it can be employed ... If the time should ever come when what is now called science, thus familiarised to men, shall be ready to put on, as it were, a form of flesh and blood, the Poet will lend his divine spirit to aid the transfiguration' (Brett and Jones's *Lyrical Ballads*, pp. 259–60).

72. Wordsworth, *The River Duddon*, p. 1 of the 'Advertisements' section at the back of the volume.

73. Ibid., p. 4 of the 'Advertisements' section.

74. Ibid.

75. Ibid., p. 2 of the 'Advertisements' section.

76. Woof (ed.), *William Wordsworth: The Critical Heritage, Vol. 1: 1793–1830*, pp. 759, 762.

77. Ibid., p. 764.

78. London: Edward Moxon, 64, New Bond Street, 1831.

79. *The Little Maid and the Gentleman; or, We Are Seven. Embellished with Engravings* (York: Printed by J. Kendrew, 1820). For an early inquiry into Wordsworth's inclusion in Kendrew's chapbooks, see H. S. Hughes, 'Two Wordsworthian Chapbooks', *Modern Philology*, 25:2 (1927), pp. 207–10. For more on Kendrew, see R. Davis, *Kendrew of York and His Chapbooks for Children* (Yorkshire: Elmete Press, 1988).

80. The first chapter 'Fame' in S. Gill's *Wordsworth and the Victorians* (New York: Oxford Clarendon Press, 1998), pp. 10–39, details Wordsworth's celebrity in the 1830s and 1840s. Although Wordsworth would make little money from his publications in the 1820s, his status and influence as a literary authority grew as a direct result of his collecting endeavors. On Wordsworth's financial gains and losses with his volumes of poetry, see Erickson's 'The Egoism of Authorship: Wordsworth's Poetic Career', as well as Owen's 'Costs, Sales, and Profits'.

WORKS CITED

Abrams, M. H., *The Mirror and the Lamp* (Oxford: Oxford University Press, 1953).

—, 'On Political Readings of "Tintern Abbey"', in K. Johnston (ed.), *Romantic Revolutions: Criticism and Theory* (Bloomington, IN: Indiana University Press, 1990), pp. 320–49.

Altick, R., *The English Common Reader*, 2nd edn (Columbus, OH: Ohio State University Press, 1998).

The Anti-Jacobin or Weekly Examiner, in Two Volumes, Fourth Edition, Revised and Corrected (London: Printed for J. Wright, Picadilly, 1799).

Arnold, M., 'Wordsworth', in *Matthew Arnold's Essays in Criticism*, ed. K. Allott (New York: J. M. Dent & Sons, 1964).

Barfoot, C. C., 'Parody and the Classic Art of Political Partisanship in *The Anti-Jacobin*', in C. C. Barfoot and T. D'Haen (eds), *Tropes of Revolution: Writer's Reactions to Real and Imagined Revolutions, 1789–1989* (Amsterdam: Rodopi, 1991), pp. 127–93.

Baron, M., *Language and Relationship in Wordsworth's Poetry* (New York: Longman Group, 1995).

Bauer, S., 'Wordsworth and the Early Anthologies', *Library*, 27:1 (1972), pp. 37–45.

Beatty, A., *William Wordsworth: His Doctrine and Art in their Historical Relations* (Madison, WI: University of Wisconsin Press, 1962).

Bell, J., *The Poets of Great Britain*, 109 vols (Edinburgh, 1778).

Benedict, B., *Making the Modern Reader* (Princeton, NJ: Princeton University Press, 1996).

Bennett, A., *Romantic Poets and the Culture of Posterity* (Cambridge: Cambridge University Press, 1999).

—, 'Wordsworth Writing', *Wordsworth Circle*, 34:1 (2003), pp. 3–8.

—, *Wordsworth Writing* (Cambridge: Cambridge University Press, 2007).

Bewell, A., *Wordsworth and the Enlightenment* (New Haven, CT: Yale University Press, 1989).

Bialostosky, D., *Making Tales: The Poetics of Wordsworth's Narrative Experiments* (Chicago, IL: University of Chicago Press, 1984).

Blair, H., *The British Poets*, 43 vols (Edinburgh: Kinkaid, 1773).

Block, A., *The English Novel 1740–1850* (1939, rev. 1961; London: Dawson, 1968).

Bloom, H., *The Visionary Company* (Ithaca, NY: Cornell University Press, 1971).

Boehm, A., 'The 1798 *Lyrical Ballads* and the Poetics of Late Eighteenth-Century Book Production', *ELH*, 63:2 (Summer 1996), pp. 453–87.

Brewer, J., *The Pleasures of the Imagination* (New York: Farrar Straus Giroux, 1997).

Brinkley, R., and K. Hanley (eds), *Romantic Revisions* (Cambridge: Cambridge University Press, 1992).

Broadhead, A., 'Framing Dialect in the 1800 *Lyrical Ballads*: Wordsworth, Regionalisms and Footnotes', *Language and Literature*, 19:3 (2010), pp. 249–63.

Burns, R., *Poems, Chiefly in the Scottish Dialect by Robert Burns* (Kilmarnock: Printed By John Wilson, 1786).

—, *Poems, Chiefly in the Scottish Dialect, In Two Volumes, A New Edition, Considerably Enlarged* (Edinburgh: Printed for T. Cadell, London, and William Creech, Edinburgh, 1794).

Burwick, F. (ed.), *Coleridge's Biographia Literaria Text and Meaning* (Columbus, OH: Ohio State University Press, 1989).

Butler, M., 'Culture's Medium: The Role of the Review', in J. Chandler and M. N. McLane (eds), *The Cambridge Companion to Romanticism* (Cambridge: Cambridge University Press, 1993), pp. 120–47.

—, *Romantics, Rebels, and Reactionaries* (Oxford: Oxford University Press, 1981).

Chandler, D., '"Twisted in Persecution's Loving Ways": Peter Bayley Reviewed by Southey, Wordsworth, and Coleridge', *Wordsworth Circle*, 24:4 (1993), pp. 256–60.

Chandler, J., *England in 1819* (Chicago, IL: University of Chicago Press, 1998).

—, *Wordsworth's Second Nature* (Chicago, IL: University of Chicago Press, 1984).

Chatterton, T., *Poems, Supposed to have been Written at Bristol, by Thomas Rowley, and Others, in the Fifteenth Century; the Greatest Part Now First Published from the Most Authentic Copies, with an Engraved Specimen of One of the Mss* (London: Printed for T. Payne & Son, at the Mews-Gate, 1777).

Christensen, J., *Coleridge's Blessed Machine of Language* (Ithaca, NY: Cornell University Press, 1981).

Christie, W., *The Edinburgh Review in the Literary Culture of Romantic Britain* (London: Pickering & Chatto, 2009).

Clery, E. J., and R. Miles (eds), *Gothic Documents A Sourcebook 1700–1820* (New York: Manchester University Press, 2000).

Colbert, B., 'Popular Romanticism? Publishing, Readership and the Making of Literary History', in E. J. Clery, C. Franklin and P. Garside (eds), *Authorship, Commerce and the Public Scenes of Writing* (New York: Palgrave Macmillan, 2002), pp. 153–68.

Colley, L., *Britons* (New Haven, CT: Yale University Press, 1992).

Coleridge, S. T., *Poems on Various Subjects, by S. T. Coleridge, Late of Jesus College, Cambridge* (London: Printed for G. G. and J. Robinsons, and J. Cottle, Bookseller, Bristol, 1796).

—, *Poems by S. T. Coleridge, Second Edition. To Which are Now Added Poems by Charles Lamb, and Charles Lloyd* (Printed by N. Biggs, for J. Cottle, Bristol, and Messrs. Robinsons, London, 1797).

—, *Christabel, &Cc, by S. T. Colerige, Esq.*, 3rd edn (London: Printed for John Murray, Albermarle Street, By William Bulmer & Co. Cleveland-Row, St James's, 1816).

—, *Biographia Literaria* (1817), ed. J. Engell and W. J. Bate (Princeton, NJ: Princeton University Press, 1983).

—, *Sibylline Leaves: A Collection of Poems* (London: Rest Fenner, 23, Paternoster-Row, 1817).

—, *Coleridge's Miscellaneous Criticism*, ed. T. M. Raysor (London: Constable, 1936).

—, *Collected Letters of Samuel Taylor Coleridge*, ed. E. L. Griggs, 6 vols (Oxford: Clarendon Press, 1956–71).

—, *The Friend*, ed. B. E. Rooke, 2 vols (Princeton, NJ: Princeton University Press, 1969).

—, *Coleridge: The Critical Heritage*, ed. J. R. de Jackson (New York: Barnes & Noble, 1970).

—, *Lectures 1808–1819 on Literature*, ed. R. A. Foakes, 2 vols, *The Collected Works of Samuel Taylor Coleridge*, K. Coburn (gen. ed.), vol. 5 (London: Routledge & Kegan Paul, and Princeton University Press, 1987).

—, *Samuel Taylor Coleridge Sibylline Leaves* (Oxford and New York: Woodstock Facsimile, 1990).

Connell, P., 'Bibliomania: Book Collecting, Cultural Politics, and the Rise of Literary Heritage in Romantic Britain', *Representations*, 70 (Summer 2000), pp. 24–47.

Cook, P. J., 'Resembling Unlikeness: A Reading of Milton's *Tetrachordon* Sonnet', *Milton Quarterly*, 26:4 (1992), pp. 121–9.

Cox, J., 'The Living Pantheon of Poets in 1820', in J. Chandler and M. N. McLane (eds), *The Cambridge Companion to British Romantic Poetry* (Cambridge: Cambridge University Press, 2008), pp. 10–34.

Crawford, R., *Poetry, Enclosure, and the Vernacular Landscape, 1700–1830* (Cambridge: Cambridge University Press, 2002).

Curran, S., 'Multum in Parvo: Wordsworth's *Poems* in Two Volumes, of 1807', *Poems in their Place: The Intertextuality and Order of Poetic Collections* (Chapel Hill, NC: University of North Carolina Press, 1986), pp. 234–53.

—, *Poetic Form and British Romanticism* (Cambridge: Cambridge University Press, 1986).

—, 'Romantic Poetry: Why and Wherefore?', in S. Curran (ed.), *The Cambridge Companion to British Romanticism* (Cambridge: Cambridge University Press, 1993), pp. 216–35.

Curtis, J. (ed.), *Wordsworth's Experiments with Tradition: The Lyric Poems of 1802* (Ithaca, NY: Cornell University Press, 1971).

— (ed.), *Poems, in Two Volumes, and Other Poems, 1800–1807* (Ithaca, NY: Cornell University Press, 1983).

— (ed.), *The Fenwick Notes of William Wordsworth* (London: Bristol Classical Press, 1993).

Darwin, E., *The Botanic Garden; A Poem in Two Parts. Part I. Containing the Economy of Vegetation. Part II. The Loves of the Plants. With Philosophical Notes* (London: Printed for J. Johnson, St Paul's Church-Yard, 1791).

Davies, H. S., *Wordsworth and the Worth of Words*, ed. J. Kerrigan and J. Wordsworth (Cambridge: Cambridge University Press, 1987).

Davis, R., *Kendrew of York and His Chapbooks for Children* (Yorkshire: Elmete Press, 1988).

De Mann, P., 'Time and History in Wordsworth', *Diacritics*, 17:4 (Winter 1987), pp. 4–17.

Devlin, D. D., *Wordsworth's Poetry of Epitaphs* (Totowa, NJ; Barnes & Noble, 1981).

Dibdin, T. F., *Bibliomania; or Book Madness* (London: Longman, 1809).

D'Israeli, I., *Curiosities of Literature*, 6:2 (London. John Murray, 1817).

—, *The Literary Character*, 3:2 (London. John Murray, 1822).

Duff, D., 'Paratextual Dilemmas: Wordsworth's "The Brothers" and the Problem of Generic Labeling', *Romanticism*, 6:2 (2000), pp. 234–52.

—, 'Wordsworth and the Language of Forms: The Collected *Poems* of 1815', *Wordsworth Circle*, 34:2 (2003), pp. 86–90.

Durrant, G. H., 'Wordsworth's "Peter Bell" – A *Pons Asinorum* For Critics', *Wascana Review of Contemporary Poetry and Short Fiction*, 1 (1996), pp. 26–43.

Dyer, G., *British Politics and the Politics of Style, 1789–1832* (Cambridge: Cambridge University Press, 1997).

Eilenberg, S., *Strange Power of Speech: Wordsworth, Coleridge, and Literary Possession* (New York: Oxford University Press, 1992).

Eisenstein, E., *The Printing Press as an Agent of Change*, 2 vols (New York: Cambridge University Press, 1979).

Erickson, L., *The Economy of Literary Form* (Baltimore, MD: Johns Hopkins University Press, 1996).

Fay, E., *Becoming Wordsworthian* (Amherst, MA: University of Massachusetts Press, 1995).

Felluga, D., *The Perversity of Poetry: Romantic Ideology and the Popular Male Poet of Genius* (Albany, NY: State University of New York Press, 2005).

Ferguson, F., *Wordsworth: Language as Counter-Spirit* (New Haven, CT: Yale University Press, 1977).

Ferris, D., 'The Question of a Science: Encyclopedic Romanticism', *Wordsworth Circle*, 35:1 (Winter 2004), pp. 2–5.

Ferris, I., 'Romantic Libraries', Romantic Circles Praxis Series (February 2004), available online at <http://www.rc.umd.edu/praxis/libraries/> [accessed 1 August 2011].

Ferry, A., *Tradition and the Individual Poem: An Inquiry into Anthologies* (Stanford, CA: University Press, 2001).

Foakes, R. A. (ed.), 'Unassigned Lecture Notes: Milton and *Paradise Lost*', in *The Collected Works of Samuel Taylor Coleridge, Vol. 5: Lectures 1808–1819 on Literature*, ed. K.

Coburn, 2 vols (London: Routledge, Kegan Paul and Princeton University Press, 1987), vol. 2, p. 428.

Fraistat, N., *The Poem and the Book* (Chapel Hill, NC: North Carolina University Press, 1985).

Franta, A., *Romanticism and the Rise of the Mass Public* (New York: Cambridge University Press, 2007).

Fry, P., 'Wordsworth in the "Rime", in *The Rime of the Ancient Mariner: Complete, Authoritative Texts of the 1798 and 1817 Versions* (New York: Bedford St Martin's 1999), pp. 319–42.

Gamer, M., '"Bell's Poetics": *The Baviad,* the Della Cruscans, and the Book of *The World*', in S. Jones (ed.), *The Satiric Eye* (New York: Palgrave Macmillan, 2003), pp. 31–53.

—, *Romanticism and the Gothic* (Cambridge: Cambridge University Press, 2000).

Garrett, J., *Wordsworth and the Writing of the Nation* (Burlington, VT: Ashgate, 2008).

Garrod, H. W., *Wordsworth: Lectures and Essays*, 2nd edn (Oxford: Clarendon Press, 1927).

Garside, P. (ed.), *English Novels 1770–1830: A Bibliographical Survey of Prose Fiction Published in the British Isles*, 2 vols (Oxford: Oxford University Press, 2000).

Garside, P., and A. Mandell, 'Producing Fiction in Britain, 1800–1829', *Romantic Textualities: Literature and Print Culture*, 1 (August 1997), available online at <http://www.romtext.cf.ac.uk//articles/cc01_n01.html> [accessed 5 July 2011].

Gaull, M., 'Romantic Humor: The Horse of Knowledge and the Learned Pig', *Mosaic*, 9 (1976), pp. 43–64.

Genette, G., *Palimpsests Literature in the Second Degree*, trans. C. Newman and C. Doubinsky (Lincoln, NE: University of Nebraska Press, 1997).

—, *Sueils*, translated in English as *Paratexts: Thresholds of Interpretation* (Lincoln, NE: University of Nebraska Press, 1997).

Gill, S., *William Wordsworth: A Life* (Oxford: Clarendon Press, 1989).

—, *Wordsworth and the Victorians* (New York: Oxford Clarendon Press, 1998).

—, 'Wordsworth and *The River Duddon*', *Essays in Criticism*, 57:1 (2007), pp. 22–41.

Gilman, P., '"To Kill and Bury the Poor Thorn Forever": "The Thorn" and Mant's *Simpliciad*', *Wordsworth Circle*, 27:1 (1996), pp. 37–41.

Glen, H., *Vision and Disenchantment: Blake's Songs and Wordsworth's Lyrical Ballads* (Cambridge: Cambridge University Press, 1983).

Gohn, J. B., 'Who Wrote *Benjamin the Waggoner*?: An Inquiry', *Wordsworth Circle*, 8:1 (Winter 1977), pp. 69–74.

Grafton, A., *The Footnote: A Curious History* (Cambridge, MA: Harvard University Press, 1997).

Gravil, R., *Wordsworth's Bardic Vocation* (London: Palgrave Macmillan, 2003).

Groom, N., *The Making of Percy's Reliques* (Oxford: Oxford University Press, 1999).

Gross, J., *The Rise and Fall of the Man of Letters: Aspects of English Literary Life Since 1800* (Chicago, IL: Ivan R. Dee, 1969).

Halliwell, J., 'Loyalist Satire, Parody; and *The Anti-Jacobin*', in S. Hull (ed.), *The British Periodical Text, 1797–1835* [electronic resource] (Penrith: Humanities eBooks, 2008), pp. 36–67.

Hamilton, C. C., *Wordsworth's Decline in Poetic Power: Prophet into High Priest* (New York: Exposition, 1963).

Hartman, G., *Wordsworth's Poetry, 1787–1814* (Harvard University Press, 1964).

—, *The Unremarkable Wordsworth* (Minneapolis, MI: University of Minnesota Press, 1987).

Hayden, J. O., *The Romantic Reviewers, 1802–1824* (Chicago, IL: University of Chicago Press, 1969).

Heffernan, J., 'Mutilated Autobiography: Wordsworth's *Poems* of 1815', *Wordsworth Circle*, 10:1 (Winter 1979), pp. 107–12.

Heinzelman, K., *The Economics of the Imagination* (Amherst, MA: University of Massachusetts Press, 1980).

Heninger, S. K., *The Subtext of Form in the English Renaissance* (University Park, PA: Pennsylvania State University Press, 1994).

Herman, J. B., 'The Poet as Editor: Wordsworth's Edition of 1815', *Wordsworth Circle*, 9 (1978), pp. 82–7.

Hess, S., *Authoring the Self* (New York: Routledge, 2005).

Higgins, D., '*Blackwood's Edinburgh Magazine* and the Construction of Wordsworth's Genius', in K. Wheatley (ed.), *Romantic Periodicals and Print Culture* (Portland, OR: Frank Cass, 2003), pp. 122–36.

Hogg, J., *The Poetic Mirror* ((London: Printed for Longman, Hurst, Rees, Orme, and Brown; and John Ballantyne, Edinburgh, 1816).

—, *Memoirs of the Author's Life*, ed. D. Mack (Edinburgh: Scottish Academic Press, 1972).

Hogle, J. (ed.), *The Cambridge Companion to Gothic Fiction* (Cambridge: Cambridge University Press, 2002).

Hollander, J., *The Figure of Echo* (Berkeley, CA: California University Press, 1981).

Hughes, H. S., 'Two Wordsworthian Chapbooks', *Modern Philology*, 25:2 (1927), pp. 207–10.

Jack, I., *English Literature 1815–1832* (Oxford: Clarendon Press, 1963).

Jackson, J. R. de. (ed.), *Annals of English Verse 1770–1835: A Preliminary Survey of the Volumes Published* (New York: Garland, 1985).

Janowitz, A., 'Coleridge's 1816 Volume: Fragment and Ruin', *Studies in Romanticism*, 24:1 (1985), pp. 21–39.

Johnson, L, *Wordsworth and the Sonnet* (Copenhagen: Rosenkilde & Bagger, 1973).

Johnson, S., *A Dictionary of the English Language: In Two Volumes, The Fourth Edition, Revised by the Author* (London: Printed by W. Strahan, 1773).

—, *The Lives of the Most Eminent English Poets* (London, 1779).

Johnston, K., 'The Politics of 'Tintern Abbey', *Wordsworth Circle*, 14 (1983), pp. 6–14.

—, *Wordsworth and The Recluse* (New Haven, CT: Yale University Press, 1984).

—, 'Romantic Anti-Jacobins or Anti-Jacobin Romantics', *RAVON*, 15 (August 1999), 36 par., available online at <http://www.erudit.org/revue/ron/1999/v/n15/005862ar.html> [accessed 10 July 2011].

—, *The Hidden Wordsworth* (New York: W.W. Norton & Co., 2000).

—, 'Wordsworth's Self-Creation and the 1800 *Lyrical Ballads*', in N. Trott and S. Perry (eds), *1800: The New Lyrical Ballads* (New York: Palgrave Macmillan, 2001), pp. 95–121.

Jones, M., 'Parody and Its Containments: The Case of Wordsworth', *Representations*, 54 (Spring 1996), pp. 57–79.

Jones, S., *Satire and Romanticism* (New York: St Martin's Press, 2000).

— (ed.), *The Satiric Eye* (New York: Palgrave Macmillan, 2003).

Kearns, S., *Coleridge, Wordsworth, and Romantic Autobiography* (Madison, NJ: Farleigh Dickinson University Press, 1995).

Keen, P., *Crisis of Literature in the 1790s: Print Culture and the Public Sphere* (Cambridge: Cambridge University Press, 1999).

— (ed.), *Revolutions in Romantic Literature: An Anthology of Print Culture, 1780–1832* (Peterborough, Ontario Canada: Broadview Press, 2004).

—, '"Uncommon Animals": Making Virtue of Necessity in the Age of Authors', in I. Ferris and P. Keen (eds), *Bookish Histories: Books, Literature and Commercial Modernity, 1700–1900* (New York: Palgrave Macmillan, 2009), pp. 41–60.

Kelley, T., *Wordsworth's Revisionary Aesthetics* (New York: Cambridge University Press, 1988).

Kent, D., and D. R. Ewen (eds), *Romantic Parodies, 1797–1831* (London: Farleigh Dickinson University Press, 1992).

Khan, J., 'The Allegories of Wordsworth's 'The Pilgrim's Dream; or, The Star and the Glow-Worm', *Studies in Philology*, 4 (Fall 1997), pp. 508–22.

—, 'Publication and Reception of Wordsworth's "The River Duddon" Volume', *Modern Language Studies*, 32:2 (2002), pp. 45–67.

Kim, B., 'Generating a National Sublime: Wordsworth's *The River Duddon* and *The Guide to the Lakes*', *Studies in Romanticism*, 45:1 (Spring 2006), pp. 49–75.

Klancher, J. *The Making of English Reading Audiences, 1790–1832* (Madison, WI: University of Wisconsin Press, 1987).

—, '"Wild Bibliography": The Rise and Fall of Book History in Nineteenth-Century Britain', in I. Ferris and P. Keen (eds), *Bookish Histories: Books, Literature and Commercial Modernity, 1700–1900* (New York: Palgrave Macmillan, 2009), pp. 19–40.

Kneale, D. J., *Monumental Writing: Aspects of Rhetoric in Wordsworth's Poetry* (Lincoln, NE: University of Nebraska Press, 1988).

Knox, V., *Elegant Extracts: or Useful and Entertaining Pieces of Poetry, Selected for the Improvement of Youth* (London: Printed for Charles Dilly, Poultry, 1784).

Lapp, R., *Contest for Cultural Authority: Hazlitt, Coleridge and the Distresses of the Regency* (Detroit, MI: Wayne State University Press, 1999).

Lewalski, B., *Paradise Lost and the Rhetoric of Literary Forms* (Princeton, NJ: Princeton University Press, 1985).

Levinson, M., *The Romantic Fragment Poem: A Critique of Form* (Chapel Hill, NC: University of North Carolina Press, 1986).

—, *Wordsworth's Great Period Poems* (Cambridge: Cambridge University Press, 1996).

Liu, A., *Wordsworth: The Sense of History* (Palo Alto, CA: Stanford University Press, 1989).

London, A., *Literary History Writing, 1770–1820* (London: Palgrave Macmillan, 2010).

McFarland, T., *Romanticism and the Forms of Ruin: Wordsworth, Coleridge, and Modalities of Fragmentation* (Princeton, NJ: Princeton University Press, 1981).

—, *William Wordsworth: Intensity and Achievement* (Oxford: Oxford University Press, 1992).

McGann, J., *The Romantic Ideology: A Critical Investigation* (Chicago, IL: Chicago University Press, 1983).

—, *The Textual Condition* (Princeton, NJ: Princeton University Press, 1991).

McKendrick, N., J. Brewer and J. H. Plumb (eds), *The Birth of a Consumer Society: The Commercialization of Eighteenth-Century England* (Bloomington, IN: Indiana University Press, 1982).

Macovski, M., *Dialogue and Literature: Apostrophes, Auditors, and the Collapse of Romantic Discourse* (New York: Oxford University Press, 1994).

Macpherson, J., *The Poems of Ossian and Related Works* (1765), ed. F. Stafford and H. Gaskill (Edinburgh: Edinburgh University Press, 1996).

—, *The Works of Ossian, The Son of Fingal. In Two Volumes, Translated from the Galic Language by James Macpherson*, 3rd edn, 2 vols (London, 1765).

Magnuson, P., *Reading Public Romanticism* (Princeton, NJ: Princeton University Press, 1998).

Manning, P. J., *Reading Romantics: Texts and Contexts* (Oxford: Oxford University Press, 1990).

Manning, S., 'Walter Scott, Antiquarianism and the Political Discourse of the *Edinburgh Review, 1802–1811*', in M. Demata and D. Wu (eds), *British Romanticism and the Edinburgh Review* (New York: Palgrave Macmillan, 2002), pp. 102–23.

Mant, R., *The Simpliciad* (1808), ed. J. Wordsworth (New York: Woodstock Books, 1991).

Martin, J. S., 'Peter Bayley and the *Lyrical Ballads*', *English Studies*, 48 (1968), pp. 533–7.

Mason, N., 'Building Brand Byron: Early Nineteenth-Century Advertising and the Marketing of *Child Harold's Pilgrimage*', *Modern Language Quarterly*, 63:4 (2002), pp. 411–40.

Mathias, T. J., *The Pursuits of Literature*, 5th edn (London, 1797).

Mayo, R., 'The Contemporaneity of the *Lyrical Ballads*', in M. H. Abrams (ed.), *Wordsworth: A Collection of Critical Essays* (Englewood Cliffs, NJ: Prentice Hall, Inc., 1972), pp. 67–74.

Meisenhelder, S., *Wordsworth's Informed Reader: Structures of Experience in his Poetry* (Nashville, TN: Vanderbilt University Press, 1988).

Miller, J. H., *The Linguistic Moment* (Princeton, NJ: Princeton University Press, 1985).

Milton, J., *Paradise Lost. A New Edition, by Richard Bentley D.D.* (London: Printed for Jacob Tonson, 1732).

—, *The Complete Poetry of John Milton*, ed. J. T. Shawcross (New York: Doubleday, 1971).

Moore, T., *Corruption and Intolerance: Two Poems with Notes, Addressed to an Englishman by an Irishman* (London: Printed for J. Carpenter, Bond-Street, 1809).

Mortenson, R., '"The Nose-Drop": A Parody of Wordsworth', *Wordsworth Circle*, 2 (1971), pp. 91–100.

Moser, W., 'Translating Discourses: Inter-Discursive Mobility in the Early Romantic Encyclopedia', *Eighteenth Century*, 22:1 (1981), pp. 3–20.

Mudge, B., '"Excited by Trick": Coleridge and the Gothic Imagination', *Wordsworth Circle*, 22:3 (Summer1991), pp. 179–84.

Murphy, P., *Poetry as an Occupation and an Art in Britain, 1760–1830* (Cambridge: Cambridge University Press, 1993).

Murray, R., *Wordsworth's Style: Figures and Themes in the Lyrical Ballads of 1800* (Lincoln, NE: University of Nebraska Press, 1967).

Nabholtz, J., *'My Reader, My Fellow Laborer': A Study of English Romantic Prose* (Columbia, MI: University of Missouri Press, 1986).

Nardo, A., *Milton's Sonnets and the Ideal Community* (Lincoln, NE: University of Nebraska Press, 1979.

Newlyn, L., *Reading, Writing, and Romanticism: The Anxiety of Reception* (Cambridge University Press, 2000).

Owens, T., 'Wordsworth, Galignani, and the Aesthetics of Piracy', *Library*, 12:1 (2011), pp. 23–36.

Owen, W. J. B., 'Costs, Sales, and Profits of Longman's Editions of Wordsworth', *Library*, 12 (1957), pp. 93–107.

—, *Wordsworth as Critic* (Toronto, Ontario: Toronto University Press, 1969).

Parrish, S., *The Art of the Lyrical Ballads* (Cambridge, MA: Harvard University Press, 1973).

Patterson, A., *Nobody's Perfect: A New Whig Interpretation of History* (New Haven, CT: Yale University Press, 2002).

Percy, T., *Reliques of Ancient English Poetry Consisting of Old Heroic Ballads, Songs, and Other Pieces of Our Earlier Poets (Chiefly of the LYRIC kind) Together with Some Few of Later Date* (London: Printed for J. Dodsley in Pall-Mall, 1765).

—, *Reliques of Ancient English Poetry*, 4th edn (London, 1794).

Pfau, T., *Wordsworth's Profession: Form, Class, and the Logic of Early Romantic Cultural Production* (Standford, CA: Stanford University Press, 1997).

Piper, A., *Dreaming in Books: The Making of the Bibliographic Imagination in the Romantic Age* (Chicago, IL: University of Chicago Press, 2009).

Ponder, M., 'Echoing Poetry with History: Wordsworth's Duddon Sonnets and their Notes', *Genre*, 21 (Summer 1988), pp. 157–78.

Pope, A., *The Dunciad. In Four Books, Printed according to the Complete Copy Found in the Year 1742, with the Prolegomena of Scriblerus, and the Notes Variorum* (London: Printed for M. Cooper at the Globe in Pater-noster-row, 1743).

Price, L., *The Anthology and the Rise of the Novel* (Cambridge: Cambridge University Press, 2000).

The Progress of Satire: An Essay in Verse with Notes, Containing Remarks on the 'Pursuits of Literature', 2nd edn (London: Printed for J. Bell, No. 148, Oxford Street, 1798).

Pricket, S., '*Biographia Literaria*: Chapter Thirteen', in D. Coleman and P. Otto (eds), *Imagining Romanticism: Essays on English and Australian Romanticisms* (West Cornhall, CT: Locust Hill Press, 1992), pp. 3–24.

Pyle, G. J., 'J. H. Reynolds's "Peter Bell"', *Notes and Queries*, 24 (1977), pp. 323–4.

Rajan, T., *The Supplement of Reading* (Ithaca, NY: Cornell University Press, 1990).

—, 'Philosophy as Encyclopedia: Hegel, Schelling, and the Organization of Knowledge', *Wordsworth Circle*, 35:1 (Winter 2004), pp. 6–11.

Raven, J., *The Business of Books: Booksellers and the English Book Trade, 1450–1850* (New Haven, CT: Yale University Press, 2007).

Reynolds, J. H., 'Peter Bell: A Lyrical Ballad', in D. Kent and D. R. Ewen (eds), *Romantic Parodies, 1797–1831* (London: Farleigh Dickinson University Press, 1992), pp. 173–84.

Richey, W., 'The Politicized Landscape of "Tintern Abbey"', *Studies in Philology*, 95:2 (1998), pp. 197–219.

Rieder, J., *Wordsworth's Counterrevolutionary Turn: Community, Virtue, and Vision in the 1790s* (Newark, DE: University of Delaware Press, 1997).

Robinson, D., '"Still Glides the Stream": Form and Function in Wordsworth's *River Duddon* Sonnets', *European Romantic Review*, 13:4 (2002), pp. 449–64.

Robinson, M., *Lyrical Tales* (London: Printed for T. N. Longman and O. Rees, Paternoster Row, by Biggs & Co. Bristol, 1800).

Roe, N., *Wordsworth and Coleridge: The Radical Years* (Oxford: Oxford University Press, 1988).

Rose, M., *Authors and Owners: The Invention of Copyright* (Cambridge, MA: Harvard University Press, 1993).

—, 'Literary Property Determined', in D. Finkelstein and A. McCleary (eds), *The Book History Reader* (New York: Routledge, 2002), pp. 231–40.

Ross, D. Jr, 'Poems "Bound Each to Each" in the 1815 Edition of Wordsworth', *Wordsworth Circle*, 12 (1981), pp. 133–40.

Ross, M., 'Romancing the Nation-State: The Poetics of Romantic Nationalism', in J. Arac and H. Ritvo (eds), *Macropolitics of Nineteenth-Century Literature* (Durham, NC: Duke University Press, 1995), pp. 56–85.

Rowland, A. W., 'Romantic Poetry and the Romantic Novel', in J. Chandler and M. N. McLane (eds), *The Cambridge Companion to Romanticism* (Cambridge: Cambridge University Press, 2008), pp. 53–75.

Ruoff, G., 'Critical Implications of Wordsworth's 1815 Categorization, With Some Animadversions on Binaristic Commentary', *Wordsworth Circle*, 9 (1978), pp. 75–82.

—, *Wordsworth and Coleridge: The Making of the Major Lyrics 1802–1804* (New Brunswick, NJ: Rutgers University Press, 1989).

Russett, M., *Fictions and Fakes: Forging Romantic Authenticity, 1760–1845* (Cambridge University Press, 2006).

Rzepka, C., 'A Gift that Complicates Employ: Poetry and Poverty in "Resolution and Independence"', *Studies in Romanticism*, 28:2 (1989), pp. 225–47.

—, 'Pictures of the Mind: Iron and Charcoal, "Ouzy Tides", and "Vagrant Dwellers" at Tintern, 1798', *Studies in Romanticism*, 42:2 (Summer 2003), pp. 155–85.

—, 'Sacrificial Sites, Place-Keeping, and "Pre-History" in Wordsworth's "Michael"', *European Romantic Review*, 15:2 (2004), pp. 205–13.

St Clair, W., *The Reading Nation in the Romantic Period* (Cambridge: Cambridge University Press, 2004).

Schoenfield, M., *The Professional Wordsworth* (Athens, GA: University of Georgia Press, 1996).

—, *British Periodicals and Romantic Identity: 'The Literary Lower Empire'* (New York: Palgrave Macmillan, 2009).

Scoggins, J., *Imagination and Fancy: Complementary Modes of the Poetry of Wordsworth* (Lincoln, NE: University of Nebraska Press, 1966).

Scott, Sir W., *The Lay of The Last Minstrel, A Poem: The Eighth Edition With Ballads And Lyrical Pieces* (London: Printed for Longman, Hurst, Rees, and Orme, Paternoster-Row, and A. Constable & Co. Edinburgh; by James Ballantyne & Co. Edinburgh, 1810).

—, *Minstrelsy of the Scottish Border, Consisting of Historical and Romantic Ballads Collected in the Southern Counties of Scotland*, 2nd edn, 2 vols (Edinburgh: Printed By James Ballantyne, For Longman And Rees, Paternoster-Row, 1803).

Seward, A., *The Letters of Anna Seward*, ed. Sir W. Scott, 6 vols (Edinburgh, 1811).

Shaw, P. (ed.), *Romantic Wars: Studies in Culture and Conflict, 1793–1822* (Burlington, VT: Ashgate University Press, 2000).

—, *Waterloo and the Romantic Imagination* (Basingstoke: Palgrave Macmillan, 2002).

Sheats, P., '"'Tis Three Feet Long, and Two Feet Wide": Wordsworth's "Thorn" and the Politics of Bathos', *Wordsworth Circle*, 22:2 (Spring 1991), pp. 92–100.

Shelley, P., *Peter Bell The Third: A Facsimile of the Press Copy*, ed. D. Reiman (New York: Garland, 1986).

Sheridan, R. B., *The School for Scandal and Other Plays*, ed. E. Rump (New York: Penguin Books, 1988).

Simpkins, S., 'Telling the Reader What to Do: Wordsworth and the Fenwick Notes', *Reader*, 26 (1991), pp. 39–64.

Simpson, D., *Romanticism, Nationalism and the Revolt Against Theory* (Chicago, IL: University of Chicago Press, 1993).

—, *Wordsworth and the Figurings of the Real* (Atlantic Highlands, NJ: Humanities Press, 1982).

Siskin, C., *The Historicity of Romantic Discourse* (New York: Oxford University Press, 1988).

—, 'The Year of the System', in R. Cronin (ed.), *1798: The Year of the* Lyrical Ballads (New York: St Martin's Press, 1998), pp. 9–31.

Smith, C., *Beachy Head: With Other Poems, by Charlotte Smith* (London: Printed for the Author: and sold by J. Johnson, St Paul's Church-Year, 1807).

—, *Elegiac Sonnets, and Other Essays. By Charlotte Smith of Bignor Park, in Sussex*, 2nd edn (Chichester: Printed by Dennett Jacques, and sold by Dodsley, Gardner, Galdwin, and Bew, London, 1784).

—, *Elegiac Sonnets, and Other Poems, by Charlotte Smith*, 9th edn (London: Printed for T. Cadell, Jun. and W. Davies in the Strand, 1800).

Smith, C., 'Robert Southey and the Emergence of *Lyrical Ballads*', *RAVON*, 9 (1998), available online at <http://www.erudit.org/revue/ron/1998/v/n9/005792ar.html> [accessed 5 February 2009].

Southey, R., *Joan of Arc. An Epic Poem* (Bristol: Printed by Bulgin and Rosser, for Joseph Cottle, 1796).

—, *Poems by Robert Southey* (London: Printed by N. Biggs, for Joseph Cottle, Bristol, and G. G. and J. Robinsons, 1797).

—, *Poems by Robert Southey, the Second Volume* (London: Printed for Biggs and Cottle, for T. N. Longman and O. Rees, Paternoster-Row, 1799).

Spenser, E., *The Shepheardes Calendar* (London, 1579).

Sperry, W. L., *Wordsworth's Anti-Climax* (Cambridge, MA: Harvard University Press, 1935).

Spivak, G., 'The Letter As Cutting Edge', *Yale French Studies*, 55/56 (1977), pp. 208–26.

Stillinger, J. (ed.), *William Wordsworth: Selected Poems and Prefaces* (Boston, MA: Houghton Mifflin, 1965).

—, *Coleridge and Textual Instability: The Multiple Versions of the Major Poems* (New York: Oxford University Press, 1992).

Stones, G., 'Parody and the *Anti-Jacobin*', *Wordsworth Circle*, 24.3 (Summer 1993), pp. 162–6.

—, 'The "Vile Art" of Romantic Parody', *Wordsworth Circle*, 27:2 (Spring 1996), pp. 87–95.

Strachan, J. (ed.), *Parodies of the Romantic Age*, 5 vols (London: Pickering & Chatto, 1999).

Thomas, G. K., 'The Lyrical Ballads Ode: "Dialogized Heteroglossia"', *Wordsworth Circle*, 20:2 (1989), pp. 102–6.

Timar, A., 'Imagination Disconnected: On Chapter XIII of *Biographia Literaria*', *AnaChronisT* (2002), pp. 79–111.

Tottel, R., *Songes and Sonettes* (London, 1557).

Trott, N., 'Wordsworth in the Nursery: The Parodic School of Criticism', *Wordsworth Circle*, 32:2 (Spring 2001), pp. 66–77.

—, 'Wordsworth and the Parodic School of Criticism', in S. Jones (ed.), *The Satiric Eye* (New York: Palgrave Macmillan, 2003), pp. 71–98.

Viscomi, J., 'Wordsworth's Dramatic Antipicturesque', in 'Scholarly Resources', *Romantic Circles*, at <http://www.rc.umd.edu/reference/> [accessed 15 December 2008].

Walker, E. C., 'Wordsworth's "Third Volume" and the Collected Editions, 1815–1820', *Bibliographical Society of America*, 80:4 (1986), pp. 437–53.

Walsh, M., *Shakespeare, Milton, and Eighteenth-Century Literary Editing* (Cambridge: Cambridge University Press, 1997).

Watson, A., 'Dark Assassin: Thomas James Mathias' Notes for The Pursuits Of Literature', in D. Lewes (ed.), *Double Vision: Literary Palimpsests of the Eighteenth and Nineteenth Centuries* (Lanham, MD: Lexington Books, 2008), pp. 37–51.

Watson, J. R., *Romanticism and War* (Basingstoke: Palgrave Macmillan, 2003).

Wheeler, K., *Sources, Processes and Methods in Coleridge's Biographia Literaria* (Cambridge: Cambridge University Press, 1980).

Wilcox, S., 'Wordsworth's *River Duddon* Sonnets', *PMLA*, 69:1 (1954), pp. 131–41.

Wood, M., *Radical Satire and Print Culture 1790–1822* (Oxford: Oxford University Press, 1994).

Woof, R (ed.), *William Wordsworth: The Critical Heritage, Vol. I., 1793–1820* (New York: Routledge, 2001).

Wordsworth, J., 'Revision as Making: *The Prelude* and Its Peers', in R. Brinkley and J. Hanley (eds), *Romantic Revisions* (Cambridge: Cambridge University Press, 1992), pp. 19–42.

Wordsworth, W., *Descriptive Sketches. In Verse. Taken During a Tour in the Italian, Grison, Swiss, and Savoyard Alps* (London: Printed for J. Johnson, St Paul's Church-Yard, 1793).

—, *An Evening Walk. An Epistle; in Verse. Addressed to a Young Lady, from the Lakes of the North of England* (London: Printed For J. Johnson, St. Paul's Church-Yard, 1793).

—, *Lyrical Ballads, with a Few Other Poems* (London: Printed For J. & A. Arch, Gracechurch Street, 1798).

—, *Lyrical Ballads, with Other Poems, in Two Volumes* (London: Printed for T. N. Longman & O. Rees, Paternoster-Row, by Biggs & Co. Bristol, 1800).

—, *Lyrical Ballads, with Pastoral and Other Poems, in Two Volumes* (London: Printed For T. N. Longman and O. Rees, Paternoster-Row, by Giggs and Cottle, Crane-Court, Fleet-Street, 1802).

—, *Poems, in Two Volumes, by William Wordsworth, Author of Lyrical Ballads* (London: Paternoster Row, 1807).

—, *Poems by William Wordsworth: Including Lyrical Ballads, and the Miscellaneous Pieces of the Author. With Additional Poems, a New Preface, and a Supplementary Essay* (London: Paternoster Row, 1815).

—, *Benjamin the Waggoner* (1819), ed. P. Betz (Ithaca, NY: Cornell University Press, 1981).

—, *The Little Maid and the Gentleman; or, We are Seven, Embellished with Engravings* (York: Printed by J. Kendrew, 1820).

—, *Selections from the Poems of William Wordsworth, Esq. Chiefly for the Use of Schools and Young Persons* (London: E. Moxon, 64, New Bond Street, 1831).

—, *The Poetical Works of William Wordsworth*, ed. E. de Selincourt, 5 vols (Oxford: Clarendon Press, 1959).

—, *William Wordsworth: Selected Poems and Prefaces*, ed. J. Stillinger (Boston, MA: Houghton Mifflin, 1965).

—, *The Letters of William and Dorothy Wordsworth*, ed. E. de Selincourt, rev. C. Shaver and M. Moorman, 8 vols (Oxford: Clarendon Press, 1967–93).

—, *The Prose Works of William Wordsworth*, ed. W. J. B. Owen and J. W. Smyser, 3 vols (Oxford : Clarendon Press, 1974)

—, *Peter Bell*, ed. J. E. Jordan (Ithaca, NY: Cornell University Press, 1985).

—, *Shorter Poems, 1807–1820*, ed. C. H. Ketcham (Ithaca, NY: Cornell University Press, 1989).

—, *Lyrical Ballads*, ed. R. L. Brett and A. R. Jones (New York: Routledge, 1991).

—, *Lyrical Ballads and Other Poems, 1797–1800*, ed. J. Butler and K. Green (Ithaca, NY: Cornell University Press, 1992).

—, *Sonnet Series and Itinerary Poems, 1820–1845*, ed. G. Jackson (Ithaca, NY: Cornell University Press, 2004).

Wu, D., *Wordsworth's Reading, 1770–1799* (Cambridge: Cambridge University Press, 1993).

—, *Wordsworth's Reading 1800–1815* (Cambridge: Cambridge University Press, 1995).

Wyatt, J., *Wordsworth's Poems of Travel* (New York: St Martin's Press, 1999).

Young, E., *Conjectures on Original Composition* (London, 1759).

Zaul, P. M., 'The Cool World of Samuel Taylor Coleridge: Vicesimus Knox, Elegant Activist', *Wordsworth Circle*, 10 (1979), pp. 345–7.

—, 'Wordsworth and the Copyright Act of 1842', *PMLA*, 70 (1955), pp. 132–44.

INDEX

Abrams, M. H., 15
Academic, 155
Anderson, Robert, 40
Annual Review, 58
Anti-Jacobin, or Weekly Examiner, 16, 18,
    23–4, 26–8
    'The New Morality', 27–8
Arnold, Matthew, 13, 92

ballad collecting, 1, 11, 18, 31, 33, 93
Barham Downs, 58
Bayley, Peter
    Poems, 58–9
Bennett, Andrew, 13, 124
Beaumont, Lady, 68, 124
Beaumont, Sir George, 68, 123
bibliomania, 19, 77–81, 85
Biggs, N., 21, 22
Blackwood's Edinburgh Magazine, 16, 20,
    142, 144, 145–50
Boehm, Alan, 43
Bowles, William Leslie, 9
British Critic, 41
British Review, 144
Bonaparte, Napoleon, 76
Burger, Gottfried, 11
Burke, Edmund, 24
Burns, Robert, 7–8, 134
Byron, George Gordon (Lord), 11, 113–14,
    145, 149–50

Canning, George, 143
Chandler, James, 13, 143
Chatterton, Thomas, 5–7, 9
Chaucer, Geoffrey, 4, 68, 87
    'The Flour', 127

Cobbett, William
    Political Registry, 16
Coleridge, Samuel Taylor
    and aesthetics, mixing high and low,
        116–19
    Ancient Mariner changes, 36–7
    Anti-Jacobin attacks in, 27
    defense of Wordsworth's genius, 121
    in 'Don Juan Unvisited', 149
    'Friend' in *Biographia Literaria*, 19,
        102–19
        see also chapter 13, *Biographia Literaria*
    and Gothic counterfeit, 102–3, 119
    Lyrical Ballads collaborator, 8, 21, 107,
        122
    making 'a bull', 108–10
    'metaphysics of typography', 8–9
    Morning Post and *Courier*, 21
    and national literary character, 103–19
    and 'the new school of poetry', 16
    and palimpsest, 104
    parody of Wordsworth's Gothic church,
        102, 111–19
    evaluation of Percy's *Reliques*, 33
    as poet-critic, 19, 111–12
    reaction to Peter Bayley's *Poems*, 29, 57
    on reputation, 109, 124
    'revelations of [the poet's] own mind', 82
    in Reynolds's 'The Dead Asses', 148
    Reynolds's 'Peter Bell', evaluation of,
        122–3
    in *The Simpliciad*, 59, 62, 65
    relationship with Southey, 29
    works
        'Advertisement' to *Lyrical Ballads*, 4,
            12, 17

'Advertisement' in *Poems by S. T.*
    Coleridge, 9
'To the Author of Poems Published
    Anonymously, at Bristol', 9
Biographia Literaria, 14, 102, 119
    Chapter 4, 108–10
    Chapter 12, 105–6
    Chapter 13, 101–19
The Brook, 153
Christabel, 104, 107, 111–15, 118
*Christabel, Kubla Khan, A Vision: The
    Pains of Sleep*, 11, 111
'An Effusion on an Autumnal Evening', 9
'Effusion XV', 10
'Epistle I', 10
The Friend, 95, 103, 125
'To a Gentleman'
    see 'To William Wordsworth'
Poems by S. T. Coleridge, 9–10
Poems on Various Subjects, 9–10
'Preface' to *Christabel*, 113–14
'Preface' to *Poems on Various Subjects*,
    10
'Preface' to *Poems by S. T. Coleridge*,
    9–10
'Preface' to *Sibylline Leaves*, 107–8
'Rime of the Ancient Mariner', 28–9,
    36–7, 104–6, 118
Sibylline Leaves, 19, 105–8, 116–17
'To William Wordsworth', 104, 111,
    115–18
Cook, Patrick, 133–5, 137
Cottle, Joseph, 8–10, 21–3, 29
Connell, Philip, 77–8, 92,
canon, contemporary, 12, 20, 92, 102, 109,
    116, 141, 144–5, 157
counterfeit, authorial and textual, 5–6
Cowper, William
    The Task, 94
Cox, Jeffrey, 2, 14
Critical Review, 29
Cumbrian poets, 40

Darwin, Erasmus
    The Botanic Garden, 8, 26
Davy, Sir Humphrey, 21
D'Israeli, Isaac, 78, 92
Donaldson v. Beckett, 3–4

Duff, David, 39
Durrant, G. H., 133
Dyer, John, 138

Eclectic Review, 145
Edinburgh Review, 8, 14, 16, 58, 61, 62, 77,
    125, 145, 147, 148
    see also Francis Jeffrey
Eilenberg, Susan, 22
European Magazine, 144

Fraistat, Neil, 32
Franta, Andrew, 13

Gamer, Michael, 102, 110
Garrett, James, 154
George III, his death, 143
Gifford, William
    The Baviad, 25, 28
    The Maviad, 25
Gill, Stephen, 79
Gilman, Priscilla, 64
Gothic
    and church/cathedral, 2, 19, 84–5, 98,
        101–4, 111–15
    and national character, 104, 108
    and popular genre, 110, 116–19
    and type script to Coleridge's 'Rime', 106

Hayley, William, 7, 26
Heinzelman, Kurt, 129
Higgins, David, 145
Hogg, James, 150
Hollander, John, 65–6
Hone, William
    The Political House that Jack Built, 143
Hunt, Leigh and John
    The Examiner, 16
Hutchinson, Sarah, 21

Janowitz, Anne, 98
Jeffrey, Francis, 14, 58, 61–2, 80–1, 145,
    147, 150
    see also *The Edinburgh Review*
Jones, Mark, 14
Jones, Steven, 15, 39
Johnson, Joseph, 3
Johnson, Samuel, 33, 86–7

Kendrew, James
  The Little Maid and the Gentleman,
    158–9
Khan, Jalal, 150
Kim, Benjamin, 154, 156
Klancher, Jon, 15
Knox, Vicisimus
  Elegant Extracts of Poetry, 32–5

Ladies Monthly Museum, 144
Lake District, 16, 18, 20, 39–43, 47, 49, 142,
  145, 147–1, 153–5, 158–9
'Lake School', 62, 64–7, 76
Lamb, Charles, 9–10, 107
Levinson, Marjorie, 6
Linnaeus, Carl, 8, 157
Literary Chronicle and Weekly Review,
  144–5
Literary Gazette, 106–7, 125, 147
Literary Keepsake, 158
London Literary Gazette, 147
Lloyd, Charles, 9–10, 107
Lockhart, John Gibson, 147
  Benjamin the Waggoner, 147–8
  see also Blackwood's Edinburgh Magazine
London Literary Gazette, 147
London Magazine, 144–5, 157
Longman, Thomas Norton, 21–3, 29, 57,
  157
Lonsdale, William Earl, 79, 123

McGann, Jerome, 16
Macpherson, James
  Ossian, 5–9, 87–8
Maginn, William, 149
  '*Don Juan* Unvisited', 149–50
Magnuson, Paul, 2, 13–14, 58
Mant, Richard
  Poems, 61–2
  The Simpliciad, 17, 18, 57–76
Mathias, T. J.
  The Pursuits of Literature, 18, 23–8
Milton, John
  Colasterion, 135
  Doctrine and Discipline of Divorce, 132
  Paradise Lost, 82, 86
  literary market, 86
  Tetrachordon, 132, 134–5

treasured classics, 89
chapter 13, *Biographia Literaria*, 101
twin sonnets 11 and 12, 131–8
Montgomery, James
  'Field Flower', 68, 127
Monthly Review, 92, 145
Moore, Thomas
  review of Coleridge's *Christabel* (1816),
    11
  Corruption and Intolerance, 11–12
More, Hannah
  *Strictures on the Modern System of Female
    Education*, 33–4
Mudge, Bradford, 103
Murray, John, 11, 113

Newlyn, Lucy, 16
  'The Nose-Drop', 155
  'Old Canon', 1, 4, 40

Parrish, Stephen, 39
Percy, Thomas
  Reliques of Ancient Poetry, 4–7, 32–4,
    88–9, 95
peruse, 30–2, 109, 117, 146–7
Peterloo Massacre, 143–4
picturesque aesthetics and travel, 8–9, 18,
  39–43, 47, 50, 151
Pope, Alexander
  The Anti-Jacobin, 28
  The Dunciad, 5
  Shakespeare edition, 87
  Joseph Warton's edition of, 25
Price, Leah, 117
Pyle, Gerald, 125

Quarterly Review, 16, 77, 149

Radcliffe, Ann
  and popular Gothic conventions, 117,
    119
  Mysteries of Udolpho, 103
reading public, 3, 7, 13, 16, 18–19, 57,
  77–81, 86–9, 102–13, 118, 131, 145,
  148–9, 154, 157
Reynolds, J. H.
  'The Dead Asses', 148–9
  'Peter Bell', 17, 19–20, 121–34, 138–9,
    147

Robinson, Mary
  Lyrical Tales, 23
Rogers, Samuel
  The Pleasures of Memory, 10
  1817 letter from Wordsworth, 150
Roxburghe, James Innes-Ker, Duke of, 77

St Clair, William
  copyright and statue law, 3–4
Satirist, 16
Schiller, Freidrich, 9
Schoenfield, Mark, 84, 128
Scott, Sir Walter
  Referred to in Wordsworth's sonnet 'On
    the Detraction', 134
  Minstrelsy of the Scottish Border, 10–11
  The Lay of the Last Minstrel, 10–11
  Percy's *Reliques*, evaluation of, 33
  in John Wilson's *Luctus*, 145
  market value of, 10, 148
self-fashioning, authorial, 7–8
Shakespeare, William, 8, 26, 86–9
Shawcross, John, 136
Shelley, Percy
  The Mask of Anarchy, 143
Sheridan, Richard Brinsley
  The Critic, 125–6
Schoenfield, Mark, 84, 128
Simpson, David, 103
Smith, Charlotte
  Elegiac Sonnets, 7–8
  Beachy Head, 7
Socrates, 12
Southey, Robert
  'Advertisement' to 1798 *Lyrical Ballads*
    and response, 36
  Annual Review, 58
  Anti-Jacobin attacks, 27
  collections of poetry, 1796–1800, 10, 29
  Joan of Arc, 9–10
    'Preface' to *Joan of Arc*, 10
  Lyrical Ballads negative review, 18,
    29–31
  'new school of poetry' and *The Simpli-
    ciad*, 16, 62
  Percy's *Reliques*, evaluation of, 33
  Peter Bayley's *Poems*, review essay of, 58–9
  'The Soldier's Wife', 10
Stoddard, John, 41
Stones, Graeme, 14

Theatrical Inquisitor, 85
Thompson, James, 40
Trott, Nicola, 15–16, 58

Walker, George Robert, Reverend, 153
Warton, Joseph, 25, 33
Wilkinson, Joseph, Reverend, 151
Wilson, John (Christopher North), 142,
    145, 150,
  '*Luctus*', 145–7
  see also Blackwood's Edinburgh Magazine
Wilcox, Stewart, 152
Wordsworth, Dorothy, 21–3, 98
Wordsworth, William
  advertisements concluding *The River
    Duddon* volume, 20, 142–3, 156–7
  branding of poetry, 2, 4, 14, 18, 22–3,39,
    43, 52, 56–7, 73, 111
  as guide, 1, 2, 18, 27, 39–41, 51, 93,
    118, 126, 138, 150–1, 158–9
  and leech gatherer, 72–5
  and library, figurative, 19, 77–99
  limits of poetry and prose, 31
  myth of his antipathy to parody, 14–15
  pastoral tradition, 18, 35–7, 39–40, 45,
    47, 52–3, 56, 118, 155
  and pleasure of readers, 32–43, 48–9,
    52, 54, 56, 64, 117
  printing and manuscript preparation of
    1800 *Lyrical Ballads*, 21–3
  stones in 1800 *Lyrical Ballads*, 40, 45–56
  and poetic system, 2, 15, 19, 28, 32, 37,
    57–9, 63, 76, 80–1, 84, 85, 91–3, 98,
    106–9, 111, 118, 121–7, 141, 144,
    156–8
  works
  'Advertisement' to *Lyrical Ballads*
    (1798), 4, 9, 12, 17, 28–30, 34–5, 48
  'Advertisement' to 'Poems on the Nam-
    ing of Places', 40, 48–9, 55
  'Advertisement' in *The River Duddon*
    volume, 141
  'Among all Things my Love had Been', 64
  'Appendix on Poetic Diction', 12
  'The Blind Highland Boy and Other
    Poems', 60–1, 68–9
  'The Brothers', 35, 39, 45–7, 50, 53
  'To a Butterfly', 61

'The Complaint of the forsaken Indian Woman', 42
'Conclusion' sonnet in *The River Duddon* volume, 153–6
'Dedicatory Sonnet' to *The Excursion*, 79
Descriptive Sketches (1793), 3, 10
  'To the Daisy' poems, 59–60, 65, 67–72, 76, 127,
Ecclesiastical Sonnets (1822), 158
'Ellen Irwin', 53
'Essay Upon Epitaphs', 12, 79, 125
'Essay Supplementary to the Preface', 7, 12, 17, 20, 85–9, 92–5, 128–30, 132, 139, 149
  An Evening Walk (1793), 3, 10, 79
  The Excursion, 1, 2, 77–81, 83, 102, 125, 141
'Expostulation and Reply', 28, 36–7, 49–51
Fenwick Notes, 95
'Fidelity', 60
'French Revolution', 93–7, 99
'Goody Blake and Harry Gill', 28–31, 93
'Hart-Leap Well', 42, 45, 47, 50, 50–4
Home at Grasmere, 83
  'The Horn of Egremont Castle', 93
'I Wandered Lonely as a Cloud', 63, 93
  'The Idiot Boy', 29
'Incident, Characteristic of a Favourite Dog', 60
'Influence of Natural Objects', 93, 96
'Inscription for the House (an Outhouse)', 54
'Inscription for the Spot where the Hermitage Stood', 54
'It is no spirit', 94, 97
  'To Joanna', 41, 47–8
'Juvenile Pieces', 97
'Lines Left upon a Seat in a Yew-Tree', 42, 50–1
'Lines Written with a Slate Pencil upon a Stone', 50, 54
Lyrical Ballads (1798), 8–10, 18, 21–2, 28–30, 35–6, 39, 48, 158
Lyrical Ballads (1800), 1–2, 7, 10, 22–3, 30, 39–56, 62, 96, 99, 122, 149
Lyrical Ballads (1802), 56
'Michael', 21–2, 40–2, 48–50, 55–6

'Miscellaneous Sonnets, 60, 69, 76, 137
Miscellaneous Poems of William Wordsworth (1820), 137, 141
'Moods of my own Mind', 57, 61, 64, 69
'Note' *To Joanna*, 47–8
'Note to *The Thorn*', 2, 30–1, 35–6, 40, 43–4, 51, 62–3, 122
'Ode to Duty', 69
'Ode: Intimations', 60, 69
'The Old Cumberland Beggar', 42, 54
'On the Detraction which Followed the Publication of a Certain Poem', 122, 131, 133–8, 150
'On Seeing a Tuft of Snowdrops in a Storm', 150
'Orchard Pathways', 64
Peter Bell (1819), 123, 125, 131–4, 136–7
  'The Pilgrim's Dream', 150
'Poems Composed during a Tour', 69
'Poems of the Fancy', 127
'Poems of the Imagination', 19, 78, 92–8, 146
Poems in Two Volumes (1807), 1, 2, 18, 23, 57–76, 77, 79–80, 123, 137, 147, 149
Poems by William Wordsworth (1815), 1, 12, 17, 20, 83, 85–99
'Preface' to *The Excursion* (1814), 2, 19, 78–9, 81, 83–5, 93–4, 98, 102, 121, 123, 128
'Preface' to *Lyrical Ballads* (1800), 4, 7, 12, 17–18, 28, 30–2, 34–7, 39, 48, 56, 57, 62, 108–11, 127, 129, 155,
'Preface' to *Lyrical Ballads* (1802), 130
'Preface' to *Poems* (1815), 12, 17, 20, 85, 89–92, 94, 97–8, 102
  The Prelude, 80, 83–4, 93–6, 116, 118, 138, 146
'Prospectus' to *The Excursion* (1814), 2, 79, 81–4, 111, 121
  The Recluse, 79, 80, 82–4, 91, 93–4, 121
  'The Redbreast and the Butterfly', 61
'Resolution and Independence', 59, 67, 69, 72–6
  The River Duddon volume (1820), 1, 2, 20, 137–8, 141–7, 150–9
River Duddon sonnet sequence, 150–9

River Duddon sonnets 31 and 32, 155–6

'Rural Architecture', 40–1, 50, 54–5, 149

Selections from the Poems of William Wordsworth (1831), 158

'She Dwelt among th' Untrodden Ways', 50, 53

'Simon Lee', 124–5

    'To Sleep' sonnets, 60

    'A Slumber did my Spirit Seal', 50, 53

    'To the Small Celandine' poems, 60

'Song'

    see 'She Dwelt among th' Untrodden Ways'

'Sonnets Dedicated to Liberty', 60, 69, 76, 142

'The Sparrow's Nest', 64

'The Tables Turned', 28, 36–7, 49

'Thanksgiving Ode', 141

'There was a boy', 93–4, 96–7

'The Thorn', 28–31, 50–1, 61–2

'Tintern Abbey', 19, 30, 42–3, 51–2, 78, 92–8

'Topographical Description of the Country of the Lakes', 3, 20, 141–2, 150–1, 154, 155

'Tribute to the Same Dog', 60

'Vaudracour and Julia', 141

    The Waggoner (1819), 133, 141, 143, 147

'We are Seven', 158–9

'Yarrow Unvisited', 150

'Yarrow Visited', 150

'Yes! full surely 'twas the Echo', 66

Young, Edward, 4

    Night Thoughts, 94